INTERNATIONAL COMPETITIVENESS

edited by

A. MICHAEL SPENCE

and

HEATHER A. HAZARD

Center for Business and Government
at the
John F. Kennedy School of Government
Harvard University

BALLINGER PUBLISHING COMPANY
A Subsidiary of Harper & Row, Publishers, Inc.

International Standard Book Number: 0-88730-250-5 (CL)
0-88730-288-2 (PB)

Library of Congress Catalog Card Number: 87-30792

Printed in the United States of America

Library of Congress Cataloging-in-Publication Data

International competitiveness / edited by A. Michael Spence,
 Heather A. Hazard.
      p.   cm.
   Includes index.
   ISBN 0-88730-250-5. ISBN 0-88730-288-2 (pbk.)
   1. Competition, International. 2. Industry and state.
 3. Trade regulation. 4. Technological innovations. 5. United
 States—Manufactures. I. Spence, A. Michael (Andrew Michael).
 II. Hazard, Heather A.
 HF1414.1575   1988
 382'.3—dc19   87-30792
 89 90 91 92 HC 5 4 3 2   CIP

INTERNATIONAL COMPETITIVENESS

Contents

List of Figures

List of Tables

Acknowledgment

Harvard University's John F. Kennedy School of Government and its Center for Business and Government wish to thank Mr. Koji Kobayashi, Chairman and CEO of Nippon Electric Company, and his company for their generosity in sponsoring the International Competitiveness Project at the Center, of which this volume is a product.

Graham T. Allison, Jr.
Dean, John F. Kennedy School
of Government

Winthrop Knowlton
Director, Center for Business
and Government

Introduction

A. Michael Spence

The problem of international competitiveness has been defined in highly diverse ways. These definitions (and the proposed solutions to the problem) are partially inconsistent, and thoroughly confusing to most academics, politicians, policy makers, and business managers. There is good reason for this confusion. The collection of problems alluded to as "competitiveness" is genuinely complex. Disagreements frequently occur not only at the level of empirical effects and of policies, but also in the very definition of the problem. Well-intentioned and reasonable people find themselves talking at cross purposes; sometimes it almost seems they are addressing different subjects.

Three years ago the NEC Corporation made a grant to the Center for Business and Government at the Kennedy School of Government at Harvard to support an exploration of perspectives on international competition. Distinguished scholars prepared papers on several different aspects of the general subject and presented them at a conference held in the spring of 1985. Our purpose was to get the pieces of the puzzle (or as many of them as we could locate) out on the table, in order to begin the process of putting them together.

Perceptions of a complex problem inevitably evolve with time and analysis. When a cartel of countries dramatically raised the price of oil in 1974, for example, the immediate reaction was a widely held view that the price hike constituted an outrageous act of international extortion on a scale never before seen. But after a period of time and some careful analysis, it became reasonably clear that at precartel prices, the prevailing level of consumption was in effect creating shortages. As a better understanding of the pricing of depletable resources developed, it became clear that there was an economic rationale to the cartel's action.

The problems and issues in the area of international competition are considerably more complex than those encountered in the oil case. The various conceptual lenses of observers cause them to see different things or to focus on different features of the problem, but analysis and discussion will predictably add to the construction of a unified picture. We hope these essays contribute to that outcome.

Among the largest industrial countries, only the United States emerged from World War II with its economy in relatively good shape. The productive capacity and the buying power of the rest of the world were substantially diminished. The Marshall Plan, whose fortieth birthday we recently celebrated, reflected a recognition of the political and international importance of economic reconstruction in Europe and elsewhere. The United States, however, came to operate on the largely correct presumption that what was economically significant from a business or policy standpoint was essentially domestic. Business operated internationally, but few businesses formulated strategies that were predicated on multinational markets.

While Americans became used to thinking of their country as largely economically self-contained, the rest of the world began to grow—quite rapidly. As a result the United States slowly and steadily became more economically interdependent. The productive capacity and purchasing power of other nations grew both individually and collectively. In some industries, the structural characteristics that create transnational scale advantages have forced successful companies to devise global strategies for multiple markets. Companies based in smaller countries may learn this lesson more quickly because they have to.

The habits of thought and analysis among economists and in business and government, which adapted quite quickly to the reality of the immediate postwar period, have since become increasingly mismatched with the present circumstances. We find ourselves today in a period of transition to a revised set of premises about the environment and economic reality.

What are the ultimate causes of concern in a world of international competition? Many have received attention. Ailing industries, particularly those that are losing market share domestically and worldwide to non-U.S. firms, are one set. Employment, the loss of jobs to other countries, is another. Many are worried about large and/or persistent trade deficits, and the associated increase in ownership of various kinds of U.S. assets by foreign individuals and institutions. Concern has been expressed about fairness and reciprocity with respect to the commitment (or lack of it) to relatively free trade. The magnitude and real value of international debt are also vexing issues. It is hardly surprising that these interconnected phenomena are difficult to bring into a coherent picture.

It is, however, possible to make some observations that help organize the issues. Let me begin with U.S. macroeconomic policy. During much of the Reagan administration, fiscal policy has been expansionary; that is, the government is running large deficits, and monetary policy has been tight. At least for a time, the result was high real interest rates and high rates of return to other kinds of investments. The dollar rose in value to levels many felt could not be permanent. American production became expensive relative to non-U.S. production. Exports declined, imports increased, and there was a deficit on current account.

Some critics, who did not like these macroeconomic policies anyway, argued that the difficulties some U.S. businesses and industries were having in international competition were due to the macroeconomic environment rather than to any failure on the part of management or labor. This perspective has some merit. The large shifts in exchange rates surely caused shifts in relative cost positions of domestic and foreign producers that were large enough to affect market shares. Yet not all the problems of domestic industries can be attributed to these shifts. In the 1970s, when the value of the dollar was dramatically lower than it has been until recently, the effectiveness of foreign competition was already apparent in many industries. By and large, American business management has recognized that many innovations in management, strategy, and manufacturing outside the United States are effective, worthy of study and sometimes emulation. And certainly these innovations are competitively important.

A second theme concerns trade barriers. It is often argued that trade barriers in other countries adversely affect domestic industries and employment. The barriers referred to are usually not tariffs but other means of preventing the importing or effective marketing of goods from outside the country. Some have urged that the United States retaliate, either to protect employment or to force the issue and have foreign trade barriers removed.

Trade barriers generally benefit the industries that are protected by them and hurt domestic consumers. More recently, it has been recognized that trade barriers, even if temporary, can aid domestic companies strategically by protecting the domestic market from foreign competition and hence tipping the balance in favor of domestic producers in a battle for worldwide market share. Clearly this strategy is effective primarily in industries where large worldwide share confers a cost or closely related advantage. It is also clear that the value of protecting the domestic market is greater for larger countries. More concretely, it makes a difference if access to the U.S. or Japanese market is denied, but few companies would care much if they were barred from competing in Luxembourg. It is not clear whether and under what circumstances, if any, the long-run benefits of tipping the balance in favor of domestic firms in a global market outweigh the cost to consumers of not being able to buy the foreign goods. The calculations that would be required to reach a conclusion are so complex that they are unlikely to be done in the near future. Because we are dealing with an entire system, these issues cannot be dealt with on an industry-by-industry basis.

Trade barriers are not the only way to support a domestic industry. For example, various forms of subsidy that lower costs can result in expanded worldwide market share. Depending on the structure and behavior of the domestic industry, they can also result in enhanced profitability or wages and salaries. In economic (as opposed to political) terms, subsidies do not make much sense as a technique for promoting industrial development unless their temporary presence leads to a more permanent competitive advantage. In certain industries where static and dynamic scale economies are important, a temporary cost advantage may provide a basis for a more permanent enhancement of competitive advantage.

Constraints on the use of capital are a somewhat less controversial but nonetheless important aspect of international competitiveness. Countries can adopt different policies with different objectives. For example, they can try to prevent the loss of jobs by limiting investment outside the country. Such a policy is unlikely to have much effect. Some countries limit direct investment by foreign companies, in part to retain control of the domestic assets, and in part to limit foreign competition in the domestic market. The latter effect may be desired as part of an industrial development strategy in which domestic firms build their domestic market and then use it as a base for competing in the global environment. The evolution of several Japanese industries suggests this pattern. From a business strategy standpoint, however, it may be unwise to fail to compete with a major potential competitor in its domestic market, even when the profitability of doing so looks marginal, or the barriers seem high. By competing in another firm's domestic market, one limits its scale and hence its competitive potential globally.

Smaller countries confront real choices with respect to trade and investment barriers. Generally, a policy of having both high trade and high investment barriers is very expensive in terms of efficiency and standard of living. Japan, which is not small, pursued such a policy and was careful to open all available channels for importing technology. Canada and Australia have maintained relatively high tariff barriers, which has led to substantial foreign direct investment. The advantage is an industrially diversified economy, with some sacrifice of efficiency because of lack of scale. And from a policy point of view, there is a control issue, since a significant fraction of domestic assets is controlled by foreign firms. Sweden is, in a sense, the opposite case. Its economy is quite open, industrially quite specialized, and, in its areas of specialization, effective in multinational competition. This approach is shared by many less developed countries with a high dependence on a limited number of industries (e.g., agriculture or natural resources). The risk is that adverse events in one of these industries can have a major negative economic impact on the country as a whole. In a larger country, such effects tend to be regional rather than national.

Discussions of competitiveness, like earlier discussions of industrial policy, have paid some attention to research and the development of technology and products. It is an important subject (as the essays in this book indicate) for a number of reasons. A significant part of the investment in the development of technology and its scientific underpinnings is public investment. Further, while markets in intellectual property exist, for structural reasons they will never be very complete. Private returns to investment in technology often fall short of the total return. There are spillover effects. In the international context, there is therefore a free-rider problem that should be the subject of international policy discussions and agreements.

Competitively, R&D is a critical aspect of the strategic investment behavior of firms. There are inherent dynamic scale economies in R&D, which tend not to be truncated at national boundaries. This transnational character distinguishes them from many other scale economies. Therefore, R&D tends to be an essential aspect of competitive interaction precisely in industries where competition is global. Moreover, the correlation between R&D intensity and growth at the industry level is strongly positive. Thus, prospectively, the R&D-intensive industries assume an even greater importance than they have now.

Let me now turn back to the macroeconomic level. One consequence of the dispersion of economic power is the increasing openness of economies. The trend has been strengthened by the reduction of tariffs over a long period under the General Agreement on Trade and Tariffs and by the European Economic Community. The openness and deconcentration of economic power has made countries increasingly interdependent in the macroeconomic sense. No country can easily pursue expansionary economic policies in isolation, in part because its trade balance would deteriorate fairly immediately. Exchange-rate adjustments, if permitted to occur, are ultimately a correcting mechanism. But recent experience in the United States suggests that the lag between the exchange-rate shift and the trade-balance response is uncomfortably long.

In the long run, competitiveness depends on investment and growth. In the United States the savings rate has fallen to unusually low levels. If one deducts from private investment the federal deficit (on the ground that it is not investment) and the trade deficit (on the ground that it is investment by citizens of other countries), savings are less than 3 percent of gross national product. That is not high enough to sustain an adequate level of economic growth in the longer term and will eventually affect U.S. competitiveness. It is a puzzle, at least to me, that savings should have reached a level well below those of most other industrial countries.

International competitiveness is a difficult subject because it is exceedingly complex. It encompasses policies, competition, and business practice with respect to trade, investment, technology, and regulation. It is also inherently linked to macroeconomic magnitudes like the savings rate and to tax, fiscal, and monetary policies that affect them. In the end, there is no substitute for the painstaking process of building the larger picture from a careful analysis of the components. This volume brings together essays on subjects ranging from trade exposure (Caves) to R&D competition (Dixit and Sato) and the management of technology development (Clark). They deal with industrial policy in general (Cooper) and in specific cases (Collis, Gregory, and Reich), with domestic regulatory policies and their impact on competitiveness (Kalt) and with capital structure and ownership in U.S. and Japanese corporations (Kester). The issue of savings and tax policy is addressed by Summers, and important aspects of the theory of international trade with differentiated products and imperfect competition are developed by Krugman and Helpmann. Taken together, these essays will give the careful reader a good sense of the range of economic, business, and public policy issues that we now confront.

I want to conclude by thanking NEC for its generous support and interest in this project, and the Kennedy School of Government and its Center for Business and Government for sponsoring the effort.

CHAPTER 1

Trade Exposure and Changing Structures of U.S. Manufacturing Industries

Richard E. Caves

The United States has experienced large deficits in its international balance of merchandise trade, driven by large capital inflows (due to a swelling public-sector deficit as well as exogenous disturbances abroad) and the resulting high foreign exchange value for the U.S. dollar. These deficits and the coincident high levels of unemployment have fueled concern about "deindustrialization" and prompted major industries to seek special forms of protection from foreign competition. The resulting appearance of industrial decline has obscured the longer-run trend, affecting most industrial countries, toward all-around increases in international trade. Between 1960 and 1980, the United States' ratio of exports plus imports to gross national product (GNP) rose from 7.1 to 17.7 percent.

The short-run situation has drawn our concern to policies regarding structural adjustment: should we help our manufacturing industries withdraw resources from sectors afflicted by import competittion? Should we fend off their foreign competition and encourage them to reinvest resources in their existing businesses, in order to raise productivity and make them viable? We have surprisingly little knowledge about how U.S. industries have adjusted structurally to international competitive threats and opportunities. Although econo-

Data for this project were mobilized with the assistance of the Project for Industry and Company Analysis, Harvard Business School. I am grateful to Michael Hemesath for research assistance and to the General Electric Foundation for financial support.

1

mists are trained to think about the process of adjustment along a supply curve, the empirical literature offers little evidence of exactly what changes occur in the population of plants and companies as an industry's output responds to export opportunities or import competition.

To begin exploring the anatomy of these adjustment processes, I have examined how U.S. manufacturing industry structure responded to changes in international rivalry over a two-decade period (1958–77). (I use the generic term *industry structure* for the various measures of an industry's size distribution of plants and companies that receive attention below.[1]) Over this period the artificial and natural barriers to international trade typically declined. The artificial barriers were reduced through periodic negotiations under the General Agreement on Tariffs and Trade (GATT) as well as the declining real incidence of specific rates of duty. Natural barriers were diminished by declining transaction and transportation costs, increasingly effective international marketing networks, and the like.

One limitation on this analysis is that the changes in trade barriers are not readily measurable; we observe their effects only in the form of expanding shares of output exported and of domestic use accounted for by imports.[2] Another problem is the impracticability of explicitly modeling supplies of U.S. imports and demands for U.S. exports. Given these constraints, I have adopted the following simple approach to studying the effect of trade changes on industry structure. Markets for most industrial goods grew substantially in real terms over the period 1958–77, both in the United States and abroad. Previous research in industrial organization has shown that a demand-side growth disturbance has substantial effects on an industry's structure. Hypotheses about the effects of changing exposure to international trade can thus be tested indirectly through the following statistical inquiries:

1. Did changing export opportunities and import competition affect the typical domestic industry differently from equal expansions or contractions of output produced and consumed domestically?

2. Did all industries' structures respond alike to export opportunities and import competition, or were the effects modified by traits particular to some industries?

The next section explains the research design and identifies the analytical support provided by previous research.

ANALYTICAL FRAMEWORK

The analytical framework sketched above will allow us to investigate a number of influences—differential competitiveness in foreign and domestic markets, the relation of trade to the extent of and bases for differentiation of the industry's product, and the role of sunk costs in delaying structural adjustment to unanticipated trade disturbances. However, the incorporation of numerous influences on industry structure exacts its cost, precluding the use of a single tight theoretical framework. We proceed in steps, addressing first the theoretical relationship between market size and industry structure in the long run, then considering differential short-term effects due to changes in international markets.

Market Size and Industry Structure

Theory suggests that changes in the size of a purely competitive market bring about only proportional changes in the number of efficient-size firms rather than changes in firms' sizes. This result also holds under Cournot competition among fewer rivals. If each seller enjoys scale economies as a result of a fixed cost per firm, but entry is otherwise free, then seller concentration (the combined market share of the n largest firms) will decline as the market grows. But firm size will still not respond positively to increases in market size.[3] Thus, both the competitive and free-entry Cournot models imply that seller concentration decreases with market size while firms' scales remain unchanged. The former hypothesis has been confirmed in a number of cross-section statistical studies of the effect of market size or market growth on seller concentration. Contrary to these models, however, the sizes of plants and firms show a robust *positive* relationship to market size, with elasticities on the order of 0.4 (see Gorecki, chap. 4, on plant sizes). Moreover, market growth is associated with proportionally faster growth of the initially smaller firms (Caves and Porter, 1980). As a result, increases in market size reduce seller concentration, but only because the deconcentrating effects of net entry and the faster growth of smaller units offset the concentrating effect of expansion by the larger production units.[4]

Since these patterns have been found in broad samples of manufacturing industries, any formal model applied to the "typical" manufacturing industry should be able to explain a positive relation between unit size and market size. Candidates are not lacking. If products are differentiated by attributes or location, unit size can respond positively to a market-size increase that takes the form of higher density of demand. Any entry barrier (other than scale economies) should have the same effect, since it implies that incumbent firms can serve an increment of demand at lower cost than can potential entrants. Because changes in market size clearly seem to affect both the sizes and numbers of production units in the market, I examine changes in several measures of industry structure, including numbers and sizes of plants and companies as well as the n-firm concentration ratio (which serves as a summary statistic for those dimensions).

Exposure to International Trade

How is the relationship of market size and industry structure affected by changing export opportunities and import competition? Again, theory offers points of departure. When an industry of Cournot oligopolists shifts from a closed national market to participation in a global competitive market, it adjusts to two changes: it faces more elastic demand, and its equilibrium output changes (the sign depending on its comparative advantage position). Greater elasticity of demand will increase the equilibrium sizes of the industry's units, assuming equilibrium output does not decline enough to eliminate the industry. The change in the number of units depends on both the elasticity change and the change in total industry output.

Recent models of monopolistic competition in international trade (for example, Krugman (1980) and Ethier (1982)) predict that when a domestic industry in monopolistic-competition equilibrium is opened to international trade, either or both of two changes will occur: more varieties of the differentiated product will be produced and consumed in the world economy, and individual varieties will be produced at larger scales. Changes in the numbers of domestic producers will depend on the industry's competitive position in general equilibrium. These models of differentiation assume that buyers divide their purchases equally among the available brands. But if varieties (all subject to the same scale economies in production) differ in their popularity and thus their shares of an autarkic national market, the differential impact of import competition will depend on whether imports are better substitutes for popular (large-share) or specialized (small-share) brands. The effects of import competition on differentiated industries' structures may thus be more diverse than on homogeneous-product industries.

Adjustment in the Short Run

The great changes in the exposure of U.S. manufacturing industries to international trade over the past quarter-century were almost certainly not fully anticipated when they put their long-lived capital investments in place. Therefore, this analysis incorporates certain theoretical considerations that devolve from models of short-run adjustments.

The first concerns trade and unexploited scale economies in production. Scitovsky (1958, chap. 3) and Owen (1983, chap. 2) explored the effects of diminished trade barriers on an industry whose producers have not exploited all available scale economies in the domestic market.[5] Assume a homogeneous product subject to scale economies in production, so that larger domestic producers enjoy a cost advantage over their domestic rivals but have not exploited all available economies of scale. Reductions in foreign tariffs or international transport costs lower domestic producers' marginal delivered costs of goods sold in foreign markets, just as reductions in the same transport costs or in domestic tariffs lower the costs of foreign goods delivered in the domestic market. Expanded export opportunities make room for more domestic producers of any given scale, and in that sense deconcentrate domestic producers. They may also increase the scale of the typical domestic producer and have differential effects on the sizes or prevalence of large and small domestic producers. Under the assumed conditions, small domestic producers are always potentially vulnerable to displacement by a rival that builds a large plant capable of producing at lower cost. Expanded export opportunities increase the potential return to such an investment in low-cost capacity—essentially because it could displace inefficient-size foreign as well as domestic producers (Owen, 1983, chap. 2). The reward for seizing such opportunities increases with the amount of vulnerably inefficient foreign production that is brought within economic reach by the disturbance in trade conditions. It is reduced to the extent that the durability and specificity ("sunkenness") of their investments lead inefficient producers to continue operating at price levels that do not cover their full costs.

The pro-concentration effects of this process unambiguously increase the size inequality of production units only in the short run, because ultimately the small domestic producers may disappear. Nonetheless, improved export opportunities should increase the size inequality of production units over a quite long-lived short run. The predicted increase in the typical unit's scale applies to both short and long runs.[6]

So far we have focused on the effect of enhanced export opportunities created by general tariff reductions. The effects of lower domestic tariffs on the structure of a sheltered industry are less well established. The preceding analysis of expanded trade with unexploited scale economies implies that inefficient-scale domestic producers will become more vulnerable when the delivered marginal costs of imports are reduced, so that size inequality will be diminished and production concentrated in the larger domestic units.[7]

Another significant short-run consideration is the role of sunk costs in delaying long-run adjustments. Because we assume the massive changes in U.S. industries' exposure to trade were not fully anticipated, the extent of the resulting changes in industries' structures should depend on the magnitude of sunk costs and the durability of the committed investments. This dependence holds especially for increased import competition: even if imports did not force an industry to contract its real outputs between 1958 and 1977, they certainly confronted some firms with lower prices or levels of demand than they had expected. Therefore, the effects of import competition on industry structure will be tempered by the extent and durability of sunk resources that retard the closure of plants and the increase in concentration of domestic producers. Import competition may also tend to equalize the sizes of companies and reduce concentration in the sense of pure size-inequality, because the larger sellers enjoy a larger return (in preserved quasi-rents) from any given reduction of capacity in a shrinking market (Ghemawat and Nalebuff, 1985).[8] Both intangible investments and conventional physical capital may represent important sunk costs.

TESTING PROCEDURE AND HYPOTHESES

Form of Estimated Model

Before proceeding to specific hypotheses, I shall describe the structure of the statistical tests. For as many U.S. manufacturing industries (defined by four-digit Standard Industrial Classification (SIC) codes) as possible, data were collected on exports, competing imports, and shipments in census years 1958 and 1977, along with various measures of industry structure, including producer concentration (share of shipments accounted for by the four largest producers), number of companies, number of plants, and proportion of resources in plants smaller than a certain minimum scale. Changes in the value of each industry's shipments were deflated by the relevant Bureau of Labor Statistics price index. Changes (from X_1 to X_2) in any of these variables were expressed in the form $2(X_2 - X_1)/(X_2 + X_1)$; this form was chosen to make the distributions of changes more nearly normal. The operator D indicates a change calculated in this manner. A partial exception was the method used to express changes in shipments, exports, and imports. A common denominator was needed for them, so that any differential effects of their changes could be observed by direct comparison of their regression coefficients. Total shipments was the natural common denominator. Thus, for each industry:

DSH = change in the real value of total shipments by U.S. industry, including exports, divided by mean 1958 and 1977 shipments

DX = change in exports divided by mean 1958 and 1977 total shipments

DM = change in imports divided by mean 1958 and 1977 total shipments

Let DMS be the change in some dimension of industry structure (measured over the same time period as the exogenous variables). Then the basic model takes the form

$$DMS = a_0 + a_1 DSH + a_2 DX + a_3 DM + u \qquad (1)$$

where $a_2 = b_0 + \Sigma_i b_i Y_i$ and $a_3 = c_0 + \Sigma_i c_i Z_i$, and Y_i and Z_i are different vectors of exogenous variables that interact with DX and DM respectively to determine their effect on DMS. This format allows a direct test whether changes in exports or competing imports overall affect industry structure differently from changes in the domestic market, as well as whether the effect of trade changes varies with exogenous features of the market. It provides a reasonable (if not rigorous) way around the unobservability of most trade-expanding disturbances. If trade changes affect industry structure the same way as changes in the domestic market, we should expect $a_2 = 0$ and $a_3 = -a_1$. The distinctive consequences of disturbances affecting trade should be reflected in violations of these conditions and significant regression coefficients for incentive variables.

Interactive Hypotheses

It is hypothesized that the response of industry structure to trade changes depends on other features of the market's structure. With several dimensions of industry structure under analysis and effects running through both imports and exports, a review of every plausible relationship would be unwieldy. I shall concentrate on interactive hypotheses about import competition, then note the few asymmetries between import competition and export opportunities. If rising imports are expected to increase domestic producer concentration (by reducing the number of viable producers), the increase should depend on the importance of sunk sector-specific resources and the character of product differentiation and other long-run environmental influences.

The sunkenness of productive assets may be measured in several ways. Sector-specific assets may include physical and human capital as well as intangibles, and fixity may result from either the physical immutability of assets or contractual stickiness. Neither economic theory nor previous empirical research tells us much about how to represent the importance of these assets, so the selection of regressors involves a certain amount of judgment.[9] The first of these variables to be interacted with DM and or DX is an indicator of how small is the proportion of value that the industry adds to its material inputs. We use:

MA = cost of purchased materials inputs as a fraction of value of industry shipments, 1977

Industries with high values of MA (low value added as a percentage of value of shipments) will have relatively little ability to withstand a reduction in the sale value of output.[10] The higher is MA, the more should changing imports alter the structure of the domestic industry.

Among the components of the industry's value added, several ratios might represent the incidence of sunk costs, including:

PW = production workers as a fraction of total employees
KL = total assets per employee
SK = payroll per employee

SK represents the industry's human-capital intensity, KL its physical-capital intensity. Concentration and other dimensions of industry structure should be less sensitive to import-based disturbances where KL and SK are high and PW low.

As discussed earlier, scale economies play an important role in generating the pro-concentration effects of both export opportunities and import competition. The concentration-increasing effect of export growth should accordingly be more pronounced in capital-intensive industries, where scale economies are normally more extensive. On the imports side, however, the long-run prediction (increased concentration) conflicts with the short-run prediction just set forth (postponement of exit), so that no sign prediction is possible. Another measure of scale economies can be used as an alternative to KL:

CD = cost disadvantage ratio, defined as value added per worker in plants smaller than the one accounting for the fiftieth percentile of output, divided by value added per worker in plants above this threshold

CD is an inverse measure of apparent scale economies in actual plants. It has shown some explanatory power in previous studies, although it is clearly a noisy indicator.[11]

In the long run the monopolistic-competition model holds that enterprises surviving an increase in exposure to international trade should increase their scales. The effect on producer concentration, however, is ambiguous because the size distribution of the survivors may change. Also, as with capital intensity (KL), the short and long runs may diverge because goodwill that is durable but depreciating can retard domestic companies' displacement by foreign rivals with a cost advantage. Product differentiation, the structural source of these predictions, hence should mediate the effect of trade disturbances on industry structure. This concept is difficult to implement statistically, because it can rest on several fundamental bases. The industry's rate of advertising expenditure, the usual choice, captures only one facet of differentiation. Factor analysis was used to compute:

$D1$ = first factor extracted from a group of variables describing aspects of differentiation; it positively reflects minor purchases made on the basis of advertised information and negatively reflects complex, customized, and/or innovative products.

$D2$ = second factor extracted from variables generating $D1$; it positively reflects innovative goods accompanied by large flows of information and auxiliary services from seller to buyer.[12]

The sign of $D1$'s interactive influence is not predictable. $D2$ should less ambiguously retard the effects of import competition on domestic producers and enlarge the long-run concentrating effects of export expansion.

The final interactive variable captures collusive behavior. If domestic producers maintain a collusively determined price in the face of increased import penetration (due to cost or other advantages), they may be expelled from the market sooner or in greater numbers than if their price responds competitively. Casual observation suggests that illegal price-fixing agreements are commonplace in certain sectors, and so the incidence of antitrust indictments is taken as an indicator of the extent of collusive pricing.

AT = total number of indictments brought against firms in the industry for violations of Section 1 of the Sherman Act.[13]

AT should amplify the effect of import penetration on concentration by speeding the elimination of domestic producers. However, no effect on exporting behavior is expected.

Some of the hypothesized interactive effects of import penetration should operate symmetrically as effects of export expansion, while others are asymmetrical or simply inapplicable. Product differentiation ($D1$, $D2$) may modify the effects of growing export opportunities, although sign predictions (as before) are hard to obtain. Capital intensity (KL) should indicate unexploited opportunities to attain scale economies that could mitigate any deconcentrating effect of export growth (or dampen the increase in the number of plants).[14] Because additional resources are usually being committed to an industry as its exports expand, however, the hypotheses associated with import penetration and sunk capital no longer apply.

Additive Hypotheses

Two exogenous variables should exert additive rather than multiplicative influences on changes in industry structure. The effect of sunk resources depends on both their proportional importance and the duration of their commitment. Importance should be captured by the variables already defined. Furthermore, one might assume that (among industries) the importance of committed resources is correlated with the duration of their commitment: what labor-intensive industry uses highly durable capital? What industry using lots of specialized capital must replace it frequently? Nonetheless, we can control directly for changes in the age structure of an industry's gross capital:

$DAGE$ = change in the average age of the industry's capital stock (weighted average of changes in the age of plant and the age of equipment)

$DAGE$ is not truly exogenous, since allowing capital to age further in place in a declining activity is an alternative to scrapping it and eliminating the production unit that employed it. That is, for an industry's capital to age, enterprise units must remain in place that would have vanished if older capital were scrapped. Thus, $DAGE$ indirectly reflects the otherwise unobservable marginal returns to keeping the older part of the capital stock in use. $DAGE$ is negatively associated with the removal of capacity, and it should be positively related to the change in the number of units in the industry and thus negatively to the change in its concentration.

The specification of the remaining variable, tariff protection, is open to debate. U.S. industries' rates of protection changed over the period 1958–77 because of multilateral tariff reductions (principally the Kennedy Round under the General Agreement on Tariffs and Trade) and the effect of inflation on the incidence of specific duties. The tariff change is only one of many factors affecting an industry's exposure to trade, but it has the advantage of submitting to reasonably accurate measurement. Can we make use of this variable, even though we assume that disturbances affecting trade exposure are generally unobservable? Yes, if U.S. tariff changes convey information about future profits that domestic producers can expect, beyond the changes' observed effects on competing imports. If tariff increases signal a willingness of U.S. public policy to preserve enterprises in an industry (and decreases signal a disinclination), then the enterprise population should increase with the tariff change even after controlling for actual import changes.

TF = import duties divided by value of imports at end of period, expressed as a fraction of import duties divided by value of imports at beginning of period[15]

The variable omits changes in nontariff barriers to trade, because adequate data are not available. Arguments can be made both for interacting TF with DM in the same fashion as the variables defined above and for treating it as an additive variable; both additive and interactive specifications were tried. Either way, with DM controlled, TF should be positively related to the change in the number of production units and thus negatively related to producer concentration.

EMPIRICAL RESULTS

The estimation period of 1958 to 1977 was chosen to reflect considerations devolving from theory, prior evidence, and the availability of data. Traded-goods shares in U.S. economic activity have expanded fairly steadily since the post-World War II recovery period, so no period is uniquely appropriate for observing the change in exposure to trade. Our emphasis on adjustment processes implies estimation over a period short enough to capture adjustment under way. However, previous research suggests that industry structures change so slowly that they should be observed for at least a decade. Hence, applying the model to a period of two decades seems reasonable.[16]

To generate a sample of industries, I started with the full population of four-digit SIC manufacturing industries (about 450), eliminating at the outset those that were redefined in the classification system between 1958 and 1977 and those to which import and export data could not be matched. That left 86 industries. Missing values of interactive variables cost some additional degrees of freedom, so that most equations reported below employ 65–70 observations.[17]

Determinants of Concentration Changes

The model was applied to explain a series of industry-structure parameters (producer concentration, the number of plants, and the number of companies). Care is needed in interpreting the results of the interactive model used in this analysis. First, the interactions unavoidably build a great deal of multicollinearity into the data set, making the magnitudes and significance levels of individual coefficients quite sensitive to changes in the specification of the model. This would not be important if a single "tight" model were available that left no doubt what variables should be included. However, when the model comprises independent theoretical considerations of varying plausibility, a definitive list of regressors is lacking. Therefore, a considered judgment about the acceptance or rejection of a particular hypothesis depends on the robustness of the result as well as standard significance tests.

Second, one must keep the interactive model in mind when interpreting the coefficients of DM and DX. Their *net* coefficients in any equation depend on the values of the interacted variables. To confirm the sign predictions for DM and DX, we must ascertain whether these net coefficients have the expected signs for "reasonable" values of the interacted variables.

Table 1–1 presents estimates of the determinants of changes in a specific measure of producer concentration (the share of shipments accounted for by the four largest producers). Equation 1 reports the core of the model.[18] The change in concentration is negatively related to the real change in shipments, as expected, and positively related to the virtual displacement of domestic production by imports. The coefficient of DM (imports) is twice that of DSH (shipments), which suggests that the smaller enterprises disproportionately lose market share to imports.[19] The export component of shipments growth (DX) takes a negative coefficient that is not significant; the sign implies that disturbances expanding exports have not favored the larger companies.

The remaining equations add various interactive terms. The interaction between DM and PW ($DMPW$) takes a significant positive coefficient and turns the coefficient of DM itself negative, implying that the concentrating effect of import competition sets in when produc-

Table 1-1. Determinants of Changes in Four-Firm Producer Concentration, 1958–1977.

Exogenous Variable	Equation				
	1	2	3	4	5
Constant	.141 (2.40)	.387 (2.68)	.435 (2.89)	.421 (2.97)	.440 (3.05)
DSH	-.239 (2.78)	-.223 (2.78)	-.195 (2.28)	-.279 (3.53)	-.214 (2.61)
DX	-.330 (.68)	-.252 (.62)	-1.556 (2.48)	-.261 (.43)	-.627 (.91)
DM	.479 (2.01)	-5.017 (2.72)	.602 (2.25)	-.718 (2.13)	-3.242 (1.61)
DXKL	—	.014 (1.45)	.034 (2.48)	.015 (1.38)	.026 (2.02)
DMPW	—	6.814 (2.89)	—	—	5.303 (2.18)
DMKL	—	—	-.026 (1.89)	—	-.018 (1.31)
DMD1	—	—	—	-1.166 (3.34)	—
DMD2	—	—	—	.216 (1.07)	—
DMCU	—	—	—	—	-.725 (1.54)
DAGE	—	-.126 (.89)	-.091 (.62)	-.149 (1.06)	-.153 (1.08)
TF	—	-.176 (2.17)	-.238 (2.47)	-.086 (1.08)	-.203 (2.18)
$\bar{R}^2$	.12	.28	.23	.32	.31

tion workers exceed roughly two-thirds of the industry's labor force, growing stronger as the nonproduction worker component becomes less important. The thickness of the industry's value-added slice has much the same interactive effect as *PW* (not shown); these two interactions compete with each other for statistical significance. Also something of an alternative to *PW* is the interaction with *KL*, significant at 5 percent in a one-tail test in equation 3 (but not equation 5), indicating that capital intensity mitigates the pro-concentration effect of imports growth. The results for *PW* and *KL* thus tend to confirm that sunk components of both human and physical capital retard the adjustment process.[20] No support emerges for the hypothesis that industries with high *KL* are affected by scale economies and hence grow more concentrated when exposed to increased import competition.

Equation 4 adds the two principal components describing structural product differentiation. *DMD1*'s significant negative coefficient indicates that competing imports knock out more domestic producers, or disfavor the smaller ones, when goods are differentiated by intrinsic complexity that when they are differentiated by advertising. This finding is a bit surprising, but may reflect greater importance of production scale economies for the complex differentiated goods. Because of the revealed importance of speeds of adjustment in the measured response of concentration to import competition, we added (after the event) the term *DMCU* to equation 5, where *CU* is the rate of capacity utilization in the domestic industry averaged over the period 1973–77.[21] As expected, low utilization postpones the resulting increase in concentration (notice that *DMKL*'s significance level declines).

Only one interaction with *DX* is shown, that with capital intensity (*DXKL*). Although its coefficient is unstable and its statistical significance depends on the presence of the same variable interacted with import growth, it does tend to confirm that expanding export opportunities increase concentration in industries subject to scale economies in production.[22] None of the variables describing the stickiness of adjustment processes proved significant for exports. The interaction of export growth with the first factor describing product differentiation, *D1*, obtains a negative coefficient significant around the 10 percent confidence level (not shown). The finding for exports thus weakly parallels that for imports (*DMD1*): export

Table 1-2. Determinants of Changes in Number of Establishments, 1958–1977.

Exogenous Variable	Equation				
	1	2	3	4	5
Constant	-.672 (5.01)	-.702 (5.42)	-.662 (5.17)	-.682 (5.49)	-.693 (5.77)
DSH	.643 (8.66)	.618 (8.58)	.632 (8.89)	.670 (9.59)	.635 (9.35)
DX	.425 (1.38)	1.400 (2.80)	-.153 (.41)	-.139 (.41)	.499 (.92)
DM	-.040 (.22)	.036 (.20)	4.166 (2.53)	.767 (2.58)	2.489 (1.50)
DXKL	—	-.021 (2.43)	—	—	-.016 (1.90)
DMPW	—	—	-5.412 (2.57)	—	-2.537 (1.12)
DMD1	—	—	—	.869 (2.84)	.577 (2.22)
DMD2	—	—	—	-.050 (.31)	—
DAGE	—	.224 (1.76)	.243 (1.92)	.244 (1.86)	.242 (2.04)
TF	—	.166 (2.30)	.174 (2.41)	.109 (1.53)	.146 (2.09)
$\bar{R}^2$	.63	.66	.66	.69	.71

growth promotes concentration for products that are intrinsically complex structurally.

Equations 2–5 incorporate the additive variables $DAGE$ (change in capital age structure) and TF (change in tariff). The latter is significant except in equation 4 and indicates that rising tariff protection tends to avert the concentration of domestic producers. $DAGE$ takes the expected sign, indicating that the continued viability of older capital preserves parts of the enterprise population and averts concentration, but its coefficient is not significant.

Table 1-3. Determinants of Changes in Number of Companies, 1958–1977.

Exogenous Variable	Equation			
	1	2	3	4
Constant	−.730	−.741	−.735	−.754
	(3.32)	(3.34)	(3.40)	(3.69)
DSH	.620	.611	.661	.677
	(5.10)	(4.94)	(5.42)	(5.77)
DX	.191	.546	.016	−.499
	(.38)	(.64)	(.03)	(.92)
DM	.011	.013	1.153	1.618
	(.04)	(.04)	(1.57)	(2.29)
DXKL	—	−.008	—	—
		(.51)		
DMMA	—	—	−2.932	−1.892
			(1.70)	(1.27)
DMD1	—	—	—	.875
				(2.22)
DAGE	.326	.326	.405	.374
	(1.51)	(1.50)	(1.86)	(1.87)
TF	.072	.078	−.040	—
	(.59)	(.62)	(.29)	
$\overline{R}^2$	.34	.39	.36	.41

Changes in Numbers of Plants and Companies

An increase in producer concentration can result from either shrink-age in the number of companies or increased inequality of their sizes. Tables 1-2 and 1-3 shed light on how the processes documented in Table 1-1 operate through these channels. In Table 1-2 the depen-dent variable is the change in the number of establishments, which is powerfully influenced by the growth rate of real industry shipments (the elasticity is about two-thirds). The export component of that growth was expected to have a negative influence, but in fact it is weakly positive unless the industry's capital intensity is high enough to make the scale-economies effect prevail (equations 2 and 5).

Import competition's effect appears only in interactive formulations: it decreases the domestic establishment population in industries that rely heavily on production-worker labor (equations 3 and 5) or make relatively complex differentiated goods (equations 4 and 5). The establishment population is enlarged where aging capital is kept in use ($DAGE$'s positive coefficient), and rising tariffs independently tend to preserve establishments. (TF's positive coefficient). The significance of several of these effects declines as variables are added to the model.

In Table 1–3 the dependent variable is the number of companies. The results closely resemble those for Table 1–2 (establishments), but significance levels are generally lower. DX exerts no significant influence, and the influence of tariffs (TF) is not significant. Thus the conclusions about producer concentration reported in Table 1–1 are closely reflected in one of its components, the number of establishments (Table 1–2), less closely in another, the number of enterprises (Table 1–3). This finding supports the emphasis placed on adjustment processes and scale economies in physical production units. Missing from the model are any determinants of how changes in the enterprise population might diverge from changes in the population of establishments because of mergers, sales of facilities, and other changes in control, although the determinants of such adjustments in the control of facilities might hold considerable interest. Testing the effects of these variables on the tails of industries' plant-size distributions yielded no additional insights.

Because adjustment processes and sunk costs dominate industry structures' responses to changing trade exposure, I pursued their effects on another dimension of structure—the product diversification of plants and enterprises. I calculated the change over the period 1958–1977 in each industry's plant specialization, defined as output of the industry's primary products emanating from establishments classified to the industry divided by the total output of those establishments. A decrease in plant specialization is consistent with increased use of plant capacity for diversified products—a possible short-run response of domestic producers to increased import competition. I also examined the change in each industry's enterprise specialization ratio, defined as the total output of plants classified to the industry and belonging to enterprises classified to the industry divided by the output of all plants belonging to those enterprises. A decrease in enterprise specialization is consistent with a reallocation

Table 1-4. Determinants of Changes in Plant and Enterprise Specialization, 1958-1977.

Exogenous Variable	Specialization Measure	
	Plant	Enterprise[a]
Constant	-.001	-.200
	(.13)	(5.24)
DSH	.007	.036
	(.40)	(.66)
DX	.235	-.831
	(2.14)	(1.59)
DM	-.081	-.348
	(2.09)	(2.37)
DXKL	-.007	.018
	(1.98)	(2.13)
DXAD	4.548	—
	(1.89)	
DXRD	—	12.876
		(.99)
$\bar{R}^2$	.14	.10

a. Data required to calculate this measure could be secured only for the subperiod 1963-72. Furthermore, data are available for only forty-three industries (sixty-six for plant specialization).

of firms' nonproduction assets toward diversified products—another possible response to increased import competition.

Table 1-4 shows that while the growth of production itself has no effect on plant or enterprise diversification, increased trade exposure does. Import penetration seems to promote defensive diversification at both the plant and enterprise levels.[23] Thus one economy of scope may be reduced costs of adjusting to disturbances to output levels of related products. Export opportunities appear to have somewhat different effects on plant and enterprise specialization. They reduce diversification of plants' output to a degree that increases with the industry's labor intensity. They reduce the diversification of companies' outputs, however, to an extent that increases with the importance of capital and research activities. (Plant diversification shows a similar sensitivity to another form of intangible capital—advertising.[24]) The effects of export opportunities on the two specialization measures do not necessarily conflict with one another, but those for enterprise specialization agree better with a priori expectations: the opportunities to reallocate resources among industries but within firms are greater where firms employ substantial tangible and intangible capital relative to other inputs.

CONCLUSIONS

This study has investigated how the changing exposure of U.S. manufacturing industries to international trade, over a two-decade period, altered their structures of production. Like other statistical analyses of changing industrial structures, the estimated models suffer from low explanatory power, and some results are sensitive to choices of specification that cannot be given firm theoretical bases. Nevertheless the study suggests that: (1) the effects of changing output levels associated with changes in trade exposure differ substantially from those of growth in the domestic economy; in that sense, trade changes distinctively affect producers' behavior and resource allocation; (2) sunk capital, tangible and intangible, strongly influences the speeds with which the structures of manufacturing industries adjust to import competition; (3) some evidence indicates that export opportunities increase the attainment of plant-scale economies; (4) structural product differentiation modifies the effect of import competition in ways consistent with the monopolistic-competition model; and (5) changes in the mixes of activities of both plants and enterprises help producers adjust to changing trade exposure.

These conclusions hold various implications for public policy. Advocates of industrial policy criticize some industries for not reinvesting to stave off foreign competition, others for not shepherding their resources into new activities that are internationally competitive. The results here suggest a substantial amount of private rationality in the adjustments that have occurred: resources were detached from industries threatened by imports at rates that were sensitive to fixed and sunk costs as perceived by private decision makers.

Although this finding does not establish that rates of adjustment were privately optimal, it suggests that the main problem for public policy lies in the price signals to which private decision makers respond. Do markets give the right signals about how long sunk resources should be kept in production? Are incumbent firms displaced too soon because their prices are inflexible downward? Are they retained too long because of the working of the tax system? Could the speeds of adjustment driven by the amount of capital owned by enterprises be too rapid for labor, the factor that embodies industry-specific capital but is not owned by the enterprise unit? Are redistributive policies applied so that they preserve the incomes of "disappointed" input suppliers without distorting their decision about when to withdraw from permanently vanished opportunities?

NOTES

1. I shall use the terms *plants* and *establishments* interchangeably to refer to physical production units sharing a common address and reporting as units to the Census of Manufactures. *Firms, companies,* and *enterprises* will denote establishments classified to an industry and under common managerial control. *Units* may indicate either plants or firms.

2. The empirical model is also consistent with disturbances to import supply (innovation; expansion of capacity), but it does not allow for supply-side effects on U.S. exports.

3. The conclusion holds if enlargement of the market is represented by an increase in the intercept of the market's linear inverse demand function. James Brander suggested the use of this reference model.

4. Curry and George (1983, pp. 216–27) surveyed the empirical research that underlies these conclusions. In some transnational comparisons the effect of market size on firm size seems to wash out any significant effect of market size on the concentration of producers.

5. The model does not explain endogenously why a domestic industry should contain different-size firms in the first place since none has exploited all available economies of scale. Satisfactory explanations involve incomplete collusion with ineffectively impeded entry or sequential entry with irreversible decisions about plants' scales of production. Clarke and Davies (1982) provided an equilibrium model with unequal-size firms, the result of diverse marginal-cost levels and Cournot behavior.

6. Improved export opportunities will shift the size distribution toward the larger domestic producers for another reason. The fixed costs of establishing a foreign marketing presence are apparently substantial, much exceeding those incurred in the domestic market. This postulate implies the corollary, confirmed by several investigators, that large firms on average export larger proportions of their outputs than do their smaller domestic rivals (Auquier, 1980, and references cited therein). A disturbance favoring the expansion of exports should therefore cause large firms on average to

undertake proportionally larger increases in their outputs, raising the concentration of domestic producers.

7. It is well established that import competition impairs the ability of concentrated domestic sellers to capture monopoly rents. The proposition has received both theoretical and empirical support; see Pugel (1980), Marvel (1980), Markusen (1981), and Geroski and Jacquemin (1981).

8. Shepherd (1964) found that the strong negative relationship between market growth and seller concentration broke down for industries with shrinking levels of activity.

9. Caves and Porter (1976) identified several categories of assets that seem to restrain the exit of firms from unprofitable activities. Besides durable physical capital they include intangible assets and intracorporate organizational linkages (shared distribution systems, for example) to other businesses of the firm.

10. We also assume, to complete the argument, that materials inputs are subject to elastic supply to the individual purchasing industry or (at least) subject to less compression of quasi-rent components in their prices than are the rewards to the industry's primary factors of production.

11. For instance, a low value of CD could indicate not diseconomies of small scale but opportunities for small establishments to use less capital-intensive technologies.

12. The variables yielding these factors include media advertising, other sales-promotion outlays, company-financed research, and a group of variables from Bailey (1975) indicating the marketing characteristics of the product. The approach to differentiation via factor analysis is discussed by Caves and Williamson (1985).

13. The variable must be considered a long shot, because it presumes that antitrust policy typically attacks industries in which collusion indeed occurs, but that it fails to eliminate the practice (except temporarily).

14. In a cross-section study of the structures of Canadian industries (not their changes), Caves, Porter, and Spence (1980) found that the effects of market size on both numbers of companies and company-size inequality were attenuated in export markets.

15. Because of constraints of the data base, the terminal year for observing this variable was 1972. Given the completion at that time of the Kennedy Round reductions, 1972 is about as appropriate as 1977.

16. Using a longer period allows us to dodge the question of whether lags may be important in the relationships hypothesized above. They probably are (Caves and Porter, 1980), but the paucity of data makes modeling the dynamics of adjustment an unpromising exercise (compare Levy, 1985).

17. We judge it reasonable to regard this erosion of the population as a random process. Losses of industries due to lack of matching trade and production data result simply from vicissitudes of the classification scheme. Losses

due to reclassification tend to filter out industries that were subject to major structural changes, rapid growth, or rapid decline, desirably retaining those without such changes.

18. Exogenous variables not mentioned in the following discussion proved insignificant or were not robustly significant. Because of multicollinearity, the significance of the typical regression coefficient in each of the following tables tends to decline as more regressors are added. Because some conclusions are sensitive to specification, several variant models for each dependent variable are presented.

19. However, the hypothesis that DM's coefficient differs significantly from that of DSH gets a t-statistic of only 1.0.

20. A supporting result emerges from a recent study of influences on seller concentration. Levy (1985) concluded that producer concentration adjusts to disturbances more promptly in unconcentrated than in concentrated industries. Because the former tend to be less intensive in both physical and human capital, that finding accords with our own.

21. Data on capacity utilization are not available at a satisfactory level of disaggregation before 1973. CU accordingly covers only the end of the period of the dependent variable, and we must assume (with ample empirical support) that industries exhibit persistent mean differences in utilization rates.

22. Interacting $DXKL$ with the cost disadvantage ratio, another indicator of scale economies, helped in some specifications but not in others.

23. Baldwin and Gorecki (1983) obtained rather different results for Canada, concluding that reduced protection during the 1970s caused Canadian plants to increase their run lengths and reduce diversification. Because the Canadian manufacturing sector is much smaller and less competitive than that of the United States, the two sets of conclusions may not be inconsistent, especially if high levels of protection in Canada had fostered high levels of in-plant diversification in order to avoid the diseconomies of operating specialized but still smaller plants.

24. In this instance the advertising/sales ratio proved a stronger explanatory variable than $D1$, with which it is positively correlated.

REFERENCES

Bailey, Earl L., *Marketing Cost Ratios of U.S. Manufacturers: A Technical Analysis* (New York: Conference Board, 1975).

Baldwin, John R., and Paul K. Gorecki, "Trade, Tariffs, Product Diversity, and Length of Production Run in Canadian Manufacturing Industries: 1970–1979," Economic Council of Canada, Discussion Paper No. 247 (1983).

Caves, Richard E., and Michael E. Porter, "Barriers to Exit," in *Essays on Industrial Organization in Honor of Joe S. Bain*, ed. R.T. Masson and P.D. Qualls (Cambridge: Ballinger, 1976), pp. 39–69.

Caves, Richard E., and Michael E. Porter, "The Dynamics of Changing Seller Concentration," *Journal of Industrial Economics* 29 (September 1980): 1–15.

Caves, Richard E., Michael E. Porter, and Michael Spence, *Competition in the Open Economy* (Cambridge: Harvard University Press, 1980).

Caves, Richard E., and Peter J. Williamson, "What Is Product Differentiation, Really?" *Journal of Industrial Economics* 34 (December 1985): 113–32.

Clarke, Roger, and Stephen W. Davies, "Market Structure and Price-Cost Margins," *Economica* 49 (August 1982): 277–88.

Curry, B., and K.D. George, "Industrial Concentration: A Survey," *Journal of Industrial Economics* 31 (March 1983): 203–55.

Ethier, Wilfred J., "National and International Returns to Scale in the Modern Theory of International Trade," *American Economic Review* 72 (June 1982): 389–405.

Geroski, Paul A., and Alexis Jacquemin, "Imports as a Competitive Discipline," *Recherches Economiques de Louvain* 47 (September 1981): 197–208.

Ghemawat, Pankaj, and Barry Nalebuff, "Exit," *Rand Journal of Economics* 16 (Summer 1985): 184–94.

Gorecki, Paul K., *Economics of Scale and Efficient Plant Size in Canadian Manufacturing Industries* (Ottawa: Department of Consumer and Corporate Affairs, n.d.).

Krugman, Paul, "Scale Economies, Product Differentiation, and the Pattern of Trade," *American Economic Review* 70 (December 1980): 950–59.

Levy, David, "Specifying the Dynamics of Industry Concentration," *Journal of Industrial Economics* 34 (September 1985): 55–68.

Markusen, James R., "Trade and the Gains from Trade with Imperfect Competition," *Journal of International Economics* 11 (November 1981): 531–51.

Marvel, Howard P., "Foreign Trade and Domestic Competition," *Economic Inquiry* 18 (January 1980): 103–22.

Owen, Nicholas, *Economies of Scale, Competitiveness, and Trade Patterns within the European Community* (Oxford: Clarendon Press, 1983).

Pugel, Thomas A., "Foreign Trade and U.S. Market Performance," *Journal of Industrial Economics* 29 (December 1980): 119–30.

Scitovsky, Tibor, *Economic Theory and Western European Integration* (London: Allen and Unwin, 1958).

Shepherd, William G., "Trends of Concentration in American Manufacturing Industries, 1947–1958," *Review of Economics and Statistics* 46 (May 1964): 200–12.

Williamson, Peter J., "Import Penetration in Imperfectly Competitive Markets: A Study of Firm and Industry Behavior under Import Threat," Ph.D. dissertation, Harvard University, 1984.

APPENDIX: DATA SOURCES

Data for this project were secured in machine-readable form from the Project for Industry and Company Analysis, Harvard Business School. The industries that could be matched between the 1958 and 1977 Censuses of Manufactures were determined from information contained in the 1977 Census. Data on producer concentration and the sizes of plant and company populations were taken from the Census of Manufactures. The measure of enterprise specialization comes from the Enterprise Statistics, Census of Manufactures, and is available for industries somewhat more aggregated (in most cases) than the four-digit SIC categories that are the principal units of observation.

To estimate the changes in real output for these industries we used price indexes provided by the Bureau of Labor Statistics for slightly more aggregated industries as defined in the input-output table. Changes in export and import components were calculated by starting with data on the shares of imports in domestic disappearance and exports in production for the beginning and ending years (data from the Census Bureau's *U.S. Commodity Exports and Imports as Related to Output*; considerable effort was expended to verify and extend the trade/output matches provided in this document). The calculation assumes that the prices of exportable output and competing imports moved proportionally to those of the domestic industry's output generally.

Some of the exogenous variables were also taken from the Census of Manufactures or the corresponding Annual Survey—numbers of employees and production workers, cost of materials as a proportion of value of shipments, total assets. Import duties as a fraction of imports come from *U.S. Commodity Exports and Imports as Related to Output*. Data on the age structures of capital equipment are available (for 1961 and 1976) on a tape provided by the Bureau of Labor Statistics, *Capital Stock Estimates for Input-Output Industries: Methods and Data*, Bulletin No. 2034. Advertising rates and other data used to construct the factors depicting product differentiation come mainly from the Federal Trade Commission's Line of Business data and Earl L. Bailey, *Marketing Cost Ratios of U.S. Manufacturers* (Conference Board, 1975). Capacity utilization rates apply to the years 1973–77 and are taken from Bureau of the Census, *Survey of Plant Capacity*. Data on numbers of antitrust cases come from J.M. Clabault and Michael K. Block, *Sherman Act Indictments, 1955– 1980* (New York: Federal Legal Publications, 1981).

CHAPTER 2

Managing Technology in International Competition: The Case of Product Development in Response to Foreign Entry

Kim B. Clark

The central role of innovation as an instrument of competitive rivalry has recently received substantial attention in both academic and popular writing about international competition. Business magazines carry articles on "chip wars," the "global telecommunications battle," and the "biotechnology race," reflecting the deep concern of both public and private executives around the world with questions about innovation and international competition. Much of the academic work on the topic, particularly in economics, has focused on explaining the competitive behavior of large aggregates— nations and national industries—in the international arena.[1] The work has examined the influences of differences in income elasticities, relative prices, rates of investment in research and development (R&D), and other structural characteristics on innovation, patterns of trade and investment, market shares in different products, and relative growth rates. Until recently less attention has been paid to the behavior of specific firms and the role that management of innovation might play in competition among international rivals.

This paper was prepared for the NEC/Kennedy School of Government Conference on International Competition. The research on which the paper was based was supported by the Division of Research, Harvard Business School. I benefited from joint work and numerous discussions with R. Jaikumar. Mark Thomas, Stephen Binder, and Takahiro Fujimoto provided excellent research assistance.

As Rosenbloom (1978) has noted, the absence of work that links management of innovation and competition reflects the very different orientations of students of competition and students of management.[2] The former focus primarily on markets, using the tools of economics and relatively simple notions about what goes on inside firms. The latter focus on the complexity of the firm's inner life, making simplifying assumptions about markets and competition. In some ways this difference in orientation reflects a healthy division of labor. But from the standpoint of policy, whether public or private, on international competition and innovation, a greater understanding of the role of management in competition seems essential. Effective executive decision and action depend on the competitive environment as well as on what happens inside the firm. Similarly, public policy on innovation and international competition will work its effect through firms, where behavior is strongly influenced by the internal structure and processes that govern decision and action.

This paper introduces a conceptual framework linking changes in technology to management and to competition. Case studies of innovation and international competition illustrate the framework and highlight the role of organization and management. All of the cases involve firms' attempts to use technology and innovation for competitive advantage. Although the framework applies to the role of management and competitive interaction in general, I focus here on one kind of competitive episode: the entry of a foreign competitor into a domestic market and the response of incumbents. Because a foreign competitor's entry changes established patterns of competition, it provides a useful window through which to view the general process of competitive interaction.

The specific questions that motivate the work concern the success of technology-based entry by foreign firms and the problems of domestic incumbents in mounting an effective response. Technological innovation in a firm involves the creation and application of knowledge. Thus I see learning and problem solving as the principal managerial task in innovation. Moreover, organizational structure and managerial process influence and interact with changes in technology. The framework suggests how the evolution of technology is linked to changes in organization and modes of problem solving. I argue that tendencies in the evolution of technology, organization, and learning, enhance the efficiency of the established products and methods of operation, but leave the enterprise vulnerable to new concepts and approaches. This vulnerability helps to explain both the successful entry by foreign firms and the response of domestic incumbents.

Both entry and the response of incumbents may involve action across a range of business functions, including marketing, manufacturing, sales, and finance. I focus here on technical innovation and specifically on the process through which the firm develops new products and processes. Decisions and actions taken in product and process development require integration of technical and commercial disciplines within the firm and execution of the central managerial tasks—problem solving and learning. The development process thus sheds light on how the firm manages innovation and technology in general.

I shall begin with brief case histories of foreign entry and competitive rivalry in selected industries. The cases help to identify the questions of interest and to introduce the notion of technology-based competition. In subsequent sections the conceptual framework that links management of innovation and competition is developed and applied in an in-depth case study of entry and competition in the auto industry. I conclude with a brief discussion of implications for further research.

INNOVATION AND ENTRY IN INTERNATIONAL COMPETITION

The entry of foreign producers into U.S. markets once dominated by domestic firms has been an important theme of international commerce in the postwar era.[3] Major technological breakthroughs have seldom been a driving force, but in some industries innovation of a more subtle variety has played an important role. Here we examine the pattern of entry in four industries: automobiles, consumer electronics, ceramic packages for integrated circuits, and plain paper copiers. These cases illustrate the scope of managerial influence in innovation and international competition. They underscore the critical aspects of competition where innovation is used for competitive advantage—what I shall call *technology-based* competition—and suggest important questions about management and competition for further analysis.

Table 2–1 summarizes the pattern of entry by foreign firms in the four industries. These examples illustrate the role of innovation in a

Table 2-1. Patterns of Entry in Selected U.S. Industries, 1955–1980.

Categories	Industries			
	Radio Receivers 1955–1960	Automobiles 1955–1980	Plain Paper Copiers 1974–1980	Ceramic Packaging for Integrated Circuits 1968–1980
Representative companies				
Established	GE, RCA	GM, Ford	Xerox	American Lava (3M)
Entrant	Sony	VW, Toyota	Canon	Kyocera
Experience base				
Established	20+ years of production experience; major R&D labs	40+ years of production experience; large technical staff	14 years of production large installed base	50+ years of experience in ceramic materials and products
Entrant	<10 years old; some experience in tape recorders, transmitters	relatively small production experience (trucks) in home market	4 years of home market experience; experience in optics and cameras	less than 10 years of experience in ceramics (founded 1959)
Product concept				
Established	console-to-tabletop receiver (home entertainment)	large, all-purpose road cruiser	large, high-volume production copier, leased to customers	job shop; cerdip/multilayer packages made to order
Entrant	miniature, mobile play-as-you-go receiver	small, fun-to-drive, efficient urban car	low-volume desktop convenience copier, sold outright	ceramic packaging system (design, package, service)
Key attributes				
Established	sound quality, cost, dealer service network	styling, dealer network, price, ride (smoothness)	cost per copy, performance, service network	low bid; available capacity and expertise
Entrant	true portability, novelty	price, quality, fun-to-drive quotient	small size, high reliability, initial price	rapid delivery, high reliability, product development

New concepts in product/process	transistors replace tubes; miniaturized antenna, speakers, components	overall package and design; efficiency with zip, maneuverability; high quality, short cycle process	proprietary cadmium-sulphide sealed drum; liquid toner operation; automated process, simplified design	proprietary processes and equipment for short-cycle/high-yield, high-volume production
Subsequent technology development	improved sound quality introduction of FM; increased miniaturization; integrated circuits	FWD, high-performance small engine; high-quality fit; new materials for efficiency	microelectronics; automated manufacturing; new toner systems; personal copiers	complex circuitry; automation; new materials
Incumbent response	slow to react; concept initially rejected despite in-house prototypes; later played catch-up	initially: introduction of small version of big car; later (10 years): redesign for small vehicle	initially avoided low end; later (5 years) offered low-end product; new products suffered reliability problems; 8 years later developed competitive designs	business as usual; focus on small volume segment in packaging and older products
Outcome	entry creates new channels of distribution/new segment; entrant (and imitators) capture significant market share and new growth	VW creates new segment, later exploited by Japanese; U.S. firms lose market share and become followers in small cars	Canon (and others) carved out significant position in low end; Xerox lost market share but mounted counterattack	Kyocera took 70% of market; U.S. firms in prototype segment

Sources:

Radio receivers: George R. White and Margaret B. W. Graham, "How to Spot a Technological Winner," *Harvard Business Review* (March-April 1978), pp. 146–52; Richard S. Rosenbloom and William J. Abernathy, "The Climate for Innovation in Industry," *Research Policy* 11 (1982): 209–25.

Automobiles: William J. Abernathy, Kim B. Clark, and Alan M. Kantrow, *Industrial Renaissance: Producing a Competitive Future for America* (New York: Basic Books, 1983).

Plain paper copiers: Yoko Ishikura, "Note on the World Copier Industry in 1983," Harvard Business School Case Services (0–384–152); "Canon, Inc. (B)," Harvard Business School Case Services (0–384–151) (Boston: Harvard Business School, 1983).

Ceramic packages for integrated circuits: Gene Bylinsky, "The Japanese Score on a U.S. Fumble," *Fortune*, June 1, 1981, pp. 68–72; Kim B. Clark and Elaine Rothman, "Management and Innovation: The Evolution of Ceramic Packaging for Integrated Circuits," Harvard Business School Working Paper 87–050, June 1986.

kind of entry that has been quite common in U.S. markets in the last thirty years (and in other countries and other times). A foreign competitor (sometimes more than one) challenges the established (and usually larger) domestic firms with a different product concept based on innovations in product and process technology. The popular press often focuses on entry based on low-cost labor and an ability to undercut the prices of domestic competitors, as does some academic writing.[4] In the industries examined here and many others (e.g., tires, cameras, machine tools, semiconductor process equipment, Swiss watches in the eighteenth century), technology and innovation occupy center stage.[5] While low labor costs and low prices can be an advantage, they are rarely sufficient for successful entry and subsequent growth.

In automobiles, for example, Renault and Fiat were unable to turn very low wage rates into a competitive advantage when they tried to enter the U.S. market in the late 1950s. Poor performance, poor reliability, and lack of a dealer or service network were decisive liabilities that a low price could not overcome. The early efforts of Toyota and Nissan met a similar fate: underpowered cars that overheated and broke down frequently could not be sold.[6] A similar pattern of minimum standards applied to new entrants is evident in all the cases in Table 2–1.

The existence of minimum standards in reliability and performance suggests that successful entry depends on offering a distinctive bundle of product characteristics. Sony's transistorized miniature radio, for example, had uses and features quite different from those of the standard radio. Had the company tried to enter with a duplicate of existing products, it might have met the same fate as the early Japanese monochrome television manufacturers, whose lower-priced standard 19-inch sets failed dismally.[7] Not until the Japanese firms pioneered the marketing of very small transistorized sets could they carve out a position in the U.S. market.

A new product that meets minimum standards while offering something distinctive has a chance at getting customers' attention. To succeed, however, the product's distinctive features must solve some problem or constraint the customer has faced. The "problem" in the case of consumer goods may involve a latent demand (e.g., a desire for convenience and mobility) that becomes apparent when the product is introduced. In industrial products the customer's problem may be quite explicit. Kyocera, for example, capitalized on the semiconductor manufacturers' expressed desire for rapid delivery and high reliability. Its product went beyond the physical ceramic package (which was similar to those offered by the U.S. manufacturers) to include the servicing of customer needs for speed and dependability.

Solving customer problems, whether latent or clearly expressed, involves changes in the standard product concept and established technology. Innovation has ranged from minor refinements to sophisticated invention. Canon, for example, developed a proprietary cadmium-sulphide sealed drum for its copier, which (along with other patented developments) allowed the company to get around Xerox patents. But Canon also introduced copier designs that were simpler to manufacture and involved relatively modest innovations in component and parts design. Both kinds of innovation contributed to the distinctive product characteristics that Canon used for successful entry. Both the proprietary drum and the design simplification, for example, were important in developing a copier with fewer parts and less complex mechanical operation—one that turned out to be at least twice as reliable as the comparable Xerox model.

Customers perceive innovation in product design and product function. Changes in process are less visible, but no less (and often more) important. Though an innovative design can sometimes be produced with established tools and procedures, there is often an intimate link between development of a distinctive product and innovation in process. Kyocera's levels of customer service and product reliability were in part a result of proprietary processes and equipment for short-cycle, high-yield production. Similarly Canon's simple modular designs and automated processes helped improve reliability and reduce cost.

Creating value for customers through new product concepts and processes helps competitors not only to enter the market, but to solidify and expand their position. In each of the cases in Table 2-1, initial entry was followed by a long sequence of technical developments affecting both product design and manufacturing processes. The early transistor radios, for example, underwent significant development; sound quality improved, frequency modulation (FM) was introduced, radios became even smaller, and components improved. In copiers, electronics replaced mechanical functions, new toner systems were introduced, automation increased, and personal copiers with cartridge systems were developed.

This pattern is consistent with historical evidence on technologies as diverse as aircraft and petroleum refining. Products do not emerge in final and finished form. They evolve in response to new demands as customers learn, to new technical options as relevant knowledge accumulates, and to the challenge of substitute products or processes. The entry product is just the first step along a development path whose outline may be only dimly perceived at first.

The importance of understanding and solving customer problems and the uncertain, evolving nature of technology determine the impact and nature of managerial influence. Effective management of innovation along the development path depends less on advance planning than on learning from experience, solving problems, and adapting to change. In the face of complex and uncertain technical and commercial problems, the role of management is to interpret, conceptualize, identify opportunities, marshal resources, nurture and motivate, implement and evaluate. In a dynamic competitive environment, management's success in that process will not come from isolated decisions (bold strokes of genius), but from the pattern of decisions and actions that determine enduring skills and capabilities.[8]

The success of the entrants described in Table 2–1 thus probably reflects the success of their management in solving technical and marketing problems and developing requisite capabilities. But this is only half the story. One must also ask why established competitors—larger, more experienced, better endowed—were not able to mount an effective response. The entrants' early market shares were small and their impact marginal. Traditional mobility barriers—capital costs, commitment to established processes, and so forth—may have influenced the incumbents' decisions. Yet even when incumbents recognized the threat and were willing to make the necessary investments, their response was slow and often ineffective. Their products suffered quality and reliability problems and were often less well adapted to the demands of customers.

The incumbents' failure to respond effectively is particularly surprising given the apparent similarity in underlying technology. In automobiles, for example, the overall product concept of the entrants was different, but the component technology—suspensions, brakes, steering, and so on—was familiar to the incumbents and similar if not identical to established approaches. Shifting from an eight- to a four-cylinder engine does not seem to be a major technological leap.

In effect, the successful new entrants relied on a form of innovation that competitors found difficult to duplicate. There was no single innovation that the established competitors could identify and respond to. The distinctive set of product characteristics resulted from several changes in concept, design, materials, components, equipment, and procedures. Further, these changes involved in-house process development. As a result, established competitors found it difficult to identify the elements of innovation ("How can they deliver with lead times that low?") and their interrelation. And, of course, the more things there were to change, the more likely that the costs of change would be high.

The evolving nature of the technology further compounded the competitive problem for established firms, which may have been traveling along a different development path from that of the new entrant. Competition tended to take the form of a series of moves attempting to exploit development of new concepts in product and process. Despite apparent similarities in individual technologies, the focus of innovative effort and the required organizational and managerial skills were sufficiently different that established competitors had difficulty making the transition from one path to another.

The cases of Table 2–1 thus suggest that to understand the incumbents' response one must understand how technologies evolve and how that evolution is linked to the development of managerial capability. The next section develops a framework for exploring that link.

PROBLEM SOLVING AND INNOVATION

Problem solving is the source of innovation and the essence of management's role in competition. Innovation has competitive impact because it solves problems for customers and creates problems for competitors. The pace and character of competitive interaction depend on how incumbents solve the problems posed by the innovating entrant. To understand management's role, one must understand differences in the problems innovation creates for competitors and in their approaches to solving them.

This section presents a framework for analyzing the interactions between innovation and problem solving; the specific focus is on product development. I first outline a typical product development process and the characteristics of knowledge underlying it. I then use these concepts and the notion of a design hierarchy to model the effect of technical evolution of the product on the organization of product development, its rules and procedures, and patterns of communication.

Product Development: A Brief Outline

Development of new technology involves several related kinds of activities that create particular kinds of problems. The literature on the innovation process often divides these tasks into three categories: idea generation, development (including design and technical problem solving), and implementation.[9] The first task a firm faces in developing a new product involves linking in concept the possibilities of the technology and the needs of the market. This may require activities on several fronts: laboratory research to identify possibilities and feasibility, discussions with customers and potential users, synthesis of diverse information, and reflection. Several kinds of problems may arise in the concept stage, including known flaws in existing designs, unmet market needs, or technical capability with an unclear application. Although these problems may be well known at the outset, the firm's first problem is often to formulate the problem before it can attempt to solve it. The outcome of the concept stage is thus a formulation of the problem in the market or the technology or both, and an overall conception of the new product (i.e., the proposed solution to the problem), including its use, potential customer base, technical content, and so forth.

Development focuses on turning into reality this broad concept of what the product (and associated processes) should be. It is an interactive process of technical goal setting, evaluation of alternatives, and problem solving. In this stage too, problems involve the fit between market requirements and technical possibilities. Established components, for example, may not deliver the performance required or may interact with a new product feature in a way that hampers performance. Sometimes a modest change to the existing component will solve the problem. In other cases the solution requires a high degree of novelty and invention. Problems also arise in the relationship between product and process, particularly if the desired performance characteristics depend on advances in process capability. Achieving the new level of process performance is likely to involve the same kind of engineering work noted above—setting goals, evaluating alternatives, and so forth. But it may also require work on procedures and systems for operating the process.

The designs, prototypes, and working models that emerge from development are put into practice in the implementation stage. Now the manufacturing process is installed, orders are placed, organizations are created, and procedures established. The problems of this stage may reflect a simple failure to execute (late deliveries of equipment) or unforeseen interrelations between process steps, or between the process and elements of product design. Assumptions underlying specific design choices may have been incorrect; information about process capability may have been inaccurate. In fact, the knowledge needed to resolve those problems may not have been available; the process or product design may have gone beyond the limits of the firm's understanding.

Complexity, Ambiguity, and Uncertainty

The innovation embodied in a new product depends on solving problems in all stages of development. Concept, prototypes, and execution of design must be successfully combined. Whenever something new is created, whether it is a new concept, a refinement of equipment design, or a new procedure for manufacture, it depends on new knowledge. Throughout the process, problem solving hinges on the search for information and new knowledge.

The problems that arise in the innovation process all reflect a misfit between the requirements placed on a technology and its actual performance. The misfit may be due to perceived changes in demand, a change in technical possibilities in one area adversely affecting another, or a move by competitors that changes what the product must do. In a general sense, a misfit becomes a problem when the firm has an incomplete understanding of future states of the world, technical relationships, and customer choice. With full knowledge and comprehension, correcting the misfit would be a trivial matter of selecting the appropriate known alternative. Typically, however, firms must search for new information, insight, and understanding.

Economists and organization theorists interested in the allocation of resources and communication in research activity have used the notion of *search* as a metaphor for what goes on in R&D labs.[10] The metaphor applies equally well to development and to implementation. However, the literature tends to treat all innovations and all problems in a similar way. As Nelson and Winter (1982, pp. 248–62) have argued, the way search is carried out, the strategies used to ferret out information, depends on the context, the objectives, and the nature of the problem. Both within the development process and across different kinds of products and processes, there are important differences in the incomplete knowledge that firms face and thus in the character of the problems that arise.

Here I note three aspects of incomplete knowledge: uncertainty, ambiguity and complexity.[11] The solution to a particular performance problem (e.g., the speed of a microprocessor) may require search for information because the relevant cause-effect relationships are unknown. The potential impact of a design choice may therefore be uncertain. The problem may also stem from ambiguity: a lack of precision or an inability to measure relevant characteristics. The cause of a particular effect may be known in general terms (e.g., more A leads to more B), but the specific relationship (why and under what conditions A leads to more B; how much more A leads to how much more B) may be poorly defined and thus ambiguous. And even if a given cause-effect relationship is specified and well defined (unambiguous), complexity may make the larger ramifications of a design choice difficult to comprehend. The specific issue— for example, how to design a logic circuit in a microprocessor—may interact with so many other dimensions that a single individual cannot master all the relevant details. In this case, knowledge is limited from an organizational perspective. Problems may be created because information and knowledge are scattered among many different heads; it may not be clear just where the information is and how to get it from one head to another.

These three aspects of incomplete knowledge—uncertainty, ambiguity, and complexity—require different responses from the organization. All may involve search and learning of some kind, but there will be differences in where to search, what to look for, how to do it, and how to organize it. If the problem is in the link between design characteristics and ambiguous market requirements, or if the issue is to identify the appropriate product concept, the firm may need to learn by metaphor. The right kind of search may be for analogies that suggest a new conceptual basis for the product. A problem involving uncertain cause and effect may be amenable to laboratory testing, but may also require learning through use or experience. For the organization to take action, moreover, there needs to be shared understanding. Solving problems may thus involve not only search by individuals, but learning by communication. This is particularly true when the problem is complex and requires search and learning on the part of many people. The mix of uncertainty, ambiguity, and complexity in a given problem will influence how it is formulated and solved; the approach chosen and its success will depend on how the process of knowledge creation and application is managed.

Problem Solving and Types of Knowledge: Know-How and Know-Why

The problems that occur in the development of new technology are often idiosyncratic, reflecting peculiar substantive issues and the specifics of time and circumstance. But they arise in the context of an existing body of knowledge. Knowledge about a technical parameter and a product's performance, for example, may range from simple pattern recognition (e.g., A and B are distinct aspects and seem to be related) to a highly developed parameterization (other things equal, a 10 percent increase in A will increase B by 2.3 percent). The nature of a firm's knowledge has implications for transfer, communication, and application to specific problems. A full treatment of the stages of knowledge is beyond the scope of this chapter; here I will make a simple distinction between *know-how* and *know-why*.[12]

The development of a new ceramic package illustrates the important differences. Production of high-performance ceramics is a notoriously difficult process: hard to control, with low yields and wide variability in results. Those who design and engineer ceramics processes know a great deal about what is required to make a good package. They know just how to specify raw material composition; they know what chemicals to add to the base material to make it pliable and formable; they know how to adjust the casting machines to make a thin layer of material that meets requirements. Further, they also know what to do (at least some of the time) when something goes wrong.

This is know-how—knowledge about what to do to accomplish a given task. Whether it is a correspondence between a machine characteristic and performance or an interaction between two characteristics, know-how is action oriented. The operators may not be able to explain what they do, and they may not be able to transfer their knowledge just by telling someone else what they do, but they know what to do to achieve a given set of performance characteristics. And much of what they know was acquired through the trials and errors of actual production.

Know-why involves a deeper understanding of relationships and interactions. Knowing why a machine setting has the effect it does demands a more complete specification of the relevant interrelationships and a firm grasp on causes and effects. Whereas know-how develops in a natural way through repetition and learning by doing, know-why may require controlled experimentation and detailed analysis. Whereas know-how is action and task oriented and provides a basis for improving individual and organizational skills, know-why is understanding oriented and permits improvement through insight into sources of problems and precision in control.

Both know-how and know-why contribute to solving problems in product development and innovation. At any point in time the firm has a stock of knowledge (know-how and know-why) that reflects its experience, the results of previous investigations into its products and processes, and information acquired from sources outside the firm. Some misfits encountered in development can be resolved by applying existing knowledge. Others, however, cast old choices in a new light and require new information for resolution. Solving problems, therefore, adds to the firm's stock of knowledge and influences the evolution of its capabilities. In this sense, problem solving is like exercising organizational muscles—it not only accomplishes work, but enhances the organization's ability to do that kind of work in the future.

This notion that firms develop the ability to handle recurring problems or tasks has deep roots in the theory of firm behavior.[13] Nelson and Winter (1982), for example, have emphasized the notion of organizational routines as the basis of organizational skill. They see routines as repetitive patterns of activity within the organization, analogous to individual skills. Routines develop over time as the organization repeatedly faces and accomplishes a given task. This notion is related to Simon's (1957A) concept of repertoires, to Allison's (1971) standard operating procedures, and to Cyert and March's (1963) emphasis on rules and procedures in organizational search and learning. All these concepts share the idea that competence is rooted in experience and is the result of past action. The same logic applies in the current framework. But the link between a firm's knowledge and the solving of problems works the other way as well. What problems the firm sees and what it does to solve them depend on its know-how (and know-why). The new knowledge the firm acquires in solving a problem may affect what it does in subsequent development projects—which misfits turn into problems, how problems are solved, what new insights are developed. The dynamic interaction of problem solving and the firm's know-how and know-why thus determines the kinds of innovation it introduces and its enduring characteristics.

What is the nature of this dynamic interaction? Can we discern patterns in the kinds of problems that arise, and thus in the evolution of capability? If so, what determines these patterns, and what is the role of management in the process? Research on technological change in specific industries has uncovered common patterns of technical development. Work by Enos (1962) on oil refining, by Miller and Sawers (1970) on aircraft development, Abernathy (1978) on automobiles, and Abernathy and Utterback on several industries has shown that product and process technologies typically evolve through a sequence of innovations that build on basic concepts laid down by an early major innovation.[14] In recent work I have shown that this general pattern is driven by the interaction of problem solving in design and the evolution of customer demands.[15] That interaction shapes and focuses innovative effort in a way that depends on the nature of the product.

Innovation and the Hierarchy of Design

A complex product like an automobile or a computer develops through a sequence of decisions about functional parameters. These decisions are responses to discrepancies between the product's characteristics and customer demands. As each succeeding version of the product is developed, the search for well-adapted designs resolves certain problems and confronts new ones. The parts of the product that get attention and the kinds of changes that are introduced thus depend on the nature of the problems and the sequence in which they occur. The pattern of innovation depends on problem solving in the design of the product and the formation of concepts that underlie customer choice. Both processes impose a hierarchical structure on the evolution of technology. In the case of design, a hierarchy of concept seems to be inherent in physical objects.

Consider the automobile engine.[16] The central functional problem in the evolution of the engine was the choice of fuel and the principle of energy transformation. Such core concepts sit at the apex of the design hierarchy and dominate all other choices within the system. That is, the choice of a core concept establishes the agenda for technical development within a particular functional domain. In the early days of the industry, engineers developed and introduced engines powered by steam, electricity, and gasoline. Once the core concept became internal combustion of gasoline, the technical agenda was set for a variety of subsidiary problems and choices. Engineers and designers concerned themselves with how to start the engine, how many cylinders to have, where to put the camshaft. But such issues would have had no place on the agenda established by the electric-powered car. There the focus for supporting technology would have included the chemistry of batteries and the parameters of electric motors.

The specific choices made in solving design problems turn partly on technical considerations but are also strongly influenced by the evolving demands of customers. As customers gain experience with the product, they gradually change their concept of what the product is and how it relates to other products and to underlying demands for services. This process also has a hierarchical structure.

In the early days of xerography, the product was treated as a substitute for carbon paper and ditto machines.[17] Without experience, new applications for copying capability in the typical office were hard to conceive. So long as the basic product concept was not well defined and market research suggested a very limited market for such a product, a concept like *desk top copier* or *personal copier* was difficult to imagine. It was only with use and only after basic ideas about the use of copiers were established that finer distinctions based on machine size, speed, and features like two-sided copying began to segment the market.

The recognition of flaws in early designs or unmet customer demands directs the focus of problem solving and innovation. In the early stages of an industry's (or product's) life, product development is focused on core concepts. Once the customers, strongly influenced by the available design, weed out alternatives and settle on a particular set of core concepts, the locus of change in product development shifts further down the hierarchy of design. This shift is predicated on stability in customer demands (at least as far as established concepts are concerned) and the absence of viable technical threats to established concepts. This pattern of technology development is consistent with a growing emphasis on cost in competition.[18] When innovation focuses on core concepts, an innovating firm may achieve significant advantage through unique or novel product performance. When core concepts are stable, cost tends to become a more important factor in competition. Competing firms then seek advantage through conservative innovation. Changes in design focus on new ideas in subparameters that refine and extend the established concepts.

Organization and Patterns of Communication

Over time, as design concepts are improved and refined, items on the technical agenda that once were "open" become "closed." Alternative design concepts are not pursued. This narrowing and deepening of focus has implications for the nature of problems encountered in product development and thus for organization and management of innovation. To identify the central tendencies in management and organization, I shall examine an archetypal firm as it travels down the design hierarchy. The analysis is not intended to portray an inevitable sequence of events, but rather to identify tendencies in managerial behavior under certain assumptions about the firm's environment. For the archetypal firm, I assume that customer demands are stable and technical options given; core concepts are established and expected to remain so.

As the firm moves down the hierarchy new products arc developed within a framework established by previous choices about basic concepts. In each succeeding round of product development, managers, designers, and engineers elaborate the existing technical concepts and thus the framework of design. The firm's know-how (and perhaps know-why) expands, and it confronts problems of a different nature. Knowledge about cause-and-effect relationships increases, and uncertainty diminishes. Parameters are better defined and measured, and problems become less ambiguous. But because knowledge grows through elaboration of the important constituent elements of the core concept, there are more and more design choices to be made, more and more nuances to be understood. Product development becomes more complex.

This pattern of decreasing uncertainty and ambiguity and growing complexity has strong implications for the management and organization of product development. Increasing complexity implies that individual designers and engineers will tend to specialize in particular aspects of the technology.[19] Specialization allows the organization to overcome the comprehension limits of individuals through parallel focus of attention and effort across the various systems and subsystems in the product. Creation of such "domains of specialization" deepens knowledge of the details of the technology, but it also creates problems of coordination. It is here that declining uncertainty and ambiguity have their impact.

The managerial challenge is to coordinate specialized groups in solving problems that are increasingly complex, but more certain and well defined. Organization theory and empirical evidence on organization structure suggest that under such circumstances the managers of product development will use two methods of coordination: hierarchy and standardization.[20] In a hierarchical organization that mirrors the hierarchical structure of design, some individuals specialize in higher-order collections of design parameters (e.g., larger subsystems and systems) and supervise the activities of people working on subsidiary parameters. Information flows up and down the organization through formal channels. Informal communication may occur within domains of specialization, but communication across domains usually occurs formally through supervisors. As Leavitt's (1962) experiments have shown, groups using hierarchical information flow are more efficient in solving well-defined problems than groups in which information flows laterally.[21] In general, informal communication absorbs time that could be devoted to designing and engineering. With stability in core concepts and a legacy of precise and certain knowledge about the product, specialized groups do not need to stay in close, informal contact with one another in order to define the important issues, or to understand each other's actions.

The hierarchical structure of responsibility and of information allows the firm to exploit the potential in the technology, while economizing on information processing. It also allows the managers in charge of developing new products to set bounds on the design choices in the domains of specialization. Once core concepts are established and the overall product concept is determined, the executive mission is to reflect down into specialized domains the limits that define their task and that together define the overall objective. These broad parameters can be communicated through the hierarchy and their execution monitored. But control can also be achieved through rules. Because higher-order concepts remain fixed from one project to the next, the executive can establish rules and procedures that pertain to the outcome of the design (e.g., execute the design within these limits) or to the way the design is made (e.g., follow this procedure in executing the design). The rules achieve coordination (and thus control) through standardization. Both rules and hierarchy tend to preserve the established concepts. In that sense hierarchy and standardization are both predicated on the core concepts (and established subparameters) and in turn reinforce development that refines and improves them.

As the firm moves down the design hierarchy, its problems change, creating pressure for changes in the organization and management of product development. But the kind of thinking and the nature of problem solving in the domains of specialization change as well. When engineers design a small part of a product that has gone through a long period of development, they are armed with a body of knowledge about the specific component or subsystem. This knowledge is not limited to isolated details about cause-effect relationships, but it includes solutions to specific kinds of problems that have arisen in previous design projects. In effect, the designers can draw on a repertoire of solutions for classes of problems.[22] In addition, because classes of design problems may recur, the groups of engineers working in the domain develop strategies for identifying and selecting ready-made solutions, as well as for modifying previous solutions to achieve a customized approach.

Moving up the Design Hierarchy: Open Questions

Product development creates more than a series of products. As the archetypal firm moves down the design hierarchy, development generates a body of organizational knowledge, a set of procedures and routines, patterns of information, and an organization structure. The organization and management of product development both shape and are shaped by the evolving technology. Innovation is conservative, but powerful; it is the repeated focus of effort that unlocks the potential in core concepts.

But innovation is not always conservative. New technical options or a change in customer demands or competitor actions may alter the calculus of product development. New demands or new options may lead firms to reopen items on the technical agenda and seek competitive advantage by departing from existing concepts. Such innovation is most dramatic when it involves core concepts, but all movements up the hierarchy destroy the value of existing commitments and competence to some degree. Whereas a path down the hierarchy depends on stability in demand and technology, a path up the hierarchy is linked to greater diversity and uncertainty in technical options and customer choice. In that sense innovation that departs from established concepts has radical effects.[23]

But how does a move up the hierarchy affect the management of product development? Problems may become more ambiguous, less certain, more like those encountered when a technology is young. Organization theory suggests that the product development organization required to handle the ambiguous, dynamic environment when core concepts are in flux will be much different from the organization that excels at developing the next version of a long-established product.[24] But existing theory about innovation and organization tends to deal with ideal types (e.g., Burns and Stalker's (1961) organic versus mechanistic) and offers limited insight into a firm's organizational dynamics as its environment becomes more uncertain. This is particularly true when the changes in technology are relatively subtle.

Some authors have recognized that a radical change in environment will pose difficulties for the firm, but the managerial influences on the firm's transition have received less attention than the nature of the firm's fixed assets.[25] Abernathy's seminal work on the technology life cycle, for example, argued that single-minded pursuit of cost reduction (efficiency) through successive refinements of an established process will create barriers to innovation.[26] He emphasized barriers formed by product-specific capital equipment, related labor tasks, and highly integrated production processes, giving less attention to organizational and managerial capability. Thus the literature does not address several questions about the likely management of product development as our archetypal firm confronts a move up the hierarchy. What will the transition be like? What if only lower-order parameters, not core concepts, are affected? Further, what might explain the pattern of change observed?

The answers to these questions are important in the development of the framework and may also help us understand incumbent response to foreign entry. If entry forces incumbents to move up the design hierarchy, then subsequent competitive problems may be based on the way product development is managed in the incumbent firms. To shed light on these issues, I shall examine product development in U.S. automobile firms in response to entry by foreign competitors. The case serves two purposes. It provides empirical evidence on the role of management in competitive response to entry and offers a basis for refining and extending the framework.

ENTRY AND INCUMBENT RESPONSE: THE CASE OF AUTOMOBILES

The framework developed above encourages us to analyze competitive interaction between domestic incumbents and foreign entrants in terms of the effectiveness of incumbent product development in response to the problems posed by the entrants' new products. Here we examine the case of automobiles, with special focus on entry by the Japanese. A brief summary of competitive interaction includes an analysis of products offered and the resulting competitive positions of Japanese and U.S. firms. I also consider alternative explanations of events, including inadequate R&D investment and lack of general experience with small cars. My main focus, however, is on the product development process as it evolved in the United States and the problems that arose in responding to foreign entry.

Imports in the U.S. Market

Beginning in the mid-1950s European producers, led by Volkswagen, began exporting small cars to the United States. They were followed by the Japanese, whose presence became significant in the mid-1960s. Figure 2–1 shows the market shares of imported cars aligned with a chronology of important product developments. Although the Big Three (General Motors (GM), Ford, and Chrysler) initially lacked any products even roughly similar to the first import wave, they responded throughout the 1960s with new products that were lighter, smaller, and less expensive than their traditional vehicles. These cars were larger than the imported products and sold for a higher price. The Corvair, the Falcon, and the Dart were followed by the Nova, the Chevy II, the Mustang, and the Maverick. Some of these products developed impressive sales figures, but as Figure 2–1 shows, imports

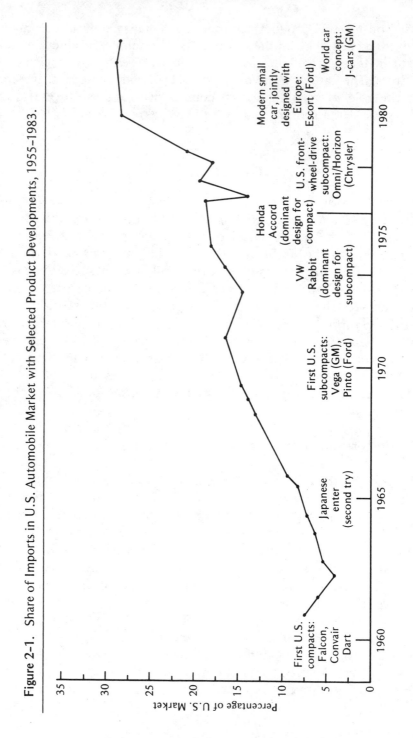

Figure 2-1. Share of Imports in U.S. Automobile Market with Selected Product Developments, 1955–1983.

made significant gains in the latter half of the 1960s after setbacks in mid-decade. Toyota and Nissan's combined market share grew from less than 1 percent in 1965 to 12.3 percent in 1980.[27]

Despite the introduction of U.S. products designed to be directly competitive with imports, the share of the Japanese firms continued to grow in the 1970s. The short-term swings in the share of the Japanese firms, particularly after the Iranian crisis of 1978, were due in part to sudden and unexpected movements in oil prices and the difficulty of U.S. firms in shifting capacity to small cars. But the longer-term increase in Japanese market share seems to reflect something more fundamental than simply inadequate U.S. small car capacity. Indeed, the introduction of significant U.S. capacity in small cars in the early 1980s did not by itself alter the basic trend.

How did the Japanese producers succeed despite a determined response by the domestic firms? Our framework suggests that the answer must have something to do with the characteristics of the products offered in the market. Table 2-2 documents the evolving product profile of Japanese and U.S. small cars. One conclusion stands out: on a variety of dimensions, the imported products were simply better. They tended to offer better acceleration and better handling, while using less gasoline. Japanese products had a substantially better record for frequency of repair. Certain Japanese models (e.g., the Datsun F-10) made a poor showing, but the average performance was superior to the U.S. average. The Japanese also did better in terms of buyer evaluation at time of delivery and defects per vehicle shipped. On all these dimensions, moreover, the Japanese products were a moving target. In 1965, for example, the Toyota Corona accelerated from 0 to 60 miles per hour in 17 seconds and had a miles-per-gallon rating of 25; in the early 1980s the Honda Accord cut acceleration time to 13.8 seconds and rated 31 miles per gallon.

The Role of Experience and R&D Spending

The U.S. firms' failure was not due to a lack of general experience with small cars or to inadequate R&D investment. Table 2-3 compares the cumulative production experience in small cars (those with a wheelbase less than 115 inches: compacts and subcompacts) of U.S. and Japanese producers. In the mid-1960s the U.S. firms had an overwhelming experience advantage in small cars. By the mid-1970s Toyota and Nissan had each produced over 10 million cars, but GM

Table 2-2. Comparison of Selected U.S. and Japanese Automobiles, 1965–1983.

Era/Model	Acceleration 0–60 mph (seconds)	Miles per Gallon	Weight (pounds)	Reliability[a]	Customer Ratings[b]	Defects per Vehicle Shipped
Late 1960s						
Toyota Corona	17.0	25.0	2,183	10	—	—
Ford Falcon	17.5	18.5	2,696	10	—	—
Early 1970s						
Datsun 510	14.5	25	2,130	15	—	—
Ford Pinto	19.0	24	2,046	10	—	—
GM Vega	19.5	20	2,264	5	—	—
Late 1970s						
Honda Civic	18.5	31.5	2,045	20	8.0	1.23
Toyota Corolla	18.2	26	1,940	20	7.8	0.71
GM Chevette	17.0	30.5	2,051	5	7.2	3.00
Chrysler Omni	14.5	30.9	2,230	5	7.4	3.70
Early 1980s						
Honda Accord	13.8	31	2,045	20	—	—
Nissan Sentra	14.4	45	1,930	15	—	—
Ford Escort	14.1	30	2,045	10	—	—
GM J-Car	18.8	25	2,421	10	—	—

a. Based on reports of repair frequency from *Consumer Reports*; points correspond to: 5 = worse than average; 10 = average; 15 = better than average; 20 = much better than average.

b. 1 = poor; 10 = excellent.

Sources: Consumer's Union of the United States, *Consumer Reports* (New York: Consumer Reports Books, 1971, 1977, 1978, 1982, 1983); William J. Abernathy, Kim B. Clark, and Alan M. Kantrow, *Industrial Renaissance: Producing a Competitive Future for America* (New York: Basic Books, 1983).

Table 2-3. Cumulative Production Experience in Small Cars, United States and Japan, 1960–1980[a] (*millions of units*).

Company	1960	1965	1970	1975	1980
Japanese Producers[b]					
Toyota	0.125	0.821	4.305	12.024	22.092
Nissan	0.131	0.755	3.508	10.238	18.877
Mazda	—	0.292	1.117	3.030	5.853
Honda	—	0.014	0.802	2.153	5.409
Total Industry	0.373	2.576	12.676	33.386	63.035
U.S. Producers					
G.M. (total)	2.598	8.839	15.032	23.216	33.778
North America	0.250	3.509	5.434	9.768	16.078
Europe[c]	2.348	5.323	9.598	13.448	17.700
Ford (total)	2.985	9.860	15.438	23.494	32.243
North America	.552	3.883	6.363	10.337	14.368
Europe	2.433	5.977	9.075	13.157	17.875
Chrysler (total)	1.569	5.224	9.094	15.413	20.011
North America	.188	1.805	3.018	5.655	8.322
Europe	1.381	3.419	6.076	9.758	11.689[d]

a. Compacts and subcompacts with wheel base less than 115 inches; specialty cars have been excluded.

b. All cars produced in Japan are assumed to be compacts or subcompacts.

c. European data cover Germany and the United Kingdom only. Since U.S. firms have large operations in Belgium and Spain, their European production is significantly understated.

d. Chrysler sold its European operation in 1978; cumulative production was then 11.689 million units.

Sources: Japan Automobile Manufacturers Association, *Motor Vehicle Statistics of Japan* (Tokyo: JAMA, 1983), pp. 14–15; Motor Vehicle Manufacturers' Association, *World Motor Vehicle Data* (Detroit, MI: MVMA, various years).

and Ford had produced over 13 million small cars in Europe and over 23 million in total.

The performance and quality problems of U.S.-produced small cars were thus not the result of inexperience. Nor did the U.S. firms lag behind in spending on R&D. As Table 2–4 shows, U.S. and Japanese firms devoted comparable proportions of sales to R&D during the 1970s; in absolute terms, U.S. firms' investments were substantially larger. Although some of these expenditures may not have

Table 2-4. Research and Development Expenditures and Sales Ratios for U.S. and Japanese Automobile Industries, 1970-1982.

	1970	1971	1972	1973	1974	1975	1976	1977	1978	1979	1980	1981	1982
Japan[a]													
Total R&D expenditure													
(billion yen)	57.0	70.8	89.7	123.2	148.1	142.5	170.3	209.8	258.7	291.6	330.3	440.8	488.7
($ billion)	0.240	0.300	0.378	0.520	0.625	0.607	0.718	0.885	1.091	1.230	1.394	1.860	2.049
R&D as percentage of sales	2.14	2.28	2.54	3.17	3.06	2.44	2.55	2.71	3.07	3.03	2.87	3.29	3.42
United States[b]													
Total R&D expenditure													
($ billion)	1.591	1.768	1.954	2.405	2.389	2.340	2.778	3.144	3.635	4.337	4.502	4.545	4.527
R&D as percentage of sales	—	—	—	—	—	2.7	2.5	2.6	2.8	3.2	4.0	3.7	4.0

a. The industry in Japan includes automobile manufacturers with more than 10,000 employees. Yen have been converted to dollars using an exchange rate of 237, the average for 1982.

b. The U.S. industry is defined as follows: 1970–71, motor vehicles and other transportation equipment; 1972–76, motor vehicles and motor vehicle equipment; 1976–82, motor vehicles (cars and trucks). In practice, the category is dominated by the OEM auto producers, and differences in classification have only a small influence on the size of expenditures.

Sources: Japan: Japan Ministry of Science and Technology, *Report on the Survey of Research and Development*, various years. United States: 1970–74, U.S. National Science Board, *Science Indicators*; 1979, table 4–2; 1975–82, *Business Week*, Annual R&D Scoreboard, various issues.

been related to small car development and production, the major R&D issues confronting the firms during this decade—fuel efficiency, pollution, new materials, electronics—were all directly applicable to small cars.

Given equivalent experience and R&D investment, why could U.S. firms not produce a small car competitive in performance, fuel efficiency, and quality with those of their Japanese competitors? Our framework suggests that the outcome may have depended on specific tradeoffs and nuances in design; it was not a question of how much money was spent, but of how it was spent and managed. Possible explanations for the U.S. firms' response range from cultural malaise to adversarial labor relations. I focus here on the issues of problem solving and the management of innovation in product development.

To gain insight into the product development process in general, and the development of small cars in the United States in particular, I reviewed published accounts of development projects, examined company documents, and interviewed engineers and managers in U.S., European, and Japanese firms.

Product Development in the Age of the Road Cruiser

When Toyota and Nissan made a serious effort to enter the U.S. market in the mid-1960s they confronted domestic competitors with long experience in producing an automobile that was peculiarly American. The U.S. auto market of the 1950s and 1960s was dominated by a product technology established in the 1930s.[28] Built around the water-cooled, carbureted V-8 engine, with automatic transmission, rear-wheel drive, power steering, and power brakes, the all-purpose road cruiser emphasized power, comfort, a smooth ride, and versatility. With basic product design concepts established in the 1930s, innovative effort in the U.S. firms from 1940 to 1965 was largely incremental in nature. The models introduced throughout the 1950s offered improved engines (e.g., plastic-insulated ignition system) and transmissions (e.g., variable-pitch blades on torque converter stator), and more noticeable product advances like rubber-tipped bumper guards, padded sun visors, and four-way power seat adjustment.[29]

The evolution of automotive product technology from 1938 to 1965 followed a pattern similar to the hierarchy of design sketched earlier: core concepts in systems and overall vehicle configuration were established early and then refined in successive rounds of innovation. The organization and management that sustained and guided this effort became more specialized and structured, more bound by rules and procedures. The contrast between development in the 1920s and the early 1970s is instructive.

In 1927 Henry Ford closed down the giant River Rouge complex in order to change the plant over to produce the new Model A. The car itself was developed in nine months by a small group of engineers headed by Ford himself.[30] The group was aided by the much larger existing production and engineering organization, but most of the design and engineering work was done in the library of the plant by the small group. By the early 1970s, product development had become a far different affair. Figure 2–2 depicts the typical activities and organizations involved in developing products in U.S. firms at that time. Four years elapsed between initial planning and the start of commercial production. Each company had several organizational units that specialized in major development fuctions: planning, design, market research, product and process engineering, component manufacturing, and assembly. Within each of these organizations there were further specialists and further levels of hierarchy. The development work—the actual investigation, design, and engineering—was governed by a formal plan in which the timing of specific actions was spelled out in detail. Project plans were based on a set of standard procedures (e.g., instrument panel layouts will be issued by the design organization 38 months before start of production), and rules established responsibility and forms of communication (e.g., design targets and key limits on vehicle structure had to be transmitted in a standard memorandum). The process also typically included a series of formal reviews, checks and cross-checks, releases and sign-offs.

The development of compacts and subcompacts to compete with the Japanese posed a significant challenge to organizations that had long focused on the all-purpose road cruiser. In the 1960s the U.S. firms generally attempted to compete in the small car market by producing smaller big cars—that is, by shrinking the size of the vehicle without changing basic design concepts.[31] But the products developed in the 1970s marked a departure from the road cruiser product technology. Not only were basic components different (e.g., four-cylinder engines, front-wheel drive), but the desired product profile,

Figure 2-2. Composite Product Development Process in U.S. Automobile Firms, Early 1970s.

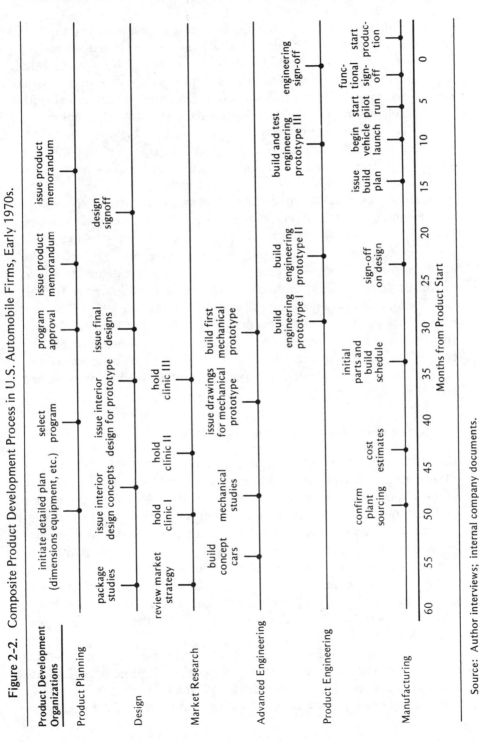

Source: Author interviews; internal company documents.

the critical characteristics that defined this segment of the market, were quite distinctive. Whereas the all-purpose road cruiser and its variants emphasized sheet metal styling, a smooth "boulevard" ride, a quiet, plush comfortable interior, and powerful engines, successful small cars in the 1970s emphasized fuel economy combined with good acceleration, nimble, sure-footed handling, and efficient use of space. Traditional products had depended on chrome, vinyl, and plush upholstery for distinctive image and appearance, but the new small car designs emphasized understated trim, lustrous paint, solid construction, and high levels of "fit and finish."

Meeting this new set of demands required U.S. firms to explore new engine designs, new kinds of materials, new uses of electronics, new kinds of componentry in brakes, steering, suspensions, and transmissions, and new concepts in process technology. Thus the effect of oil shocks, foreign competition, and market demands was to move the focus of innovative effort up the design hierarchy. Technical diversity flourished in engines and drive trains. In 1970, U.S. producers offered only five engine/drive train packages. One of the five (the V-8 engine, rear-wheel drive, automatic) accounted for 80 percent of all vehicles produced.[32] By 1980, U.S. firms offered twenty-one different engine/drive train packages; by 1984 that number had grown to thirty-four.

Changes in Communication and Collaboration

U.S. firms encountered significant internal problems in responding to these changes in technology and in market requirements. One source of poor performance appears to have been inadequate information and communication, a finding consistent with the logic of the design hierarchy. When the focus of development effort shifts to new concepts and previously unexplored (or lightly explored) paths, the problems encountered are likely to require new information flows and patterns of communication and collaboration across functional units. The auto producers' problem is illustrated by the role of design and manufacturing in product quality and by the relationship between R&D and manufacturing.

Producing a small car with fewer parts, automated processes, and superior fit and finish and reliability requires significant collaboration between product engineering and manufacturing. To obtain well-fitting body panels, doors, windows, and trim without extensive rework and repair, the car must be designed with "manufacturability" as a prime criterion. At very early stages of development, engineers and designers need insight into the capabilities of processes (e.g., how well tolerances can be held; how hard it is to develop a die to do a given shape). Manufacturers need to make clear both the abilities and limitations of their equipment, processes, and systems. Yet the established order in U.S. automobile firms in 1970 did not include such close cross-functional collaboration and early manufacturing involvement in design. Manufacturing had little role in product development until well after the basic design was established. Product engineering and manufacturing communicated through formal means like blueprints, mockups, and standard memos. Manufacturability was of secondary concern in design; the assumption was that any problems with fits, difficult parts, or finish could be handled in production with inspection and rework or repair. At Chrysler, for example:

> One of the flaws in the R-body cars was rattling windows. In examining the blueprints, Butts' people found a flange that was originally designed to extend in a straight line across the door panel to hold the glass firmly in place. In the production cars, however, the flanges were always curved. Engineers at the Twinsburg, Ohio, stamping plant were contacted and reported that they'd never been able to make the flange straight; they just couldn't build it as it was designed. The problem was solved only when Butts took the problem all the way back to the original product engineers, who redesigned the piece so that it could be made properly.[33]

Problems of collaboration and communication also were evident in the relationship between advanced technical departments and manufacturing. Technical specialists (including scientists and engineers involved in research and advanced development) had by 1970 become an elite within the organization and had very little contact with operating groups (either marketing or manufacturing). Thus at a time when the demands of the marketplace and competition required application of new technology, the technical organization was out of touch with the plants and customers. One company developed a new engine design in the 1970s incorporating new concepts in combustion and extensive advanced computer control of engine operations. Some of the systems in the engine were very complex and delicate. When the manufacturing organization evaluated the engine (long after the basic design was established), they argued (successfully) that the complexity of the design made it inappropriate for volume production in their processes and systems.[34]

Successful development would have required collaboration (and probably simultaneous development of new manufacturing capability) between organizations that had only a tenuous connection with each other. Such failures were not just the fault of engineers; often the manufacturing organization failed to make use of the available technical expertise. Another company, for example, encountered a major quality problem with a new product because of dust particles in the paint. For months, manufacturing tried unsuccessfully to solve the problem on its own. Only under the prodding of a senior executive was the R&D group consulted; they found a solution.[35]

These examples suggest that new design concepts may create new interdependencies and interactions—and thus new limits on knowledge—different from those on which existing rules, procedures, and information channels are based. Further, there appears to be a natural tendency for domains of specialization to become isolated. Specialization breeds expertise through focus of effort and attention. People working within a particular domain experience common problems and develop a common set of priorities and methods. Organizing around common tasks and developing common approaches contribute to the development of organizational expertise. But as Lawrence and Lorsch (1967) have argued, such focus of effort creates problems of coordination.[36] Firms tend to rely on formal mechanisms involving hierarchy and standardization to achieve communication and coordinate effort across groups. Clearly, under some conditions the firm will use other integrative devices like committees. But as development moves down the design hierarchy, the work of such groups is itself likely to become formalized and governed by standard procedures and routines.

Informal communication across groups also becomes more difficult, partly because of the differences in orientation, but also because specialization breeds differences in language and semantics. Marketers see the product and the world in terms of niches and segments, and they speak the language of price points and psychographic profiles. Manufacturers see the world in terms of volumes, costs, and reliability, and they speak the language of process control and quality assurance. Engineers and designers see the world in terms of their technical specialty, and they speak the language of fracture toughness, nanoseconds, and fluid mechanics.

The problems of communication and knowledge transfer are well illustrated in the relationship between the European and North American divisions of the U.S. automakers. Until the 1970s the divisions' product development efforts were not closely integrated. One might have expected that the shift in U.S. market requirements during the 1970s would have placed a premium on learning from the European organizations, with their greater experience in small cars. But the framework suggests that transferring know-how from Europe to the United States would not be easy. The two parts of the firm were divided by differences in language, procedures, know-how, and orientation. Because of specialization within the organization and the importance of organizational routines and repertoire, knowledge transfer would not be accomplished by exchanging blueprints or getting a few individuals together. Injecting European small car know-how into the U.S. organization would require transfer of individuals and working groups, and training on a large scale.

Although the U.S. firms tried to achieve closer European involvement through joint design projects in the 1970s, they did not attempt the more fundamental changes required for extensive transfer of European know-how. Some insights and understanding into specific aspects of small car design may have been transferred, but as late as 1984, the European and North American organizations remained quite different in approach and structure, and in their products (even those originally begun as joint projects).[37]

Moving up the design hierarchy thus confronts the organization with problems that require new information and new patterns of communication. Solutions to new problems may require not only that information flow outside or across existing channels, but that the organization's specialists learn a new language and ways of interpreting what they hear. The kind of problem solving required also changes. The new kinds of problems are less routine and more ambiguous, and the range of solutions is less certain. Even though the organization may once have solved such problems well, skill in formulating problems and dealing with uncertainty is unlikely to come back naturally. It is not like riding a bicycle. Since such skills are used less and less as the organization moves down the design hierarchy, they are unlikely to remain part of its repertoire. The skills on which the organization can draw are those of current routines, those supported by the existing structure and policies of management.

Gaps in Know-How and Know-Why

Failures of information flow and the atrophy of skills in problem formulation and in coping with uncertainty are matters of procedure, method, and organization. There is also the question of substance. A move up the hierarchy is a move into design concepts that may be unfamiliar. Gaps in know-how and know-why are likely to be revealed, not only for major changes in core concepts, but also for apparently modest departures from past practice.

After the oil shocks of the 1970s, reducing overall vehicle weight became a design imperative. Particularly in the small car market where miles-per-gallon ratings played a significant role in customer choice, each pound was critical. At the same time the design agenda included new objectives for fewer parts and far more efficient use of space. And, of course, weight had to be reduced without sacrificing objectives for crash protection, ride, noise, and so forth.

The issue of weight challenged the development organizations' traditional approach to design and engineering problem solving. In the era of the all-purpose road cruiser, weight was not a major issue, and manufacturers did not hesitate to add pounds (and additional parts) to the vehicle to overcome weaknesses in design. Noise problems, for example, might be solved by adding heavy sound insulation, while rattles and excessive vibration might be handled with a metal reinforcement or cross member. Problems with the hang and fit of doors might be solved with a few metal shims under the hinges. The development of the Chevrolet Vega illustrates both the tension between weight reduction and structural integrity, and the weight-increasing approach to problems.

> Chevrolet engineers took the prototype Vega to the GM test track in Milford, Michigan. After eight miles, the front of the Vega broke off. The front end of the car separated from the rest of the vehicle. It must have set a record for the shortest time taken for a new car to fall apart. The car was sent to Chevy engineering where the front end was beefed up. Already the small, svelte American answer to foreign car craftmanship was putting on weight—20 pounds in understructure to hold the front end intact. Thus began a fattening process of the "less-than-2,000-pound" mini-car that would take it to ponderous proportions. . . .[38]

General Motors' experience with the J-car project in the late 1970s illustrates how pervasive traditional design concepts can be and how hard they are to change. A subcompact introduced in 1981, the J-car, was probably 300–400 pounds heavier than originally conceived. A project manager described the problem:

> "I guess you could say the Japanese have been more mass conscious than we have," admits Brewbaker. He describes their tradition of building small, light, efficient cars, noting that Detroit has had to change its philosophy of design— one in which weight and size were not as critical. "It's a lot easier to make a component larger than it is to reduce it in size. That's what we're having to do, and it doesn't happen overnight."[39]

Once again, natural tendencies seem likely to leave the archetypal firm vulnerable to the effects of a new agenda. Members of the organization may be working with the wrong repertoire of solutions. What they know how to do depends on the problems they have encountered in the past. Movement down the design hierarchy reduces the range of contingencies faced and reinforces a focus on recurring problems; this tendency creates vulnerability as well as know-how. Knowledge of particular cause-effect relationships may be quite well developed, but knowledge of other relationships, along unexplored branches of the hierarchy, is likely to be quite limited. These limits pertain not only (and perhaps not even primarily) to technical matters, but to the relationship between the technical choices and market demands. The problems encountered may thus involve both unfamiliar technical details and new tradeoffs between dimensions of performance created by new technical alternatives. The old repertoire of solutions will be inadequate to this new agenda; further, the organization's strategies for searching out solutions and choosing among them may not work.

But the problem of knowledge cuts deeper. If the organization has developed deeper knowledge (know-why), one would expect it to have a basis for solving problems that fall outside its range of immediate experience. But does the development and refinement of technology provide the basis for new solutions? Does know-why tend to emerge naturally as the firm moves down the design hierarchy?

The answer appears to be a qualified no. Problems in the introduction of high-strength (HS) steels in automobile bodies illustrate the development of know-how without know-why. The introduction of HS steels during the 1970s allowed body panels to be made much thinner and lighter. But the new materials also introduced new design problems. One automaker's engineering group, for example, designed new HS hoods in the traditional fashion and had several prototypes made. Testing revealed that the new hoods resonated with engine vibration and even oscillated in some cases. Baffled by the problem, the engineers went back to the steel company with a simple message: it doesn't work.

For the steel engineers this response was perplexing. The body designers wanted the problem fixed, but had no clear idea what should be done. Of the several possible variables to be considered, it was not clear what action to take on any one, or which combination would yield the best fit with requirements. The problem might be with the thinness of the steel, the shape of the hood, the metallurgical or mechanical properties of the steel, or the stamping process. On further investigation it became clear that the body and stamping engineers had developed significant know-how in working with conventional steel, but had no idea why their traditional methods produced a part that did not resonate or oscillate. Established rules of thumb, probably derived from some long-forgotten process of trial and error, sufficed to meet traditional requirements.[40]

As this example suggests, the knowledge base of the archetypal firm is likely to be dominated by know-how. In certain situations, however, know-why may emerge as part of the normal course of development. In some cases learning by doing may create deep understanding not only of what works, but why. In other circumstances, development of the technology may require know-why. An effort to solve specific problems or a policy of competing on advanced technology may take the organization to the limits of the technology. In either case, meeting objectives may require pushing beyond those limits, which in turn may require know-why.

Overall, however, the firm's search for know-why is likely to be limited as it moves down the design hierarchy. The natural tendency is for know-how to dominate. The competitive imperative in any particular development project is to find something that works. When misfits appear, the issue is to find a change in the design that will remove them. If that search process creates know-how and know-why simultaneously, or if know-why is essential to the solution, then know-why will be developed. But otherwise, search stops when the developers find something that satisfies the requirements. There is no incentive to ponder why their solution works. There is no reward for spending the time and resources to conduct experiments that might add to know-why. In the development process, all the pressure is on solving the problem and moving on. Know-how thus develops in a natural way, but (except rarely) know-why does not.

Explicit policies to pursue know-why also tend to have limited impact. In the first place the development of know-why requires controlled experimentation and subsequent analysis. If time, attention, and resources are devoted to building know-why that will be of value in the future, the current development project may suffer. The usual solution to this tradeoff is to create another domain of specialization—a group devoted to pursuing know-why. This move may focus attention and improve performance on current projects, but it is unlikely to create a base of know-why supporting all of the firm's relevant know-how.

As a given design hierarchy is developed, it becomes more elaborate, its constituent elements better defined, its definition more detailed. Know-how builds up around the various elements, and specialization reinforces focused attention on the nuances of the design. This growing complexity of knowledge confronts the group specializing in know-why with several problems. Creating know-why in every aspect, every nuance of the technology is a daunting task. There are so many nuances, so many little details that the group probably cannot afford to pursue them all. Further, most of the nuances and details appear to work just fine. In the absence of problems (either commercial or technical) related to a particular aspect of the design, it will be difficult to justify allocating scarce resources to it.

Given scarcity and complexity, the know-why specialists are unlikely to pursue everything. In addition, the nature of know-how makes it difficult to enumerate and codify the nuances and details of the design. As Nelson and Winter (1982, pp. 76–82) have argued, much relevant know-how is not found in blueprints or specifications, but is tacit—that is, known (and usable), but difficult to explain or codify. Insight into the important details and transfer of know-how may require close involvement with the specific technology and the actual process of development. But in an organization where that know-how is created in a domain of specialization and the pursuit of know-why is likewise specialized, the experts in pursuing know-why are unlikely to get those insights. They are subject to the same tendency toward isolation, specialized language, and hierarchical information flow as the other domains.

Without close involvement in other domains, without unlimited resources, the know-why specialists are likely to focus their efforts where the significant problems are, where limits on the technology are impeding performance, where major performance advantages are possible. Even in their areas of focus, they may not appreciate all the relevant nuances and details. Consequently, when the focus of development shifts up the design hierarchy, gaps in both know-how and know-why are likely to make that transition difficult.

OBSERVATIONS AND IMPLICATIONS: MANAGEMENT AND COMPETITIVE INTERACTION

The evidence on patterns of communication, on isolated domains, and on know-how suggests an interpretation of foreign entry and competitive interaction in the U.S. auto industry. U.S. auto producers had difficulty mounting an effective response to Japanese competitors because market demands forced them to move up the hierarchy of design. They had a legacy of structure, procedure, practice, and repertoire very different from what they now needed. In effect, the game changed. The U.S. firms needed more than just new capacity or equipment. They needed new managerial processes, new patterns of communication, new knowledge.

The new technologies were sufficiently different and the nuances sufficiently important to cause competitive problems for U.S. firms. They had difficulty coping with the new requirements and were slow to develop competitive vehicles. In retrospect, the similarity of the new and old products probably contributed to the lack of response. The notion that a car is a car died hard. Had the foreign entry been a small nuclear-powered hovercraft, the U.S. firms might have realized the extent of changes demanded by the new environment. As it was, the depth and extent of the changes required became apparent only after several competitive disappointments. (As recently as 1980 many framed the competitive problem in terms of government regulation in the United States and cheap labor in Japan.[41]) Successful product development efforts by U.S. firms in the early to mid-1980s came only with major changes in people, practices and procedures, organizational structure, policy, and attitude and orientation.

But change (and particularly effective change) has taken a long time, and managers of U.S. firms have been criticized for their performance. The pattern of actions by U.S. and Japanese firms is not just a matter of management, however. At least part of the explanation involves a confrontation between two technological, organizational, and managerial regimes: one rooted in the logic of the all-purpose road cruiser, the other in the logic of small, efficient, high-quality, nimble vehicles. The strength and swiftness of the Japanese success in the United States reflected new market demands that favored the latter regime over the former.

The new environment and the problems of moving up the design hierarchy created opportunities that the Japanese firms exploited. For some of the smaller Japanese producers, changes in the United States created opportunities that were not available in the home market. Honda, for example, capitalized on developments in the United States to carve out a relatively strong position there.[42] Its success in Japan, where the changes of the 1970s were far less dramatic and established competitors were far more accomplished in the small car regime, has been more limited. In 1980 Honda exported 77.5 percent of its Japanese car production; its market share in Japan was 5.8 percent.[43]

A move up the design hierarchy will create problems even for the firm whose move *down* the hierarchy has been superbly managed. The Japanese firms succeeded in large part because they had a different, more appropriate, legacy of practices, procedures, repertoires, and know-how. But managers can influence the nature of that legacy and the kinds of vulnerabilities it poses. In the first place, pursuit of a development path that leads far down the design hierarchy is a strategic choice. Managers may choose instead to compete by introducing new design concepts that require the design, engineering, and manufacturing organizations to be open to new ideas and to cope with more ambiguous, uncertain problems. Such a development strategy may expose the firm to risks of cost disadvantage and design failure, but reduce its vulnerability to shifts in demands or technology.[44]

Even as the firm pursues refinement of existing designs, management can modify the tendencies toward overspecialization and isolation. How well a firm adjusts to technological and market shifts may depend on just how the move down the hierarchy is managed. Managerial action may modify and alter the natural tendencies of the archetypal firm. The U.S. auto firms seem to have carried the organizational and managerial tendencies (e.g., specialization, use of rules) quite far; in some cases the tendencies became dysfunctional. In contrast, the Japanese firms counteracted some of the same tendencies as they moved down their own design hierarchy.[45] Specialization by function, for example, exists in Japanese product development, but cross-functional collaboration and communication are more extensive than in the traditional U.S. operation. Product engineers regularly interact with manufacturing personnel on the plant floor, and there is more use of multifunctional teams, so that issues of manufacturability can be raised early in the design process. Personnel assignments give some engineers exposure to other parts of the business, and status barriers (e.g., pay differences, rank, dress) are much lower.

These practices may have reduced the isolation of functional groups and encouraged sharing of understanding and insight. They may also reflect a distinctive managerial orientation toward technology. During the 1950s and 1960s, U.S. firms refined and enhanced existing concepts without significantly improving performance; labor productivity, for example, changed little in U.S. auto firms during the period.[46] In effect, U.S. firms were in a kind of technological steady state. The Japanese firms, in contrast, experienced a period of dynamic growth, in both volume and technical sophistication. While they too moved down a particular design hierarchy, the domestic competitive environment and their position as upstarts on the world scene focused attention on sustained improvement of product performance. The Japanese organizations pursued their opportunities with a vigor not matched by their U.S. competitors.

With their emphasis on continual improvement and the lower barriers to communication and collaboration, Japanese organizations may have been less vulnerable to unexpected shifts in market demands or technical possibilities. Had they undergone the same kind of competitive shock as the U.S. firms, they might well have encountered gaps in know-how and needed to develop new patterns of communication—but the hypothesis is that they would have adjusted more rapidly and effectively. Some evidence for this proposition is provided by Mazda's ability to transform itself in the space of a few years from a high-cost, technology-oriented producer of rotary-powered vehicles to a highly efficient producer of high-quality small cars.[47] The most important lesson of Japan's success may be that conservative innovation can be pursued in a way that preserves the firm's ability to respond to unexpected changes in its environment. This notion deserves further study.

Implications for Research

In exploring why domestic incumbents have had difficulty responding effectively to the entry of foreign competitors, we have focused on the management and organization of product development. This perspective suggests that a contest among competing bodies of organizational knowledge and competing paradigms of management and organization underlies the contest among rival products in the marketplace. The framework presented here suggests that those organizational forms and managerial practices grow out of the interactions among problem solving, innovation, and organizational knowledge as an industry and a technology develop. Much further work remains to be done in developing the ideas sketched here and applying them to other competitive contexts. Work is under way to give the behavioral propositions in the framework a more rigorous foundation and to make clearer the connections between the competitive environment and the development of organizational knowledge.

The evidence presented here suggests that incumbent firms forced by market shifts to move up the design hierarchy are likely to experience a difficult period of transition. Whatever the merits of government aid in that context, traditional public policies aimed primarily at changing the firm's financial resources or its incentive to invest, either in R&D or in plant and equipment, are unlikely to work well. The competitive problem of the U.S. auto producers in the 1970s was not simply one of capital investment. In such situations an infusion of money, equipment, or scientists will not solve the problem without changes in management and organization. It is not clear what the government can do to foster internal change, particularly given the important role that the competitive pressure of foreign producers plays in creating incentive for change, and the central role of highly specific knowledge in charting a course of action.

Further research on management and on international competition might usefully focus on the role of "base markets" in international competition and the organizational and managerial foundations of their influences. Firms in different countries may have quite distinctive organizational knowledge and paradigms of management, reflecting differences in historical experience and domestic customers. Further, the nature of competition in the base market may influence the skills the firm develops. These differences in experience create differences in organizational knowledge and capability that may be a source of competitive advantage.

On the managerial side, a central research problem is how an experienced firm can manage itself so as to reap the competitive benefits of technological development, without eliminating (and perhaps enhancing) its ability to take advantage of new, possibly unforeseen opportunities. This is part of a set of broader questions about the nature and management of learning in organizations. On the competitive side, we need to learn more about the nature of advantages stemming from organizational knowledge. Under what conditions do they exist, and are they durable? Must the firm's know-how be acquired through experience, or can it be developed in other ways? Under what conditions can the firm's organizational and managerial capability be deployed in operations outside the base market? Analysis along these lines may shed light not only on international competition, but on other competitive issues, including the development of competitive advantage in general and in market niches in particular. All these questions require a better understanding of organizational knowledge and the management of problem solving and learning.

NOTES

1. There is a particularly influential body of work on trade and the product life cycle. Wells (1972) contains several important papers. Recent work has focused on the R&D content of trade and on innovation as a source of product differentiation. See Krugman (1979, 1983).

2. Rosenbloom (1978) proposed the notion of strategy as a way of integrating the two orientations.

3. This phenomenon is well documented for industries like autos, steel, and consumer electronics, but has also been important in textile machinery, semiconductors, telecommunications equipment, small forklift trucks, and many others.

4. The product cycle literature, for example, tends to emphasize the labor cost explanation for a rise in imports from newly industrializing countries.

5. David Landes's work on the rivalry between Britain, Switzerland, and later the United States in the watch industry shows that new technology was a critical factor even in an artisan-based industry.

6. The early experience of Toyota is described in Kamiya (1976); for Nissan, see Rae (1982).

7. Abernathy and Rosenbloom (1982) discuss the experience of Japanese television set manufacturers.

8. This distinction recently has been discussed in the literature on business strategy, where the traditional emphasis on linear, analytical strategic thinking has been challenged by an incremental, adaptive approach to strategy development. See Chaffee (1985) and Wheelwright (1984).

9. Examples of this paradigm are presented in Myers and Marquis (1969) and reviewed in Utterback (1974). Rosenbloom (1985) has recently adapted this paradigm to what he calls extraordinary innovation.

10. See Nelson and Winter (1982), chap. 11, for an extended discussion of the economic issues. The classic work on communication in R&D labs is Allen (1977). Related work on problem solving in engineering and design can be found in Marples (1961) and Allen and Frischmuth (1969).

11. These aspects of knowledge and much of the subsequent discussion are the focus of joint work with R. Jaikumar.

12. A more extensive analysis of the stages of knowledge is the subject of joint work with R. Jaikumar.

13. See, for example, Simon (1957a, b); Cyert and March (1963), Allison (1971), and Nelson and Winter (1982).

14. The broad outlines of evolution of technology are traced by Enos (1962) for oil refining, Miller and Sawers (1970) for aircraft, and Abernathy (1978) for automobiles.

15. See Clark (1985) for a discussion of the interaction between problem solving in design, and the evolution of customer needs.

16. This example is taken from Clark (1985).

17. For a discussion of the introduction of xerography, see Jewkes et al. (1960), pp. 405–8. Additional background on copiers is provided in Ishikura (1983).

18. This pattern of competition has been documented in a number of historical studies. See, for example, Porter (1980), chap. 8, and Abernathy (1978).

19. The connection between complexity and specialization seems to be fundamental to organizations as diverse as ant colonies, Eskimo hunting parties, and primitive as well as modern factories. The organization theory literature contains many studies. See, for example, Simon (1957a), p. 102, and Filley et al. (1976), p. 337. There is also a close connection between complexity and decentralization; see Mintzberg (1979), pp. 272–78, for an extended review of the literature.

20. The combination of complexity with stability is related to increased bureaucratization of organizations and to the use of standardization to achieve coordination. This is the thrust of work by Burns and Stalker (1961). A more formal, information-theoretic model of the relationship

between limits on knowledge and organization structure is the subject of joint work with R. Jaikumar.

21. See Leavitt (1962) for a discussion of the managerial implications of this research. In other experiments, Guetzow and Simon have shown that when left to their own devices, individuals in an unstructured group tend to adopt a hierarchical information structure to handle recurring problems. See Mintzberg (1979) for a review of these experiments.

22. Some choices may be highly proceduralized and routinized; in other cases there may be a range of options available without predetermined selection. Allison (1971) and Nelson and Winter (1982) present models that incorporate the notion of routine or standard procedure in decision making.

23. The definition of radical innovation in terms of its impact on existing systems of production is developed more fully in Abernathy and Clark (1985).

24. This proposition is a central implication of the contingency theory of organizations. See Lawrence and Lorsch (1967) for an early statement; much of the literature is reviewed in Mintzberg (1979).

25. Some efforts in this direction are evident in the work of Cooper and Schendel (1976), who document the difficulty established competitors have in responding to radical technological change. Bennett and Cooper (1984) argue that success in a product that becomes mature creates barriers in the form of complacency, myopia, and sunk costs that inhibit innovation. Nystrom and Starbuck (1984) emphasize the importance of the top manager's dominating ideas and world view in creating organizational inertia.

26. See Abernathy (1978) and Abernathy and Wayne (1974). Although managerial capabilities are noted in passing in the latter work, their nature and role are not explained.

27. These data were taken from Salter et al. (1984).

28. Abernathy (1978) provides a history of product technology; further data are available in Appendix A of Abernathy et al. (1983).

29. The incremental nature of innovation is documented in Abernathy et al. (1983).

30. See Nevins and Hill (1962) for a history of the Model A development project.

31. The exception to this rule was the Corvair, which incorporated several concepts (e.g., rear-mounted engine) that departed from established practice. However, the Corvair did not establish a new design direction; with its withdrawal from the market, application of those concepts came to an end.

32. Data on technical diversity, along with definitions and sources, may be found in Abernathy et al. (1983), chap. 8 and Appendix C.

33. Moritz and Seaman (1984), p. 205.

34. Author interviews with participants.
35. Author interviews with the senior executive involved.
36. Lawrence and Lorsch (1967) examine organizational differentiation (which grows out of specialization(and integration. They define integration as the "quality of collaboration that exists among departments." They are concerned with a broad notion of relationships among departments, and thus with conflict resolution. I focus here on the somewhat narrower problem of information flow and communication.
37. Author interviews with executives in Europe and North America. The lack of transfer is evident in the Ford Escort and the GM J-car, which are produced in both North America and Europe. The European versions share few parts with their North American counterparts and have very different operating characteristics.
38. Wright (1980), p. 190. The speaker quoted is John DeLorean, the general manager of Chevrolet when the Vega was introduced.
39. Yates (1984), pp. 55–56. The speaker quoted is Bob Brewbaker, manager of the J-car project.
40. The hood example is based on interviews with the heads of R&D from the steel and auto companies involved.
41. This view was expressed in industry white papers and congressional testimony. See, for example, Katz (1980).
42. Many U.S. industry observers have called the Honda Accord a breakthrough vehicle. See Yates (1981), pp. 37–42. Honda's market share in the United States was 4.6 percent in 1982.
43. Japan Automobile Manufacturers Association (1983), p. 9. Toyota exported 51.2 percent of production and had 38.3 percent of the domestic market.
44. This seems to have been the strategy of Hewlett-Packard in calculators, particularly in comparison with Texas Instruments. See Wheelwright (1984) for a comparison.
45. These observations are based on interviews with executives and engineers in Japanese auto firms. See also Imai et al. (1985) for additional discussion.
46. Comparative data on productivity over this period can be found in Cusumano (1985).
47. See Clark (1981) for evidence on the dramatic changes made at Mazda.

REFERENCES

Abernathy, William J., *The Productivity Dilemma: Roadblock to Innovation in the Automobile Industry* (Baltimore: Johns Hopkins University Press, 1978).
Abernathy, William J., and Kim B. Clark, "Innovation: Mapping the Winds of Creative Destruction," *Research Policy* 14 (1985): 3–22.

Abernathy, William J., Kim B. Clark, and Alan M. Kantrow, *Industrial Renaissance: Producing a Competitive Future for America* (New York: Basic Books, 1983).

Abernathy, William J., and Richard S. Rosenbloom, "The Climate for Innovation in Industry," *Research Policy* 2 (1982): 209–25.

Abernathy, William J., and James Utterback, "Patterns of Industrial Innovation," *Technology Review* (June-July 1978): 40–47.

Abernathy, William J., and Kenneth Wayne, "Limits of the Learning Curve," *Harvard Business Review* 52 (September-October 1974): 109–19.

Allen, Thomas J., *Managing the Flow of Technology* (Cambridge: M.I.T. Press, 1977).

Allen, Thomas J., and Frischmuth, "A Model for the Description and Evaluation of Technical Problem Solving," *IEEE Transactions on Engineering Management,* no. 16 (June 1969), pp. 58–64.

Allison, Graham T., *Essence of Decision: Explaining the Cuban Missile Crisis* (Boston: Little, Brown, 1971).

Bennett, Roger C., and Robert G. Cooper, "The Product Life Cycle Trap," *Business Horizons* (September-October 1984), pp. 7-16.

Burns, Tom, and G. M. Stalker, *The Management of Innovation* (London: Tavistock, 1961).

Chaffee, Ellen Earle, "Three Models of Strategy," *Academy of Management Review* 10 (January 1985): 89–98.

Clark, Kim B., "Toyo Kogyo (A), (B)," HBS Case Services, Nos. 9–682–092 and 9–682–093 (Boston: Harvard Business School, 1981).

———, "Interaction of Design Hierarchies and Market Concepts in Technological Evolution," *Research Policy* 14 (1985): 235–51.

Cooper, Arnold C., and Dan Schendel, "Strategic Response to Technological Threats," *Business Horizons* (February 1976), pp. 61–69.

Cusumano, Michael, *The Japanese Automobile Industry: Technology and Management at Nissan and Toyota* (Cambridge: Council on East Asian Studies/ Harvard University Press, 1985).

Cyert, Richard M., and James G. March, *A Behavioral Theory of the Firm* (Englewood Cliffs, NJ: Prentice Hall, 1963).

Enos, J. L., *Petroleum Progress and Profits: A History of Process Innovation* (Cambridge: M.I.T. Press, 1962).

Filley, A. C., R. J. House, and S. Kerr, *Managerial Process and Organizational Behavior,* 2d ed. (New York: Scott, Foresman, 1976).

Imai, Ken-ichi, Ikujiro Nonaka, and Hirotaka Takeuchi, "Managing the New Product Development Process: How Japanese Companies Learn and Unlearn," in *The Uneasy Alliance: Managing the Productivity-Technology Dilemma,* ed. Kim B. Clark et al. (Boston: Harvard Business School Press, 1985).

Ishikura, Yoko, "Canon, Inc. (B)," HBS Case Services (0-384-151) (Boston: Harvard Business School, 1983).

_____, "Note on the World Copier Industry in 1983," HBS Case Services (0-384-152) (Boston: Harvard Business School, 1983).

Japan Automobile Manufacturer's Association, Motor Vehicle Statistics of Japan (Tokyo: JAMA, 1983).

Jewkes, John, David Sawers, and Richard Stillerman, The Sources of Invention (London: Macmillan & Co. Ltd., 1960).

Kamiya, Shotaro, My Life with Toyota (Tokyo: Toyota Motor Sales Co., 1976).

Katz, Abraham, "Statement of Abraham Katz, Assistant Secretary of Commerce for International Economic Policy, before the Subcommittee on Trade of the House Ways and Means Committee, March 18, 1980," cited in National Academy of Engineering, The Competitive Status of the U.S. Auto Industry (Washington, D.C.: National Academy Press, 1982).

Krugman, Paul, "A Model of Innovation, Technology Transfer and the World Distribution of Income," Journal of Political Economy 82 (April 1979): 253-66.

_____, "New Theories of Trade Among Industrial Countries," American Economic Review 73 (May 1983): 343-47.

Landes, David, Revolution in Time: Clocks and the Making of the Modern World (Cambridge: Harvard University Press, 1983).

Lawrence, Paul R., and Jay W. Lorsch, Organization and Environment (Homewood, IL: Irwin, 1967).

Leavitt, Harold J., "Unhuman Organizations," Harvard Business Review (July-August 1962), pp. 90-98.

Marples, David L., "The Decision of Engineering Design," IEEE Transactions on Engineering Management, EM-8, no. 2 (June 1961), pp. 55-71.

Miller, Ronald, and David Sawers, The Technical Development of Modern Aviation (New York: Praeger, 1970).

Mintzberg, Henry, The Structuring of Organizations (Englewood Cliffs, NJ: Prentice Hall, 1979).

Moritz, Michael, and Barrett Seaman, Going for Broke: Lee Iacocca's Battle to Save Chrysler (Garden City, NY: Anchor Press/Doubleday, 1984).

Myers, Sumner, and Donald G. Marquis, Successful Industrial Innovations (Washington, DC: National Science Foundation, 1969).

Nelson, Richard R., and Sidney G. Winter, An Evolutionary Theory of Economic Change (Cambridge: Harvard University Press, 1982).

Nevins, Allan, and Frank E. Hill, Ford: Decline and Rebirth (New York: Charles Scribners, 1962).

Nystrom, Paul C., and William H. Starbuck, "To Avoid Organizational Crises, Unlearn," Organizational Dynamics (Spring 1984): 53-65.

Porter, Michael, Competitive Strategy: Techniques for Analyzing Industries and Competitors (New York: Free Press, 1980).

Rae, John B., *Nissan/Datsun: A History of Nissan Motor Corporation in U.S.A., 1960–1980* (New York: McGraw-Hill, 1982).

Rosenbloom, Richard S., "Technological Innovation in Firms and Industries: An Assessment of the State-of-the-Art," in *Technological Innovation: A Critical Review of Current Knowledge*, ed. P. Kelly and M. Kranzberg (San Francisco: San Francisco Press, 1978).

_____ , "Managing Technology for the Longer Term: A Managerial Perspective," in *The Uneasy Alliance: Managing the Productivity-Technology Dilemma*, ed. Kim B. Clark et al. (Boston: Harvard Business School Press, 1985).

Salter, Malcom S., Alan M. Webber, and Davis Dyer, "U.S. Competitiveness in Global Industries: Lessons for the Auto Industry," in *U.S. Competitiveness in the World Economy*, ed. Bruce R. Scott and George C. Lodge (Boston: Harvard Business School Press, 1984).

Simon, Herbert A., *Models of Man* (New York: Wiley, 1957).

_____ , *Administrative Behavior*, 2d ed. (London: Macmillan, 1957). Cited in Mintzberg (1979).

Utterback, James, "Innovation in Industry and the Diffusion of Technology," *Science*, no. 183 (February 15, 1974), pp. 620–26.

Wells, Louis T., Jr., ed., *The Product Life Cycle and International Trade* (Boston: Harvard Business School, 1972).

Wheelwright, Steven C., "Strategy, Management and Strategic Planning Approaches," *Interfaces* (February 1984).

Wright, J. Patrick, *On a Clear Day You Can See General Motors: John F. DeLorean's Look Inside the Automotive Giant* (New York: Avon, 1980).

Yates, Brock, *The Decline and Fall of the American Auto Industry* (New York: Vintage Books, 1984).

CHAPTER 3

The Machine Tool Industry and Industrial Policy, 1955–82

David J. Collis

T he recent industrial policy debate has focused on three major
issues. The first is whether industrial policy actually increases
national welfare and improves macroeconomic performance; this has
largely been the concern of economists, particularly the new international economists.[1] The second issue concerns the appropriate targets of a country's industrial policy and its structure: which industries should be picked as winners? which merit assistance in the face
of international competition? should U.S. antitrust law be rewritten?
This debate has been conducted primarily in the public arena.[2] The
third issue, which has concerned political scientists, is how the political process affects the emergent form of industrial policy and whether
unique cultural and institutional factors determine the viability of
industrial policy in different countries.[3] Research in each of these
areas has tended to take a single country as the unit of analysis and
has been primarily concerned with the aggregate industrial policy of
that country and its comparison with that of other countries.

This chapter instead takes a micro-level approach to address two
more fundamental issues. First, does industrial policy make a difference to an industry's performance in a particular country? Second, if

This chapter summarizes a paper of the same name presented at the Kennedy School of
Government/NEC conference on international competition. Readers are referred to that
paper for a more extended treatment of this topic. The author thanks Bo Carlsson for his
many valuable comments.

if it does, how can industrial policy best be implemented at the industry level? To explore these questions, I have taken a single worldwide industry as the unit of analysis and focused explicitly on how industrial policy influenced the development of that industry in different countries over time.[4]

METHODOLOGY

The machine tool industry was selected for study because it has been a global industry since World War II. It has experienced many changes during the last twenty-five years and has been the focus of active industrial policy in many countries.[5] In particular, the introduction of numerical control (NC) transformed the industry from one based on a mature nineteenth-century technology to one that, as an essential part of the "factory of the future," stands at the forefront of modern electronics technology. This technological revolution created opportunities for firms and countries to exploit new dynamic sources of advantage rather than merely await the evolution of comparative advantage, and so opened up a role for industrial policy.

Industrial policy toward the machine tool industry over this period varied significantly among countries, ranging from perceived nonintervention in the United States to broad activism in Japan. Because a wide spectrum of such policies could be evaluated across countries whose industry performance was radically different, it has been possible to make comparative judgments on the efficacy and desirable form of industrial policy.[6]

To isolate the role of industrial policy, the effect of other factors on a national industry's performance must also be examined. Prime among these are relative comparative advantage, macroeconomic performance, and the appropriateness and quality of companies' strategies.[7] Each of these factors significantly influences the performance of a country's machine tool industry and limits the impact of domestic industrial policy. No experiment could possibly control these factors, so this analysis relies on historical rather than scientific methodology to argue the role of industrial policy.

Even if industrial policy can be shown to improve the industry's performance, one can still ask whether it contributes to the optimization of the nation's social welfare. However, in focusing on the effect of industrial policy in a single industry, we leave aside the issue of whether the machine tool industry was an appropriate target for intervention in every country and define performance by the size and competitiveness of the industry in each country. Since almost every country defined a successful machine tool industry as one that increased national welfare (either for defense purposes or because of linkages to the country's manufacturing industries), and since the industry is imperfectly competitive, so that economic rents are available for capture, the difference in the definition of performance may not be substantial.[8] We must still, however, pay attention to the direct costs and economic efficiency of industrial policy in order to determine how it can best be implemented at the industry level.

COUNTRY PERFORMANCE IN THE MACHINE TOOL INDUSTRY

Countries' varying performance in machine tools is reflected in their shares of world production and world exports and is paralleled in their trade balances (Table 3-1).[9] From less than 1 percent of world production in 1955, Japan had grown to be the world leader in machine tool output by 1982, although it is important to note that Japan became a major exporter only in the late 1970s, when it was already a major world producer.[10] During the same period, the United States declined from just under half to just over 10 percent of world production, and in 1985 the $1.3 billion deficit represented 33 percent of U.S. consumption.[11] The United Kingdom's share of world production declined from nearly 10 percent to 3 percent, and France's share more than halved, while Italy nearly tripled its share. The relative stability of the shares of West Germany and Switzerland, and the emergence in the late 1970s of the NDCs as machine tool producers, is also apparent in the data.[12] To what extent were these differences due to differences in macroeconomic performance? Figure 3-1 shows that in the countries that increased their share of world machine tool production, the industry was growing faster than gross national product (GNP). Table 3-1 also shows that the countries most successful in machine tools showed a revealed comparative advantage in that industry (i.e., they had a greater 1985 share of the world's machine tool exports than of all exports). Thus a country's superior performance in the world machine tool industry is not merely due to superior macroeconomic performance but also reflects a superior relative performance of the industry within that country.

Table 3-1. Machine Tool Industry Performance.[a]

		United States	Japan	West Germany	United Kingdom	Italy	France	Switzerland	Taiwan	South Korea
Share of world production (%)	1955	40.4	0.6	14.1	8.7	1.8	5.2	3.3	0.0	0.0
	1985	11.7	24.0	14.2	3.3	4.8	2.1	2.1	1.2	0.8
Share of world exports (%)	1955	22.7	0.5	24.5	10.5	2.6	3.2	10.0	0.0	0.0
	1985	4.7	22.1	20.0	3.5	6.4	2.4	8.8	2.2	0.3
Country share of all manufactured goods exports (%)	1985	10.7	8.8	9.2	5.0	3.9	5.0	1.4	1.0[b]	1.6
Net trade balance ($ million)	1962	113	(143)	271	4	(46)	(30)	58	NA	NA
	1985	(1280)	1877	1308	(7)	418	(122)	658	97	(135)
NC share of production (% of value)	1966	15	1	2	3	6	4	NA	NA	NA
	1984	40	67	49	32	20	58	NA	15	NA

a. Data are for the entire world, including East bloc countries.
b. 1980 data.
Source: National Machine Tool Builders Association, *American Machinist.*

Figure 3-1. GNP and Machine Tool Growth, 1960–1980.

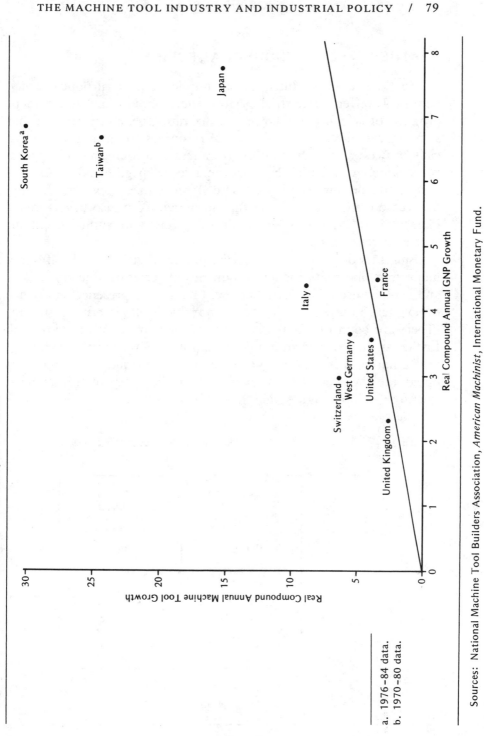

a. 1976–84 data.
b. 1970–80 data.

Sources: National Machine Tool Builders Association, *American Machinist*, International Monetary Fund.

THE EFFECT OF INDUSTRIAL POLICY

In principle, every country has an implicit industrial policy, which necessarily affects industrial performance, because any government program or action (from corporate tax rates to welfare benefits) has some effect on the commitment of resources to an industry. Typically, however, *industrial policy* is understood to mean explicit measures targeted at improving performance in specific industries, and that is the definition adopted here. I recognize, however, that the indirect consequences of government activity can also have a major impact on an industry's performance, especially in countries without such an intentional policy.

Using this definition of industrial policy, Figure 3–2 classifies the major machine tool-producing countries in terms of industry success and explicit use of industrial policy. Clearly, the presence or absence of explicit industrial policy does not by itself determine success. (There are countries in all quadrants of the matrix.) We need to look further at the exact form of industrial policies in particular countries.

Ultimately it is the strategic decisions of individual companies that determine the success of an industry. The first step of this analysis, therefore, will be to describe the changes over time in the economics

Figure 3–2. Industrial Policy and Machine Tool Industry Success.

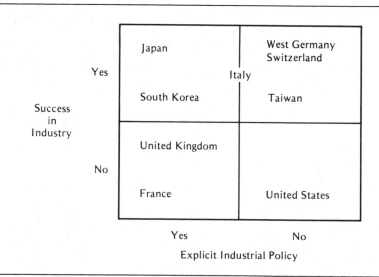

and the key strategic variables of the industry. Then I detail the history of industrial policy as it affected the machine tool industry in each country. Finally I examine how those policies helped or hindered the performance of firms.[13]

THE MACHINE TOOL INDUSTRY

Machine tools are of two generic types—metal cutting and metal forming—both of which are divided into more specific categories such as drills, lathes, and milling machines. These tools are further subdivided according to such criteria as size, type of tool holder, and vertical or horizontal action. In the 1950s, firms specialized in one or two narrowly defined types of machine tool, because the technology of each was different. To develop a lathe required a different design expertise from that needed to develop a grinding machine or a drill, and a lathe for the high-volume auto industry was substantially different from one for a job shop metalworking establishment. Machine tool type and end-use industry were therefore the key dimensions of segmentation, and many of today's machine tool companies were product and market specialists at that time.

This pressure for product specialization was reinforced by the reduction in production costs that resulted from accumulated learning in the manufacture of a particular machine tool model; by the ability of firms to build a reputation and an installed base of a given type of machine tool; and by the high costs of switching that customers faced when they held stocks of engineering drawings and jigs, and had accumulated operator learning on a particular machine tool.

The key to success in those days was to have a large cumulative output of a single model of a machine tool. The fixed cost of model design (estimated on average to be 10 percent of unit cost) could then be amortized over greater volumes, and companies could benefit from longer production runs and accumulated experience. My estimates of economies of scale suggest a 95 percent scale curve on model production costs and a 90 percent price experience curve during the 1950s and 1960s.[14]

In contrast, economies across model types or in large plants were severely limited by the sheer variety of models and the absence of modularization. Pratten, who studied economies of scale in the machine tool industry in the late 1960s, summarized his work by "emphasiz[ing] the economies for large outputs of individual models" and noting that "economies attributable to larger factories appear to be small in relation to other factors."[15]

As a result, each country's machine tool industry was composed of small specialist firms. The largest 20 firms in the United Kingdom in 1960, for example, were estimated to account for only half of industry output.[16] Even in the United States, after several mergers in the early 1970s, the metal-cutting machinery industry was in the bottom 20 percent of all manufacturing industries ranked by concentration levels.[17] However, because firms were specialized, the effective concentration was much higher. Pratten, for example, found only 6 of 200 firms competing on average in each of 44 classes of machine tool.[18]

Nor were these small firms at a disadvantage in sales or service networks. Machine tools in the 1950s were a relatively simple, mature-technology product that could be sold through distributors who offered a full line to customers. Similarly, since an installed machine tool required little service beyond regular oiling and replacement of the cutting tool itself, there was no need for an extensive service network offering rapid emergency repairs.

The segmentation of the machine tool industry in the 1980s is noticeably different, having been altered by the introduction of numerical control and by the establishment of the industry in the newly industrializing countries. Combined, these forces have led to the globalization of competition.[19] The industry now comprises four distinct segments.

The standard manual machine tools have been adopted by low-wage economies as the core of their developing machine tool industries. These are products that require no R&D and can be manufactured without a highly skilled work force and sold through distributors on the basis of price alone. Japan, Brazil, Taiwan, and South Korea have specialized in turn in engine lathes and universal drills.[20] In this segment of the industry, the evolution of comparative advantage has probably played a more important role than industrial policy in enabling developing countries to exploit their relatively low wages to build competitive machine tool industries.

Certain nonnumerically controlled machine tools are inappropriate for manufacture by the newly industrializing countries. Because of the complexity and customization of their metalworking technology, manufacturers of these tools must have substantial R&D programs, accumulated learning in design and production, and a direct sales force. In fact, this is the reason these tools have not yet been numerically controlled. Grinding, for example, is intrinsically a more complex process than drilling, less susceptible to analysis and automation. In 1983, only 9 percent of U.S. grinding machine tool production was numerically controlled, while three-quarters of all lathes and well over half the drilling machines were. Such machine tools remain close to their 1950s counterparts, and success still hinges on specialization by product type and large accumulated model sales volume. The major change in this segment has been a shift from national to global competition.

Numerically controlled machine tools are now the dominant segment in the industries of the developed countries (Table 3-1). This sector has undergone the most fundamental change in the nature of competition. First, manufacturers who wanted to compete had to develop computer and electronics expertise. Many chose to develop their own numerical control units; even those who purchased them from outside suppliers still had to adapt the control unit to their own tools, program the unit for the specific capabilities and dimensions of each tool, and install and service the complete machine tool. This required not only electronics and computer hardware knowledge, but also software programming capabilities. Manufacturers also needed sophisticated electrical and fluid engineering know-how because the cutting head was controlled by servomotors and hydraulic systems. Finally, the mechanical engineering requirement also expanded as the physical construction of the tool changed from castings to weldings in order to provide greater rigidity.

Since the 1950s, accordingly, the R&D investment required for each model redesign has increased; at the same time, the pace of product change has quickened. Numerical control technology has evolved rapidly, and no single innovation has revolutionized the industry with a once-and-for-all technological transformation. Instead an accumulation of small changes in related technologies and small improvements in design have required manufacturers to update their models continually in order to offer state-of-the-art numerically controlled machine tool technology. This continuous change has halved the average life of machine tool models since the 1950s.[21] The manual Bridgeport Series I milling machine, for example, had only two minor redesigns between 1938 and 1972, but by 1980, over half of Cincinnati Milacron's sales was in products less than five years old.[22] Broader requirements and faster change in technology together have increased R&D expenditures to about 8 percent of industry value added.[23]

Sales and service networks have also become more important, and their cost is now about 18 percent of industry value added.[24] A machine tool company needs trained salesmen to demonstrate the complex and expensive numerically controlled products to a relatively conservative group of buyers, particularly because the advantages of the product can often be seen only by analyzing total factory costs, not simply by comparing machine hour rates. Similarly, since the high capital cost of a numerically controlled machine makes it critically important to limit downtime, manufacturers must maintain an effective service network that can rapidly service any component of the tool, whether mechanical, electrical, or electronic.

Each of these changes has increased the fixed costs and the minimum efficient scale of firms competing in the numerically controlled machine tool segment. The industry level of concentration has increased correspondingly. In Japan in 1980, the six largest firms produced 37 percent of industry output, and in the much smaller U.K. industry in 1975, the seven largest firms produced 60 percent of industry output.[25] Moreover because the expertise and R&D in the new technology are applicable to more than one product type, as are the companies' sales and service networks, there are now substantial economies of scope that were not present with the old technology. Indeed, the machining center, which is the archetypal numerically controlled machine tool, combines on one tool several different metal cutting operations. As a consequence, success now depends more on company sales volume than on accumulated model sales volume. Although having successful models is still important in determining profitability, the successful numerically controlled machine tool company has to be larger and involved in a wider range of products than its predecessor.

The high-technology end of the numerically controlled market, the specialty numerically controlled machine tools, and flexible manufacturing systems (FMS) carry these economies of scope further. Given the need for robot, automatic pallet, computer system, and custom engineering know-how, competitors in this segment must not only be large in world terms, but have an extraordinarily wide range of products. Such companies have had to become more than simply machine tool companies; indeed, some of the potential competitors, like IBM and General Motors, are not even traditional machine tool manufacturers. In this segment, the machine tool has become merely a piece of hardware in a much larger system package.

A certain amount of international specialization has been apparent throughout the postwar period, with firms in one country tending to produce the same type of machine tool. The newly industrializing countries have concentrated on standard manual machine tools, but within the developed countries, there has also been specialization. West Germany, for example, has been a major producer of grinding, gear cutting, and metal forming machinery. Since 1970 Japan has specialized in numerically controlled lathes and machining centers, which together represented one-third of its output and two-thirds of its exports in 1982. This appears to be due to Marshallian economies in areas such as R&D, design, and assembly labor, which result from the transfer of accumulated knowledge and skills between firms within a single country. This supposition is reinforced by the geographic concentration of the industry within countries.

To be successful, machine tool firms have, therefore, had to adapt to many changes in the postwar period. In particular, they have had to consistently make the correct strategic decisions along a number of critical dimensions. The most obvious was which machine tool segment to compete in, a decision that hinged on product choice, the breadth of machine tool types produced, and the degree of standardization and compatibility with other manufacturers. Company size and levels of R&D expenditure had then to be appropriate to meet the requirements of the chosen segment. Finally, there were important decisions to be made on when and how to raise capital (in an extremely cyclical business[26]), develop sales and service networks (particularly for export promotion), and attract and retain high-quality managerial and technical personnel.

THE HISTORY OF INDUSTRIAL POLICY

Japan

In the early 1950s Japan's machine tool industry was recognized as strategically vital to the development of a manufacturing infrastructure, and yet it was not internationally competitive.[27] As a result, it was designated a high-priority industry for government support, and the June 1956 Extraordinary Measures Law for the Promotion of the Machinery Industry outlined a policy to create an industry based on standard manual machine tools.

Specific programs included the provision of capital to the industry. Loans to the industry were made by the Japan Development Bank. Although not large in themselves, these loans provided implicit approval of the machine tool industry as a priority borrower from private banks. A series of tax breaks, such as accelerated depreciation, reserve funds, and export deductions, was also instituted, which reduced the overall corporate tax rate by 20 percent.[28]

On the trade front, the Ministry of International Trade and Industry (MITI) controlled imports of machine tools through differential tariffs on various types of machine tool and direct exchange controls. It permitted imports only of machinery that could not be made in Japan at that time. Moreover foreign companies were not allowed to invest in Japanese plants, as capital inflows were effectively prohibited. A machine tool export association was also established, but until the 1970s, exports were used primarily as a safety valve during domestic recessions and were often tacitly acknowledged to be sold at "dumping" prices.

To control the flow of technology, a 1950 law required that MITI approve all technology licenses from overseas. Thus the government was able not only to choose which technologies to license, but also to prevent competitive bidding by allocating the licenses to one company. Very little direct support for Japanese R&D was offered at that time.

An "administrative guidance cartel" attempted to control entry to the industry and removed any threat of antitrust action. This institution had little effect during the rapid growth phase of the industry as each of the large Japanese bank groups set up its own machine tool company, but in 1965, during the first of the severe Japanese recessions, MITI intervened to rationalize the industry. It first specified a minimum company size of $1.39 million in sales and then encouraged firms to obey a 5-and-20 rule—they should not manufacture a product unless it had a 5 percent Japanese market share and represented more than 20 percent of the firm's output. Finally MITI organized the companies into ten groups, which were to rationalize production among themselves and undertake sales and exports on a joint basis. Although this direct integration quickly broke down as the economy recovered, the groups remained as "social gatherings."

In the early 1970s, a major shift in national industrial policy redirected the Japanese industrial structure from one of resource intensity to one of knowledge intensity. For the machine tool industry, which still retained its strategic role, this implied a shift from standard manual machine tools to numerical control. MITI set a goal for half of output to be numerically controlled by the end of the decade.

The Japanese machine tool industry focused on developing simple, low-cost numerically controlled lathes and machining centers. The industry established standards for tool-changing mechanisms, size increments, and so on. Within those guidelines, firms tended to specialize in one type of numerically controlled tool and developed simple, modular designs. As a consequence, the number of parts in a machine tool was reduced by up to 30 percent, and a 10–40 percent overlap of parts between models was achieved.[29]

Japanese industrial policy took several approaches toward helping the machine tool industry develop competitive advantage in this new market. It encouraged one company, Fujitsu FANUC, to become the dominant supplier of control units to the industry. After developing the first Japanese numerically controlled unit in 1956, FANUC had decided not to manufacture machine tools itself. Its decision was supported by the 1965 proposals of the Nakayama committee for MITI and by the 1973 MITI reorganization, which merged the control unit and machine tool industry bureaus. FANUC became merely a supplier of the control unit and designed the simplest possible such unit for each type of machine tool, which it then sold to the whole Japanese industry. The resulting symbiotic relationship between FANUC and the machine tool industry was so successful that by 1971, only one Japanese machine tool company produced its own control unit, and FANUC had 80–90 percent of the Japanese numerically controlled control unit market.[30] Building on this success at home and using a simple design of the new microprocessor numerical control technology (CNC) originally developed for the Government Laboratory, FANUC went on to capture a 40–50 percent share of the worldwide market for control units by the 1980s.[31]

Aside from its encouragement of FANUC, the main role of the Japanese government in the 1970s was to provide a broad 10–15 percent R&D subsidy to the machine tool industry, effected through tax credits, subsidized loans, and a direct subsidy from the proceeds of the government monopoly of bike, motorbike, and offshore powerboat racing.[32] Firms were encouraged to use this subsidy to compete in the application of NC to machine tools rather than in basic research, and during this period a new crop of entrepreneurial companies successfully entered the numerically controlled machine tool market.

On the trade front, Japan was under great pressure in the early 1970s to cut tariffs and liberalize capital flows after it joined the General Agreement on Tariffs and Trade (GATT). To accommodate these pressures in the machine tool industry, the government drastically reduced tariffs on standard drills and lathes, but maintained those on numerically controlled tools by classifying them as computers. Capital inflows were also allowed so that foreign firms could establish joint ventures in Japan—but on Japanese terms. In return for establishing factories in Japan to manufacture cheap, standard manual machine tools, foreign companies had to license NC technology to their Japanese joint venture partner.

To support exports, the industry association and the MITI-funded Japan External Trade Organization (JETRO) sponsored exhibitions, disseminated information, and offered advice and assistance, but the machine tool industry missed out on the wide range of export subsidies that had been offered in the 1960s. In advance of the industry's major export drive the government did, however, encourage the machine tool companies to establish their own overseas sales and service networks to replace their previous reliance on the Japanese trading houses.

Exports nevertheless remained of secondary concern to the Japanese industry until it had exploited the domestic market and gained technological leadership in low-cost CNC machine tools. It was only after the 1975 recession that exports reached 20 percent of output and became central to the industry's development. The initial export emphasis was on selling low-cost numerically controlled lathes and machining centers to the United States. This effort was so successful that in 1978 it was necessary to implement a cartel that set minimum export prices on these tools to assuage U.S. protectionist demands. This cartel was extended to Europe in 1981 as Japanese selling efforts intensified there. Soon, ironically, Japanese companies were licensing CNC machine tool designs to the very companies they had licensed from twenty-five years earlier.

In the midst of this success, Japanese industrial policy changed again. In 1976, MITI funded a $60 million, eight-year flexible manufacturing system research project in which nine machine tool, seven electronics, four industrial machinery firms, and FANUC cooperated. Its fundamental goal was to develop basic standards for an FMS that would enhance the productivity of small and medium-sized Japanese firms. When the project concluded in 1983, aid switched from R&D assistance to low-interest loans for financing installation of these systems, and by 1985 Japan led the world in FMS installations—the most advanced of which were in the machine tool companies' own facilities.

United Kingdom

The United Kingdom adopted interventionist policies toward the machine tool industry beginning in 1964, after the Labor government's election on the promise of the "white heat of technological change."[33] A number of policies were implemented to remedy the extremely fragmented structure of the industry, the lack of R&D expenditure, the separation of the machine tool and the numerical control unit manufacturers, the lack of product standardization, the extreme cyclicality of the industry, and the lack of technical and managerial expertise.

First, the government's new Industrial Reorganization Corporation (IRC) encouraged a series of mergers and takeovers that radically changed the structure of the industry in order to correct the small size of U.K. companies in comparison with their U.S. counterparts.

Between 1965 and 1968, six major machine tool companies acquired twenty-three other machine tool companies. These acquisitions were largely complementary, and the acquired firms were often run as separate subsidiaries rather than integrated into a single firm. Alfred Herbert, for example, which became the world's largest machine tool company in 1966, under the pressure of "old family influences" remained as twenty-four separately run companies until 1969 and made gears in nine factories. Only the Cohen 600 Group acquired companies in order to rationalize product ranges, and it became the world's largest producer of lathes during the 1960s.

To bolster R&D, the government began to grant substantial aid to individual firms for particular development programs—pursuing a policy, as with Concorde in the same period, of trying to pick winners.[34] It gave $1 million to one company to develop an "extremely ambitious general-purpose tape controlled machine tool" in 1962,[35] but the major sums went in 1967 to Molins, a cigarette machinery manufacturer to build a digital numerically controlled (DNC) system (the forerunner of FMS); to a joint venture company that would manufacture the world's most advanced technology machine tools for the U.K. auto industry; and for the development of advanced numerically controlled tools at a start-up company founded with government venture capital.

The Molins System 24 failed in 1969 because the machine tools could cut only light alloys in restricted sizes, not hard steels. The joint venture company closed its greenfield factory in 1972 because its breakeven capacity was too high to be supported by the cyclical U.K. auto industry. The tiny start-up company, Marwin, also floundered along until a merger partner was found for it in the late 1960s. Only a £10 million program for the purchase and loan of advanced machine tools to metalworking establishments was more successful in encouraging industry R&D.

The control unit industry was also reorganized during the 1960s, culminating in 1969 in a merger of the three largest producers into one company that held 70 percent of the U.K. market and was the second-largest European control unit manufacturer. Until then, although only one U.K. machine tool company had developed its own control unit, machine tool companies had failed to cooperate with the control unit manufacturers. These companies had therefore pursued design and development alone, and had had to invest in their own European service networks to build sales there.

The policy toward standardization encouraged by the British Standards Institute examined color coding, tool testing, and power pack standards. A broader move to standardization was hindered by the government's encouragement of import substitution. The industry itself had supported this emphasis and asked for a finer breakdown of the trade statistics in order to discover exactly what products were being imported so that they could manufacture them instead.

Cyclicality, and the consequent cash flow problem and loss of skilled workers in a downturn, was addressed by establishing an insurance scheme to protect manufacturers if they failed to sell machine tools built for stock in a downturn. No company applied for this benefit, however. Finally, to improve technical education, when a 1960 report had found only twenty-five graduate engineers employed at the top ninety machine tool companies, a cooperative industry/university training scheme was introduced, centered on Birmingham University.

Despite those efforts the industry in 1970 was still seen as suffering from the same underlying weaknesses as in 1964. Government policy throughout the 1970s then consisted of reactive moves to the gradual failure of specific companies.

Initially aid went to Alfred Herbert, which was under pressure to update its product line but which had insufficient cash flow to fund R&D. A line of CNC machine tools using a general purpose control unit designed by a small U.K. electronics company was introduced unsuccessfully. The vast product list was trimmed and the labor force was almost halved, but losses widened until the company was acquired by the National Enterprise Board (NEB) in 1975—effectively nationalizing it. Further injection of funds totaling £45 million was fruitless, and the company was liquidated in 1980. The other major writeoff occurred when the continually underfunded successor company to Marwin—hailed as producing in a £10 million turnover company the broadest range of NC machine tools in Europe—was sold.

A change of policy finally came in 1975 after it was found that two of the top five U.K. producers of numerically controlled machine tools were U.S. subsidiaries, and that one of them produced a quarter of all U.K. numerical machine tool output. A blanket scheme open to any machine tool manufacturer was introduced that provided cut-rate loans for NC product development and an outright grant for investment in plant and equipment. This scheme and similar successors helped triple the NC share of U.K. production between 1975 and 1984, but the £100 million that the government had spent in the industry between 1966 and 1978 had done little to remedy the erosion of its competitive position.

United States

The United States has done little in the way of Japanese-style interventionist industrial policy. After initial Department of Defense involvement in the development of numerical control in the 1950s, explicit government policy toward the machine tool industry was almost nonexistent. Policies aimed at industry in general or at non-economic targets influenced the machine tool industry, however. The

Kennedy tax cuts (particularly the investment tax credit), together with the Vietnam War and the National Aeronautics and Space Administration's race for the moon, fueled a decade-long boom in the machine tool industry. This provided funds for the development of NC technology, for the injection of capital by conglomerates that acquired machine tool companies in order to share in the capital spending boom, and for a degree of internal industry rationalization through merger.

The U.S. industry's emphasis during this boom was on high-technology numerically controlled products. After the success of the original NC development project for the Air Force at M.I.T. in the early 1950s, the Pentagon purchased millions of dollars worth of NC machine tools each year to encourage their use. (Until 1970, the Department of Defense owned over $1.5 billion worth of machine tools that it loaned to defense contractors.) Since NC had been designed for jet aircraft wing production, the first civilian purchaser of NC machine tools was the aircraft industry, which accounted for one-third of numerical control sales as late as 1970.[36] Their purchases, and those by another large buyer, the auto industry, were of complex machine tools costing up to $1/2 million each (1967 prices). In line with this orientation, several of the largest machine tool companies had even prematurely developed DNC for the aerospace industry by 1970.[37]

The development of simple, low-cost numerically controlled machine tools during this period was generally left to smaller companies. They tried to develop cheap numerically controlled drills around 1960, but had little success in selling them to the small firms that dominated the metalworking industry.[38]

A major debate during the 1960s focused on whether machine tool manufacturers should develop their own control units. The industry association throughout this period felt restrained by the threat of antitrust action from developing any form of standardization, let alone joint R&D programs. In the end, at least ten machine tool companies and five outside suppliers developed NC control units. These were incompatible with each other and were relatively complex and expensive, because the limited market for one firm's control unit required enough versatility for it to be used on several different models of machine tool.

Nevertheless, throughout the 1960s, the industry believed itself to be handling the evolution of comparative advantage effectively. The

Kennedy Round of GATT brought machine tool tariffs down to 7.5 percent, and import penetration reached 10 percent of domestic production in 1967. Although the industry association sought protection, the growth of imports was believed to be primarily due to lengthening U.S. delivery times in the boom, and to consist of standard manual machine tools in which the larger U.S. companies accepted their lack of competitiveness. Indeed, these companies began to use their European subsidiaries as the global source for such tools and later opened manufacturing facilities for these products in Japan, Brazil, or the Far East, while continuing to produce sophisticated special-purpose and more custom-designed machine tools in the United States.

In the 1970s and early 1980s, even as U.S. machine tool production expanded and industry profitability increased, some fundamental changes were felt. The smaller companies that had targeted the low end of the numerically controlled machine tool market in the early 1970s and performed well until 1976 found themselves overwhelmed by Japanese imports in the 1980s. Japanese companies now clearly held technological leadership in these products, and a secret visit of U.S. machine tool manufacturers to Japan in 1981 found the Japanese to be twice as productive as American tool manufacturers.[39] Many companies pressured the industry association to sue for protection, which it did in 1982 under Section 232 of the Trade Act (the vital defense industry clause).

The larger U.S. companies, encouraged by high demand from the auto companies retooling for small car production after the oil price shock, continued their emphasis throughout the 1970s on large complex machine tools, and increasingly on systems. These companies continued to spend heavily on R&D and began to acquire other machine tool companies. Just as they had abandoned production of manual machine tools in the 1960s, in the 1970s they began to cease design and manufacture of their own low-cost numerically controlled machine tools. As the recession of the early 1980s took hold, merger and acquisition activity intensified among the larger firms, until in 1984 the second- and third-largest machine tool companies merged in order to rationalize excess capacity and compete effectively in flexible manufacturing systems.

In that same year, government again began funding R&D. The Bureau of Standards opened a laboratory whose aim was to set standards for interchangeability between companies' FMS equipment.

The threat of antitrust action against cooperative R&D was also removed when the government approved such a program for semiconductor research and recommended that the machine tool industry follow suit. Nevertheless, the industry remained in chronic recession, and even the largest firms felt threatened by the Japanese advances in FMS. Even if the United States had a technological lead, they feared, the closer links between Japanese producers and users (which were often the same company) gave Japan the lead in the installation of FMS.

West Germany

By 1955 West Germany had recovered from the devastation of World War II and re-established itself as the world's leading exporter and second-largest producer of machine tools. The German industry specialized in a number of machine tool types, notably grinding, gear cutting, and metal forming, and was at the forefront of technology in those specialties. Many small specialist firms each produced a limited range of these sophisticated machine tools.

This industry structure survived into the 1980s because the introduction of numerical control was delayed in the German specialty areas. In 1983, for example, only 9 percent of grinding machinery production, less than 10 percent of gear cutting machinery, and less than a quarter of forming machines were numerically controlled in the United States. About half of German production is in these categories of machine tools, which has reduced the penetration of NC and consequently the pressure for rationalization within the industry. Nor is the German industry under much pressure from low-wage countries, because its specialties are relatively sophisticated machine tools. Nevertheless, the industry has had to meet some challenges. It has evolved a unique institutional structure and has been supported by a limited industrial policy.

Industrywide cooperative R&D programs have been important. Led by a strong association, the industry cooperates in basic R&D work and competes only in the application of that research to individual companies' machine tools. Through contracts with eight major technical institutes, the association provides research small companies could not undertake, and companies themselves can sponsor a project that will be cofunded by local and federal government, provided the results are published within two years of completion.

Aachen, the primary machine tool research institute, is the focal point for this activity, not only as a teaching institution for undergraduates, but as the link between industry and academia. Graduates who have worked in the industry for a few years often return to pursue research for a limited time. This close relationship, together with the scale of such activity, encourages cooperation between toolmakers in other areas. Indeed, the West German industry has been described as a "group of clubs," and cooperation extends through standardization of product specifications to sales and service activity in foreign markets.[40]

In foreign trade, government policy advocated East bloc barter trade (to such an extent that in the late 1970s, a quarter of all West German exports were to the East bloc), and it allowed the German network of bank holdings in companies to channel funds to specialist producers. Thus, though "the Government has not pushed the industry into shape it wanted," industrial policy encouraged and supported the industry.[41] Problems began to emerge only in the late 1970s, as numerical control began to penetrate even the traditional West German specialty machine tools, and as Japanese imports increased.[42]

THE ROLE OF INDUSTRIAL POLICY

The optimal industrial policy for a growing industry would involve:[43]

1. Defining the role for the industry in the country's economy.
2. Understanding the strategy that firms within the industry will have to adopt to fulfill that role.
3. Determining where the important market failures or externalities exist within that strategy.
4. Implementing a coherent and consistent set of policies to correct those market imperfections.

I have assumed that the goal of all countries considered in this chapter was a large and successful machine tool industry. In the broader statement of industrial policy implied here, the first step must be to determine if a particular industry should be supported. The discussion elsewhere has enumerated some principles that might be applied to this decision (are there production externalities, increasing returns to scale in an upstream industry, or Marshallian economies of scale? is the industry imperfectly competitive, so that it produces rents for the country that dominates the industry?).[44]

Once it is decided that building a large and viable industry should benefit a country, the question remains how best to intervene. Welfare economics and trade policy argue that a simple direct subsidy is seldom desirable, but (in the absence of other distortions) direct intervention to correct an externality or market failure is optimal. Since each industry has its own imperfections, the appropriate form of intervention will differ among industries and must be addressed on a case-by-case basis.

This case-by-case analysis begins with understanding the appropriate strategy for firms within the industry, the second task of industrial policy. It is here that the existing firms' current strengths and weaknesses, competitive positions, and so on, are related to the overall structure desired for the economy and the potential bases of comparative advantage in that country. Essentially, the optimal dynamic strategy for the industry must be identified, along with the strategic dimensions that are critical to success within the industry.

The third task of industrial policy is then to correct any market imperfections that impede firms' ability to perform along the important strategic dimensions, and that, by definition, the industry cannot correct itself. If industrial policy limits itself to these actions, its role will be complementary to that of the industry, even though it involves interventionist policies. By implication, explicit interventionist policies are not required where there are no market imperfections affecting the industry's ability to fulfill its strategic goals.

The fourth task of industrial policy is to implement a consistent set of policies. Conflicting policies have often been adopted, particularly where industrial policy has been implicit rather than explicit. In the U.K. machine tool industry, for example, the government simultaneously impeded cash flow in the industry (by altering the investment credit from a cash grant to a tax credit) and introduced several schemes to provide additional finance to the industry. While some conflicts are inevitable between policies adopted to affect industry in general and those directed at specific industries, they must be minimized if industrial policy is to be implemented effectively. In particular, the industry-specific effects of general policies need to be analyzed.[45] It is equally important to examine the internal consistency of separate policies, not just the single most obvious direct consequence of each policy.

What market imperfections existed in the machine tool industry? The first concerned research and development. As a public good, intervention is needed to provide incentives for firms to undertake R&D and yet generate adequate information spillover.[46] The education and training of a work force in specific skills is also a public good and a source of market failure if workers' skills are transferable between firms, but workers cannot be tied to a single employer or required to invest in their own training.[47]

If a capital market failure exists, industrial policy has a role to play in allocating capital. There is no reason to believe that the capital market systematically undervalues distant potentially risky earnings. Yet given differential taxation of corporations, dividends, and capital gains, transaction costs, insider information, and the risk of bankruptcy, it is not clear that the capital market is fully efficient. In some countries, moreover, particular institutions replace a freely working capital market. Thus it is appropriate to analyze the country's institutional structure for the provision of capital to the particular industry.

Industry structure can also be a source of market failure. Traditional economic theory assumes that managers of firms are rational maximizers of an objective function subject to exogenous constraints. In contrast, Schumpeter saw entrepreneurs as individuals who broke those constraints and moved the economy forward in a gale of "creative destruction." While Schumpeter was referring mainly to technology and product innovations, he included "reorganizing an industry" as one example of breaking the constraints.[48]

When competition in the machine tool industry altered during the 1960s and 1970s, many small specialist firms made a rational, "managerial" response. They did not increase R&D, since they could not compete with larger companies, or introduce numerical control, which was too expensive to develop. Instead they retreated to the traditional markets, now in decline. Lacking entrepreneurs to consolidate firms into the larger, broader-based companies needed for success in the NC era, the industry went into "rational" decline. Industrial policy could have provided the "entrepreneurial" stimulus to industry rationalization, playing a valid role beyond the traditional (and often negative) use of antitrust legislation.

In an uncertain world that lacks a complete set of futures markets, the series of temporary equilibria that emerge are dynamically inefficient, unless expectations are rational, in the sense of consistent with all markets clearing.[49] Industrial policy can therefore have a role in shaping and providing some convergence (or rationality) to expectations. The establishment of standards is perhaps the best example of this kind of role. Recent work in industrial organization suggests that the market equilibrium generates insufficient compatibility if expectations and information are independently formed.[50]

The final set of market imperfections comprises those arising from the production externalities and increasing returns to scale that contributed to the Marshallian economies within the machine tool industry. To rectify these imperfections requires either establishing new markets, assigning new property rights, or a direct subsidy.

THE EFFECTIVENESS OF INDUSTRIAL POLICY

We are now in a position to evaluate nations' overall industrial policies, by assessing the efficacy of the programs each adopted to remedy the six market imperfections identified above that hindered the ability of machine tool firms to perform along the key strategic dimensions outlined earlier. Figure 3-3 shows the linkages between market imperfections and strategic dimensions. Some strategic dimensions, and hence some market failures, were more important than others in particular industry segments, and therefore in particular countries.

Japan

Japan very clearly articulated the desirable product choice for the machine tool industry throughout the postwar period. In the 1950s and 1960s this was standard engine lathes and universal drills. By the 1970s and 1980s it had become low-cost simple NC lathes and machining centers. Initially this choice was to some extent forced on Japan because the United States and West Germany had superior technology in the more sophisticated machine tools; nevertheless it reflected a conscious industrial policy decision to assign the machine tool industry the role of improving the productivity of industry in general by developing machine tools suitable for the mass market.

Figure 3-3. Key Strategic Dimensions and Market Imperfections.

Market Imperfections	Strategic Dimensions						
	Product Choice	Company Size	Level of R&D	Source of NC Unit	Overseas Sales and Service Networks	Financing	Management and Labor Quality
R&D			√	√			
Education							√
Industry structure		√		√			
Capital market failure						√	
Expectational convergence/ standards	√			√			
Production externalities/ increasing returns to scale/ Marshallian economies	√			√	√		

Initially, MITI's control of technology licenses and foreign exchange, together with selective tariffs, forced Japanese manufacturers to concentrate on the simpler manual tools. Working with the powerful industry association, it also encouraged the standardization of machine tool components.

As policy changed in the 1970s, tariff rates were altered to maintain protection of the newly favored general-purpose NC machine tools, while support for FANUC as the dominant supplier of control units to the industry encouraged the industrywide development of simple low-cost NC machine tools. Finally the cooperative research program for FMS was explicitly established to develop a general-purpose, flexible system, and not a highly specialized one appropriate for only a few sophisticated users.

This basic philosophy supported the establishment of a machine tool industry specialized in the general-purpose, simpler tools and enabled it to exploit the available Marshallian economies in the high-volume segment of the market at each point in time. The cumulative benefits of experience and larger scale in these products, combined with an emphasis on low-cost design and manufacturing technique and investment in the most modern machine tools, have given the Japanese industry its current leadership position.

Industrial policy also aimed at influencing company size and type. An early period of free market competition (with foreign investment prohibited to prevent overseas firms from preying on the domestic industry) yielded a number of "winners." Thereafter policies, such as the 5-and-20 rule, aimed at increasing industry concentration and specializing companies on particular machine tool models, with the goal of increasing volume per model in each company—then the key to competitive success in manual machine tools.

With the industry's transition to the NC segment, FANUC's role reduced the requirements for electronics capability and research in the machine tool companies and so limited the increase in the minimum efficient company size. The availability of R&D subsidies and funding from related bank groups enabled the large machine tool companies, which by the early 1970s were comparable in size to their U.S. counterparts, to reach the minimum efficient scale.

When the industry became involved in flexible manufacturing systems, where breadth of expertise was a key to success, MITI explicitly intervened to integrate companies with the required technologies and allow specialist machine tool manufacturers to develop FMS know-how without being broad-line producers themselves. The cooperative research program actively transformed the industry structure in the way required for competitive success.

Japan's R&D policy, which has been a cornerstone of its industrial policy in the machine tool industry for fifteen years, has been notably successful in improving the industry's technical sophistication. In the early years, MITI did not support any indigenous R&D projects, but instead controlled the flow of technology licensing agreements into Japan.[51] This was the low-cost way to acquire technology for the relatively mature, standard manual machine tools produced at that time. Later, as the absolute level of R&D became important in the early 1970s, the key feature of the government's policy was to make the R&D subsidy and the core NC technology broadly available. Japanese industrial policy therefore developed the public-good nature of basic research while broadly subsidizing downstream R&D to maintain a desirable level of expenditure. In the third stage of industry development, the basic FMS technology was similarly made widely available through the cooperative R&D project. Government aid then switched to financial assistance for installing FMS, to encourage companies to compete in applying that basic technology to specific systems.

Many of the market failures that might have arisen from the relationship between the NC and machine tool industries were resolved by FANUC's symbiotic relationship with the machine tool industry. The establishment of an NC standard that stressed simplicity and low cost, the avoidance of duplicative expenditures in NC development, and the exploitation of learning and economies of scale by a single NC supplier, all resulted from FANUC's unique position. The creation of a de facto industry standard also remedied a potential market failure to generate sufficient compatibility between suppliers and encouraged the rapid diffusion of NC to all metalworking establishments by reducing the risk of obsolescence for early investors in the new technology.

Unlike other Japanese industries, machine tools did not receive export subsidies, but to the limited extent that externalities exist in export promotion, Japanese industrial policy played some role in their exploitation. Similarly, in the context of Japan's relatively controlled capital markets, the role of industrial policy in providing capital to the machine tool industry was not especially significant. However, when there was a capital shortage in Japan in the 1950s, industrial policy was particularly active in this respect. When access to capital was no longer a critical resource, such government aid was phased out.

Finally, with respect to training and education, Japanese industrial policy took few actions directly aimed at the machine tool industry, relying instead on the Japanese education system and the pseudo-contractual solution of lifetime employment to remedy the market's underinvestment in worker and management skills.

Overall, Japanese industrial policy consistently adopted a coherent set of specific programs that acted directly on the market imperfection and not in a second-best manner by, for example, simply subsidizing the industry. This was the most efficient form of intervention and minimized the negative repercussions of the policies. Indeed, in the many cases where policy exploited an externality, economic efficiency was promoted independently of the competitive benefit for the machine tool industry. The most notable case where economic efficiency conflicted with benefit to the industry was the use of tariffs in the 1960s and 1970s to protect certain machine tools, but an argument for bureaucratic simplicity might even justify that policy.

At each stage in the industry's evolution Japanese industrial policy assisted firms in successfully performing along the key strategic dimensions. This successful and efficient approach to implementation helped establish Japan's machine tool industry as the dominant world producer of standard low-cost NC machine tools (Figure 3–4).

Some questions remain, however. First, is this experience applicable to industries at the forefront of technology? As in most other instances of Japanese industrial policy successes, the machine tool industry was effectively playing catch-up with other countries. In such cases it may be relatively easy to target a desirable segment of the market, understand the keys to success, and choose to focus on one technology, since correct answers are, at the very least, amenable to analysis. In other industries the implementation of an industrial policy may be less straightforward and more difficult. The Japanese themselves must face this challenge as they move into leadership positions in many industries for the first time and must trail-blaze for themselves, rather than merely avoid the mistakes of their predecessors.

A second question is whether the effort was truly worthwhile. Was the net return on the investment in the machine tool industry posi-

Figure 3-4. Effectiveness of National Industrial Policies.

	United States	West Germany	United Kingdom	Japan
R&D support				
Broad subsidy				✓
Cooperative R&D		✓		✓
Purchase loans			✓	✓
Direct procurement	✓			✓
Pick winners			x	
Capital				
Subsidy			✓	✓
Tax breaks	✓		✓	✓
Insurance/stockpiling			x	
Bailouts			x	
Trade				
Imports				
Tariff				✓
Nontariff				✓
Export				
Finance	x	✓	✓	✓
Sales promotion		✓		✓
Prohibition	x			
Capital flows				✓
Technology licenses				✓
Industry rationalization				
Direct			x	✓
Industry association/cartels	x	✓	x	✓
Standard setting	x	✓	x	✓
Nationalization			x	
Antitrust	x			
Training/education		✓	✓	
Planning agency			x	✓
Government purchases	x			

tive, or did Japan recklessly build its position without regard to the expense? Such a question is difficult to answer in the scope of this chapter. No firm estimate of total government expenditures is possible (although they were probably less than $500 million over the whole period), nor can one know the profitability of the industry in its early years or the indirect welfare consequences of tariff barriers, exchange rate movements resulting from machine tool trade surpluses, and so on. On the positive side, spill-overs into other manufacturing industries from the successful machine tool industry cannot easily be calculated.

However, since most of the actions taken to benefit the industry corrected rather than created distortions to the economy, there is a strong presumption that the policy was beneficial. In addition, of course, the industry now accounts for one-fourth of the world's production of machine tools, is profitable (the average posttax return on equity for the largest Japanese machine tool companies over the last cycle was 12.6 percent),[52] and has a sustainable position from which it can expect to reap the rents for a long period of time.

United Kingdom

Interventionist policy can be counterproductive, as the U.K. experience shows. Although at various times the U.K. government used almost all the same policies as the Japanese, and at least in principle appeared to understand where the relevant market imperfections lay, it consistently misjudged the appropriate strategy for firms in the industry.

In the area of product selection, for example, the U.K. government failed to encourage an industry specialization or even a consistent product choice. (The United Kingdom is notable among the developed countries for a lack of industry specialization, perhaps resulting from its history of factoring.) Government supported substitution for whatever imports the domestic industry felt it could manufacture economically. Nor did it develop effective industry standards, though it correctly identified the need in 1960. Its main efforts in that direction were sidetracked to trivial items, so that in 1970 the Department of Trade and Industry was still bemoaning the lack of component and design standards. Moreover, its R&D support went to extremely advanced technology projects unrelated to the existing industries' strengths and certainly not relevant to the broad mass of end-use metalworking industries. It thus failed to exploit the Marshallian economies that would have resulted from developing an industry specialization.

To remedy the perceived failure of the industry to rationalize itself in the 1960s, the government intervened to encourage massive restructuring. Unfortunately, it confused mere size and efficiency, and failed to see that the key to competitive success at that time was high model volumes, not large company size. As a result it created unwieldy conglomerates of independent and unrelated machine tool divisions. Only the Cohen 600 Group (now Europe's largest machine tool company) independently pursued the correct policy of merger and product rationalization. Yet in the 1970s, as U.K. companies made the transition to numerically controlled machine tools and company size became important to support the required increase in R&D expenditures, government support went to the weakest or the smallest U.K. companies. U.K. industrial policy thus managed to support exactly the wrong industry structure at both stages of the industry's development.

U.K. industrial policy also failed to overcome the market's under-provision of R&D, as it pursued a strategy of picking winners, a relatively ineffective form of R&D support.[53] The decision to support specific extremely advanced technology products at specific companies did not raise the overall level of industry R&D, which hopefully would have generated its own winners. Moreover, none of the chosen "winners" turned out to be an economic success. The success of the more recent blanket schemes for R&D support in raising the NC share of U.K. output only highlights the earlier failure.

To exploit the benefits of a single major control unit supplier, the government facilitated a merger in 1969. Afterward, however, the United Kingdom could not engineer a close relationship between companies, and any potential benefits were left unrealized. U.K. industrial policy was not the responsibility of a single body like MITI, but reflected advice from the National Economic Development Committee (NEDC), representing labor, management, and government. Its recommendations were implemented haphazardly by the various ministries responsible for particular activities, so that R&D was under the Ministry of Technology, financial aid under the Department of Trade and Industry, and so on. The resulting dispersion of authority led to conflicting policies, an absence of accountability, and a substantially less directive role for industrial policy.

The lack of a single body empowered to implement a plan also limited the ability of industrial policy to provide expectational consistency. France's indicative planning suffered similarly before the Mitterrand government intervened in the industry after 1982. Industry participants in both countries neglected advice and ignored the implications of plans they could assume, in a self-reinforcing prophecy, would not be fulfilled.

No specific trade support was offered the U.K. machine tool industry, although it benefited from the general effects of entry into the European Economic Community, low-cost export financing, sponsorship of trade missions, and so on. However, the government did try to remedy a perceived capital market failure through nationalization and assistance when the private capital market did not supply finance. These company-specific bailouts were not fruitful, however, since they were not attempts to solve marketwide problems but short-term responses to noneconomic, political pressures. A more successful way to inject capital would have been through such industrywide programs, as the 1966 preproduction ordering scheme, the 1982 Small Engineering Firms and FMS investment schemes, and similar schemes used in Italy and France. If the justification for intervention is market failure, then the solution should be marketwide, not company specific.

The U.K.'s success in increasing the number of graduate engineers employed in the industry can be directly attributed to its introduction of programs at Birmingham University. However, the engineers appear to have arrived too late to penetrate the ranks of senior management (who were still often family members) and awaken them to the realities of competition in an electronic environment. Indeed poor British management must share much of the blame for the U.K. industry's performance.

This raises the question, to what extent does a nation's success depend on its industrial policy, to what extent on its companies' strategies? Effective company strategy is a necessary, but not sufficient condition for success. If industrial policy takes as its role the correction of market imperfections, it can, as we saw in the Japanese example, contribute more than the firms themselves to the likelihood that the industry will succeed. Good industrial policy undoubtedly works together with good company strategies; it can assist but not supplant them.

Macroeconomic policy failure may also have contributed to the U.K. machine tool industry's relative failure. Most of a nation's machine tool production is for domestic consumption, so that the performance of the domestic economy is amplified in the industry. Even without industrial policy, domestic growth would probably have impelled the Japanese to a substantial machine tool industry. Even with an effective policy, the U.K. machine tool industry would still have been hurt by the stop-go cycles of the 1960s and 1970s. The performance of the overall economy clearly limits what can be accomplished through (Figure 3-1), but still does not render it utterly futile. Moreover, it implies that industrial policy should be appropriately designed for the macroeconomic environment in which it will operate, rather than based, as U.K. and French policy were too often, on unrealistically optimistic scenarios for economic growth. Effective macroeconomic policy is probably the best sort of policy, but it does not invalidate the use of specific industrial policy in addition.

West Germany

West Germany has had less need of an interventionist industrial policy since its industry has specialized in non-NC special machine tools in which the basis of success has not altered since the 1950s. Assistance in the rationalization of the industry, for example, has been irrelevant until recently because the traditional specialist company was still viable in that segment of the industry. Nor was a policy toward the control unit industry required because relatively little of West German machine tool production was numerically controlled. The main role of industrial policy has been to correct the only market failures that did exist in R&D, training, and export promotion. The subsidization of cooperative R&D has enabled West Germany to retain its technical lead in its areas of specialization. Indeed, it has explicitly generated spill-overs to reinforce that specialization. Aacher provided an industrywide source of training, while the provision of generalized export assistance was particularly valuable to the smaller firms in reducing the fixed costs of exporting.

The lesson of the West German example is that in the absence of major market imperfections, explicit industrial policy is not required to sustain a viable industry. Today, numerical control is penetrating even the German specialties, and this period of minimalist industrial policy may be drawing to a close, as changes in strategic success factors affect the West German industry for the first time.

United States

The absence of an explicit U.S. industrial policy failed to remedy certain inherent market failures and allowed the country's implicit policy to hinder its industry's performance in several ways.

With respect to product choice, the U.S. Department of Defense's involvement in the development of numerical control encouraged an advanced technology emphasis within the industry and delayed the introduction of low-cost NC machine tools for the mass market. Beginning in the 1950s, the easiest and most profitable place to sell numerical control was to a limited number of large-scale, technologically advanced industries. The resulting close liaison between these customers and major firms in the machine tool industry led to specialized end-use developments, incompatibilities between suppliers, and the premature establishment of advanced manufacturing systems to satisfy their particular needs.

The industry was then inappropriately configured to develop a mass-produced, low-cost-design numerically controlled machine tool in the 1970s. The larger U.S. firms' relatively slow and unprofitable entry into that part of the market allowed the Japanese to establish technical leadership there and pushed these U.S. firms even further into the high-technology end of the market. The smaller U.S. firms that tried to develop low-cost NC machine tools were hindered by the incompatibilities between NC standards, which made smaller metalworking firms reluctant to invest in NC machine tools, and by their limited R&D capabilities and production volumes. When the larger Japanese companies entered the United States after 1976, these small firms were swept away.[54]

To the extent that the early specialization in high technology that developed in the U.S. appeared at the time to be a viable position, it is hard to fault the outcome. As the industry leader, the United States may not have realized in the 1960s and even the early 1970s that a mass market would develop in low-cost NC machine tools. If so, even an active industrial policy might have ignored the market's potential. However, to argue that the machine tool industry merely responded to the evolution of comparative advantage in re-treating to the more technologically advanced segment of the ma-chine tool industry severely restricts the set of industries in which the U.S. can be seen to have a comparative advantage. If, as Law-rence argues, the U.S. comparative advantage lies in high-technology R&D intensive capital goods, the loss of traditional standard manual tools can be accounted for, but not the poor performance in numeri-cally controlled machine tools since even the relatively low-cost NC machine tools are prime examples of high-technology, R&D-intensive capital goods.[55] The failure of the U.S. industry is even more pro-nounced when seen in this light. Beyond the basic industry speciali-zation, moreover, the absence of explicit industrial policy and the effect of implicit industrial policy had more direct and harmful con-sequences in other areas.

The only intervention in R&D until recently was the early Depart-ment of Defense involvement in NC development, which produced the U.S. industry's original orientation to complex and sophisticated products. Given the ensuing absence of R&D support, the deterrent effect of antitrust legislation on cooperative R&D, and the lack of university-level machine tool research, the market underprovision of R&D went uncorrected. The result was wasteful duplication of effort (particularly in NC development) and potentially a lost opportunity for cooperation in FMS, where it is most necessary. This failure is now recognized by the industry itself, which sees cooperative basic research as a major way to restore U.S. competitiveness.[56]

The need for standards, which a wary industry association would not impose, is best illustrated in the numerical control field, where most major machine tool companies and five outside suppliers devel-oped their own systems in the 1960s. This pattern of events dupli-cated R&D expenditures, proliferated alternatives for metalworking industries to consider (which slowed the diffusion of NC by increas-ing the risk of obsolesence), and increased each unit's complexity so that its development cost could be amortized over a range of each company's tools. Moreover, the industry failed to exploit economies of scale and learning, and so incurred substantially higher production costs. This of itself delayed its development of low-cost NC machine tools.

Some degree of competition in NC development was probably appropriate in the early 1960s, but to have fifteen different developments was not optimal. It may be difficult to know when to curtail alternatives and settle on one approach, but the effect of running too many for too long is all too apparent.

The United States probably did not suffer from a failure to rationalize the industry, since its leading firms were always of sufficient size to compete effectively. Nor did it suffer from a failure of capital provision, unless the tendency of conglomerates using portfolio management techniques to curtail investment in their subsidiaries after 1980, or the nonneutrality of the tax system is seen as a capital market failure. However, there probably was a market failure in worker training that went unremedied, and the U.S. government's support of restrictions on trade with the East bloc hurt the machine tool industry by effectively prohibiting it from exporting to nearly 20 percent of the world's market.

Whereas West Germany had few market imperfections to rectify, the absence of explicit industrial policies and the unintended effects of some other policies in the United States were detrimental to the performance of its machine tool industry. Protectionism may turn out to be the first recent component of explicit U.S. industrial policy toward the machine tool industry. If introduced, it would not remedy any market imperfection, but would merely represent the response to past failures to remedy market imperfections that contributed to the U.S. industry's declining competitiveness.

CONCLUSION

Industrial policy can make a difference to the performance of an industry. It is best implemented not by being *explicit* per se, but by being *appropriate* in meeting four criteria: defining the industry's role, understanding company strategy, identifying market failures, and implementing coherent policies to correct those failures.

Japan used industrial policy to correct market imperfections and support firms that were pursuing a viable and dynamic long-term strategy; it succeeded in its goals. The United Kingdom used industrial policy without understanding the keys to success in the industry, thereby distorting firm behavior and contributing to the industry's failure. West Germany had limited need for industrial policy because the segment of the market in which it competed remained largely unchanged; the few policies it did adopt remedied the relevant market failures. The United States had no explicit industrial policy and thus was not able to provide critical assistance to the industry. At the same time the unintended industrial policy that resulted from pursuing other types of policy objectives fostered a strategic approach that foundered in the long term.

For industrial policy at the industry level to succeed, it must first clearly understand what company strategies are viable in the light of shifting international comparative advantage and the changing structure of the global industry. Operational policies must then be appropriate for that strategy and complementary to firms' own activities along the critical strategic dimensions. Intervention is appropriate only in those cases of market imperfection where firms cannot successfully act alone.

NOTES

1. See, for example, R. Bolling and J. Bowles, *America's Competitive Edge* (New York: McGraw-Hill, 1982); Ira C. Magaziner and Robert B. Reich, *Minding America's Business* (New York: Random House, 1983); and Paul R. Krugman, ed., *Strategic Trade Policy and the New International Economics* (Cambridge: M.I.T. Press, 1986).

2. For example, Robert Z. Lawrence, *Can America Compete?* (Washington, DC: The Brookings Institution, 1984); and Ezra F. Vogel, *Comeback* (New York: Simon and Schuster, 1985).

3. For example, Robert B. Reich, *The Next American Frontier* (New York: Times Books, 1983); David B. Yoffie, *Power and Protectionism* (New York: Columbia University Press, 1983); and Chalmers Johnson, *MITI and the Japanese Miracle* (Stanford: Stanford University Press, 1982).

4. In that it examines more than two countries, this effort differs significantly from previous industry studies, mainly in the semiconductor, footwear, and textile industries, which typically contrast two nations with and without an industrial policy.

5. The president of the National Machine Tool Builders Association stated explicitly that "America is the defender of the industrial west and machine tools are the foundation of our industrial defense preparedness" (foreword, *Economic Handbook of the NMTBA*, 1983).

6. The machine tool industry was not chosen because "it can be claimed as [a] success for Japanese industrial policy," as stated in the *Economic Report of the President, 1984* (Washington DC: U.S. Government Printing Office), p. 98. When the study began we were not aware that this was the case.

7. In his discussion of this paper, at its original presentation, Bo Carlsson stressed that country performance was affected as much by company strat-

egy as by industrial policy. See B. Carlsson, "Firm Strategies in the Machine Tool Industry in the U.S. and Sweden," Working Paper: Research Program in Industrial Economics, Case Western Reserve University, 1984.

8. The machine tool industry meets at least part of the seven criteria Spencer suggests for selecting strategic industries for targeted support. See B. J. Spencer, "What Should Trade Policy Target," in Krugman, op. cit.

9. Except where otherwise stated, all data quoted in the text are from the National Machine Tool Builders Association Economic Handbook for various years.

10. In 1970, for example, Japan had 14.2 percent of the world production of machine tools but only 3.5 percent of world exports.

11. Even though the U.S. dollar was overvalued in 1985, it was in 1980, when the dollar was at its lowest recent rate and 16 percent below its 1972 level in real trade weighted terms, that the U.S. machine tool trade deficit first exceeded $½ billion.

12. The exception is West Germany, whose share of production grew to a peak of 22 percent in 1971 before declining.

13. Extensive use of primary and secondary bibliographic source material was supplemented by limited field interviews.

14. Data on costs and economies of scale were drawn from C. F. Pratten, "Economies of Scale For Machine Tool Production," *Journal of Industrial Economics* 19 (April 1971): 148–65, and for the experience curve from accumulated price and production data of the Bridgeport Series I milling machine reported in *American Machinist* (August 10, 1970): 98.

15. Pratten, op. cit.

16. Department of Trade and Industry, *The Machine Tool Industry* (London: Her Majesty's Stationery Office, 1970), p. 16.

17. F. M. Scherer, *Industrial Market Structure and Economic Performance*, 2d ed. (Boston: Houghton Mifflin Company, 1980), pp. 62, 68.

18. Pratten, op. cit.

19. The share of world production exported was 18 percent in 1955 and 43 percent in 1985.

20. In 1959 over half of Japan's output was in those two categories of machine tool. By 1983 Japan had less than 8 percent of its output in those categories and Taiwan had 45 percent.

21. According to the general manager of Cincinnati Milacron, quoted in *Business Week*, October 11, 1969, p. 66.

22. Cincinnati Milacron annual report, 1984.

23. Figure for West German industry average, quoted in a Boston Consulting Group interview, July 1984.

24. Metalworking machine tool industry average figure from Federal Trade Commission, Line of Business Report, 1976.

25. International Trade Commission, *Competitive Assessment of the U.S. Metalworking Machine Tool Industry* (Washington, DC, 1983); *Financial Times*, June 16, 1975, p. 27.

26. In 1983 U.S. real output was 60 percent below that of 1981.

27. This historical section is an abbreviation of material in the original paper and does not cover several countries discussed there.

28. Tsuruta estimate noted in Johnson, op. cit., p. 235.

29. Estimate from E. C. Sciberras and B. O. Payne, *Machine Tool Industry* (London: Longman, 1985).

30. Reported in *Iron Age*, April 23, 1970, p. 91.

31. Share in unit terms derived from *American Metal Market* annual production data for various years.

32. Estimated in Ira C. Magaziner and Thomas Hout, *Japanese Industrial Policy* (London: Policy Studies Institute, 1980), p. 99.

33. The first industrial policy toward the machine tool industry was actually enacted during World War I. See, for example, D. H. Aldcroft, "The Performance of the British Machine Tool Industry in the Interwar Years," *Business History Review* 40 (1966): 281, and D. H. Aldcroft and H. W. Richardson, *The British Economy 1870–1939* (London: Macmillan, 1969), particularly pp. 185, 232.

34. This policy of the Ministry of Technology to offer government development contracts to civil industry had been backed by the Trend Committee report of 1963.

35. *Economist*, June 23, 1962, p. 1239.

36. Reported in *Industry Week,* June 29, 1970, p. 53.

37. DNC failed in the early 1970s because the single central computer that ran the various machine tools in the system was overtaxed. FMS has been successful in the 1980s because CNC machine tools allow for the decentralization of processing tasks.

38. In 1965 only 6 percent of numerically controlled machine tools had been sold to those firms employing less than 100 employees, which made up 87 percent of metalworking industry establishments. *American Machinist*, August 30, 1965, p. 85.

39. Reported in *American Metal Market*, December 21, 1981, p. 10.

40. *Economist*, July 1, 1972, p. 55.

41. *Economist,* July 1, 1972, p. 55.

42. Between 1976 and 1985 West Germany's share of world production fell from 18.3 percent to 14.2 percent, and its export share fell from 30.5 percent to 20 percent.

43. Since the worldwide machine tool industry was growing at an average compound annual growth rate of 3.25 percent during the period covered here, I do not consider the ideal industrial policy for an industry in decline.

44. See P. Krugman, "Introduction: New Thinking About Trade Policy," in Krugman, op. cit.

45. The most obvious example is the nonneutrality of the tax system (see Chapter 5). This argument supports those like Reich (op. cit.) and Lawrence (op. cit.), who argue for a more explicit analysis of the net effect of all government policies on an industry, and not of just the industry-specific policies.

46. See A. Michael Spence, "Cost Reduction, Competition and Industry Performance," *Econometrica* 52 (January 1984): 101.

47. This is the case in a nonslave society where loans for investment in human capital are difficult to get and equity investment in human capital runs into agency problems. See the human capital literature—for example, J. Mincer *Schooling, Experience and Earnings* (New York: Columbia University Press, 1974).

48. J. A. Schumpeter, *Theory of Economic Development* (London: Oxford University Press, 1934).

49. See H. R. Varian, *Microeconomic Analysis* (New York: W. W. Norton & Company, 1978), pp. 175–79.

50. M. Katz and C. Shapiro, "Network Externalities, Competition and Compatibility," *American Economic Review* 75 (June 1985): 424, and J. Farrell and G. Saloner, "Standardization, Compatibility, and Innovation," *Rand Journal of Economics* 16 (Spring 1985): 70.

51. In 1963, for example, a University of Michigan Institute of Science and Technology report noted only two government-sponsored R&D projects. Reported in *Iron Age,* July 25, 1963, p. 51.

52. Calculated for 1977–83 from Daiwa Securities Analysts data.

53. See in particular R. Nelson, "Government Support of Technical Progress: Lessons from American History," Yale University, 1982. Mimeo.

54. Currently average production rates of CNC lathes in Japanese firms are five times those of U.S. firms. See Sciberras and Payne, op. cit.

55. See Lawrence, op. cit., pp. 66, 70.

56. An FMS laboratory has been established with Navy support.

CHAPTER 4

Industrial Policy and Trade Distortion: A Policy Perspective

Richard N. Cooper

Industry in the United States currently feels itself under siege from foreign competitors, as imports claim a rising share of the domestic market and U.S. exports' share of world markets declines. A host of foreign government practices have been cited to explain this increase in competition, ranging from specific export promotions and import prohibitions to broadly drawn industrial policies that allegedly provide impetus to foreign exports while discouraging imports from the United States and elsewhere. These practices, in one form or another, are used not only by other industrial countries, but by less developed countries as well, particularly the newly industrialized countries such as Korea and Brazil. Japan is held up as the main culprit, not so much because its so-called unfair trade practices are more extensive than those in other countries, but because it has become the most successful competitor in certain industries previously dominated by Americans. It is foreign success rather than the practices themselves that has given rise to such widespread concern, and has led to calls for U.S. actions ranging from retaliation to emulation.

How should the U.S. government respond to these foreign practices and their alleged impact on the foreign trade—and even the industrial viability—of the United States? This chapter will consider the objectives and instruments of foreign industrial policy, focusing on Japan, and inquire into governmental influences on the American

Repinted by permission of the publisher from Dominick Salvatore, editor, *The New Protectionist Threat to World Welfare*, © 1986 by Elsevier Science Publishing Co., Inc.

economy and its structure of trade. On close inspection, these turn out to be more pervasive than most Americans think and have some unexpected twists. I then consider the issue of whether comparative advantage is given or whether it can be produced by government policy. Finally, I examine alternative approaches to U.S. policy for dealing with the pervasive influence of foreign governments on the composition of output and trade, acting either in a cooperative framework and on its own.

MACROECONOMIC CONTENT

A fundamental analytical error underlies much discussion of so-called unfair trade practices and other policy distortions to international trade. That is the supposition that the overall trade balance and, lying behind that, economic growth and employment are strongly influenced by foreign government policies or practices that limit particular imports or promote particular exports. This error is an example of the "fallacy of composition": the sum of separate actions that have well-defined effects (e.g., enlarging the Japanese import quota on citrus will surely lead to larger Japanese imports of citrus products) will not produce the expected overall effect. Even if the Japanese changed every policy measure and practice foreigners point to as restricting imports, the large Japanese trade surplus would not be reduced and overall Japanese imports might not even increase. The fallacy arises from ignoring an identity in national accounts, namely the trade balance equals the difference between national saving and national investment. Only insofar as actions influence saving and investment can they influence the trade balance:

$$X - M = S + (T - G) - I$$

Here the difference between exports (X) and imports (M) equals net foreign investment (unilateral transfers are neglected). Net foreign investment in turn must equal the difference between national saving and national investment (I), where national saving equals private-sector saving (S) plus the government operating surplus (taxes [T] minus government expenditures [G]). Decisions that affect one of these aggregates automatically must affect one or more others in a consistent way.

This relationship is of fundamental importance in assessing overall trade performance. For example, lifting the Japanese citrus quota will almost certainly raise Japan's imports of citrus and will probably raise overall Japanese imports (but by less than the increase in citrus imports); it will not reduce the large Japanese trade surplus except insofar as lifting the quota affects national saving and/or investment (i.e., probably negligibly if at all). Given a large saving-investment imbalance, a rise in a particular import will be offset by a decline in other imports and/or a rise in exports. Paradoxically, it is even conceivable that a stripping away of all Japan's protective practices would lead to a *rise* in the trade surplus, if the sudden import competition reduced Japanese investment more than it reduced saving.[1] On the other hand, since saving includes corporate earnings, this change could equally plausibly reduce the trade surplus by reducing corporate profits while stimulating corporate investment, in order to survive in the new, more competitive environment. The point is that the overall impact of policies cannot be assessed without looking beyond the specific commodities affected.

After 1981, the United States had a rapidly growing trade deficit, whereas Japan and several European countries developed large surpluses. This trend in overall imbalances had a strong influence on the rise in import shares in the U.S. market and the decline in U.S. export shares. It correspondingly increased the competitive pressures felt by American firms. But these pressures arose from overall macroeconomic developments, not from "unfair trade practices," however extensive such practices may be. It is unrealistic to expect industries affected by severe foreign competition to sort out the macroeconomic influences from the effects of specific policies and to take issue only with the latter. But for policy purposes it is essential to make this distinction; failure to do so inevitably leads to frustration, since even a vigorous use of the wrong instruments will not achieve the desired objective.

In 1985, the United States ran a current account deficit of $115 billion, or 2.9 percent of gross national product (GNP), a record high until then. Gross private saving was 17.2 percent of GNP, a normal level since 1945. Gross investment was 16.5 percent of GNP, a typical level for a year in which the economy was in neither boom nor recession. But the deficit on governmental account (including state and local governments) was 3.4 percent of GNP, down slightly from 1983 but nearly a historical high, excluding World War II. Under these circumstances, the United States was bound to have a large trade deficit. Paradoxically, additional investment stimulated by additional tax concessions to investment (often sought by the business community as a means to enhance international competitiveness) would actually worsen the trade balance during the period of investment. It would do so both by increasing investment and by increasing the budget deficit.

An analogous development occurred in Japan. Private saving and investment rates have been considerably higher in Japan than in the United States over the past three decades and were roughly equal to one another on average until 1975. Investment fell sharply after 1975 and has remained low by Japanese standards ever since then. Japan greatly expanded its social welfare programs in the early 1970s; together with an economic slowdown, that move produced large government deficits, reaching over 4 percent of GNP in 1979. Since then, it has been Japanese policy to reduce the budget deficit; but private saving has continued to exceed investment, so a large current account surplus emerged in 1981, and by 1985 it had reached over 3 percent of GNP.

How are these movements in saving and investment, inclusive of government, translated into trade surpluses or deficits? A simple version of the answer is that the excess private saving of Japan, to the extent it could not be used to finance the government deficit, sought investment abroad. This in turn put downward pressure on the yen, which depreciated and made Japanese goods more competitive in world markets. In the United States, in contrast, a combination of government deficit and private investment in excess of private saving strengthened interest rates and thereby attracted capital from abroad, leading to appreciation of the dollar and worsening the competitive position of American products both at home and abroad. So the main mechanism of equilibration was the exchange rate. Under a system of fixed exchange rates, this pressure of a desired increase in net private saving cannot weaken the currency. Instead, it causes incomes to fall to the point at which the reduced saving, the increased budget deficit (due to lower tax revenue), and the improvement in the current account balance (due to lower imports) preserve the equality between net national saving and net foreign investment. The recession may also put downward pressure on wages and prices, thus improving international competitiveness.

Either way, the link between the overall trade position and overall saving-investment behavior is inescapable, and no tinkering with particular trade policies or practices will get around it. For instance, the occasional call for a U.S. import surcharge would improve the trade balance mainly by increasing revenue to the government (reducing its dissaving); that improvement would be undermined by the increased investment some proponents want it to stimulate unless accompanied by higher private saving.

An individual industry may perceive these macroeconomic developments as less important than the industry-specific policies of countries, which can strongly influence the commodity structure and geographic direction of trade. But the industry perspective is naturally myopic; in assessing the impact of industrial policy on trade as a whole, it is crucial to take into account the macroeconomic environment.

COMPETITIVENESS AND GOVERNMENT POLICY

Industrial policy has no well-defined boundaries. In its broadest sense, we can take the term to mean any government policies that affect the structure of output or, slightly more narrowly, that deliberately attempt to influence the structure of output. But perhaps the best way to characterize industrial policy of the type that concerns many Americans now is to discuss briefly but concretely the policies of the country that seems most threatening: Japan.

This task is somewhat more difficult than it might seem, since Japanese policies have changed substantially over the past twenty-five years, and some of the measures most frequently cited belong largely to the past. So Japanese industrial policy will be described here in the three phases frequently cited by Japanese analysts: (1) from the end of postwar price controls in 1952 to the early 1960s, when the goal was to establish the base for a modern industrial economy; (2) 1960–72, following the elimination of foreign exchange controls, when the goal was to excel in exports; and (3) from 1972 to the present, when Japan has tried to shift the structure of its economy from capital-intensive to knowledge-intensive activities.[2] These divisions are intended to reflect substantial changes in both policy orientation and instruments of policy that have occurred over the last forty years.

Japan in the 1950s

In the early 1950s, the Japanese desired to build a modern industrial society, drawing insofar as possible on their existing strengths, which included a skilled work force in steel making, shipbuilding, and optics (for binoculars) built up during World War II. Strong government guidance in modernization had been part of Japanese history during the previous eighty years, and it was used again. Crucial industries were identified, forecasts of demand were made, and the industries were encouraged to invest accordingly. A rationalization program was begun for steel in 1951. Special industry promotion laws were passed for synthetic fibers (1953), petrochemicals (1955), machinery (1956), synthetic rubber (1957), electronics (1957), and aircraft (1958). Assembly of automobiles was made a priority in Japan in 1952 (Warnecke, 1978, p. 127). The occupation-imposed Anti-monopoly Act was amended in 1953 to permit the formation of "recession" and "rationalization" cartels with government approval in order to prevent cutthroat price competition and to induce orderly reduction in capacity during periods of slack demand (such as immediately following the Korean War, when the revisions were passed). The Export and Import Trading Act was also passed in 1953, permitting cartels to fix prices and to limit imports. By 1971, 195 cartels were legally recognized under the Export-Import Trading Act, 13 under the Anti-monopoly Act, and 23 under separate legislation pertaining to the machinery, electronics, and fertilizer industries (Yamamura, 1982, p. 82). The total had declined by about 20 percent from the mid-1960s (Caves and Uekusa, 1976, p. 148).

During this period the Fiscal Investment and Loan Program (FILP) was created, whereby postal saving accounts (historically an important depository of household saving) and public pension funds were channeled into a series of trust funds (about forty today) for the promotion of public policy. These trust funds include the Japan Development Bank (JDB) and the Export-Import Bank of Japan.

Investment by the favored industries was encouraged by special tax incentives and by loans from the JDB. Japanese industry drew 13 percent of its external financing from the JDB in 1952–55, and another 15 percent from other FILP programs (these figures had declined to 4 and 10 percent, respectively, by 1971–75). Four key selected industries—electric power, shipping, coal, and steel—got 24 percent of their external financing from the JDB, and another 13 percent from other FILP programs in 1952–55 (Noguchi in Yamamura, 1982, p. 131). This government finance was a key instrument of policy; moreover, a JDB loan often provided a signal for lending (at commercial terms) by the quantitatively more important private banks, on the grounds that the favored firms were likely to involve lower risk than other business loans.

Finally, foreign exchange was controlled throughout this period, and import licenses were used to further the industrial policy. For instance, as the taxi industry revived and thrived, its demand for foreign cars rose (including used cars from American forces resident in Japan). Foreign cars were more durable and commodious than domestic ones. Purchase of such cars was limited under foreign exchange regulations in 1951. While imports were liberalized in 1952, they were tightened sharply again in early 1954, and a "buy domestic" campaign was started with the taxicab companies. Japanese production with improved quality required foreign technology. In 1952, the Ministry of International Trade and Industry (MITI) promulgated guidelines for auto assembly licensing agreements that stipulated, among other things, that within a specified time period, eleven key auto parts had to be produced in Japan (Yakashiji in Aoki, 1984, pp. 278–81). Foreign exchange regulations were used to limit imports in many other industries as well and to shape the development of each favored industry.

Japan in the 1960s

Although Japan recognized the importance of exports as early as 1949, when export promotion was adopted as MITI's main goal, the 1950s were principally a period of import substitution, as Japan began to produce more sophisticated products itself. In 1960, there was a major foreign exchange liberalization, associated with pressure from the United States and Europe to move toward currency convertibility and to accept fully the obligations of the General Agreement on Tariffs and Trade (GATT). Japan had joined the GATT in 1955, as preparation for admission to the Organization for Economic Cooperation and Development (OECD), the club of industrialized countries, in 1964. This move eliminated exchange controls and general use of overt import restrictions as a major instrument of industrial policy, although some approved cartels continued to limit imports, presumably with MITI knowledge. The relative importance of the JDB also declined sharply, as the private banks became both stronger and more assertive.

With the liberalization of foreign exchange regulations and the growing strength of sources of domestic credit in Japan, MITI had to rely more on moral suasion and less on directives. This approach did not always work. An effort to pass a new law supporting selected industries unexpectedly failed because of domestic opposition in the early 1960s, and in 1965–66, the Sumitomo steel company flouted MITI's administrative guidance to cut back steel production. The growth of independent banks inhibited the development of "national champions" in Japan, since each bank wanted its own family of firms to include a representative from each major industry. The degree of competitiveness among major Japanese banks and firms and the difficulty it sometimes poses for government were already apparent in 1955, when a MITI plan to create a single small inexpensive people's car (along the lines of Volkswagen) to open the mass market was leaked to the press. (Japan's press is more competitive and more aggressive than that in the United States.) A storm of protest from actual and would-be automakers forced MITI to abandon the plan, and vigorous competition developed among Japan's automakers.

A general policy can continue despite even major exceptions and derogations. But such exceptions remind officials of the limits to their authority. These limits influence what MITI calls for, and what industry calls on MITI to call for if the industry is not unanimous. It is not true, as foreigners sometimes believe, that Japanese business leaders are unwilling to take risks on their own and to stand out from the crowd.

By the 1960s, steel and shipbuilding were commercial successes, and relative emphasis shifted to encouragement of the machine tool industry. Close observation of the American economy had convinced the Japanese that, like steel, machine tools were a prerequisite for a modern industrial economy. This industry continued to benefit from tax breaks, modest subsidies, and favored procurement.

Japan in the 1970s

In the early 1970s, there was a marked shift in Japanese policies in several respects. The Japanese public had become restless about growing pollution, the inadequate welfare system, and even the fact that they had to pay much higher prices for some Japanese products than Japan's overseas customers did (television sets, especially, became a local cause celebre). Moreover, MITI and other officials became concerned about the rapid growth of Japan's imports of oil, even before the oil shock of late 1973. In 1972, in response to general public pressure, Japan adopted a much more generous social security system and introduced stiff pollution standards. After the dollar crisis of 1971–72, Japan took a number of steps to liberalize imports, to liberalize direct investment inflows, and to monitor exports with a view to restraining too rapid growth. Japan also eliminated its "buy only Japanese" policy with respect to government procurement, and loans under FILP were made subject to Diet approval, something that had not been required before 1972 and that greatly reduced their flexibility as an instrument of policy.

Looking to the future, MITI emphasized the growing importance of knowledge-intensive industries and encouraged Japanese industry to move in that direction. The Agency for Industrial Science and Technology (AIST) was created within MITI to finance research projects in ceramics, computers, seabed mining, and flexible computer-aided manufacturing systems. The criteria for AIST support are that the item in question is not yet available on the commercial market and that the research effort required is too large or too risky for private firms to undertake alone. An early success was a desalination process that was later commercialized by private firms and sold in the Middle East. MITI in 1983 had a total research and development budget of about $250 million, which was divided between the ministry's own fifteen laboratories and support for research and development by private firms. Japanese firms themselves spent about $10 billion a year on research and development.

The most heavily publicized cases of government research and development support concern the VLSI (very large-scale integrated circuit) project, for which the government made some $120 million in conditional loans (repayable only in the event of commercial success) between 1976 and 1979, and government support of a fifth-generation computer in the early 1980s. But high-technology industries have other sources of support than research grants and conditional loans. Since 1978, the National Aeronautics and Space Development Agency has given preference in its procurements to satellites with high local content (which now exceeds 60 percent). However, Japan's semiconductor market was described in 1984 as "completely open to American-owned companies" (U.S.-Japan Trade Study Group, 1984, p. 54).

Besides helping the products of the future, Japan has since 1978 had a program to restructure industries that are depressed, for whatever reason. Firms accounting for two-thirds of a depressed industry's output can petition the government for a restructuring plan, which involves an agreed reduction in capacity, with loan guarantees and tax benefits accruing to firms that scrap capacity under the plan.

In mid-1984, there were twenty-two officially designated depressed industries; of these, five (paper, ethylene, compound fertilizer, polyolefins, and PVC resin) had formed legal cartels to restrict output and price competition (U.S.-Japan Trade Study Group, 1984, p. 64).

This represents a substantial decline in the use of cartels from twenty years earlier. In addition, FILP support for Japanese industry is very much less (proportionately) than it used to be, and the government loan rate differential below market rates dropped from around 3 percentage points in the early 1960s to about 1 percentage point in the early 1980s (Noguchi in Yamamura, 1982, p. 137). In general, the Japanese government is far less involved in determining industrial structure than it once was—in part because the two instruments of foreign exchange licensing and credit control are now unavailable for disciplining large firms. But it continues to provide hortatory guidance in MITI's "Visions" and other government pronouncements, and to back these up with direct or indirect funding on a modest scale and with directed government procurement.

Europe

Other countries have industrial policies similar to those in Japan, but generally they are more extensive. Britain, France, and Italy all have had organizations analogous to the JDB that channel publicly raised funds to private enterprises. All provide tax breaks to encourage investment in general and favored investment (by industry and by region) in particular. All have extensive state-owned enterprises (a phenomenon rare in Japan) that receive periodic infusions of new "equity" capital, which is difficult to distinguish from subsidies when firms are running operating losses. All have given extensive support to their steel and textile industries to consolidate operations and scrap obsolete capital. Britain, France, and Germany have also provided government support to cushion declining demand in their shipbuilding industries. In the high-technology area, all have provided extensive government funding and favored government procurement in aerospace, computers, and telecommunications (for a survey of actions, see Carmoy in Warnecke, 1978). For instance, national Post, Telephone, and Telegraph (PTT) organizations in these countries rarely procure foreign-made equipment, nor do national power companies buy heavy electrical generating equipment abroad.

Newly industrializing countries also have adopted strong industrial policies, beyond the traditional technique of restricting imports that compete with the production of favored industries. Korea has adopted a novel incentive at least in one area: some Koreans who work on contract engineering and construction products in the Middle East have allegedly been exempted from the draft and given priority in public housing when they return home (Warnecke, 1978, p. 133).

OBSERVATIONS ON INDUSTRIAL POLICIES

We have seen how widely industrial policy is used and what diverse instruments of support governments employ. How can such extensive interference with market forces be reconciled with a liberal trading system predicated on the mutual gains that flow from reliance on comparative advantage to determine each country's structure of output and trade (with certain acknowledged exceptions having to do with national security)?

The discovery that foreign governments intervene extensively in national economic development, even at the sectoral level, and that these interventions may impinge on the markets for American products has recently led to a number of recommendations for U.S. policy (see, for example, LICIT, 1983, and Magaziner and Reich, 1983). It has been suggested that the U.S. government should:

Insist that other countries give up the practices that allegedly represent unfair competition for American firms.

Adopt measures similar to foreign actions that are deemed to have been successful (e.g., create a revived Reconstruction Finance Corporation modeled on the Japan Development Fund).

Raise sectoral import barriers against goods enjoying "unfair" advantages, either as a threat or as a last recourse when other policies fail.

Match the foreign competitive measures in third country markets (e.g., through generous Exim Bank financing).

Restrict imports into the United States from countries engaging in unfair competition in third markets.

What would be the overall economic impact of these suggestions? Several observations should be made. First, most of these policies have been around for a long time, so whatever real stimulus they once provided should already have been adjusted to through adaptation elsewhere in the economic system. For example, France, Italy, and Japan, among major countries, began extensive industrial policies in the early 1950s. Britain launched on this course in the mid-1960s. If anything, the impact of industrial policies has been declining in Japan in recent years, and the Thatcher government has attempted to reduce Britain's sectoral policies in the early 1980s. Second, government often exacts a costly quid pro quo for support of a firm or industry, limiting flexibility in decisions regarding employment, plant closings, new investment, and diversification. Directly or indirectly, this loss of freedom increases costs. Such factors are typically not recognized as negative consequences offsetting the benefits of government support. Third, it is often forgotten that although the United States does not have an industrial policy as such, it has adopted many measures that directly or indirectly assist American business. Fourth, measures that discriminate in favor of certain firms or industries necessarily discriminate *against* other firms or industries. In economics, there are only rarely opportunities for a free lunch, and someone has to pay for the special aids that are granted to others.

The U.S. government has long had extensive sectoral involvement in the economy. For example, in the nineteenth century it gave land grants to the railroads, and more recently it has constructed a vast highway system to open up areas of the country and provide cheap inland transport. It provides cheap, underpriced water to irrigate Arizona and California farms, producing the citrus that growers complain they cannot sell "fairly" to the Japanese and Europeans. Extensive Department of Defense and the National Aeronautics and Space Administration research and development programs generate commercially valuable spin-offs such as jet engines, helicopters, and the Boeing 747 (see Nelson, 1982). While Europeans and Japanese exaggerate the commercial impact of U.S. defense R&D, most American analysis of foreign government policies similarly leaves the impression of greater quantitative importance than is warranted. The allowance of extensive charitable deductions under the U.S. tax system permits the United States to provide higher education to a much larger percentage of the labor force than the Europeans could afford with their tax-supported systems. The U.S. educational system thus operates in "unfair competition" with the private universities of Japan.

In fact, the U.S. government engages in a host of activities that influence the competitiveness of American exports. These range from direct actions encouraging exports to activities stimulating production, general support for business activity, and actions encouraging certain industries by discouraging others. The following list (adapted from Cooper in Warnecke, 1978) proceeds from the most direct form of export encouragement to less direct forms.

1. Economic and military assistance to less developed countries has been tied to the procurement of American goods. The U.S. government in effect buys the American goods and gives them away, or lends them on very easy terms. Foreign aid represents an extreme form of export subsidization, but it is accepted as contributing to the economic development or national security of the recipients. The importing countries in this case would be unlikely to accuse the United States of unfair import competition or to impose countervailing duties, but third countries may lose export orders because of foreign aid shipments tied to U.S. procurement. The subsidization of American exports would cease if foreign aid grants and loans were freely usable for the purchase of goods and services from any source, as is the case with loans from the World Bank. U.S. foreign assistance and military credit sales amounted to about $15.5 billion dollars in 1982, or about 4.5 percent of total U.S. exports of goods and services. Many other aid donors of course also tie some or all of their aid to domestic procurement.

2. Under U.S. tax laws until 1984, corporations that derived at least 95 percent of their gross receipts from exports could qualify as domestic international sales corporations (DISCs) and could defer payment of corporate profits tax until dividends were remitted to the parent corporation. This provision, by which more than $1 billion in annual tax revenue was foregone in the mid-1970s, amounted to an interest-free loan from the government for expenditures involved in the promotion of exports. The subsidy element—about $60 million a year—was thought to be much less than the foregone revenues, since the taxes eventually would have to be paid. In fact, the 1984 Tax Act (which eliminated the DISC concept and permitted the Foreign Trade Corporation in its place), waived many of the unpaid taxes, so the interest-free loan turned out to be a direct subsidy.

3. The U.S. government subsidizes both the construction and operation of merchant vessels under U.S. registry. Construction subsidies do not increase exports of ships since such subsidies are available only to purchases by U.S. flag companies. Operating subsidies, however, make it easier for Americans to export shipping services. Both programs are of long standing, and in the mid-1970s the oper-

ating subsidy amounted to around $200 million a year. Governments throughout the world are heavily involved in ship construction and shipping services.

4. The Export-Import Bank provides medium-term credit for American exports. For a number of years, the interest rates were below market rates, so a direct subsidy was involved. More recently, the Bank has tried to keep its lending rates above its borrowing rates by enough to cover its operating costs, except when necessary to meet foreign competition. The subsidy to American exports is thus now the more subtle (and smaller) one that arises from the use of U.S. government credit in borrowing in the capital market plus the absence of a requirement to pay dividends on the Bank's capital.

5. Until 1973 the Commodity Credit Corporation (CCC) gave substantial subsidies to U.S. exports of many agricultural products, the difference between high domestic price supports and lower world prices for grains, cotton, tobacco, and so on. The high price supports stimulated output, so the program also involved limitations on acreage. This system was reinstituted in the early 1980s. It is difficult to say whether agricultural exports are larger or smaller than they would have been without the government support program, since the support prices and the acreage controls could be expected to have opposite effects on farm production.

6. Investment in plant and equipment in the United States until 1986 enjoyed a 10 to 25 percent tax credit. The credit in effect lowered the cost of domestic investment by that amount and thus stimulated the productive capacity of the economy. The credit operated for all investment, however, so it is not obvious whether it did more to stimulate exports or imports. The first-round effects of increased production and income could go either way. The major long-run effect of the investment tax credit was to make American industry somewhat more capital intensive than it would be without the credit, both in individual industries and in the overall industrial structure. In addition, from 1981–86, write-off provisions for the depreciation of new investment were extremely generous. These provisions had an effect similar to that of the investment tax credit.

Depletion allowances for oil and other minerals stimulate domestic production of such products and thus serve to reduce imports or to increase exports of these products. Until 1975 this tax privilege was available to American-owned mineral investment anywhere in the world, but now it is limited to production in the United States.

7. The U.S. government makes many direct expenditures that support business enterprise. Examples are federal spending, net of user charges, for airports and air traffic control, for dredging rivers and harbors, and for providing postal service. Billions in government funds have been devoted to development of water resources. This provides cheap hydroelectric power, and cheap water for irrigation in the southwestern part of the country, greatly stimulating agricultural output there. In addition, the Rural Electrification Administration has subsidized the electrification of the rural parts of the American economy for nearly fifty years, at low interest rates, thus making farming less costly than it would otherwise be.

8. Price controls on domestically produced natural gas cheapen energy for Americans with access to the price-controlled gas and hence "subsidize" American exports as well as domestic sales of goods whose production requires the use of gas. (Government revenues are not reduced by this form of support.) In 1985 some, but not all, gas price controls were removed, so this "subsidy" will diminish in importance over time. For nearly a decade before 1981 U.S. oil prices were also held below world market prices, with similar effect.

9. Government expenditures on research and development help to cover the initial cost of new economic activities, which often lead to exports later. The classic example is agriculture research, which has been financed by the government for over a century and has vastly improved the productivity of American agriculture and the quality of agricultural products. Sometimes large export sales are a distant by-product of military research development and development expenditures, as was the case with the jet engine. The government has spent substantial sums on research and development in the energy sector, both on nuclear power and on such possibilities as liquefaction of coal. For years the United States was a major exporter of nuclear plants. To the extent that liquefaction proves to be economically feasible, it may augment future exports of American coal.

10. Extensive government purchases sometimes lead to the development of products that are highly competitive in world markets, by helping private firms spread their own R&D costs and other overhead expenditures over a larger number of sales. This factor is quantitatively important in relatively few industries, such as military equipment, avionics, some kinds of telecommunications equipment, and ground tracking stations for satellites.

11. A pervasive influence, probably the most important stimulus to exports of particular goods, but also the least obvious, is the host of government regulations on U.S. production that aim to improve the working environment or the natural environment. Effluent controls, safety regulations, minimum wage legislation, and restrictions on child labor can all have a profound effect on the competitiveness of particular industries, and hence on the relative competitiveness of other industries less directly affected. Most observers would not mention such government actions in a list of export subsidies, and indeed they do not normally lead to a loss of government revenue, except where the government occasionally incurs some of the costs. To illustrate the reality of these regulatory effects, it is worthwhile to trace through the influence on exports of the minimum wage requirement. The key assumptions in this analysis are that over time balance is maintained in international payments, for example by movements in the exchange rate of the dollar, and that the government takes whatever steps are necessary to assure full employment of the labor force. Here we are concerned with the *sectoral* effects, the relative stimulation or retardation of production in particular sectors of the economy that arise from the regulation in question.

For example, if the minimum wage is set high enough to exceed the wages that would otherwise be paid in some industries, it reduces their international competitiveness by raising their costs. Such industries will find it is more difficult to compete with products from abroad. Imports will rise, and restoration of equilibrium in the balance of payments will require some depreciation of the dollar relative to its level otherwise. The depreciation, in turn, will *increase* the competitiveness of all sectors where wages are not influenced by the minimum wage. Put more concretely, it is likely in the United States that the minimum wage discourages the production of apparel (which is displaced to some extent by imports) and encourages the production and export of machinery. Thus, in an indirect fashion, through adjustment of the exchange rate, the export of machinery is "subsidized" (but without reducing government revenue). A similar argument holds for other government regulations. For example, meeting required safety standards will raise costs more in some industries than in others and through adjustments in the exchange rate will increase the competitiveness of industries or firms whose costs for safety have increased least. (See Chapter 8 for a finding that environmental regulations have affected the composition of U.S. trade.)

*   *   *

Government actions thus exercise a persuasive influence on international competitiveness. That influence may flow from actions whose goals have nothing to do with stimulating exports and may be so indirect that it cannot be traced in detail with any confidence. Nevertheless it may be substantial.

The United States has the federal structure of its government, a special characteristic that it shares with only a few other countries, such as Canada, Australia, and West Germany. The federal government accounts for only one-third of total government expenditures in the United States and about one-fifth of total civilian government employment. For the most part, the influence of state and local governments on the structure of production and costs falls into categories (7) and (11) in the foregoing list: expenditures that support business enterprise in a general way, and regulation of the conditions of production or marketing. In addition, local governments sometimes support particular firms by providing cheap land, low utility rates, or cheap credit. Starting in the 1950s a number of localities used their privilege of floating tax-exempt securities to provide cheap credit to new firms by issuing so-called industrial development bonds, a practice that continues. The business-promoting activities of state and local governments are not, of course, aimed at encouraging national exports, but rather the sale of goods from the particular state or locality to the rest of the United States, and only incidentally to other countries.

Just as the minimum wage hurts some industries and helps others, discrimination in favor of certain firms or industries automatically involves discrimination against firms and industries that are not specially favored. If subsidies, tax breaks, or below-market credits are given to favored firms, others have to make up the difference by paying more taxes or more for credit than would be true in the absence of the discriminatory measures. To the extent that exports are stimulated, the currency will appreciate, thus putting others at a disadvantage with respect to foreign competition. When Japan allows the formation of cartels in periods of recession or for industrial restructuring, it hurts those who buy from the cartel, which will hold domestic prices above the level they would otherwise be at. If consumers bear the additional cost, as in the notorious color television case, exports are not adversely affected. But if a cartel raises the price of steel, industrial chemicals, machinery, or a host of other products, downstream purchasers' costs are increased. (Of course, for domestic prices to remain above world market prices, some form of import restriction must exist.) It may also be true, as Yamamura (1982) points out, that the possibility of creating recession cartels has generated higher capacity than otherwise would occur, by removing from investing firms some of the risk of a major downturn in the market, and that this excess capacity in turn encourages exports at something below average cost. If Yamamura's hypothesis holds, the yen will be stronger, and cartelization will put other firms at a disadvantage for that reason too. These points are generally neglected by those who criticize the unfair trade practices of Japan and other countries.

A similar argument applies to favored procurement of domestic products. The American heavy electrical generating equipment industry has long complained that potential purchasers in other major industrial countries buy exclusively domestic products, regardless of cost. This is true especially in Europe, where electricity supply is typically provided by public authorities, but also in Japan, which like the United States has extensive private utilities. In contrast, the American market for heavy generating and transmission equipment is relatively open, and perhaps one-fifth of U.S. purchases are from abroad, mainly Japan. Foreign utilities' requirement to buy domestic will raise the costs of generating electricity in those countries, and those costs must be either subsidized by the government or passed on to consumers, including industrial consumers. So while U.S. heavy electrical equipment industry suffers from this practice, the rest of American industry in general benefits, by virtue of paying lower electricity charges than their foreign competitors must do. Similar arguments apply to the requirement in some countries that computers should be purchased locally. Over time, unless the local computers are competitive in quality and price, the (mostly state-owned) enterprises that are burdened by this obligation will suffer in competitiveness.

We can now return to a point raised at the outset: can comparative advantage be created? Of course it can. A tradition going back at least to Frank Taussig (1927) has recognized that comparative advantage is determined not only by a country's natural endowments, but also by its social, political, and educational systems.[3] Comparative advantage depends on the quality as well as the quantity of the nation's labor force, the motivation of its workers, and their willingness to work diligently. Insofar as government provides for inland transport, education, efficient banking, and other financial transactions, these too can influence comparative advantage, as can the long list of policies and practices discussed above for the United States, especially the regulatory environment. It would be absurd to pretend otherwise and to treat each geographic area as a *tabula rasa* with natural endowments but with no social or political system.

That is perhaps not what is meant when people talk about "making" comparative advantage rather than "finding" it. Rather, they may have in mind the permanent cost advantages that can be generated by a head start or by extensive production of a particular product. If important and durable economies arise from learning by doing, then doing can give an advantage, however it is brought about, as analyzed by Krugman (1985). Two cautionary points should be made, however. First, undertaking production that is not immediately profitable in order to reap the advantages of learning by doing represents an investment. The mere supposition of future positive rates of return is not sufficient justification for any investment. Rather the yield on the investment should be at least as high as that on alternative investments. If, on analysis, that seems to be the case, then as with any new investment opportunity, many parties may simultaneously want to undertake it, and that would not necessarily be a bad thing.

Second, "decisive" cost advantages for a given product or product group often turn out to be remarkably transient, given the large number of products that have had their commercial introduction in the United States, but whose production has subsequently been relocated abroad. Evidently there are cost factors that eventually overwhelm the cost advantages achieved even by a relatively long head start in production. Perhaps other countries do not recognize these two points and therefore undertake government support for activities that ultimately turn out to be bad investments, but meanwhile create competition for otherwise successful American firms. What, if anything, should be done about it?

POSSIBLE POLICY DIRECTIONS

The problems posed above are not new. What we now call industrial policy goes back, in the strictly commercial arena, at least to the early eighteenth century, when France tried (successfully) to create a high-quality porcelain industry in competition with the Saxon industry in Dresden. The effort in textiles dates back even further, to the early seventeenth century, when England attempted (unsuccessfully) to start a finished textile industry in competition with the Flemish cities, by prohibiting the export of wool.

Existing Arrangements

The General Agreement on Tariffs and Trade of 1947 dealt with the problem of subsidies and international trade by suggesting (in Article 16) that export subsidies on manufactured goods (note the exclusion of primary products) should generally be eschewed, and permitting contracting parties to impose countervailing duties when such subsidies cause material injury. (In addition, Article 19 provides a general escape clause from GATT commitments, permitting countries to reimpose tariffs, on a nondiscriminatory basis, whenever a domestic industry is subject to substantial injury by imports.) A GATT working party attempted to define export subsidies more precisely in 1960. In the mid-1970s the United States introduced its "traffic light" proposal, distinguishing between subsidies that were prohibited (red), subsidies that were clearly permitted (green), and subsidies that were potentially troublesome and hence subject to consultation and possible countervailing action when they caused injury to another contracting party to the GATT (yellow). This proposal was not adopted in the form in which it was presented, but it provided a framework for the Code on Subsidies and Countervailing Duties that was adopted in 1979 as part of the Tokyo Round of multilateral trade negotiations.

The 1979 code prohibits export subsidies except on certain primary products and except by developing countries. Code signatories undertake not to use such subsidies (Article 9); their use creates a (rebuttable) presumption of adverse effects and is thus subject to countervailing duties without an injury test, but subject to international approval. The code also provides, in its annex, an illustrative list of export subsidies, which goes a long way toward defining them. The code acknowledges the widespread use of, and permits, many other subsidies, but signatories recognize that these can hurt the trade interests of other countries and they therefore "seek to avoid causing such effects through the use of subsidies." In evaluating the use of subsidies in pursuit of domestic economic objectives, signatory countries are to "weigh . . . possible adverse effects on trade" (Article 11). If other countries are injured, they can countervail the subsidies in question (see the appendix for the relevant code articles and the illustrative list of export subsidies).

This general language leaves much room for interpretation, not to mention the cracks and overlaps in the illustrative list of prohibited subsidies. U.S. practice is gravitating toward an interpretation that requires a domestic subsidy to provide a "special favor" to a firm or industry before it is countervailable under U.S. law. That is, such broad legislative favors as accelerated depreciation, investment tax credits, and R&D tax credits would not be considered countervailable subsidies. A domestic subsidy is countervailable if it causes material injury to an American industry through stimulated exports *and* if the subsidy is selective rather than general in its impact on the foreign firm or industry.

On the whole, the approach embodied in the GATT Code and in evolving U.S. practice seems very sensible: Export subsidies are prohibited, and other subsidies are permitted as long as they are not selective and there is no clear injury to another party. But several practical problems remain. First, we must await sharper definition of the distinction between selective and general subsidies on a case-by-case basis. Second, until this sharper definition is obtained, it will be possible to harrass importers by bringing test cases and creating uncertainties through "suspension of liquidation" whenever there is a preliminary finding of subsidy. (This puts an importer on notice that he may have to pay a higher duty later, but does not specify what the duty will be.) Third, there is no assurance that other countries will move in the same direction as the United States in their interpretation of the distinction between selective and general subsidies. The United States tends to be the most active country in developing the case law, perhaps because other countries can use less formal mechanisms for restricting imports if they choose to.

In their detailed study of the treatment of subsidies to international trade, Hufbauer and Erb (1984) suggest that the list of prohibited export subsidies needs to be tightened and that the distinction between general and specific subsidies needs to be substantially clarified. But they basically accept the existing framework. Their most novel suggestion is to propose a countervailing *subsidy* as a remedy, to be financed by an (internationally approved) import duty on goods coming from the country providing the offending subsidy (Hufbauer and Erb, 1984, p. 129). Unlike a countervailing duty, a countervailing subsidy would permit the injured country to continue to sell in third-country markets and even in the home market of the subsidizing country. Its obvious disadvantage is that it would affect other foreign competitors, which would have to compete with two subsidizing countries. That might engender a race toward subsidies, perhaps ultimately followed by a "disarmament" negotiation to remove the subsidies, as happened during the late 1970s and early 1980s with respect to official export credits, thereby reducing the distortions to international trade. But once subsidies are introduced, eliminating them is a prolonged, difficult, and often not wholly successful process, as the effort to gain consensus on official export credit illustrates.

Three Alternative Criteria

Public debate often mixes three quite different criteria for assessing subsidies: distortions to resource allocation, fairness or equity, and injury. If there were no injury, the issues of fairness and distortion would probably not arise in the practical world of policy (although academic economists would still be concerned with the misallocative effects of distorting subsidies). However, when injury does arise, the three different criteria tend to be commingled; unfortunately, each points to a rather different solution.

The first policy approach is to eliminate subsidies. In principle, subsidies, domestic or export, distort the allocation of resources. Hence they should be eliminated or offset in the interest of economic efficiency (except if the subsidy is itself designed appropriately to offset some other distortion, such as an externality of some kind). This principle underlies the GATT prohibition on export subsidies and the permissible imposition of a countervailing duty. As noted earlier, however, the countervailing duty cannot undo the distortion of competition in third markets. A plan to eliminate all of the distortions introduced by government action would be a counsel of perfection, given the extensive government intervention in modern economies. It would even be difficult to eliminate all selective subsidies, since these are invariably justified on grounds of correcting a distortion in capital or labor markets, exploiting an externality, being vital to national security, or (in extreme cases) ensuring domestic peace and political harmony. Governments are likely to abandon their extensive array of domestic subsidies only when they believe that the costs, defined broadly, of preserving them are greater than the rewards.

Emphasis on equality or fairness leads to other approaches to policy: the cooperative option would be to harmonize domestic measures among countries. If an activity has positive externalities or national security value, that attribute is presumably not limited to a particular country. Most countries are concerned about having substantial local production of the staple food, perhaps of steel, perhaps of small arms, and increasingly of electronics, on grounds of national security. Nations can negotiate broad ground rules on what is and is not acceptable. Such an effort would offer one concrete meaning to the evocative but basically obscure phrase, providing a "level playing field." The rules would be permissive rather than obligatory, but they would also be limiting, in that countries could not subsidize beyond what was agreed.

The United States tried to negotiate a more detailed elaboration of acceptable but possibly troublesome subsidies during the Tokyo Round, but the result was the less specified code described above. However, the United States could try again to secure greater international agreement as to which domestic subsidies are permissible and which are so potentially troublesome that they should be avoided. Inevitably, such a negotiation would have to propose a conditional most-favored-nation basis, such as that employed in the subsidies code, since the interests of GATT members are too diverse to permit any meaningful harmonization among all ninety countries. By general consensus, developing countries are held to a lesser standard than are the fully industrialized countries, although the extent to which the standard should be relaxed is still a matter of considerable dispute.

If other countries decline to cooperate willingly, the United States could approach the matter unilaterally and perhaps use threats to force conformity. One way to do this is through the notion of reciprocity as embodied in Senator Danforth's telecommunications bill. In major European countries, government-owned monopolies purchase virtually all telecommunications equipment domestically, closing the market to foreign suppliers. Danforth's bill would require other countries to open their individual markets to imports of U.S. telecommunications equipment within three years or face a sharp increase in U.S. tariffs on their exports of telecommunications products, from roughly 8 percent today to about 35 percent. The underlying principle is that the terms of access should be the same in each product field and that the United States should persuade others to adopt its practices—which, with the recent breakup of AT&T, means relatively open procurement by private telecommunications companies. If other nations do not adopt U.S. practice, their access to the U.S. market will be greatly reduced.

This general approach encounters two problems. First, it does not address the question of exports to third countries. (That is perhaps not a major problem in telecommunications; indeed the United States continued to hold 38 percent of the world market in telecommunications products in 1982, compared with only 11 percent for Japan, despite its alleged export prowess.) Second, the impact of the threat embodied in the Danforth bill is likely to vary from country to country. Japan has a large stake in the U.S. market. France, whose practices are if anything even more exclusive than Japan's, does not. Japan might comply in its negotiations with the United States, Britain and Germany might comply partially, and France might not comply at all. At the end of three years, the United States would have to impose different levels of restriction on products from each country and develop value-added criteria to prevent geographic arbitrage among them. The issue is even more complicated when one allows for the difference between national ownership and location of production, through foreign subsidiaries. Thus new distortions would be introduced into international trade, the discrimination implied would represent a sharp break with the most-favored-nation principle embodied in the GATT, and the consequence would be much closer surveillance over imports, with correspondingly greater opportunities for threats and harrassment. These developments would not be in the overall U.S. interest.

Another unilateral approach designed to produce a "level playing field" (or, more accurately, to reduce the protectionist mischief that can be done under that label) would be to introduce a uniform tariff of, say, 10 percent on all U.S. imports of manufactures, against a presumed entitlement of zero. These tariff levels would be combined with a stipulation that any industry wanting additional protection would bear an exceptional burden of proof to show that it was significantly injured by a substantial foreign subsidy, one that was well above 10 percent (except in the case of prohibited subsidies).

Imposing a levy on all imports of manufactures would greatly reduce the uncertainty that foreign exporters now face with respect to U.S. administrative law in the area of subsidies and countervailing duties. Unfortunately, this kind of measure imposes a burden on all consumers of imports. Moreover, through the macroeconomic mechanisms discussed earlier, tariffs reduce the competitiveness of U.S. exports. Where tariffs cause higher input prices, the damage done to U.S. manufacturers can be mitigated only in part by giving drawbacks of the duty. Also, over time it might be difficult to sustain the principle that the 10 percent duty covered most foreign subsidies, against an asserted entitlement of no duty, as firms came to consider it a right rather than a policy of convenience.

The third major approach shifts the emphasis to injury and away from the subsidies as such (except for the clearly prohibited subsidies). It recognizes that government influence is pervasive and of long standing, and that in many ways such influence has been absorbed into existing prices and economic structures. It focuses instead on large *changes* in government policy and the injury they may cause. This approach would call for prior notification of all major changes in government policy and gradualism in the implementation of these changes. When gradualism was not followed, it would permit degressive (that is, gradually phased-out) relief to the injured party, with a view to encouraging ultimate adjustment to the new situation. Procedures would be established for discussing proposed new policies and for considering measures that would achieve the same objective with less external impact. They would cover any major change in policy that would have external repercussions on particular industries, with the objective of minimizing the costs imposed on other countries. A gradual introduction of the new measures, like the multiyear staging of tariff reductions, is one way to reduce the costs of adjustment. The principles involved here cover subsidization of domestic production that competes with imports as well as subsidization of exports.

Instead of demanding a harmonization of policies, an exacting requirement in a world of independent nation states, this approach calls for extensive prior consultation on any industrial policy changes that are likely to cause injury, with a view to avoiding those changes or at least mitigating injury.

Attempts at harmonization are not incompatible with an approach emphasizing injury. Even if reduction of injury is the main strategy, countries could negotiate to reduce the discrepancies among their industrial policies. But extreme harmonization would not be necessary.

Advice to the United States

In framing U.S. policy, it is necessary to consider what is in the best interest of the United States, given its capabilities and limitations. The United States cannot favor particular industries secretly; that is not consistent with the way American government operates. Should it do so openly? My answer would be that particular industries should be openly supported only if a strong public policy case can be made for such support on its merits: either on grounds of national security or because such support would engender strong and demonstrable externalities. This approach, while sounding blandly obvious, has strong implications with respect to some of the proposals that have been made. It argues for restraint in the use of threats and indiscriminate reliance on reciprocity.

For example, the Labor-Industry Coalition for International Trade has complained of closed markets in other industrial countries for electric power generating equipment, whereas imports have sometimes accounted for 20 percent of U.S. purchases. This, they contend, is unfair (see LICIT, 1983, pp. 79–82). Despite these closed markets, U.S. firms enjoy any economies of scale that they might obtain because of their sales in the large domestic market, augmented by exports. In fact, the U.S. share of world exports actually rose between 1965 and 1980, from 5 to 10 percent. In addition, Americans presumably get lower-cost power by permitting import competition, and power is an important input into industry. It is possible, for instance, that part of the difficulties of aluminum refiners in Japan is due to their preferred procurement of domestic electric generating equipment. Clearly it would be desirable to be able to sell U.S. equipment in France and Japan. But it may not be in the U.S. interest to stop purchases from those countries even if they decline to open their markets to U.S. equipment. Indeed the existing regime may on balance favor U.S. industry as a whole. We simply do not know about the general equilibrium effects.

Furthermore, U.S. policy should not be motivated by arguments that rest on the fallacy of composition—that assert an action would generate employment or improve the overall trade balance. Employment and the overall trade balance are determined by the macro-economic conditions of each economy, not by particular trade policies.

In short, the United States should monitor other countries' practices to detect violations of GATT and its codes; in the process it may observe policy measures that have useful application in the United States. But in the end the United States should adopt measures that are best for itself in its own institutional setting, rather than those that have seemed to work well abroad. Many actions by foreign governments have been costly and largely unsuccessful; those that have been successful would not necessarily or generally be successful in the American context. It would be unwise to adopt many of the practices of Europe or Japan. In particular, Americans should have to make a specially strong case for discriminatory treatment in favor of any particular industry. It is much easier for foreign countries to "pick winners" because they observe successful new industries as they develop first in the United States. How would the U.S. government pick the industries of the future? To what experience could America turn? Its practice has been to rely on private rewards to thousands of firms and individuals, each making a guess as to which activities will be winners in the future. Most will be wrong. Some will be right.

How can the United States bargain with other countries on their practices? Might it not be desirable to introduce Danforth-style reciprocity or in other ways to threaten to close U.S. markets with a view to getting foreign countries to open theirs? Here we must recognize the nation's limitations. The U.S. government cannot bargain subtly in the economic arena, and it has always found it difficult to back away from a publicly stated and argued position introduced for bargaining reasons, but not fully acknowledged as such. Many citizens will believe the arguments that have been advanced. In short, a pluralistic, open society cannot get away with bluffing. Foreigners will be skeptical of any non-serious threat, and once domestic political support has been built for the threat, the threat becomes serious but it ceases to be a bluff. For this reason the United States should threaten actions only when it is clearly willing to undertake them. And in general it should be willing to undertake them only if they are in its best interests, not simply as a bargaining tactic.

The ambiguity surrounding decision making in the United States, and particularly the relationship between the president and the Congress when it comes to trade matters, is sometimes helpful in bargaining with foreigners, since they can never be certain that Congress will not take the upper hand and move in a way that disadvantages them. This uncertainty is a reality of American politics, and it can sometimes be used successfully in the bargaining context. But it is rather different from the deliberate bluff of a poker player.

If other countries continue to pursue practices that the United States considers unacceptable, should the United States retaliate just to show it is willing to take action hurtful to the other country, even if it hurts itself as well? As suggested above, the general answer to this question is no. Such action cannot absolutely be ruled out, however, if it has a reasonable prospect of inducing a change in the other country's behavior that benefits the United States. But this prospect is so heavily conditioned on the exact manner, timing, and context of the threatened retaliatory action that general rules are not likely to be helpful. Playing by ear is likely to work better than trying to follow a score or, to mix metaphors, a recipe. That is where the art of diplomacy comes into the economic arena.

APPENDIX
Key Articles Pertaining to Subsidies in the 1979 GATT Code on Subsidies and Countervailing Duties

Article 8 Subsidies—General Provisions

1. Signatories recognize that subsidies are used by governments to promote important objectives of social and economic policy. Signatories also recognize that subsidies may cause adverse effects to the interests of other signatories.
2. Signatories agree not to use export subsidies in a manner inconsistent with the provisions of this Agreement.
3. Signatories further agree that they shall seek to avoid causing, through the use of any subsidy:
   (a) injury to the domestic industry of another signatory,*
   (b) nullification or impairment of the benefits accruing directly or indirectly to another signatory under the General Agreement,* or
   (c) serious prejudice to the interests of another signatory,*
4. The adverse effects to the interests of another signatory required to demonstrate nullification or impairment* or serious prejudice may arise through

*Denotes footnote in original document.

(a) the effects of the subsidized imports in the domestic market of the importing signatory,

(b) the effects of the subsidy in displacing or impeding the imports of like products into the market of the subsidizing country, or

(c) the effects of the subsidized exports in displacing* the exports of like products of another signatory from a third country market.*

*Article 9   Export Subsidies on Products Other than Certain Primary Products**

1. Signatories shall not grant export subsidies on products other than certain primary products.

2. The practices listed in points (a) to (l) in the Annex are illustrative of export subsidies.

Article 10   Export Subsidies on Certain Primary Products

1. In accordance with the provisions of Article XVI:3 of the General Agreement, signatories agree not to grant directly or indirectly any export subsidy on certain primary products in a manner which results in the signatory granting such subsidy having more than an equitable share of world export trade in such product, account being taken of the shares of the signatories in trade in the product concerned during a previous representative period, and any special factors which may have affected or may be affecting trade in such product.

2. For purposes of Article XVI:3 of the General Agreement and paragraph 1 above:

(a) "more than equitable share of world export trade" shall include any case in which the effect of an export subsidy granted by a signatory is to displace the exports of another signatory bearing in mind the developments on world markets:

(b) with regard to new markets traditional patterns of supply of the product concerned to the world market, region or country, in which the new market is situated shall be taken into account in determining "equitable share of world export trade":

(c) "a previous representative period" shall normally be the three most recent calendar years in which normal market conditions existed.

3. Signatories further agree not to grant export subsidies on exports of certain primary products to a particular market in a manner which results in prices materially below those of other suppliers to the same market.

Article 11   Subsidies Other than Export Subsidies

1. Signatories recognize that subsidies other than export subsidies are widely used as important instruments for the promotion of social and economic

policy objectives and do not intend to restrict the right of signatories to use such subsidies to achieve these and other important policy objectives which they consider desirable. Signatories note that among such objectives are:

(a) the elimination of industrial, economic and social disadvantages of specific regions.

(b) to facilitate the restructuring, under socially acceptable conditions, of certain sectors, especially where this has become necessary by reason of changes in trade and economic policies, including international agreements resulting in lower barriers to trade.

(c) generally to sustain employment and to encourage re-training and change in employment.

(d) to encourage research and development programmes, especially in the field of high-technology industries.

(e) the implementation of economic programmes and policies to promote the economic and social development of developing countries.

(f) redeployment of industry in order to avoid congestion and environmental problems.

2. Signatories recognize, however, that subsidies other than export subsidies, certain objectives and possible form of which are described, respectively, in paragraphs 1 and 3 of this Article, may cause or threaten to cause injury to a domestic industry of another signatory or serious prejudice to the interests of another signatory or may nullify or impair benefits accruing to another signatory under the General Agreement, in particular where such subsidies would adversely affect the conditions of normal competition. Signatories shall therefore seek to avoid causing such effects through the use of subsidies. In particular, signatories, when drawing up their policies and practices in this field, in addition to evaluating the essential internal objectives to be achieved, shall also weigh, as far as practicable, taking account of the nature of the particular case, possible adverse effects on trade. They shall also consider the conditions of world trade, production (e.g. price, capacity utilization etc.) and supply in the product concerned.

3. Signatories recognize that the objectives mentioned in paragraph 1 above may be achieved, *inter alia*, by means of subsidies granted with the aim of giving an advantage to certain enterprises. Examples of possible forms of such subsidies are: government financing of commercial enterprises, including grants, loans or guarantees; government provision or government financed provision of utility, supply distribution and other operational or support services or facilities; government financing of research and development programmes; fiscal incentives; and government subscription to, or provision of, equity capital.

Signatories note that the above form of subsidies are normally granted either regionally or by sector. The enumeration of forms of subsidies set out above is illustrative and non-exhaustive, and reflects these currently granted by a number of signatories to this Agreement.

Signatories recognize, nevertheless, that the enumeration of forms of subsidies set out above should be reviewed periodically and that this should be done, through consultations, in conformity with the spirit of Article XVI: 5 of the General Agreement.

4. Signatories recognize further that, without prejudice to their rights under this Agreement, nothing in paragraphs 1-3 above and in particular the enumeration of forms of subsidies creates, in itself, any basis for action under the General Agreement, as interpreted by this Agreement.

Annex   Illustrative List of Export Subsidies

(a) The provision by governments of direct subsidies to a firm or an industry contingent upon export performance.

(b) Currency retention schemes or any similar practices which involve a bonus on exports.

(c) Internal transport and freight charges on export shipments, provided or mandated by governments, on terms more favourable than for domestic shipments.

(d) The delivery by governments or their agencies of imported or domestic products or services for use in the production of exported goods, on terms or conditions more favourable than for delivery of like or directly competitive products or services for use in the production of goods for domestic consumption, if (in the case of products) such terms or conditions are more favourable than those commercially available on world markets to their exporters.

(e) The full or partial exemption, remission, or deferral specifically related to exports, of direct taxes* or social welfare charges paid or payable by industrial or commercial enterprises.*

(f) The allowance of special deductions directly related to exports or export performance, over and above those granted in respect to production for domestic consumption, in the calculation of the base on which direct taxes are charged.

(g) The exemption or remission in respect of the production and distribution of exported products, of indirect taxes* in excess of those levied in respect of the production and distribution of like products when sold for domestic consumption.

(h) The exemption, remission or deferral of prior stage cumulative indirect taxes on goods or services used in the production of exported products in excess of the exemption, remission or deferral of like prior stage cumulative indirect taxes on goods or services used in the production of like products when sold for domestic consumption; provided, however, that prior stage cumulative indirect taxes may be exempted, remitted or deferred on exported products even when not exempted, remitted or deferred on like products when sold for domestic consumption, if the prior stage cumulative indirect taxes are levied on goods that are physically incorporated (making normal allowance for waste) in the exported product.*

(i) The remission or drawback of import charges in excess of those levied on imported goods that are physically incorporated (making normal allowance for waste) in the exported product: provided, however, that in particular cases a firm may use a quantity of home market goods equal to, and having the same quality and characteristics as the imported goods as a substitute for them in order to benefit from this provision if the import and the corresponding export operations both occur within a reasonable time period, normally not to exceed two years.

(j) The provision by governments for special institutions controlled by governments of export credit guarantees or insurance programmes, of insurance or guarantee programmes against increases in the costs of exported products* or of exchange risk programmes, at premium rates, which are manifestly inadequate to cover the long-term operating costs and losses of the programmes.*

(k) The grant by governments (or special institutions controlled by and or acting under the authority of governments) of export credits at rates below those which they actually have to pay for the funds so employed (or would have to pay if they borrowed on international capital markets in order to obtain funds of the same maturity and denominated in the same currency as the export credit), or the payment by them of all or part of the costs incurred by exporters or financial institutions in obtaining credits, in so far as they are used to secure a material advantage in the field of export credit terms.

Provided, however, that if a signatory is a party to an international undertaking on official credits to which at least twelve original signatories* to this Agreement are parties as of 1 January 1979 (or a successor undertaking which has been adopted by those original signatories), or if in practice a signatory applies the interest rates provisions of the relevant undertaking, an export credit practice which is in conformity with those provisions shall not be considered an export subsidy prohibited by this Agreement.

(l) Any other charge on the public account constituting an export subsidy in the sense of Article XVI of the General Agreement.

NOTES

1. I use the term *practices* because I believe much difficulty in import penetration in Japan is due to deeply engrained purchasing practices by Japanese firms and mid-level ministry officials, rather than to government policy.

2. The following description is a blend from several sources: Namiki in Warnecke (1978); U.S.-Japan Trade Study Group (1984); Yakushiji in Aoki
   (1984); Yamamura (1982); and interviews with MITI officials.
3. Taussig (1927, pp. 57–58) pointed to Germany's well-trained chemists and
   lab assistants as the basis for that country's comparative advantage in
   chemical dyes and other chemical products.

REFERENCES

Aoki, Masahiko, ed., *The Economic Analysis of the Japanese Firm* (Amsterdam:
Elsevier, 1984).

Caves, Richard E., and Masu Uekusa, *Industrial Organization in Japan* (Washington, DC: Brookings Institution, 1976).

Cline, William R., *Reciprocity: A New Approach to World Trade Policy?* (Washington, DC: Institute for International Economics, 1982).

_____, ed., *Trade Policy for the 1980s* (Washington, DC: Institute for Interna-
tional Economics, 1983).

Hufbauer, Gary Clyde, and Joanna Erb, *Subsidies in International Trade* (Washington, DC: Institute for International Economics, 1984).

Jacquemin, Alexis, ed., *European Industry: Public Policy and Corporate Strategy* (Oxford: Clarendon Press, 1984).

Kalt, Joseph P., "The Impact of Domestic Regulatory Policies on International
Competitiveness," Chapter 8.

Krugman, Paul, "Notes on Trade in the Presence of Dynamic Scale Economies,"
March 1985, Mimeo.

Labor-Industry Coalition for International Trade (LICIT), *International Trade,
Industrial Policies, and the Future of American Industry* (Washington, DC,
1983).

Magaziner, Ira C., and Robert B. Reich, *Minding America's Business* (New York:
Vintage Books, 1983).

Ministry of International Trade and Industry (MITI), *The Vision of MITI Policies in the 1980s* (Tokyo, 1980).

Nelson, Richard R., ed., *Government and Technical Progress: A Cross-Industry
Analysis* (New York: Pergamon Press, 1982).

Patrick, Hugh, and Henry Rosovsky, eds., *Asia's New Giant* (Washington, DC:
Brookings Institution, 1976).

Taussig, Frank W., *International Trade* (New York: Macmillan, 1927).

U.S.-Japan Trade Study Group, *Progress Report: 1984* (Tokyo, 1984).

Warnecke, Steven J., ed., *International Trade and Industrial Policies* (London:
Macmillan, 1978).

Yamamura, Kozo, ed., *Policy and Trade Issues of the Japanese Economy* (Seat-
tle: University of Washington Press, 1982).

CHAPTER 5

International R&D Competition and Policy

Avinash Dixit

M ost analyses of American industrial strategies attach special importance to the industries at the frontier of technological advance. The report of the President's Commission on Industrial Competitiveness (1985), p. 16, for example, stated that a risk of "loss of the U.S. position in vital high-growth technology markets has enormous implications for our future competitiveness." The commission recommended several policy measures "to create, apply and protect technology." These include tax incentives for firms to undertake more R&D; a lower cost of capital; stronger patent protection for our innovations, achieved by lengthening the effective period of protection and negotiating with other countries to improve the enforcement of such protection there; and relaxation of some regulatory restrictions.

Many Americans believe that the Japanese government promotes the advance and the commercialization of technology in Japan by means of all these policies and others, including protection of the home market, promotion of exports, and rationalization of the innovation process, achieved by restricting the field to a few chosen firms. A comprehensive statement of this view can be found in Borrus, Millstein, and Zysman (1983). The extent and the efficacy of

I am grateful to Carl Shapiro for valuable discussions and to the National Science Foundation for research support under grant SES-8509536.

all these measures have been questioned, for example by Krugman (1984a), but the prevailing view in policy circles is of an activist and successful Japanese industrial policy toward high-tech industries. These activities are often described as "creating comparative advantage."

The corresponding fear is that the United States' comparative advantage is being determined as a residual and may lie in unproductive and undesirable industries. "A nation of hamburger stands" and "sweeping the floor around Japanese computers" are the vivid phrases used to describe this prospect. The implication is that the United States should rise from its passive, reactive policy posture and actively seize the leadership in the game of international R&D competition.

This chapter examines these arguments in greater detail. I shall identify several market failures that justify policies to promote high-technology industries. Other market failures, however, suggest restraining the level of activity in those industries. Thus it becomes important to assess the relative strengths of the two arguments. Previous theoretical work fails to resolve the issue, since each contribution to the literature focuses on one feature or the other. Therefore I shall construct a simple but more general model that juxtaposes the competing forces. The results point to the conditions under which the market mechanism will channel too few or too many resources into R&D. We can also see how policies can remedy the problems when necessary.

In the next section I review the economic arguments for policy intervention in the process of R&D. Then I construct and analyze the formal model and shall sum up its policy conclusions.

AN OVERVIEW OF THE ISSUES

Economists and policy makers alike recognize two broad classes of problems that can justify government support for high-technology industries. The President's Commission on Industrial Competitiveness (1985, p. 18) expresses the issues as follows: "State-of-the-art products have commanded premium prices in world markets, and technological advances have spurred productivity gains throughout the economy." The first point recognizes that markets for products at the forefront of technology are by their nature imperfectly competitive and allow pure profits. The second point concerns positive externalities or spill-over benefits generated by R&D. The policies listed above can be seen as tackling these two classes of problems. Krugman (1987) discusses the two categories in more detail.

The concept of "creating comparative advantage" reflects a relatively recent view of policy as a strategic commitment that can change the conditions of international competition to the advantage of the active country. Several papers in Krugman (1986) discuss this view.

Here I shall examine some of these points in more detail, to identify the features that must be incorporated in a formal model.

Externalities

One firm's R&D success can confer economic benefits on other firms and consumers in many ways. Knowledge of the new product or process may leak out. Patents can be circumvented. Employees with the necessary specific skills can be bid away. When there is licensing, whether required by law or arising from the firms' mutual interests (see Katz and Shapiro, 1985), the licensees may get a share of the rent accruing to the innovation. When perfect price discrimination is not possible, the innovator cannot capture all the consumer surplus that is generated.

The resulting tradeoff is well known from the work of Arrow (1971) and was most recently analyzed by Spence (1984). If the benefits flowing from an innovation cannot be fully appropriated, then the incentive to undertake R&D is reduced. But after an innovation becomes available, the marginal cost of transmitting it is small, and giving the innovator monopoly rights can result in too little dissemination. The usual second-best policy is to find the optimal finite patent life. With perfect information, an up-front subsidy for R&D costs, coupled with antitrust policy to enforce competitive pricing of the outcome, can achieve the first-best outcome, but in practice this approach raises serious moral hazard problems. A more realistic policy may be to raise the rewards for achieving R&D success, using either prizes for winners or subsidies for subsequent production and sales.

Policy analysis of spill-overs frequently stops here. However, there are three important balancing considerations. First is the obvious caveat. As Krugman (1986, p. 17) puts it, "by definition a spillover does not command a market price, and therefore leaves no paper trail by which we can trace it." Therefore we have little objective sense of the magnitude of such effects. Assertions about their ubiquity and importance usually come from people within the industries, whose motives are suspect since they stand to gain from the proposed policies. Therefore we should discount these claims, perhaps quite substantially, unless the magnitudes are objectively calculated, as Bresnahan (1986) has done for the case of computers.

The second point is particularly important in connection with international competition. Many of these external effects are not confined to one country; Krugman (1984a) discusses the point with special reference to the electronics industry. But policy in one country does not take account of the benefits it would confer on others. On the contrary, each has the incentive to cut back its own effort and to gain some free-rider benefits from other countries' promotion policies for R&D.

The final point is potentially the most important—not all external effects are beneficial. A familiar example is environmental pollution, which can harm consumers and other firms. These literal spill-overs can also have an international dimension. Another kind of negative spillover is especially important in R&D competition. Since each firm's R&D effort worsens the others' prospects of success, all make excessive efforts in a race to be first. The problem is similar to that of overexploitation of a common resource pool. Independent operators of separate oil wells tapping a common deposit each have incentives to extract as much as possible before the other does. The general issue is discussed by Hirschleifer (1971) and appears in the formal models of Barzel (1968), Loury (1979), and Lee and Wilde (1980).

A mere listing of all the spill-overs, positive and negative, national and international, associated with R&D does not help us find their net balance. We need a model that incorporates them all, sees how they interact, and yields an overall criterion for the direction of policy. After a general discussion of profits and strategic commitment, that will be my task in the next section.

Profits

When international competition allows pure profit, it is in each country's interest to capture it. When the government has better strategic instruments for doing so than do firms, a case can be made for policy intervention. This insight, developed in a number of papers by Brander and Spencer, is illustrated for the case of R&D in Spencer and Brander (1983). They consider the case of a duopoly with one firm in each country. If one government subsidizes domestic R&D, the domestic firm achieves a lower unit cost than the foreign firm. This shifts the equilibrium of the output competition in its favor.

Handsome profits have often been obtained by successful innovators of new products as well as of lower-cost processes. The existence of such profits seems to lend support to the Brander-Spencer view that the government can and should act to capture them for domestic firms. However, both their theory and these observations have a serious flaw. R&D is an inherently uncertain undertaking. For every successful innovator, there are many who fail. The Brander-Spencer model ignores such uncertainty. So do casual observers who notice only successful innovations and fail to look for the costs of failure. These costs are admittedly hard to locate in accounting data, but they must be included in a correct calculation of social costs and benefits. To affect incentives, the policy regarding R&D support has to be fixed before the outcome is known. Unless the government can somehow recognize the winner ex ante and exclude all others, it must consider the effect of its policies on the structure of an entire industry. The criteria by which policies are judged should likewise include the expected profits of the whole industry, and not just those of the winner.

Of the policies listed above, most are not directed to specific firms. They establish a framework of taxes, subsidies, patent laws, trade practices, and so on, that apply to all. Indeed, it is doubtful if the U.S. constitution and politics would allow making the benefits of R&D policies available only to selected firms. Consequently, when favorable policies are announced, new firms will enter the business until the expected profit to an additional entrant becomes negative. In the case of a large group of identical entrants, the industry as a whole will have zero expected profit, and the profit-capture motive for policy will disappear.

Other countries (like Japan) may sometimes successfully restrict entry, but one suspects that even those governments are subject to political pressure from the firms they seek to exclude. In any event, unless the Japanese can pick winners ex ante and exclude all losers, they can only achieve a target probability of winning by allowing enough firms to enter, most of whom will be ex post losers. This chain of events will have a similar effect on the industry profit. To handle such effects, the formal model to be built in the next section should incorporate uncertainty and the calculation of ex ante expected profits of the entire industry to which R&D support is directed.

Strategic Commitment

When a government pursues a policy of profit capture, it makes a strategic irreversible commitment that alters the domestic firm's behavior in a credible way. The foreign firm then responds by changing its behavior. An export subsidy, for example, lowers the private marginal cost of the domestic firm, which leads it to act more aggressively in output competition. The foreign firm's best response in any particular conflict is usually an accommodating output reduction. In this way the outcome is altered in the domestic firm's favor. In game-theoretic terms, the domestic firm's output reaction function shifts outward, and the equilibrium moves along the foreign firm's downward-sloping reaction function. It is this forced change in the foreign firm's action that yields strategic advantage to the domestic firm.

In the case of R&D, the home country generally wants the foreign country's firms to reduce their effort level. This is accomplished by committing to an increased level of effort if the foreign firm's reaction function is downward sloping. However, its reaction function may slope upward. A commitment to greater effort domestically will increase the optimal level of foreign effort if it raises the *marginal* return to foreign effort. This can occur at least in some circumstances, even though increased domestic effort reduces the *total* return to foreign effort. The general game-theoretic issues of this kind are discussed by Fudenberg and Tirole (1984). Once again, we need a model that is sufficiently rich to allow us to sort out the possibilities.

THE MODEL

I shall develop the simplest model that meets the requirements discussed in the previous section. (In fact, the results are valid far more generally, as I show in a separate technical paper (Dixit, 1986b).) The model is a combination and extension of Dasgupta and Stiglitz (1980), Loury (1979), and Lee and Wilde (1980).

Each basic unit conducting R&D is called a firm, but could equally well be thought of as a laboratory. There are many such firms; where convenient I shall treat the total number X as a continuous variable. This is a reasonable assumption. At the start of most R&D races in the semiconductor or biotechnology industries, for example, there are a dozen or more competitors. This number is large enough to make the problems of small and integer numbers of negligible importance.

While the R&D effort is going on, each firm has the probability of success, λdt, in any small interval of time, dt. This is a conditional probability, given that the R&D race has not ended by the beginning of this interval. Statistical theory refers to λ as the hazard rate. I assume that it is constant over time and the same for all firms. The former assumption is restrictive, but it is hard to do without it. The latter assumption is relaxed in Dixit (1986b), where each firm chooses its λ and the choices can differ across firms; the policy conclusions that follow are unaffected.

The chances of success are taken to be independent across firms, because any correlated R&D efforts would be better handled in a single merged firm. With X firms, the conditional probability that one of them succeeds in a small interval of time, dt, is Xdt; the probability of a tie is of order $(dt)^2$ and can be ignored. The probability that the race is still going on by time t is found (by splitting this time into a large number, N, of intervals of small length, t/N, each) to equal

$$\lim_{N \to \infty} (1 - \lambda Xt/N)^N = e^{-\lambda Xt} . \qquad (1)$$

When one firm succeeds, the R&D race ends. The prize of the successful firm is the prospect of a discounted (back to the date of innovation) present value P of future gains. These gains will usually be the rents it gets from exploiting its monopoly power or licensing its patent, but could include the rationally forecast value of any advantage this victory gives it in any future R&D races. Thus P is the appropriable part of the benefit. The spill-over benefit to the rest of society, in present value terms as of the date of innovation, is denoted by S; this includes consumer surplus, other firms' free-rider benefits or rent shares, and so on, net of any negative externalities of the pollution kind. The common pool externality is built into the nature of R&D competition, and will emerge below.

So far I have ignored the international dimension of R&D competition. Suppose there are Y foreign firms in the race as well as the X domestic ones. If one of them is the winner, its appropriable benefit is no part of our country's social welfare, but we may receive some spill-over benefits. However, we should expect our spill-over benefit to be smaller if the winner is a foreign firm than if it is a domestic firm. First, leakage of knowledge may be somewhat slower across national boundaries. Second, it may be more difficult to bid away skilled foreign workers than those in our own country. Finally, a foreign firm may be able to exert monopoly power more readily. I shall capture all these effects by supposing that our spill-over benefits from a foreign firm's victory are αS, where S denotes as before our spill-over benefits due to the victory of a domestic firm, and α is a parameter, lying between 0 and 1, that measures the fractional international transmission of spill-overs.

Now consider the costs of conducting R&D. These can be of two kinds: lump-sum costs that are sunk at the outset, and flow costs that are incurred each year while the race is going on. For conceptual convenience think of the former as capital costs (building a lab with few alternative uses) and the latter as labor costs (salaries of scientists who could move on to other projects when this one ends). Since the two kinds of costs play different roles with regard to the common pool externality, both must be incorporated in the model. Dasgupta and Stiglitz (1980) and Loury (1979) consider only initial lump-sum costs, while Lee and Wilde (1980) include only flow costs.

For mathematical simplicity, I shall assume that the capital-labor ratio is the same for all firms, and so a parameter characteristic of this project. A more general treatment allowing capital-labor substitution that can also differ from one firm to another is in Dixit (1986b); again the results are unaffected.

Firms may differ in their overall ability to conduct R&D. Some companies may be innately better; some may have advantages rooted in past success. In any case, we can rank them in order of increasing cost. Suppose firm number x has capital costs $kG(x)$ and labor costs $\ell G(x)$ per unit of time. Here k and ℓ are fixed parameters and $G(x)$ is an increasing function; the use of the same function for the two kinds of costs reflects the assumption of a fixed capital-labor ratio. When there are X firms active, they will be the least-cost ones, whether they are selected by a competitive market mechanism or by an industrial policy that pays due regard to economic efficiency.

Then the total capital costs will be $kH(X)$ and total labor costs per unit time will be $\ell H(X)$, where $H(X)$ is just the sum of all the included firms' $G(x)$'s, and $G(X)$ is the marginal $H(X)$:

$$H(X) = \int_0^X G(x)dx \,, \quad H'(X) = G(X) \,. \tag{2}$$

Now we are ready to look at the race as a whole at time 0, the starting point, and find out how many firms will take part in a market equilibrium, and how many should for social optimality. This determination involves calculations of expected costs and benefits.

Begin with the expected private benefits for any one of our firms. As seen at time 0, the probability of its winning in the small time interval from t to $(t + dt)$ is $e^{-\lambda(X+Y)t}\lambda dt$, namely the probability that no firm, domestic or foreign, has won before time t, times the conditional probability of victory for our chosen firm in the next interval dt. In this eventuality, this firm's benefit is P discounted back to t, or Pe^{-rt} discounted to time 0, where r is the rate of interest. Multiplying the benefit by the probability, and summing over all possible values of t, the expected value of the private benefit is

$$\text{expected private benefit } (EPB) = \int_0^\infty Pe^{-rt} e^{-\lambda(X+Y)t} \lambda dt$$

$$= P/(X + Y + r/\lambda) \,. \tag{3}$$

Observe that the expected private benefit decreases as the number $(X + Y)$ of firms in the race increases. This is because the probability of victory for any one selected firm falls uniformly over time as there are more contestants. This is an aspect of the "common pool" negative externality that was discussed before.

Next consider expected costs for the xth firm. Capital costs $kG(x)$ are incurred at time 0 if this firm enters the race. Labor costs $\ell G(x)$ are incurred as long as the race is going on. The probability that the race ends during the time interval $[t, t + dt]$ is $e^{-\lambda(X+Y)t} \lambda(X + Y)dt$; in this event the discounted present value of labor costs is given by $\ell G(x) [1 - e^{-rt}]/r$. Then

expected labor costs for firm x

$$= \int_0^\infty \ell G(x) \frac{1 - e^{-rt}}{r} e^{-\lambda(X+Y)t} \lambda(X + Y)dt$$

$$= (\ell/\lambda) G(x)/(X + Y + r/\lambda) \,. \tag{4}$$

For any given x, an increase in the total number $(X + Y)$ of firms reduces the expected labor costs of firm x. The race is likely to end sooner when there are more contestants. Therefore any given firm, whether or not it wins, is likely to incur its labor costs for a shorter duration. Thus the common pool externality is positive in its effect on labor costs. Of course in equilibrium we will be looking at firms with positive expected profits. So the harmful effect on the expected gain will exceed the beneficial effect on expected labor costs, and there will be a net negative common pool externality. The externality affects labor (flow) costs but not capital (initial sunk) costs. That is why R&D projects with different capital-labor ratios give rise to different kinds of market failure and require different policies. That is also why it is important to allow both types of costs into the model.

Now the overall expected cost of firm x, when there are X domestic firms in the race, can be denoted $EPC(x, X)$, and written as

$$EPC(x, X) = \left\{ k + \frac{\ell/\lambda}{X + Y + r/\lambda} \right\} G(x) . \qquad (5)$$

In a market equilibrium, firms will enter the race until the expected private benefit (EPB) equals the expected cost of the marginal firm $(EPC(X, X))$. This condition is

$$\frac{P}{X + Y + r/\lambda} = \left\{ k + \frac{\ell/\lambda}{X + Y + r/\lambda} \right\} G(X) . \qquad (6)$$

This determines the equilibrium number of domestic firms X_e, given all the parameters of the problem and the number of foreign firms, Y.

To determine the full international equilibrium, I should write down an analogous equation for the foreign country (or countries) and solve for the equilibrium numbers X_e and Y_e simultaneously. I shall not go into that complication. However, our discussion of policy issues must consider both reactive policies (those that respond to a given committed level of foreign R&D effort) and active ones (those that seek to alter the foreign effort by making a strategic commitment domestically).

To set the stage for the policy analysis, let us find the social benefits and costs. First the benefits. The probability of victory for any one of the domestic firms in the time interval $[t, t, + dt]$ is $e^{-\lambda(X+Y)t} \lambda X dt$; the present value discounted back to time 0 of the consequent social benefit is $(P + S)e^{-rt}$. For the case where a foreign firm is the winner, the corresponding probability is $e^{-\lambda(X+Y)t}\lambda Ydt$, and the domestic benefit is αSe^{-rt}. Therefore:

expected total social benefit (ETSB)

$$= \int_0^\infty (P + S)e^{-rt} e^{-\lambda(X+Y)t} \lambda Xdt + \int_0^\infty \alpha Se^{-rt} e^{-\lambda(X+Y)t} \lambda Ydt$$

$$= \frac{(P + S)X + \alpha S Y}{X + Y + r/\lambda} .\qquad(7)$$

The corresponding marginal is

expected marginal social benefit (EMSB)

$$= \partial(ETSB)/\partial X$$

$$= \frac{P + S}{X + Y + r/\lambda} - \frac{(P + S)X + \alpha S Y}{(X + Y + r/\lambda)^2}$$

$$= \frac{P + S - ETSB}{X + Y + r/\lambda} .\qquad(8)$$

Compare this with the expected private benefit of each firm, which was $P/(X + Y + r/\lambda)$ in equation 3. The social marginal benefit differs on two counts. The term $S/(X + Y + r/\lambda)$ obviously reflects the positive spill-over effect. The other term, $-ETSB/(X + Y + r/\lambda)$, is the net common pool externality, which is negative. An additional firm raises the prospect of an earlier end to the race. This acts like an increase in the discount rate and lowers the present value of the expected benefit attributable to all inframarginal firms.

Expected total social cost with X firms is simply the sum of the expected costs of all firms x between 0 and X. Using equations 5 and 2, we can write

$$ETSC = \left\{ k + \frac{\ell/\lambda}{X + Y + r/\lambda} \right\} H(X) .\qquad(9)$$

Expected marginal social cost is

$$EMSC = \left\{ k + \frac{\ell/\lambda}{X + Y + r/\lambda} \right\} G(X) - \frac{\ell H(X)/\lambda}{(X + Y + r/\lambda)^2}$$

$$= EPC (X, X) - \frac{L(X)}{X + Y + r/\lambda} ,\qquad(10)$$

where

$$L(X) \quad = \quad (\ell/\lambda)\, H(X)\, /\, (X + Y + r/\lambda) \tag{11}$$

is simply the expected total labor cost. Thus we have the positive common pool externality on the cost side: marginal social cost is less than the private cost of the marginal firm because of the beneficial effect on the labor costs of all inframarginal firms. As mentioned before, we should expect this positive effect to be weaker than the corresponding harmful effect on the benefit side, since we will be looking at equilibria or optima where the benefits exceed the costs.

CORRECTIVE POLICIES

The next step is to compare the market equilibrium with the socially optimal outcome and characterize the Pigovian subsidy or tax policies that will correct the various externalities discussed above. In this section I shall do this while holding the level of the foreign R&D effort Y fixed. This approach can be interpreted in one of two ways. The first would be to suppose that the foreigners have indeed made a strategic commitment of their effort, and all that can be done domestically is to find the best response. Some may argue that the United States is now in such a reactive situation; then the analysis will tell the United States how to make the best of it. The next section will examine what can be done by seizing the initiative.

The second view of this section's approach is that it forms a part of the analysis of a complete multicountry equilibrium. The best choice of X corresponding to various possible levels of foreign Y traces out a "reaction curve," shown as the curve R in Figure 5–1. Typical contours of the domestic national net benefit are also sketched. The assumption is that more intensive foreign R&D harms domestic interests, so contours lower down correspond to a higher net benefit domestically.

The market equilibrium level of X can also be shown in relation to the foreign effort level Y in the same diagram. Then the analysis of this section, which compares the equilibrium and the optimal levels of X for a fixed Y, tells us whether the market equilibrium locus lies to the left of the socially optimal one, like M_1 in Figure 5–1, or to the right, like M_2. In the former case, the Pigovian policy calls for a subsidy, and in the latter for a tax.

Figure 5-1. Reactive Policies and Market Equilibria.

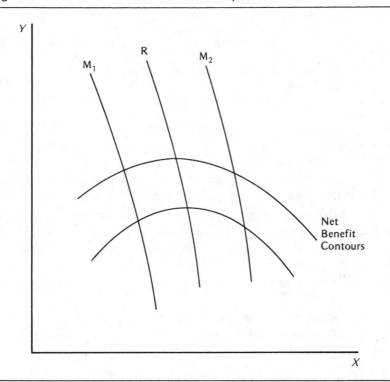

Let us begin the analysis. The condition for social optimality, equating the expected marginal social benefit *EMSB* and the expected marginal social cost *EMSC*, is found using equations 8 and 9 as

$$\frac{P + S - ETSB}{X + Y + r/\lambda} = EPC(X, X) - \frac{L(X)}{X + Y + r/\lambda} . \qquad (12)$$

Compare this with the market equilibrium condition of equation 6:

$$\frac{P}{X + Y + r/\lambda} = EPC(X, X) .$$

The two differ because of the external effects: the spill-overs and the common pool externality on the benefit side, and only the latter on the cost side. The same inspection tells us what to do. The government should decide on a tax or subsidy policy such that if the winning firm is a domestic company, its private benefit will be P' instead of P. Then the market equilibrium condition will become

$$\frac{P'}{X + Y + r/\lambda} = EPC(X, X) \ .$$

We can make this coincide with (12) by setting

$$P' = P + S - ETSB + L(X) \ . \tag{13}$$

The corrective terms on the right-hand side give us the appropriate Pigovian policy. With both positive and negative terms involved, the net effect depends on their relative strengths.

The simplest way to bring private and social interests in line is to give the winning firm a lump sum prize of $(P' - P)$ if $P' > P$, and levy a lump sum penalty of $(P - P')$ if $P > P'$. Other measures, such as lengthening (or shortening) patent lives, and subsidies (or taxes) on the post-innovation production, will have other effects on monopoly powers and spill-overs; we will have to augment the model with a more detailed treatment of the variables P and S to examine these aspects.

To implement the optimum, we must calculate the proper X from the condition in equation 11 and then evaluate the corrective terms in equation 13 at *that* X. However, if we are initially at the free market equilibrium, we can more easily find the beneficial *direction* of policy reform by evaluating the corrective terms at the *market* value of X. If this balance is positive, then at the market outcome the expected net marginal social benefit from an increase in X is positive. Let us work this condition into a form that will convey a rough idea of the magnitudes involved.

Here it helps to introduce two parameters. First suppose labor costs are a fraction β of expected total costs, so

$$L(X) = \beta \left\{ k + \frac{\ell/\lambda}{X + Y + r/\lambda} \right\} H(X) \ . \tag{14}$$

Next recall how $H(X)$ is defined in equation 2. Figure 5–2 depicts the process. $H(X)$ is the shaded area, while $XG(X)$ is the whole rectangle. Let

$$H(X) = \theta XG(X) \ . \tag{15}$$

Figure 5-2. R&D Costs of Domestic Firms.

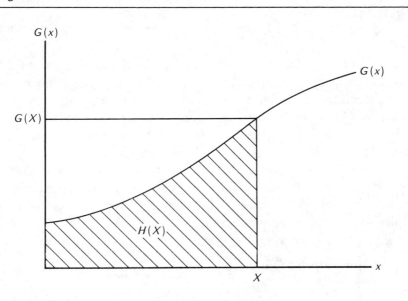

We can regard θ as a measure of the relative importance of marginal versus inframarginal firms in this industry. If all domestic firms are marginal, because the country is new in the R&D game, with few or no experienced low-cost firms, then $G(x)$ will be nearly constant and θ will be nearly equal to one. If most domestic firms are low-cost inframarginals, then $G(x)$ will rise suddenly and θ will be low.

Now the condition under which the positive externalities prevail, and the optimal corrective policy is a subsidy, is

$$S > ETSB - L(X) \ .$$

Using the expression in equation 7 for $ETSB$, and equations 14 and 15, we have

$$S > \frac{(P + S)X + \alpha S Y}{X + Y + r/\lambda} - \theta \beta X \left\{ k + \frac{\ell/\lambda}{X + Y + r/\lambda} \right\} G(X) \ .$$

We are evaluating this at the market equilibrium, where equation 6 holds. There the condition becomes

$$S > \frac{(P + S)X + \alpha S Y}{X + Y + r/\lambda} - \theta \beta X \frac{P}{X + Y + r/\lambda} \ .$$

After some algebra, this simplies to

$$\frac{S}{P} > (1 - \beta\theta) \; \frac{X}{(1 - \alpha)Y + r/\lambda} . \tag{16}$$

If this holds in the free market situation, then the domestic R&D effort should be promoted by offering the domestic winner a suitably calculated subsidy. If the inequality goes the other way, the effort should be discouraged by means of an appropriate tax.

We can now get a better feel for the condition by trying out some values. Suppose $S/P = 0.5$; this will happen if the winner operates a monopoly with constant marginal cost and a linear demand, and fails to capture the consumer surplus. Suppose $\alpha = 0.5$ (international spill-overs are half as strong as the domestic ones), $\beta = 0.5$ (labor and capital costs are equally important), and $\theta = 0.5$ (inframarginal and marginal firms are roughly equally important). Finally, suppose $X = Y = 10$, $r = 0.1$, and the expected time to success is 5 years, so $20\lambda = 1/5$ and $\lambda = 0.01$. Then the right-hand side of 16 becomes 0.5, the same as the left-hand side. The various externalities just happen to cancel one another. Therefore this is a useful central case from which the departures of any actual instance can be judged.

We can also see how the magnitudes of the various parameters affect the condition and whether they strengthen or weaken the case for a subsidy on externality grounds. The larger is β (i.e., the more important are flow costs in relation to sunk costs in the R&D process), the more likely it is that the condition for a subsidy will be met. This is because of the beneficial common pool effect on flow costs. The case for a subsidy is stronger when θ is larger (i.e., when there are few inframarginal firms). In this sense a newly emerging country in the R&D game may have more reason to use subsidies than an old established one. The negative common pool externality acts on the benefit *minus* the industry's labor costs. If all firms have labor costs nearly as high as those of the marginal firm, then the negative externality is less important, and so the case for a subsidy is stronger.

The case for a subsidy is stronger when X is smaller and Y is larger. Here the issue is who suffers more from the common pool externality. Countries that are smaller players in the game are the ones with a better externality case for subsidies. Finally, the case for a subsidy is stronger when S/P is larger (i.e., spill-overs are more important) and when α is smaller (i.e., when there is less international leakage of spill-overs).

STRATEGIC POLICIES

In this section I consider the strategic commitment of a domestic R&D effort level, designed to put the foreign country in a reactive position and thereby induce it to alter its effort to the domestic benefit. The first question is whether the home country would like the foreign country to reduce or to increase its effort. A reduction will help by weakening the common pool effect on domestic net benefit, but an increase can help because of the international transmission of spill-overs. I shall concentrate on the first effect, expected to be the more important, leaving out the second altogether (i.e., by setting $\alpha = 0$).

Thus the strategic aim of the home country is to secure a reduction of the foreign R&D effort. How this is done depends on the slope of the foreign reaction function. Figure 5–3 shows the possibilities. First suppose the foreign reaction function is downward

Figure 5-3. Foreign Reactions and Domestic Strategic Policies.

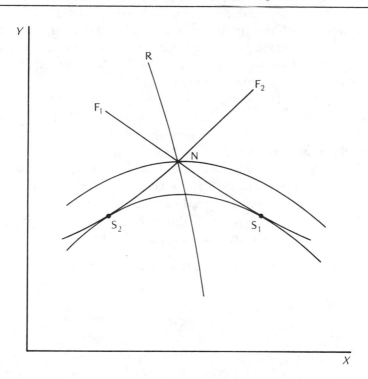

sloping, like F_1. In the absence of any strategic commitment, the outcome would be at the point N, where the domestic reaction function R meets F_1. By making a commitment to a higher effort level, the home country can induce the foreign country to lower its effort along F_1. Of the outcomes that can be achieved in this way, S_1 is the best domestically.

In a competitive market, domestic firms cannot make such a commitment on their own. Policy can achieve the desired end, however. A subsidy to domestic R&D will shift the domestic reaction function R to the right. The magnitude of the subsidy can be chosen to make it pass through S_1. If the foreign reaction function is upward sloping (F_2), then the domestically preferred outcome (S_2) will be achieved by a domestic commitment to an effort level lower than that at N. The proper policy is a tax or other restraint on domestic R&D.

To find the slope of the foreign reaction function, we should construct an explicit model of the determination of that nation's Y for any given X. This is just a restatement, in different notation, of the model discussed earlier. I shall avoid the need for this repetition, simply reinterpreting the earlier notation by switching the country labels. In the algebra of this section, therefore, Y will be the precommitted number of the domestic R&D firms and X the foreign response. Different cases must be considered, according to whether the foreign country follows a pure laissez-faire policy toward R&D or a reactive policy that simply corrects for externalities.

Begin with the laissez-faire case. The market equilibrium condition 6 equates the expected private benefits and costs. Now an exogenous increase in Y will reduce the equilibrium level of X, but by less than the increase in Y. The intuition is simple. With X held temporarily fixed, the increase in Y lowers the expected benefit to the foreign country because of the common pool effect. It lowers the expected cost by less, since only the labor component is affected. To restore equality, X must fall. But it cannot fall by so much as to reduce ($X + Y$), or the common pool effect will be reversed.

Mathematically, we differentiate equation 6 to obtain

$$\frac{dX}{dY} = \frac{-1}{1 + PG'(X)/[kG(X)^2]} \tag{17}$$

and $-1 < dX/dY < 0$.

The conclusion is that if the home country observes the foreign country to be purely passive and can precommit to a level of R&D effort, it should do so at a higher level than the one it would choose without precommitment. For example, if the United States had a laissez-faire R&D policy, then the Japanese may have been rational in using policies to promote R&D as a strategic commitment to raise their effort.

Now suppose the foreign country has a reactive policy that corrects externalities. Its choice of X equates the expected social benefits and costs as expressed in equation 12. The effect of Y on this is quite complex. A better approach is to start again with the expected net social benefit. From equations 7 and 9, we have

$$ENSB = \frac{(P + S)X}{X + Y + r/\lambda} - \left\{ k + \frac{\ell/\lambda}{X + Y + r/\lambda} \right\} H(X) . \qquad (18)$$

(Remember we have set $\alpha = 0$.) The net marginal social benefit is

$$NMSB = \frac{(P + S)(Y + r/\lambda)}{(X + Y + r/\lambda)^2} - \left\{ k + \frac{\ell/\lambda}{X + Y + r/\lambda} \right\} G(X)$$

$$+ \frac{(\ell/\lambda) H(X)}{(X + Y + r/\lambda)^2} , \qquad (19)$$

and the first-order condition determining X for given Y is $NMSB = 0$.

If an increase in Y raises the value of $NMSB$ at the old X; that is, if $\partial(NMSB)/\partial Y > 0$, then X must rise to restore the optimality condition. Similarly, if $\partial(NMSB)/\partial Y < 0$, then X will fall as Y rises.

$$\frac{\partial(NMSB)}{\partial Y} = \frac{P + S}{(X + Y + r/\lambda)^2} - \frac{2(P + S)(Y + r/\lambda)}{(X + Y + r/\lambda)^3}$$

$$+ \frac{(\ell/\lambda) G(X)}{(X + Y + r/\lambda)^2} - \frac{2(\ell/\lambda) H(X)}{(X + Y + r/\lambda)^3}$$

Evaluating this expression at the optimal point, we have

$$\frac{\partial NMSB}{\partial Y} = \frac{P + S}{(X + Y + r/\lambda)^2} - \left\{ 2k + \frac{\ell/\lambda}{X + Y + r/\lambda} \right\} \frac{G(X)}{X + Y + r/\lambda} . \qquad (20)$$

Since the answer depends on the relative importance of capital and labor costs in R&D, it is useful to examine the two extreme cases.

First consider the case in which there are only labor costs, so $k = 0$. Then, using equations 17 and 18, we find that 20 simplifies to

$$\frac{\partial (NMSB)}{\partial Y} = \frac{ENSB}{(X + Y + r/\lambda)^2} \tag{21}$$

This must be positive: $ENSB = 0$ can be achieved by choosing $X = 0$, so the optimal X must yield higher net benefit. In this case, therefore, the foreign country's reaction function is upward sloping, and the domestic strategic interest is best served by precommitting to too small a number of R&D firms.

Now suppose there are only capital costs ($\ell = 0$). We find

$$\frac{\partial NMSB}{\partial Y} = \frac{(P + S)}{(X + Y + r/\lambda)^3} \; (X - Y - r/\lambda) \; . \tag{22}$$

In this case the answer depends on the relative size of the two countries. If the number of domestic firms Y would be sufficiently high, even without strategic reasons, to make the sign of this expression negative, then the strategic motive dictates raising Y still further. But if Y would otherwise be sufficiently small, the home country will want to commit it at an even smaller level. Thus the strategic motive amplifies any existing dominance in R&D. For a similar phenomenon in the general theory of contests, see Dixit (1986a).

The general case, with both capital (sunk) and labor (flow) costs, yields a mixture of these two polar cases. If the home country is relatively small in the world R&D activity, then its strategic policy should restrain R&D irrespective of its capital intensity. If the home country is a sufficiently large actor in this arena, however, its strategic incentive is to promote domestic firms' R&D if sunk costs are sufficiently more important than flow costs.

All of this assumes that the home country can implement a policy of strategic commitment while the foreign country is passive or reactive. What happens if both countries heed their strategic incentives and commit themselves to the appropriate tax or subsidy policies? To answer this question, we must consider a two-stage game, where the governments choose their policies at the first stage, taking into account the effect on the market equilibrium that will ensue at the second stage. It turns out that the *nature* of the desirable tax policy (tax versus subsidy) found above is unchanged, but the exact *magnitude* of the chosen instrument is altered. Since my whole analysis is largely qualitative, no purpose would be served by demonstrating this point in detail.

A SUMMING UP

I have considered several aspects of R&D competition that call for policy intervention and attempted to get a rough idea of the relative importance of the various forces involved. A more precise calculation is ultimately an empirical matter, although it will require some theoretical refinements and improvements in the model. But it is useful to take stock of the qualitative results obtained above.

The model has three especially important features: (1) negative common pool externalities as well as positive spill-overs, (2) strategic motives for policy as well as corrective ones, and (3) an ex ante viewpoint that recognizes the costs of prospective failure as well as the profits from possible success. These elements interact to produce some new insights.

Perhaps the most striking point comes from juxtaposing the results of our analyses of corrective and strategic policies. In reality both motives are present, and the overall policy should combine the two considerations. But in every case the corrective incentives and the strategic ones tend to run counter to each other. For example, if sunk costs are a large fraction of total costs, then the corrective measure is more likely to be a tax on R&D (because the negative common pool externality is more important), but the strategic argument is more likely to indicate a subsidy (and will do so if the country is large). Both tendencies are reversed if flow costs are the more important. If the country is small, then the corrective policy is more likely to be a subsidy (because the common pool problem is less bothersome), but the strategic policy is more likely to be a tax (because the rival's reaction function slopes upward). The opposite is true if the country is large. Of course, we cannot be sure that these opposing tendencies will cancel each other exactly. But we should realize that the recognition of both corrective and strategic considerations makes the net case for policy weaker than it would appear if one of the forces were ignored.

We can also draw some qualitative conclusions about the conduct of U.S. policy in this area. As an important country in the R&D business, the United States should be significantly concerned about the negative common pool externality and therefore wary of promoting the domestic level of effort. If the United States practices total laissez-faire, the domestic reaction function will be downward sloping, and rivals might use strategic commitment to drive the country down that slope, to their benefit. If the United States wants to seize the strategic initiative, the right policy depends on the relative importance of flow and sunk costs of R&D. If flow costs dominate, the strategic incentive is to tax domestic R&D. If sunk costs dominate, then as a large country the United States may want to promote domestic R&D for strategic commitment. But that is precisely the case in which the common pool problem is at its most serious, and corrective motives suggest taxing domestic R&D. Finally, as an established presence in R&D with many inframarginal firms, the United States is more likely to want to tax R&D for corrective reasons. Overall, the economic case for a U.S. policy to promote R&D seems likely to prove weak or nonexistent. But this is a conjecture based on qualitative theoretical reasoning; confirmation or refutation must await empirical research on the relevant parameters.

REFERENCES

Arrow, Kenneth J., *Essays in the Theory of Risk-Bearing* (Amsterdam: North-Holland, 1971.

Barzel, Yoram, "Optimal Timing of Innovations," *Review of Economics and Statistics* 50 (August 1968): 348–55.

Borrus, Michael, James E. Millstein, and John Zysman, "Trade and Development in the Semiconductor Industry: Japanese Challenge and American Response," in *American Industry in International Competition*, ed. John Zysman and Laura Tyson (Ithaca: Cornell University Press, 1983).

Bresnahan, Timothy F., "Measuring the Spillovers from Technical Advance," *American Economic Review* 76 (1986): 742–55.

Dasgupta, Partha S., and Joseph E. Stiglitz, "Uncertainty, Industrial Structure, and the Speed of R&D," *Bell Journal of Economics* 11 (1980): 1–28.

Dixit, Avinash, "Strategic Behavior in Contests," 1986a, Working paper.

———, "A General Model of R&D Competition and Policy," 1986b, Working paper.

Fudenberg, Drew, and Jean Tirole, "The Fat Cat Effect, the Puppy Dog Ploy and the Lean and Hungry Look," *American Economic Review* 74 (May 1984): 361–66.

Hirschleifer, Jack, "The Private and Social Value of Information and the Reward to Inventive Activity," *American Economic Review* 61 (September 1971): 561–74.

Katz, Michael, and Carl Shapiro, "On the Licensing of Innovations," *Rand Journal of Economics* 16 (1985): 504–20.

Krugman, Paul R., "The U.S. Response to Foreign Industrial Targeting," *Brookings Papers on Economic Activity*, 1984a, pp. 77–131.

_____ , "Targeted Industrial Policies: Theory and Evidence," in *Industrial Change and Public Policy* (Kansas City: Federal Reserve Bank of Kansas City, 1984b).

_____ , ed., *Strategic Trade Policy and the New International Economics* (Cambridge: M.I.T. Press, 1986).

_____ , "Strategic Sectors and International Competition," in *U.S. Trade Policies in a Changing World Economy*, ed. Robert M. Stern (Cambridge, M.I.T. Press, 1987).

Lee, Tom, and Louis L. Wilde, "Market Structure and Innovation: A Reformulation," *Quarterly Journal of Economics* 94 (1980): 429–36.

Loury, Glenn C., "Market Structure and Innovation," *Quarterly Journal of Economics* 93 (1979): 395–410.

President's Commission on Industrial Competitiveness, *Global Competition: The New Reality* (Washington, DC: U.S. Government Printing Office, 1985).

Spence, A. Michael, "Cost Reduction, Competition and Industry Performance," *Econometrica* 52 (January 1984): 101–121.

Spencer, Barbara J., and James A. Brander, "International R&D Rivalry and Industrial Strategy," *Review of Economic Studies* 50 (1983): 707–22.

CHAPTER 6

A Sad and Sorry Story: Industry Policy for the Australian Motor Vehicle Industry

Robert G. Gregory

INTRODUCTION

M anufacturing industry has always been a central policy concern in Australia. During the first two decades after World War II it was generally accepted among policy makers and the community that rapid expansion of the manufacturing sector would lead to higher standards of living and, perhaps more importantly, provide employment for a wide range of unskilled European immigrants. Unfortunately, manufacturing industry did not take naturally to the Australian economic environment. The government responded by actively encouraging industrialization through the widespread use of import tariffs and quotas.

Within manufacturing the motor vehicle industry was to play a key role. Motor vehicle production, with a high degree of local content, absorbs a large proportion of resources, and the input requirements extend into many industries. To encourage the industry fully, it was clear that special policies would be needed. These were most fully developed during the mid-1960s. In many ways the evolution of these policies and their effect on the industry illustrate the worst features of Australian industry policy. From this history many lessons can be learned, almost all of which point to the dangers of in-

This chapter was written in collaboration with V. Ho; we have received helpful comments from R. Wilson.

volvement in special policies to favor the development of particular industries.[1]

By 1984 the combination of government policies for the motor vehicle industry and changing economic circumstances had produced the following outcomes.

In an industry where economies of scale were important, five manufacturers—Ford, General Motors Holden (GMH), Nissan, Australian Motor Industries Ltd. (Toyota/Australian ownership), and Mitsubishi—shared a market about one-twentieth the size of the United States'.[2]

The Australian industry was so inefficient by world standards that (even after imports had satisfied 20 percent of the domestic market) motor vehicle buyers, at the margin, were prepared to pay a tariff of just over 90 percent for the right to import an additional vehicle.

The average effective rate of assistance to the motor vehicle industry had doubled and was still increasing (Table 6-1). It was currently about 160 percent for assembly and around 100 percent for parts.

Over the last decade productivity growth had been well below the norm for manufacturing (Table 6-1).

Employment had fallen to around 90 percent of its level of 10 years earlier (Table 6-1).

THE MOTOR VEHICLE PLANS

Four Key Features

The motor vehicle industry consists of two parts: the assembly process and component manufacturing. Aiming to develop a motor vehicle industry with the largest possible impact on the manufacturing sector, the Australian government needed to encourage both assembly and component manufacturing.[3] (Otherwise, given international trade, it could clearly have participated in one part without the other.) The ingredients of this special policy became important after the abandonment of import controls in 1960. The four key features that have dominated the evolution of the industry were refined and extended from 1963 to 1965.

First, the industry was to be encouraged by high tariffs levied on imported vehicles and components. This aspect of the policy had

Table 6-1. Tariffs, Import Shares, Employment and Labor Productivity
Indices, 1968-1982.

	1968-69	1973-74	1977-78	1981-82
Average nominal rates (percent)				
Motor vehicles	36	27	47	59
Motor vehicle instruments	40	30	40	49
Motor vehicle parts n.e.c.	30	22	43	53
Manufacturing Total	24	17	15	16
Average effective rates (percent)				
Motor vehicles	52	41	108	158
Motor vehicle instruments	51	39	84	106
Motor vehicle parts n.e.c.	40	29	88	119
Manufacturing Total	36	27	26	26
Import share of transport equipment [a] (percent)	10	26	19	24
Employment index				
Transport equipment	100	110	94	91
Manufacturing Total	100	106	90	91
Labor productivity index				
Transport equipment	100	108	114	128
Manufacturing total	100	116	131	147

a. Calendar years 1969, 1974, 1978, and 1982.
Sources: Average nominal and effective rates: Assistance to Manufacturing Industries in
Australia 1968-69 to 1973-74, Annual Report 1982-83, Industries Assistance Commission,
Australian Government Printing Service, Canberra 1986. Import share of transport equip-
ment: Industries Assistance Commission (1974, Table 5.2, p. 66; 1981, Table 4.2, p. 36)
Employment index; ABS Manufacturing Establishments, Details of Operations by Industry
Class, Cat. No. 8203.0 (various issues). Labor productivity index; ABS Constant Price Esti-
mates of Manufacturing Production Cat. No. 8211.0 (various issues); ABS Manufacturing
Establishments, Details of Operations by Industry Class, Cat. No. 8203.0 (various issues).

several adverse effects on the industry. In principle, a tariff on components would encourage local production as a substitute for imported components. The tariff, however, would also act as a tax on
the assembly process, without which the component industry could
not develop. In effect, the tariff on components would encourage the
import of fully assembled cars. *A way was needed to offset this*

aspect of the policy and to protect assemblers from the high cost of components created by tariffs.

The second feature of the policy was intended to solve this problem. For a number of decades the government had operated a general by-law scheme that provided for a waiver of tariffs on imported inputs of production for which no suitable substitute was produced locally. The motor vehicle industry made extensive use of the by-law provisions, which allowed the assemblers to reduce the cost of imported components. During the early 1960s the government became concerned by its failure to encourage domestic production. The industry seemed increasingly to use by-law concessions and import components rather than to source locally. *A way was needed to offset this aspect of the policy and to encourage component production.*

The third feature of the motor vehicle policy was intended to solve this problem. Very detailed local content plans were to apply individually to each basic vehicle produced. For example, under Plan A, introduced in 1965 for the models of the major car manufacturers, local content was to be raised to 95 percent.[4] Plans for small-volume producers required lower levels of local content (40–60 percent). These small-volume plans were eventually discarded, and a general 95 percent plan was extended to all.

Manufacturers who entered the plans would have restricted access to by-law provisions. If they remained outside the plans, the full tariff, usually 25 percent, would be levied on all imported components. It was made fairly clear that policy would be set so that the large manufacturers had no choice but to enter the plans. But imposing local component requirements would hurt the assembly process. *A way was needed to offset this aspect of the policy.*

The fourth feature of policy, intended to address this problem, was a tariff trigger that would increase the tariff on completely built-up vehicles (CBUs) from 35 to 45 percent if CBU imports exceeded 7.5 percent of the local market. *No plans were made to offset the effect of this aspect of policy on consumers.*

A Diagrammatic Exposition

Figure 6–1 illustrates the costs and revenues associated with a representative vehicle produced in Australia under the complex policy outlined above.[5] The cost of an imported vehicle net of duty is shown along the horizontal axis, divided into two elements: assembly

Figure 6-1. Cost Components of a Locally Produced Vehicle.

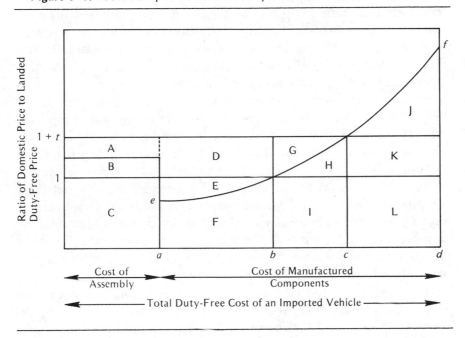

Note: It is assumed that the landed duty-free price is equal to the world free trade price.

and manufactured components. On the vertical axis is the ratio of the domestic price of a vehicle or component to the landed duty-free price. The duty-free price is assumed to be equal to the free trade price. Unity, then, is the point at which the domestic price is equal to the free trade price. We assume a common tariff t for components and imported vehicles so that the landed duty-paid price of components or a vehicle is $1 + t$. The curve ef traces out the ratio of the cost of production of components in Australia to the duty-free imported price. It is assumed that automobiles will be sold at a t percent premium over free trade prices. Local assemblers and manufacturers will receive windfall profits as a result of this market distortion.

If motor vehicles and components could be imported duty free, there would be Australian production of motor vehicles at a local content level (of assembly and component manufacturing), provided that area E is greater than or equal to area B—that is, provided that the cost advantage E of local component manufacture exceeds or is equal to the cost disadvantage B of local assembly.

If imported vehicles and components are subject to the tariff t, then local content is increased to c and the economic rent gained from local production is the area A + D + E + G. Area H is the economic cost over the world price of the extra components manufactured in response to the tariff t. The components cd are still imported and subject to the tariff payments equal to area K.[6]

Now assume that with the tariff in place, the government introduces a by-law scheme with no local content requirements. Under these circumstances, assemblers would appeal to the government to waive the tariff, claiming that no suitable local products exist; their goal would be to reduce local content back to b and earn the extra economic rent, area H. Local component manufacturers, however, would counterappeal to the customs department, arguing that they can make suitably equivalent components bc and be profitable under the tariff. If the component manufacturers won, the by-law concessions would not be granted and the local assemblers would not be allowed to reduce the local content below the level that would prevail under the tariff. If the by-law concessions were granted, then local assemblers would replace bc of local parts with duty-free imported parts. This would increase the rents to the assemblers, since they would now reap the rents that would otherwise have been dissipated through the inefficiency of the Australian component manufacturers. The by-law concession, then, subsidizes local assemblers by area H. (The local buyers of motor vehicles, needless to say, still bear the burden of paying a t percent premium over the world free trade price.)

In the early 1960s, assemblers were quite successful in obtaining tariff exemptions. The government felt that a mechanism was needed to encourage component production. In 1965, the government modified the plan as shown in Figure 6–2 through the introduction of a local content scheme and required extra components, cd', to be sourced locally. This forced the motor vehicle assemblers to increase their use of Australian component production from c to d'. Consequently, some of the assistance provided to local assemblers in the form of rents was lost. Assemblers were burdened with increased costs (area K) through the removal of the by-law concession from the additional local content (cd'). In addition, the cost of local sourcing now exceeded the landed duty-paid price of a component for cd', so there was an extra cost factor added to the industry, area J. As a result of these two factors, the local cost of car assembly became

Figure 6-2. A Local Content Scheme.

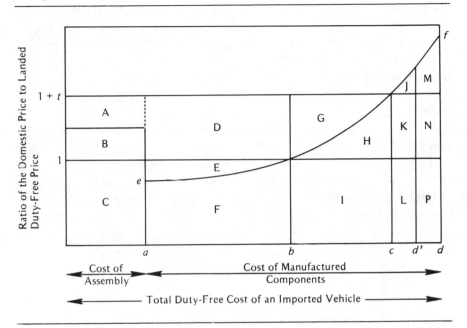

Cost of Assembly

Cost of Manufactured Components

Total Duty-Free Cost of an Imported Vehicle

Note: It is assumed that the landed duty-free price is equal to the world free trade price.

considerably higher than when manufacturers had unlimited access to a general by-law scheme. As might be expected, in response to this increase, the government introduced the trigger tariff.

An Evaluation

The local content plans posed considerable difficulties for the development of a rational industry policy for the motor vehicle industry. In the first place, they created a great deal of uncertainty and considerable lobbying activity. The government knew neither the precise relationship of the domestic price to the world price for any car model, nor how the function varied with the scale of manufacture. Consequently, there was considerable scope for putting together local content-volume combinations that seriously distorted assistance between large and small producers.[7]

As might be expected under these circumstances, government advisers depended on the industry for information. As a result, there was close cooperation between the two parties and the plans were subjected to continual change as one car assembler after another claimed to be specially disadvantaged by the latest set of plans. The expectation rapidly developed that the details of the plan were subject to revision and that the government would respond to lobbying from individual manufacturers. Plans were drafted and changed at bewildering speed. Each time a local manufacturer succeeded, the local component producers were usually hurt, and they responded by trying to change the plan to their own advantage.

No precise idea of the allocation of assistance between assembly and component manufacture was possible. It was not really possible to identify the areas H and J. Furthermore, since manufacturers had to achieve a given local content, the level of assistance to the marginal component could be quite high. The plan compounded this problem by adopting "reversion rules" that more or less ensured that a locally sourced component could not be replaced, not even for another local component.

THE CRISIS OF 1974-75

When the 95 percent local content plan was introduced, the Australian motor vehicle industry was dominated by six-cylinder cars. The two leading producers, GMH and Ford, held more than half the market, and their leading six-cylinder models were already close to 95 percent local content. The scheme thus did not impose a significant additional cost on them, except to the degree that the special conditions of the low-volume plans favored the small producer.

Soon, however, the demand for motor vehicles began to shift toward smaller four-cylinder cars and a wider variety of models. Local producers could not economically extend their production range, however, given the small size of the Australian market and the now general scheme of 95 percent local content. The production volumes were too low and the price ratio curve, ef, therefore too high, so that the area J became prohibitive. As a result the new demand for smaller vehicles was met by Japanese imports.

By August 1966, within two years of the introduction of the extensive local content plans, the trigger tariff had become operative, and all imported cars were subject to a 45 percent tariff. Even so, the Japanese vehicles continued to make inroads into the Australian market. On July 19, 1973, in response to the general macroeconomic environment, all import tariffs were reduced by 25 percent. The tariff on motor vehicles fell to 33.5 percent. Between 1972 and 1974 imported motor vehicles increased their share of the market from 9 to 28 percent.

On July 10, 1974, the Industries Assistance Commission (IAC) reported to the government on the Passenger Motor Vehicle Industry. The report emphasized that:

Economies of scale were of vital importance to the industry. The four manufacturers of that time—Ford, GMH, Chrysler, and British Leyland—were clearly too many for such a small market.

The local content scheme significantly increased the costs of car manufacture in Australia and should be disbanded.

The tariff on CBU should gradually be reduced to 25 percent by 1982.

At this tariff level the Australian market would need to accept a larger volume of imports and a smaller number of producers.

The report was ignored. The economic downturn of 1974 and the growth of Japanese imports led the government to adopt policies that in many instances were directly opposed to the commission's recommendations and that ensured continuing trouble for the industry. Within four months of the IAC report, the tariff was restored to 45 percent in an attempt to maintain 80 percent of the market for local producers (a new goal). Within another two months it became clear that a 45 percent tariff was not sufficient to restrict imports to 20 percent of the market; as a result, import quotas were introduced. Although the government refused to reduce the local content requirements to any significant degree, it made some marginal adjustments in the right direction. The new plan was defined on a company rather than a model basis, and each producer was now to achieve 85 percent local content. Finally, in 1976 the Australian government prevailed on Nissan and Toyota to enter the plans.[8] The number of producers thus increased to five (British Leyland withdrew from manufacturing in 1976), and one source of pressure for change was muted as the dominant importers were co-opted into the Australian industry. The government press release put forward the following argument:

Because of the strong demand in the Australian market for Toyota and Nissan products, their exclusion from local manufacture would create a continuing need for import restrictions. This would be contrary to GATT and could

Table 6-2. Relationship between Local Content Levels and the Price Disadvantage of the Complete Vehicle.

Form	Assembled Model	Manufactured Model				
Small Light Vehicle (Corolla)						
Local content level	37%	60%	70%	75%	80%	85%
Major components sourced in Australia	Tires, battery, glass, seat, carpet, trim, electrical equipment, etc.	(plus) Engine, transmission, propeller shaft, rear axle	(plus) Clutch, brake drum, shock absorber, etc.	(plus) Pressed parts, etc.	(plus) Headlamp combination meter, etc.	(plus) Brake with booster, pedals, brackets, small parts, etc.
Import duty required to adjust cost difference between built-up import and assembled model or manufactured model	19%	41%	46%	51%	59%	72%

Medium Vehicle (Corona)

Form	Assembled Model	Manufactured Model				
Local content level	31%	56%	70%	75%	80%	85%
Major components sourced in Australia	Tires, battery, glass, seat, carpet, trim, electrical equipment, etc.	(plus) Engine, transmission, propeller shaft, rear axle	(plus) Clutch, brake drum, shock absorber, etc.	(plus) Pressed parts, etc.	(plus) Headlamp combination meter, etc.	(plus) Brake with booster, pedals, brackets, small parts, etc.
Import duty required to adjust cost difference between built-up import and assembled model or manufactured model	14%	35%	39%	43%	47%	52%

Source: Industries Assistance Commission, *Passenger Motor Vehicles and Components—Post 1984* (Canberra: Australian Government Printing Services, 1981).

damage our relationships with Japan. On the other hand, their entry into manufacture would provide additional business for the Australian component manufacturers and additional employment opportunities.

The Japanese car producers were to be bought off, and Australian consumers were to pay a higher price for cars. Rather than enriching the Treasury with import duties, a significant portion of the increased price was to go into the cost of producing cars in Australia. Once the Japanese were subjected to the high-cost Australian conditions and imports could no longer increase their market share, the situation in the motor vehicle industry deteriorated further. More manufacturers had to share the same small market. The extent of the deterioration was shown both in the prices paid in bid for quota allocations and in the excess costs of the local content scheme.

The cost disadvantages implied by the local content scheme varied according to the size of the production run, the motor vehicle model, and the country of origin of the imported component. A rough idea of the extent of the cost disadvantages in 1979 is given in Table 6–2. For an Australian version of the Toyota Corolla produced at 85 percent local content, a 72 percent nominal import duty was required to negate its cost disadvantage to a CBU import. At a 75 percent level of local content the needed import duty falls to 51 percent, a very significant reduction. At the margin, therefore, the magnitude of the cost disadvantage of domestic production was very sensitive to the local content level. At the 85 percent local content level, the IAC estimated that the cost disadvantage of the last component was at least 500 percent. A similar relationship existed for the Toyota Corona, but for medium-sized cars the cost disadvantages were not so great. Between 1979 and 1984 all cost disadvantages increased further.

The same deterioration of performance was reflected in the change in the system of allocating import quotas. Import quotas were initially allocated free of charge on the basis of import clearances during 1973 and 1974. As comparative advantage continued to move against the Australian industry, the price premium resulting from import quotas increased considerably.[9] In response, the government's 1978 budget increased the tariff from 45 percent to 57.5 percent to divert some of these rents toward the Treasury. As time went by and it became clear that import quotas would continue for some time, the government turned its attention to improving the allocation process. In October 1979 it was decided to allocate a proportion of the quotas by tender. The quotas delivered the right to import a given volume of vehicles each year until the next change of the plan. The bidding was to be conducted in terms of an ad valorem duty rate *additional* to a base rate of 45 percent. In November 1979 the tender allocation was sold at an additional tariff of 50.5 percent, making a total duty of 97.5 percent. In March 1980 the tender allocation was sold at an additional tariff at 86.5 percent, making a total duty of 131.5 percent.[10]

Things were obviously becoming worse. In December 1980, perhaps embarrassed by the very high prices that were being paid, perhaps responding to industry lobby pressure, the government announced that import quotas would no longer be sold but would instead be allocated free of charge by administrative rule. In December 1984, following a change of government, quotas were again made subject to tender, but now on a year-by-year basis. A proportion of quotas were auctioned, and the combination of the tender price and tariff led to an aggregate tariff of 94.5 percent.

THE END OF THE ROAD AND NOWHERE TO TURN

It was clear in 1974, as indicated by the IAC report, that if the motor vehicle industry was not to deteriorate further, the government had to accept a lower level of local content and a greater volume of imports than had prevailed in the past. The government refused to make these decisions and instead invited Japanese producers to enter the motor vehicle plans. First Nissan and Toyota began production, and later Mitsubishi replaced Chrysler. Then there was nowhere to turn. With five local producers, the economic performance of the Australian motor vehicle industry was guaranteed to deteriorate further. The 1965–74 history was to be replayed with a new cast of characters—and the government probably knew it.

The repetition of the history of the industry, and the sense of déjà vu in the development of policy, is ironic at times. In 1984, for example, the president of Nissan called for the complete prohibition of Japanese imports, which, at the margin, were paying something like a 100 percent tariff. He reportedly said, "We would like the Australian government to make completely clear to us whether or not it would like the motor vehicle industry to be viable. They should not pursue a half-hearted policy and if they are to promote a motor industry in Australia, they should shut off CBU imports into Australia" (*Australian Financial Review*, December 17, 1984).

The policy fiasco is fully documented in the Motor Vehicle Plan of the previous Liberal government that was announced in December 1981 to be operative for eight years beginning in 1984. The details were as follows:

The current arrangement that 80 percent of car sales would be produced in Australia and 20 percent imported was to be replaced by a tariff quota system. The duty on above-quote imports was to be set at *150 percent* and progressively reduced in steps of 5 percent beginning in 1988 to reach *125 percent* in 1991. (The Liberal government was announcing that if necessary (i.e., if cars were imported outside the quota system and under the tariff), it was prepared to see the price of cars in Australia increase to at least twice the level of world prices.)

Those who held import quotas would continue to pay a tariff of only 57.5 percent. (That is, those fortunate enough to hold a quota were to receive a permanent gift of between 70 and 95 percent of the landed duty-free price of each imported vehicle.)

Some of the quotas were to be subject to tender sale, the proportion rising to 40 percent in 1992.

Local content was to be maintained at 85 percent.

A special allocation of import quotas was to be given to a producer who could not survive behind a long-run tariff ceiling of 125 percent and chose to withdraw from the plan.

Before the Liberal government plan was introduced, the new Labor government announced its version in May 1984, to be operative in 1985. (The industry tradition of the perpetually changing plan continued.) This new plan accepted the elements of the Liberal government plan with two sets of modifications. First, the Labor government *increased* the level of assistance immediately available by allocating $150 million to research and development grants for the industry, to apply over a five-year period, and tightening import quotas by extending them to include derivatives of passenger vans and certain four-wheel drives, which were gaining market share as substitutes for passenger motor vehicles. A second set of modifications proposed to make *all* import quotas subject to tender sale by 1989 (the Liberal government had restricted the proportion to 40 percent), and to set the 1985 tariff quota at 100 percent (the Liberal government proposed 150 percent in 1988), to be pared down to 57.5 percent by 1992 (the Liberal government proposed 125 percent).[11]

How might costs be reduced to be compatible with a long-run tariff of 57.5 percent and still maintain a motor vehicle industry of reasonable size? The government seemed to have in mind three possible avenues for cost reductions: (1) export facilitation; (2) fewer producers, longer production runs, and therefore greater opportunity for achieving economies of scale; and (3) more production integration among competitors.

Export Facilitation and Local Content

As the economic situation in the motor industry deteriorated, Liberal and Labor governments turned toward exports as a possible way out.[12] But if the industry could not compete against imports without tariff near 90 percent, how were exports to be possible? The government's answer was a special policy called export facilitation.

Under the export facilitation scheme, a car manufacturer could substitute exports for local content, up to a value of 7.5 percent of the cost of the vehicle. An Australian producer that manufactured for export incurred costs higher than those encountered elsewhere, but gained the right to substitute components purchased off-shore at the world price for expensive, locally produced components.[13]

The IAC estimated that the export disadvantage in Australia was somewhere between 18 and 50 percent for those components that could be produced most cheaply in Australia. It also estimated that the cost of the marginal component produced locally and incorporated in local cars under the local content scheme was about two and a half times the world price. Other things being equal, the export facilitation scheme was designed to maintain the production of local components but to change the patterns of production toward components in which Australian production was relatively efficient.

The scheme also allowed for a further 7.5 percentage points of export credits, but it was not clear that the industry would be able to utilize this provision fully because the potential gain was not as great as the first set of credits. The government imposed several requirements that would increase the cost of exporting.[14] In addition, the extra cost of the marginal component over and above world prices would fall as local content moved from 85 percent to 77.5 percent, reducing the saving achieved by switching from local sourcing.[15]

Export facilitation was a step in the right direction. It involved the replacement of an uneconomic activity, production of local components (requiring assistance of 200 percent or more), by an activity that was less uneconomic (perhaps requiring assistance of between 18 and 50 percent). However, the scheme had all the disadvantages of the original local content plans, and in the long run would presumably be subject to the same sort of problems.

First, the level of assistance offered to manufacturers under export facilitation was not known. It would vary according to the changing cost conditions of the local components that were replaced. For example, the amount of assistance delivered to engine exports would depend on the cost disadvantages of the unrelated items that were no longer produced but imported—components such as brakes, windshield wipers, and so on. In a good industry policy, the amount of assistance should be known and measurable.

Second, those manufacturers who responded to the export subsidies now had an interest in perpetuating the 85 percent local content scheme. Any further reduction in local content requirements would redirect assistance toward those who had not responded, since this group would then be able to switch marginal components from expensive domestic sources to inexpensive foreign sources without incurring the extra cost of exporting. The export facilitation scheme, therefore, created another lobby group (manufacturers who export) in favor of local content provisions. Of course, once all producers exported, the local content scheme could be dismantled without generating this difficulty; in this way, the export facilitation scheme might be thought of as a device for indirectly removing local content.

Finally, although export facilitation would reduce costs, the reductions were not likely to be sufficient to enable an industry of the current size and structure to survive. The recent sale of quotas suggested that the industry needed a tariff of about 90 percent. The evidence submitted to the IAC for 1979 indicated that the combination of savings from the reduction in local content and the extra costs of exporting might, on balance, reduce the tariff needed by 7–10 percentage points. This is far short of the cost reduction necessary to achieve a long-run tariff of 57.5 percent.

Fewer Producers, Longer Production Runs, and Greater Access to Economies of Scale

During the late 1960s and the early 1970s the Australian motor vehicle industry was dominated by GMH, which produced a six-cylinder family car that in 1964, for example, had an annual production run of 130,000 (Table 6-3). At that time the average production run per model for an Australian producer, excluding the Holden, was about 18,000. It was generally thought that the low-volume, low-local-content plans subsidized small production runs relative to large production runs, thereby making GMH less able to reap the benefits of economies of scale. Consequently, the belief developed that scrapping the local content plans would remove the bias in favor of low-volume producers, and the companies specializing in these vehicles would cease to produce in Australia. The low-volume cars would then be imported at a price higher than that prevailing under the plans, and demand would be diverted toward the larger producers, which would now be able to realize greater economies of scale. This was the mechanism by which the tariff could be reduced without jeopardizing the future of the two large producers (GMH and Ford).

Table 6-3. Range of Locally Produced Passenger Motor Vehicles, 1964, 1973, 1977, and 1980.

	1964	1973	1977	1980
Number of producers	5	4	5	5
Number of models	8	12	17	14
Number of body styles	13	23	31	24
Average registrations per model (thousand)	32.1	24.8	< 19.5	22.8
Range of registrations per model (thousand)	1.7–130.1	4.6–95.3	2.2–53.8	1.3–68.2
Average registrations per body style (thousand)	19.7	13.0	< 10.7	13.3

Note: In each of these years a GMH model has achieved the maximum number of registrations.

Source: Industries Assistance Commission, *Passenger Motor Vehicles and Components—Post 1984* (Canberra: Australian Government Printing Service, 1981), p. 63.

The essential link in the argument was the bias in the local content plans that reduced the relative price of small cars. This bias was removed by the adoption of the 85 percent local content plans although many still accepted the argument that fewer producers would mean greater volume of production for those that remained. The press statements accompanying the new plan stressed that it would result in fewer producers, a fewer local models, and consequently greater access to economies of scale.

Full implementation of the new plan would clearly mean fewer producers and models made in Australia. It was not clear, however, how the remaining producers would achieve longer production runs. The process bringing about the change would be different from that upon which the earlier argument was based. The new mechanism would be tariff reductions. As the tariff was reduced *all* manufacturers would begin to lose markets to imports (i.e., their ability to achieve economies of scale would be reduced). Eventually a producer, say Toyota, would cease manufacturing in Australia and (presumably) substitute imported cars for local production. The imported cars would probably not be more expensive than before the tariff reductions began, and they would be very close substitutes for the domestic production they replaced (e.g., a Japanese-produced Corolla might be substituted for the Australian version). As a result, little of the Toyota market would spill over to the remaining local producers. If Ford or GMH were to leave the market, there would be greater scope for a spill-over because these companies specialize in family cars tailored for Australia. It is difficult to imagine, however, the government accepting the withdrawal of either Ford or GMH.

Thus the government's belief that the new plan would result in larger production runs and resultant economies of scale seemed to be misplaced.

Integration of Models and Components among Producers

In the early 1980s some manufacturers had begun to assemble each other's models under different names. Ford was producing Lasers (the Mazda 323 with a new name) in Australia while the Mazda 323 was being imported. GMH was assembling the Nissan Pulsar under the GMH label and marketing the car as the Astra. Similarly there had been a trend toward the common sourcing of components. For example, GMH was planning to buy Nissan six-cylinder engines for the new range of Commodores.[16]

These tendencies toward "badge engineering" and common components offered considerable scope for cost reductions. As the tariff was reduced and imports became more competitive, however, the economic gains from *assembling* Japanese cars under badge engineering would presumably disappear as it became cheaper to import CBUs. Common sourcing of components might increase but local assembly and production was not likely to develop.

CONCLUDING REMARKS

Since 1984 the Australian government has continued to add new policy measures to offset the effects of earlier initiatives. The fortunes of the motor vehicle industry have been more significantly affected by the sudden and unexpected exchange rate movements between the yen and the Australian dollar, however.

The principal source of import competition over the last decade and a half has been Japan. European cars, relatively unimportant overall, have had a small presence in the luxury market. Between January 1985 and December 1986, the exchange rate between the Australian dollar and the Japanese yen devalued in nominal terms by just over 50 percent; in real terms (adjusting for the changes in the price level of each country), the exchange rate devaluation was just under 50 percent. This change had a significant impact on the motor vehicle market, given the existence of import quotas and local content plans, the pattern and levels of industry assistance have been completely altered.

First, the value of import quotas has been considerably reduced; quotas currently are not filled and can be obtained without payment.[17] The net result is that there will be a 57.5 percent nominal tariff rate on imported vehicles until the quotas are filled. Then, depending on the price paid for quotas, the tariff is variable up to the marginal tariff rate, which is currently 90 percent but is being reduced to 57.5 percent over the next five years. Suddenly, the prospects for local production look much better. The important point, of course, is that this improvement did not stem from any change in the cost structure of the industry, or from any policy, but from a large fall in the prices of primary products that led to an Australian dollar devaluation. Exchange rate changes seem to bring about larger changes in the local industries' ability to compete than do adjustments to policy. The current devaluations, which have improved competitiveness, seem to be as important as the large revaluations duing the 1972–74 period that affected competitiveness so adversely.

Second, the realignment of exchange rates has been hardest on importers who do not manufacture in Australia, while their competitors, the local producers, have benefited from the large exchange rate devaluation and the export incentive scheme. There has been a sudden and dramatic change in the industry, and, as might be expected of a government that pursues a conservative welfare function and accepts responsibility for the health of the industry, new policies have been devised.

In response to lobbying, the government has extended the export credit scheme to importers even though they do not produce in Australia. The scheme works as follows. Companies who import (e.g., Mazda and BMW), currently pay an import tariff of 57.5 percent. If these companies order Australian components to be included in their overseas production of cars, they will be allowed a duty concession on imports of built-up cars. For each dollar of components exported, the 57.5 percent duty will be waived on fifty cents of built-up car imports. The concession is limited to a maximum of 25 percent of the value of each importer's imports.

This scheme offers the importer some protection from exchange rate changes—the subsidized exports of components from Australia offset devaluation-induced increases in the price of imported cars. The extension of the export facilitation plan to importers is a continuation of the government policy, despite statements to the contrary, to encourage component manufacture. What component manufacturers lose through export facilitation of local manufactures, they recoup through export facilitation to importers. (The export facilitation scheme has also been extended to component manufacturers.)

Third, the very large devaluations have increased the cost of primary materials and therefore components, so that many manufacturers now find they cannot satisfy the 85 percent content plan. The government has responded by allowing a notional exchange rate—a sixteen-quarter moving average of past exchange rates—to be applied to the cost of components. This procedure smooths out the effects of rapid exchange rate movements.

Successive governments have believed that the market produces too many motor vehicle models in Australia, a tendency encouraged by the government's own industry assistance measures. Changes have been announced to reduce the number of models. Access to duty concession through the local content scheme is to be removed in 1987/88 for models produced in runs of fewer than 15,000 units. The minimum production run needed for concessions will increase to 20,000 in 1989 and later to 30,000 to 40,000.

It will be difficult to enforce this requirement if the implementation period coincides with a period of reduced demand that depresses production runs. The government would then appear to be exacerbating industry problems. Nor is it clear how models will be defined. With the growth of badge engineering and the new technologies of producing cars, the definition of a model in economic production terms has become more complicated, since cars share common engines, gear boxes, and chassis in different combinations.

The history of the last two years reinforces some of our observations based on Australia's earlier experience with policy for the motor vehicle industry. First, such plans cannot be static. Because the government is so heavily involved each time the industry experiences economic difficulties, the plans are inevitably changed. Consequently, each company needs to invest considerable time and effort in lobbying and maintaining good relations with the government.

Second, the government always feels a need to extend assistance to all parts of the industry. Each new measure hurts some section of the industry and sets up a reaction, so a new measure is initiated to offset this hurt, thus shifting it somewhere else. This complex process continues without end. Witness, for example, the extension of export facilitation to offset the losses being experienced by importers and to boost the production of local component makers.

Third, as the government assistance packages become more complex, it is nearly impossible to understand what is happening to the level of protection. The relationship between car assembly, component manufacture, and import keeps changing in complicated and significant ways. The extension of the export facilitation plan to importers, for example, has offered them assistance, but the incidence is difficult to calculate. At the same time, this policy has reduced protection for assemblers, who in turn reduce their demand for local components.

Fourth, the short-run exchange rate movements have a very large effect on industry performance. The interaction of exchange rates changes and the responding industry policy initiatives seems to be dragging the Australian government further and further into industry planning.

Finally, current and future exchange rates are absolutely crucial in determining industry profitability and its long-run prospects. When the bulk of the research reported here was done, all interested parties, except importers, were pessimistic about the long-run future of the Australian motor vehicle industry. Today, there is much greater optimism as Australia is now beginning to export vehicles to the United States, Japan, and Europe.

NOTES

1. The best source of information on the Australian motor vehicle industry is a series of inquiries by the Tariff Board and the Industries Assistance Commission. See Tariff Board (1965), Passenger Motor Vehicles,etc. (1974), Passenger Motor Vehicles and Components—Post 1984 Assistance Arrangements (1981), Industries Assistance Commission (1974, 1981, 1985 (Appendix C)).

2. For 1984 the market shares were Ford 24 percent, Toyota 20 percent, GMH 18 percent, Nissan 11 percent, and Mitsubishi 10 percent. The top-selling car was the Ford Falcon, at 68,313 units. Ford Laser was the top-selling small car (24,927 units).

3. During the 1960s, Minister for Trade and Industry, John McEwan, stated government policy as "ensuring the sustained development of an economic and efficient automotive industry in Australia, in relation to the production of *complete* motor vehicles with *maximum* Australian content" (from the terms of reference to the Tariff Board Enquiry, October 1963).

4. There had been earlier local content schemes—the 1957 Tariff Board Report had stipulated 70 percent local content—but they had little effect on the industry. For a full discussion of these plans, see Stubbs (1971).

5. The Australian motor vehicle plans are very similar to those suggested for Canada by D. Bladen in the 1961 Report of the Royal Commission on the Automotive Industry; see Johnson (1963).

6. In equilibrium the economic rent, $A + D + E + G$, would be competed away by new models or new manufacturers. New models and manufacturers reduce the ability of an individual producer to reap economies of scale, and ef moves upward as does area B, thus reducing the rent. Along the way the level of local content falls further.

7. Economies of scale are so important in component manufacturing that if a single plan were operative and required a high degree of local content,

it would *magnify* the advantages of scale. Low-volume producers would not be able to offset their scale disadvantage by importing a greater proportion of components. Consequently a high local content plan would force low-volume producers out of the market. Accordingly, low-volume plans were needed with less stringent local content requirements.

8. Special transition plans were designed for Nissan and Toyota (Australian Motor Industries). Local content was to increase in steps from 62.5 percent at January 1, 1976, to 85 percent by January 1, 1980. By-law concessions began at 25 percent of imported components and were to be gradually reduced to 15 percent by January 1, 1980.

9. In November 1976 the Australian dollar was devalued significantly, and import quotas were removed in December. Imports again increased rapidly, and quotas were reintroduced in July 1977. Within a few months, it was announced that import quotas would apply until 1979. In 1979 it was announced that import quotas would continue until 1981.

10. The associate director of GWA Ltd., which imports Mazdas and BMWs, remarked that "quotas were almost a license to print money" (*Australian Financial Review*, July 27, 1984).

11. The quota allocation subject to 57.5 percent tariff was to be 75 percent in 1986, 50 percent in 1987, 25 percent in 1988, and 0 in 1989.

12. A detailed discussion of export facilitation is contained in IAC (1981, Appendix 1.5).

13. A second source of saving cannot easily be illustrated in this diagram. Where economies of scale are important, the cost of the exported components used in local vehicles will also fall.

14. For example, the value added of the exports should exceed the industry average value added ratio; exports should involve diverse production activities, rather than a single process; a reasonable level of skill should be utilized; the export program should contribute to the government aim of reducing the number of vehicle models. A new authority, the Automotive Industry Authority, was to judge whether the exports met these criteria. On economic grounds these criteria are disinctly odd; once again policy had the effect of negating the cost savings that could accrue from economies of scale. The stated justification for these restrictions was to ensure that "Australian skill levels are protected where export facilitation exceeds 7.5 percent" (Australian Government press release, May 29, 1984).

15. What can be exported by an industry that currently needs a nominal tariff of about 90 percent? Obviously not CBUs, although Mitsubishi has attempted to export Sigmas to the United Kingdom with little success. Nissan is exporting cylinder heads and front covers to Japan, and GMH is exporting engines to Britain and West Germany as part of its J-car production.

16. In addition, Mitsubishi has reportedly been exploring the possibility of cooperation with the local manufacturer of Toyota vehicles, Australian Motor Vehicles Ltd.
17. When import quotas are in place, exchange rate variations lead to very large changes in industry assistance. When the new motor vehicle plan was introduced in 1983, the government gave the car assemblers an allocation of 6,000 import quotas without charge. It has been reported that GMH very quickly sold these for $2,000 each. In effect, the Australian government gave them an instantly realizable asset of $12 million. The other assemblers have kept their import quotas and suffered a capital loss as a result of the exchange rate changes, as have those who bought the quotas under the tender system.

REFERENCES

Assistance to Manufacturing Industries in Australia, 1968-69 to 1973-74, annual statistics.

D. Bladen, *Report of the Royal Commission on the Automotive Industry* (Ottawa: Canadian Government Printer, 1961).

Industries Assistance Commission, *Passenger Motor Vehicles, Etcetera*, July 1974.

Industries Assistance Commission, *Passenger Motor Vehicles and Components—Post 1984 Assistance Arrangements* (Canberra: Australian Government Printing Service, 1981).

Industries Assistance Commission, *Annual Report, 1982-83* (Canberra: Australian Government Printing Service, 1983).

Industrial Assistance Commission, *Annual Report, 1983-84* (Canberra; Australian Government Printing Service, 1985).

Johnson, H. G., "The Bladen Plan for Increased Protection of the Canadian Automotive Industry," *Canadian Journal of Economics* 29 (May 1963).

Sampson, G. and G. Woodbridge, "An Analysis of the Post 1984 Arrangements for Motor Vehicles," 1984, Mimeo.

Stubbs, Peter, "The Australian Motor Industry" (Cheshire: University of Melbourne, 1971), Mimeo.

Tariff Board, *Report on Motor Vehicles and Concessional Admission of Components* (Canberra: Australian Government Printing Service, 1985).

CHAPTER 7

Imperfect Competition and International Trade: Evidence from Fourteen Industrial Countries

Elhanan Helpman

Recent developments in the theory of international trade in the presence of economies of scale and imperfect competition have shed new light on observed trade patterns. Particularly useful in this respect has been the work on monopolistic competition in differentiated products (see Lancaster, 1980; Dixit and Norman, 1980, chap. 9; Krugman, 1981; and Helpman, 1981).

Although the success of the new models in explaining stylized facts is encouraging, it is very desirable to examine more carefully their consistency with actual observations for at least two reasons. First, certain empirical hypotheses are implied by these models but have not been tested (see, for example, Helpman, 1981). Second, by subjecting the implications of models to empirical testing, one may hope to discover weak points that need further theoretical development.

This chapter reports evidence on three empirical hypotheses that emerge from models of international trade based on monopolistic

Most computations for this study were performed by Per Skedinger and Peter Sellin at the Institute for International Economic Studies, University of Stockholm, to whom I am very grateful. The last stages of the project were carried out with the aid of the Foerder Institute for Economic Research. I would like to thank the Bank of Sweden Tercentenary Foundation, for financing the acquisition of the data set and parts of the computations; the Foerder Institute; and especially NEC for financing most of this research through a grant to the Kennedy School of Government.

This chapter is adapted from an article by the same name that appeared in the *Journal of the Japanese and International Economics* 1 (1987): 62–81 (copyright © 1987 by Academic Press, Inc.).

competition in differentiated products. Two of these hypotheses concern the behavior of the share of intraindustry trade. The third hypothesis concerns the behavior of the volume of trade. The theoretical derivation of these hypotheses relies on Helpman and Krugman (1985, chap. 8). The theory and evidence concerning the volume of trade are present in the next section, followed by the theory and evidence concerning the share of intraindustry trade.

THE VOLUME OF TRADE

The factor proportions theory contributes very little to our understanding of how the volume of trade in the world economy, or within groups of countries, is determined. Nor does the Ricardian view of comparative advantage offer much help in this respect. Nevertheless, there seem to exist certain regular relationships between income levels of trading partners and the volume of trade, which economists have tried to explain for many years (Deardorff, 1984). Models of monopolistic competition in differentiated products can contribute to the explanation of these links.

Consider a $2 \times 2 \times 2$ economy (two goods, two factors, two countries), in which capital and labor are the only factors of production. If both sectors, X and Y, produce homogeneous products with constant returns to scale, then the factor price equalization set is represented by the parallelogram OQO^*Q' in Figure 7-1, where OQ is the vector of employment in X (the employment level in industry X) and QO^* is the vector of employment in Y in an equilibrium that would result if labor and capital could move freely across countries as they do across industries within a country. The origin of the home country is O and the origin of the foreign country is O^*.

In a trading equilibrium without international factor mobility, allocations in OQO^* make the home country import Y and export X. The volume of trade is defined to be the sum of exports. Assuming identical homothetic preferences and free trade, the volume of trade is given by:

$$V = p_x (X - s\overline{X}) + p_y (Y^* - s^*\overline{Y})$$

where $s(s^*)$ is the share of the home (foreign) country in world spending, X is the output level of X in the home country, Y^* is the output level of Y in the foreign country, and $\overline{X}$ and $\overline{Y}$ are world output levels of X and Y, respectively. Thus, $s + s^* = 1$, $X + X^* = \overline{X}$, and

Figure 7-1. A Typical Factor Price Equalization Set.

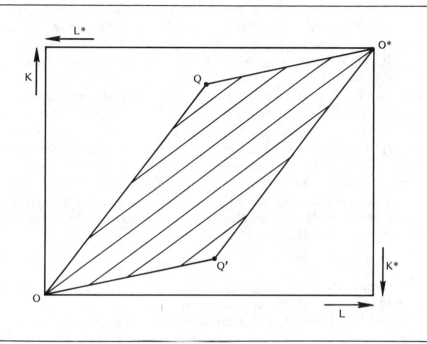

$Y + Y^* = \overline{Y}$. Assuming balanced trade, the volume of trade is equal to:

$$V = 2p_x (X - s\overline{X}) \tag{1}$$

for endowments in OQO*.

Now, at all endowment points in the factor price equalization set, p_x is constant and both X and s are linear functions of the home country factor endowment point. Hence the iso-volume-of-trade curves that correspond to this model are straight lines. Moreover, they must be parallel to the diagonal OO*, and they are therefore represented by the lines within the parallelogram of Figure 7-1 (see Helpman and Krugman, 1985, chap. 8). The farther away a line is from the diagonal, the larger is the volume of trade that it represents.

In this model, as Figure 7-1 shows, larger volumes of trade are associated with larger differences in factor composition. Differences in relative country size, as measured by gross domestic product (GDP), have no particular effect. This prediction, which is inconsistent with the evidence (Deardorff, 1984), does not change when the model is extended to many countries and goods.

Next change the model, and suppose that X is a differentiated product. There are economies of scale in the production of every variety, and monopolistic competition prevails in the industry. In the equilibrium attained with free factor mobility, industry X comprises a large number of firms, each producing a different variety and making zero profits. Suppose that all varieties are equally priced and produced in the same quantity. The vectors OQ and QO* still represent employment in sectors X and Y, respectively. But this time OQ is employed by n firms, each one producing a different variety. Contrary to the constant-returns-to-scale model, here the number of firms, n, is well determined and of great importance for many issues. The world output level of x, $\overline{X}$, is still a valid measure of aggregate output in the industry, but this time it consists of $\overline{n}$ varieties, with output per variety being

$$x = \overline{X}/\overline{n} \ .$$

The parallelogram OQO*Q' remains the factor price equalization set for trading equilibria without factor mobility.

Figure 7–2 reproduces the relevant features of Figure 7–1. Suppose E is the endowment point; the home country is relatively capital rich. Then full employment with factor price equalization is attained when the home country employs OP_X in the differentiated product sector and OP_Y in the homogeneous product sector. By drawing through E a downward-sloping line BB' whose slope equals the wage rental ratio (w_L/w_K), we obtain point C, which represents the distribution of income across the two countries. Then, if trade is balanced, OC_Y represents consumption of Y in the home country and OC_X represents aggregate consumption of X in the home country, provided we normalize units of measurement so that $\overline{X}$ = OQ and $\overline{Y}$ = OQ'. It is clear from the figure that the home country imports Y and it is a *net* exporter of X.

The fact that every firm produces a different variety of X and the assumption that all varieties are demanded in every country imply that there is intraindustry trade in differentiated products. The home country produces

$$n = \frac{\overline{OP_X}}{x} = \frac{X}{x}$$

Figure 7-2. A Typical Allocation.

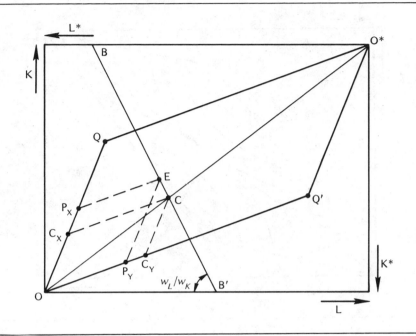

varieties, and the foreign country produces

$$n^* = \frac{P_x Q}{x} = \frac{X^*}{x}$$

varieties. Provided preferences are identical and homothetic in both countries, the value of X-exports from the home country is

$$s^* p_x nx$$

and the value of X-exports from the foreign country is

$$s p_x n^* x \; .$$

Hence, there is two-way trade in X products. The volume of trade is now equal to:

$$V = s^* p_x nx + s p_x n^* x + p_y (Y^* - s\overline{Y}) \; .$$

Figure 7-3. Equal Trade Volume Contours for the Mixed Case.

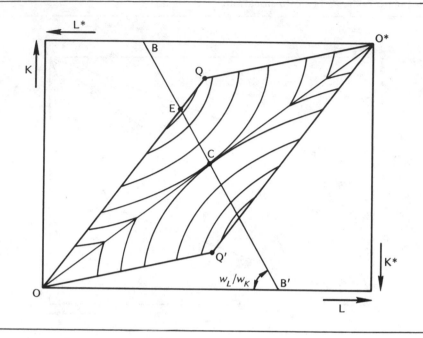

Again assuming balanced trade, this expression reduces to:

$$V = 2s^*p_x nx \tag{2}$$

for E∈OQO*.

Helpman and Krugman (1985, chap. 8) show that the curves on which (2) obtains constant values look like the curves in Figure 7-3. They are tangent on BB' (which passes through the center of OO*) to rays through O. The farther away a curve is from the diagonal, the larger is the volume of trade that it represents. In OQO* the volume of trade is maximized at E, where the difference in factor composition is largest for countries of equal size. A comparison of Figures 7-3 and 7-1 shows that product differentiation introduces a new dimension, relative country size, to the determinant of the volume of trade. Now the larger is the difference in factor composition and the smaller is the difference in relative size, the larger is the volume of trade.

Relative country size becomes *the* determinant of the volume of trade when both X and Y are differentiated products. In this case the volume of trade is:

Figure 7-4. Equal Trade Volume Contours for the Pure Differentiated Product Case.

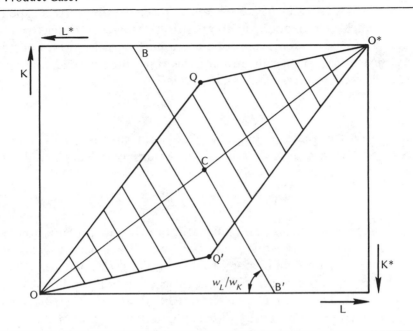

$$V = s(p_x X^* + p_y Y^*) + s^*(p_x X + p_y Y) = sGDP^* + s^*GDP \ .$$

But $GDP^* = s^*\overline{GDP}$ and $GDP = s\overline{GDP}$, so this yields:

$$V = 2ss^*\overline{GDP} \qquad (3)$$

where $\overline{GDP}$ is gross domestic product in the world economy. Hence the volume of trade depends only on ss^*, or relative country size. Figure 7-4 describes the corresponding equal-volume-of-trade curves. They are downward-sloping lines whose slope is equal to the wage rental ratio. The farther a line is from BB$'$ (which represents equal-size countries), the lower is the volume of trade that it represents.

Figures 7-1, 7-3, and 7-4 show that the larger is the share of output accounted for by differentiated product industries, the more important is relative country size in the determination of the volume of trade. More generally, when no good is produced in more than one country, the distribution of country size is the sole determinant of the share of world GDP that is traded. Thus, the more specialization there is in production, the more important is the role of relative country size. The existence of differentiated products that are produced with economies of scale leads to specialization of this type (in the presence of monopolistic competition). However, other forms of specialization that stem from scale economies will also do for current purposes. For with specialization of this type, the bilateral volume of trade between country j and country k is:

$$V^{jk} = s^j GDP^k + s^k GDP^j$$

where s^j is the share of country j in world spending and GDP^j is gross domestic product of country j. Assuming balanced trade this yields:

$$V^{jk} = 2s^j s^k \overline{GDP} . \tag{4}$$

This provides a theoretical explanation of the gravity equation (see Anderson, 1979, and Krugman, 1980), which has been successfully estimated using data on bilateral trade flows (e.g., Linnemann, 1966). It also has an important implication for the relationship between the ratio of world trade to GDP, on the one hand, and the distribution of country size, on the other. By direct calculation we obtain

$$\frac{V}{\overline{GDP}} = \frac{1}{2} \sum_{j} \sum_{k \neq j} s^j s^k = [1 - \sum_{j} (s^j)^2] . \tag{5}$$

(See Helpman, 1983.)

Equation 5 suggests a possible explanation of the fact that the volume of trade has grown faster than income since World War II. During this period the differences in relative GDP have decreased, so that the dispersion index on the right hand side of (5) has grown over time. To examine this hypothesis, we need to develop a formula that is applicable to *groups* of countries and takes into account trade imbalances.

Let A be a set of indexes for a group of countries. Then the group's gross domestic product is

$$GDP^A = \sum_{j \in A} GDP^j$$

and we define

$$e_A^j = \frac{GDP^j}{GDP^A} , \qquad e_A = \frac{GDP^A}{GDP}$$

as the share of country j in the group's GDP, and the share of the group in world GDP, respectively.

Also define t^j to be the excess of exports over imports in country j and

$$t^j_A = \frac{t^j}{GDP^A} , \qquad t_A = \sum_{j \in A} t^j_A .$$

Then the within-group volume of trade is

$$V^A = \sum_{\substack{j \in A}} \sum_{\substack{k \in A \\ k \neq j}} s^j GDP^k$$

$$= \sum_{\substack{j \in A}} \sum_{\substack{k \in A \\ k \neq j}} s^j e^k_A GDP^A = GDP^A \sum_{j \in A} s^j (1 - e^j_A)$$

However,

$$s^j = \frac{e^j_A GDP^A - t^j}{GDP} = e_A (e^j_A - t^j_A) .$$

Hence,

$$\frac{V^A}{GDP^A} = e_A [1 - t_A + \sum_{j \in A} e^j_A t^j_A - \sum_{j \in A} (e^j_A)^2] . \qquad (6)$$

In this case the intragroup trade volume grows faster than its combined income if the adjusted size dispersion index, given by the bracketed term on the right-hand side of (6), grows over time (given a constant share of the group in world income).

Table 7-1 calculates size dispersion indexes, both adjusted for trade imbalances and unadjusted, for a group of fourteen industrial countries during the years 1956–81. Clearly trade imbalance adjustments do not change the time series properties of this index significantly. Trade imbalances, including the external imbalances generated by shocks in oil and primary commodity prices, were quite small as a proportion of income for those countries. Table 7-1 also presents the time series of the ratio of intragroup trade to the group's income. During this period the ratio of trade to income rose, and so did the dispersion index (the latter resulting from a reduction in relative country size). The trade imbalance-adjusted size dispersion index is plotted in Figure 7-5 against the trade-income ratio, revealing a positive relationship. Thus the decline in relative country size contributes to the explanation of the differential rates of trade and income

Table 7-1. Trade and Income-Related Statistics for the Industrialized Countries, 1956–1981.

Year	Size Dispersion Index[a]	Trade Imbalance— Adjusted Size Dispersion Index[b]	Trade-Income Ratio[c]
1956	0.631	0.634	0.048
1957	0.638	0.640	0.049
1958	0.643	0.643	0.045
1959	0.645	0.638	0.048
1960	0.654	0.655	0.051
1961	0.670	0.670	0.052
1962	0.672	0.675	0.052
1963	0.680	0.677	0.053
1964	0.690	0.686	0.056
1965	0.691	0.686	0.057
1966	0.696	0.691	0.059
1967	0.695	0.690	0.058
1968	0.691	0.686	0.062
1969	0.723	0.718	0.070
1970	0.715	0.710	0.068
1971	0.725	0.725	0.069
1972	0.744	0.738	0.071
1973	0.767	0.763	0.080
1974	0.773	0.776	0.092
1975	0.782	0.776	0.083
1976	0.776	0.776	0.088
1977	0.778	0.778	0.088
1978	0.791	0.788	0.088
1979	0.799	0.805	0.097
1980	0.804	0.811	0.100
1981	0.776	0.777	0.092

Note: The countries in the sample are Canada, the United States, Japan, Austria, Belgium-Luxembourg, Denmark, France, Germany, Ireland, Italy, Netherlands, Sweden, Switzerland, and the United Kingdom. The calculations were made by converting all national currency variables into U.S. dollars by means of the average exchange rate (row *af* in the IFS).

a. This index is: $\left[1 - \sum_{j \in A} \left(e_A^j\right)^2\right]$.

b. This index is: $\left[1 - t_A - \sum_{j \in A} \left(e_A^j t_A^j + \sum_{j \in A} e_A^j\right)^2\right]$.

c. The trade-income ratio is the within-group volume of trade divided by the group's income.

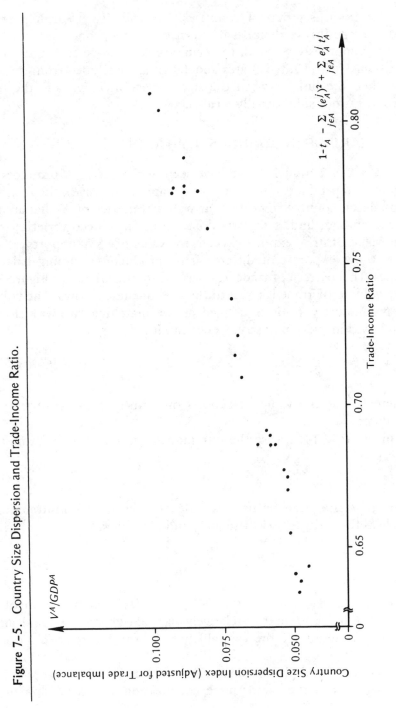

Figure 7-5. Country Size Dispersion and Trade-Income Ratio.

growth for this group of countries. However, two warnings are in order. First, this evidence is no substitute for a proper statistical test of the hypothesis. Second, the evidence is sensitive to country composition. If the United States and Japan are excluded from the sample, then the link between the size dispersion index and the trade income ratio is substantially weakened.

SHARE OF INTRAINDUSTRY TRADE

In a $2 \times 2 \times 2$ model, as we have seen, when sector X produces differentiated products (and is relatively capital intensive), the relatively capital-rich country imports Y as well as varieties of X that are produced abroad, and it exports domestically produced varieties of X. The value of its X-exports exceeds the value of its X-imports, so that it is a net exporter of differentiated products (assuming balanced trade). This pattern of trade is described by the arrows in Figure 7-6. The volume of trade is equal to the sum of these arrows. The volume of intraindustry trade is defined as the matching two-way flow of goods within every industry. Generally, it is:

$$V_{i-i} = \sum_j \sum_k \sum_i \min (E_i^{jk}, E_i^{kj}) = 2 \sum_j \sum_{k>j} \sum_i \min (E_i^{jk}, E_i^{kj})$$

where E_i^{jk} is the value of exports of country j to country k of i-products.

In our $2 \times 2 \times 2$ case the intraindustry trade volume formula reduces to:

$$V_{i-i} = 2sp_x n^*x \ . \tag{7}$$

This expression can be used to calculate the share of intraindustry trade as the ratio V_{i-i}/V. Using (2) and (7), this ratio is:

$$S_{i-i} = \frac{sn^*}{s^*n} \ . \tag{8}$$

Helpman (1981) showed that S_{i-i} is a declining function of the capital-labor ratio in the relatively capital-rich country and an increasing function of the capital-labor ratio in the relatively capital-poor country.

Constant intraindustry-share curves are depicted in Figure 7-7 for endowments in the factor price equalization set (see Helpman and

Figure 7-6. Trade Composition.

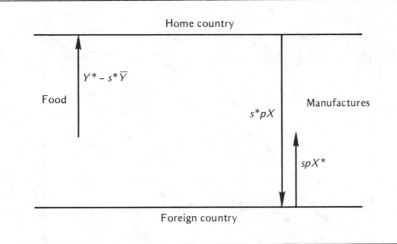

Krugman (1985, chap. 8) for a proof of the properties of these curves). The diagonal represents a share equal to one, while O*Q represents a share equal to zero. The share is lower the farther away a curve is from the diagonal. Clearly larger differences in factor composition are associated with smaller shares of intraindustry trade, and the larger the country that is a net exporter of differentiated products, the smaller the share of intraindustry trade. The second relationship, however, may be rather weak.

More insight into the determination of the share of intraindustry trade can be obtained by considering a many-country many-goods environment with only two factors of production, this time allowing for unequal factor rewards. A case of three countries and four industries is depicted in Figure 7–8 by means of a Lerner diagram. (Strictly speaking, this diagram is valid only when production functions are homothetic; see Helpman and Krugman (1985, chap. 8) for details.) Every inoquant represents a dollars' worth of output, and every downward-sloping line represents a dollars' worth of factor costs. Superscripts indicate countries (e.g., w_L^j / w_K^j is the wage rental ratio in country j), while the rays through the origin describe the capital-labor ratios available in the three countries.

Given the structure described by Figure 7–8, country 1 produces products 1 and 2, country 2 produces products 2 and 3, and country 3 produces products 3 and 4. If these are differentiated products,

Figure 7–7. Equal Intraindustry Trade Share Contours.

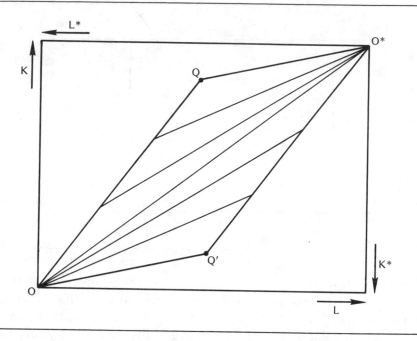

then there will be intraindustry trade between countries 1 and 2, and between countries 2 and 3, but not between countries 1 and 3. This insight can be generalized: with unequal factor rewards and many countries, the share of intraindustry trade in the *bilateral* volume of trade should be larger for countries with more similar factor compositions. On the other hand, for a group of countries, larger shares of intraindustry trade in the within-group trade volume should be associated with smaller within-group dispersions in factor composition.

The difference across countries in factor composition can be measured by cross-country differences in income per capita. This method is accurate when there are only two factors of production and all goods are freely traded. Given this proxy, our analysis suggests two hypotheses, one about the composition of bilateral trade flows and one about the composition of within-group trade flows (see Helpman, 1981):

1. The share of intraindustry trade in bilateral trade flows should be larger for countries with similar incomes per capita.

Figure 7-8. Unequal Factor Rewards.

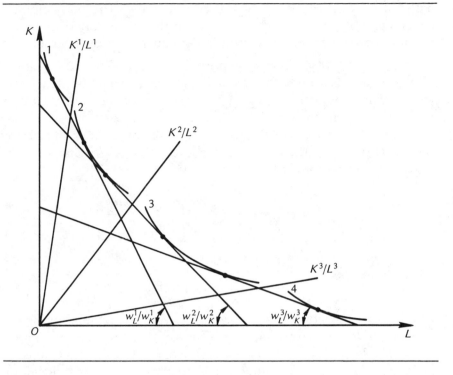

2. The share of intraindustry trade in the within-group trade volume should be larger in periods in which the within-group dispersion of income per capita is smaller.

To examine the consistency of these hypotheses with the data, I calculated bilateral and within-group intraindustry trade shares for the fourteen industrial countries in the sample for each year from 1970 to 1981. The bilateral shares were calculated as:

$$S_{i-i}^{jk} = \frac{2 \sum\limits_{i} \min (E_i^{jk}, E_i^{kj})}{\sum\limits_{i} (E_i^{jk} + E_i^{kj})}. \tag{9}$$

This was done for every pair of countries in every year.

It is well known that this index is biased in the presence of trade imbalance (see Aquino, 1978). The bias can be seen in Figure 7-6. If the trade imbalance arises because the home country exports less of X (thus having a trade deficit), then this will reduce the denominator of (9) but will not change the numerator, therefore yielding a larger share of intraindustry trade. If, on the other hand, the foreign country exports fewer differentiated products, S_{i-i}^{jk} will be smaller. Finally, if the foreign country exports less Y, then S_{i-i}^{jk} will be larger. Thus the bias generated by trade imbalance depends on its source, and no simple adjustment is possible. For this reason, I report results that were estimated using (9).

To test the consistency of the data with the hypothesis concerning the bilateral trade flows, I estimated the following equation on the cross-section data for every year from 1970 to 1981:

$$S_{i-i}^{jk} = \alpha_0 + \alpha_1 \log \left| \frac{GDP^j}{N^j} - \frac{GDP^k}{N^k} \right|$$

$$+ \alpha_2 \min (\log GDP^j, \log GDP^k)$$

$$+ \alpha_3 \max (\log GDP^j, \log GDP^k)$$

where N^j is the population of country j. The minimum and maximum of GDP levels were introduced in order to capture the importance of relative size. (Loertscher and Wolter (1980), who estimated a similar equation for manufacturing industries, emphasized the importance of the combined size of the trading countries as represented by their joint GDP.) The equation was estimated on four-digit SIC data, using manufacturing as well as nonmanufacturing sectors. The results are presented in Table 7–2, with t-values appearing in parentheses.

As Table 7–2 shows, there is a negative partial correlation in the sample between the share of intraindustry trade and dissimilarity in income per capita, which weakened toward the end of the sample period. The size of the smaller country has a positive effect, and the size of the larger country has a negative effect, on the share of intraindustry trade, which is consistent with the hypothesis that the more similar countries are in size, the larger will be the share of intraindustry trade. Moreover, since the estimates of $\alpha_2 + \alpha_3$ are positive, the joint size of two countries has a positive effect on the share of intraindustry trade between them. These results justify the use of a combined size variable, as in Loertscher and Wolter (1980), although

Table 7-2. Bilateral Trade Flows: Regression Coefficients, 1970–1981 (*t-values in parentheses*).

	α_1	α_2	α_3	R^2
1970	-0.044 (-3.141)	0.055 (4.153)	-0.014 (-1.105)	0.266
1971	-0.041 (-3.495)	0.053 (4.003)	-0.016 (-1.260)	0.271
1972	-0.029 (-2.311)	0.056 (4.036)	-0.018 (-1.393)	0.233
1973	-0.017 (-1.389)	0.048 (3.390)	-0.019 (-1.428)	0.146
1974	-0.033 (-2.236)	0.038 (2.744)	-0.020 (-1.471)	0.146
1975	-0.032 (-2.252)	0.039 (2.602)	-0.18 (-1.185)	0.148
1976	-0.040 (-2.516)	0.035 (2.379)	-0.021 (-1.381)	0.141
1977	-0.021 (-1.361)	0.033 (2.109)	-0.018 (-1.150)	0.084
1978	-0.000 (-0.005)	0.043 (2.617)	-0.018 (-1.137)	0.076
1979	-0.023 (-1.860)	0.034 (2.079)	-0.011 (0.715)	0.100
1980	-0.022 (-1.397)	0.027 (1.641)	-0.013 (-0.812)	0.064
1981	-0.006 (-0.370)	0.027 (1.686)	-0.020 (-1.283)	0.039

Note: Values shown are estimates of the equation

$$S_{i-i}^{jk} = \alpha_0 + \alpha_1 \log \left| \frac{GDP^j}{N^j} - \frac{GDP^k}{N^k} \right| + \alpha_2 \log \min \left(GDP^j, GDP^k \right)$$

$$+ \; \alpha_3 \log \max \left(GDP^j, GDP^k \right) \, ,$$

where S_{i-i}^{jk} has been calculated on the basis of sectors in the four digit SIC system. The sample consists of the fourteen industrial countries cited in Table 7-1.

caution should be exercised in this interpretation because α_3 is not different from zero at the usual significance levels.

To examine directly the separate effects of combined size and relative size, Table 7–3 reports estimates of the following equation:

$$S_{i-i}^{jk} = \alpha_0' + \alpha_1' \log \left| \frac{GDP^j}{N^j} - \frac{GDP^k}{N^k} \right| + \alpha_2' \log(GDP^j + GDP^k)$$

$$+ \alpha_3' \log \left[1 - \left(\frac{GDP^j}{GDP^j + GDP^k} \right)^2 - \left(\frac{GDP^k}{GDP^j + GDP^k} \right)^2 \right] .$$

These results support the previous conclusion, although the effect of combined size appears to be rather weak in the second half of the sample period. The coefficient α_3' represents the effect of relative country size.

To examine the second hypothesis, we need to calculate both the share of intraindustry trade in the within-group volume of trade and a measure of the within-group dispersion of income per capita. The within-group total volume of trade was calculated by adding up bilateral exports within the group—that is, as:

$$V^A = \sum_{j \in A} \sum_{k \in A} \sum_i E_i^{jk} .$$

The within-group volume of intraindustry trade was calculated as:

$$V_{i-i}^A = \sum_{j \in A} \sum_{\substack{k \in A \\ k \neq j}} \sum_i \min (E_i^{jk}, E_i^{kj}) = 2 \sum_{j \in A} \sum_{\substack{k \in A \\ k > j}} \sum_i \min (E_i^{jk}, E_i^{kj})$$

Then the within-group share of intraindustry trade was calculated as:

$$S_{i-i}^A \equiv \frac{V_{i-i}^A}{V^A} = \frac{2 \sum\limits_{j \in A} \sum\limits_{\substack{k \in A \\ k > j}} \sum\limits_i \min (E_i^{jk}, E_i^{kj})}{\sum\limits_{j \in A} \sum\limits_{k \in A} \sum\limits_i E_i^{jk}} . \tag{10}$$

The time series of these calculations for the years 1970–81 is reported in the first column of Table 7–3. These calculations are based on the four-digit SIC data for the sample of fourteen industrial countries listed at the bottom of Table 7–1. *All* sectors, not just manufacturing, were used in the calculation.

The shares S_{i-i}^A reported in Table 7–4 are smaller than other available calculations. Hevrylyshyn (1983), for example, reports a share

Table 7-3. Bilateral Trade Flows, Expanded Model, Regression Coefficients, 1970-1981 (*t-values in parentheses*).

	α'_1	α'_2	α'_3	R^2
1970	-0.044 (-3.108)	0.041 (3.003)	0.065 (3.728)	0.254
1971	-0.041 (-3.483)	0.037 (2.716)	0.065 (3.697)	0.262
1972	-0.029 (-2.290)	0.037 (2.646)	0.068 (3.738)	0.213
1973	-0.017 (-1.403)	0.028 (1.893)	0.059 (3.199)	0.138
1974	-0.033 (-2.251)	0.017 (1.157)	0.048 (2.662)	0.141
1975	-0.032 (-2.248)	0.021 (1.267)	0.048 (2.443)	0.142
1976	-0.040 (-2.507)	0.014 (0.862)	0.044 (2.278)	0.136
1977	-0.022 (-1.383)	0.015 (0.867)	0.041 (1.989)	0.078
1978	-0.000 (-0.029)	0.024 (1.337)	0.053 (2.445)	0.069
1979	-0.023 (-1.885)	0.022 (1.283)	0.040 (1.875)	0.095
1980	-0.023 (-1.414)	0.013 (0.773)	0.031 (1.424)	0.057
1981	-0.005 (-0.343)	0.007 (0.444)	0.035 (1.621)	0.034

Note: Values shown are estimates of the equation

$$S_{i-i}^{jk} = \alpha'_0 + \alpha'_1 \log \left| \frac{GDP^j}{N^j} - \frac{GDP^k}{N^k} \right| + \alpha'_2 \log \left(GDP^j + GDP^k \right)$$

$$+ \alpha'_3 \log \left[1 - \left(\frac{GDP^j}{GDP^j + GDP^k} \right)^2 - \left(\frac{GDP^k}{GDP^j + GDP} \right)^2 \right] ,$$

where S_{i-i}^{jk} has been calculated on the basis of sectors in the four-digit SIC system. The sample consists of the fourteen industrial countries cited in Table 7-1.

Table 7-4. Within-Group Shares of Intraindustry Trade, 1970–1981.

	S_{i-i}^{A}	$\sigma^{A}/\bar{g}^{A}$
1970	.342	.373
1971	.346	.354
1972	.356	.306
1973	.367	.260
1974	.362	.257
1975	.378	.245
1976	.379	.268
1977	.386	.246
1978	.387	.213
1979	.394	.201
1980	.389	.180
1981	.375	.192

$$S_{i-i}^{A} = \frac{2 \sum\limits_{j\in A} \sum\limits_{\substack{k\in A \\ k>j}} \sum\limits_{i} \min \left(E_{i}^{jk}, E_{i}^{kj}\right)}{\sum\limits_{j\in A} \sum\limits_{k\in A} \sum\limits_{i} E_{i}^{jk}}$$

$$\frac{\sigma^{A}}{\bar{g}^{A}} = \frac{\sqrt{\sum\limits_{j\in A} \pi_{j}^{A} (g_{j} - \bar{g}_{j}^{A})^{2}}}{\sum\limits_{j\in A} \pi_{j}^{A} g_{j}}$$

of .638 for a group of industrial countries in 1978. This is about 1.5 times larger than the figure reported in Table 7–4.

The differences between my results and those of others may be explained in three ways. First, typical calculations (including Havrylyshyn, 1983) are based on manufacturing industries only, therefore biasing the results upward. In contrast, the hypotheses derived at the beginning of this section are based on *all* sectors, for theoretical reasons. Therefore, the appropriate index of intraindustry trade for the examination of these hypotheses must include all sectors, not only the manufacturing industries. Second, typical calculations of within-group intraindustry trade shares average out single-country intraindustry trade shares in their trade volume with the rest of the world, using one or another system of weights. This procedure is not equivalent to calculating equation 10, and it introduces a bias whose direction and magnitude depend on the weighting system.

However, (10) seems to be the variable suggested by the theory. Finally, typical calculations are done at the three-digit SIC level of aggregation, whereas I have used the four-digit level.

To examine the relationship between the within-group share of intraindustry trade and the degree of dispersion in income per capita, we need a dispersion index. For current purposes it seems appropriate to use the ratio of the standard deviation of income per capita to its mean. Thus, taking g_j to be income per capita in country j, our index is:

$$\frac{\sigma^A}{\overline{g}^A} = \frac{\sqrt{\sum_{j \in A} \pi_j^A (g_j - \overline{g}^A)^2}}{\sum_{j \in A} \pi_j^A g_j} , \tag{11}$$

where π_j^A is the share of country k in the group's population (i.e., $\pi_j^A = N^j / \sum_{k \in A} N^k$) and $\overline{g}^A$ is mean income per capita.

The second column of Table 7–4 presents the time series of equation 11 for the fourteen countries in the sample. A comparison of the two columns of Table 7–4 shows that the share of intraindustry trade is negatively correlated with dispersion in income per capita, as suggested by the second hypothesis. This relationship is exhibited in the scatter diagram of Figure 7–9.

In summary, the experience of fourteen industrial countries during the 1970s supports both hypotheses concerning the behavior of the share of intraindustry trade—one applying to bilateral trade flows and the other applying to within-group trade flows (the former applying to cross-section data, the latter to time series data).

CONCLUDING COMMENTS

Changes over time in the size of *GDP* of the industrial countries relative to each other can help explain rising trade-income ratios. On the other hand, Table 7–4 suggests that the decline over time of differences in factor composition (measured by the index of dispersion in income per capita) cannot contribute to the explanation of a rising trade-income ratio. More importantly, it has been shown that the evidence on trade volume composition is consistent with hypotheses derived from models of trade in differentiated products. This conclusion holds for both cross-section comparisons and comparisons over

Figure 7-9. Scatter Diagram of Intraindustry Trade and Dispersion in Income per Capita.

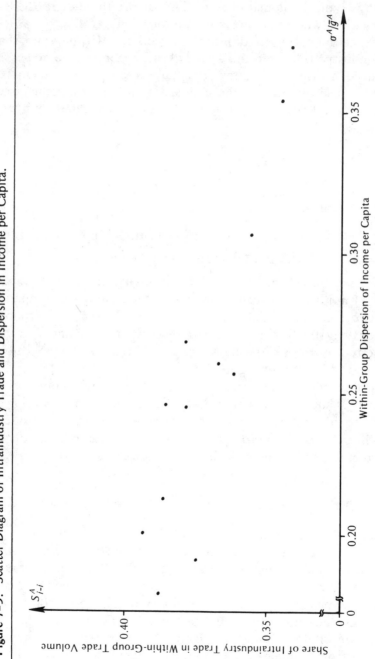

time. (Previous studies have not made comparisons over time.) These results are encouraging, particularly since highly disaggregated data have been used and calculations were based on both manufacturing and nonmanufacturing industries. The use of manufacturing industries only would be inappropriate, because the hypotheses of trade volume composition were derived from theoretical models that account for all industries. In fact, even our data set is incomplete in this respect because it does not include services.

This analysis indicates that in bilateral trade flows, the link between the share of intraindustry trade and differences in factor composition has weakened over time. This trend may be the result of data contamination by differential trends in inflation rates and exchange rate movements. However, it may well be the result of real economic developments, and it deserves careful investigation. One possibility is that it reflects the rising share of multinational corporations in world trade. This hypothesis would be consistent with the theoretical findings in Helpman and Krugman (1985, chaps. 12, 13). For the moment, however, the explanation remains an open question.

REFERENCES

Anderson, J. E., "A Theoretical Foundation of the Gravity Equation," *American Economic Review* 69 (1979): 106–16.

Aquino, A., "Intra-industry Trade and Inter-industry Specialization as Concurrent Sources of International Trade in Manufactures," *Weltwirtschaftbiches Archiv* 114 (1978): 275–96.

Deardorff, A. V., "Testing Trade Theories and Predicting Trade Flows," in *Handbook of International Economics*, vol. 1, ed. R. W. Jones and P. B. Kenen (Amsterdam: North Holland, 1984).

Dixit, A., and V. Norman, *Theory of International Trade* (Cambridge, England: Cambridge University Press, 1980).

Havrylyshyn, O., "The Increasing Integration of Newly Industrialized Countries in World Trade," October 1983, Mimeo.

Helpman, E., "International Trade in the Presence of Product Differentiation, Economies of Scale, and Monopolistic Competition: A Chamberlin-Heckscher-Ohlin Approach," *Journal of International Economics* 11 (1981): 305–40.

_____ , "A Note on the Relationship Between the Rate of GDP Growth and the Rate of Growth of the Volume of Trade," October 1983, Mimeo.

Helpman, E. and P. R. Krugman, *Market Structure and Foreign Trade* (Cambridge: M.I.T. Press, 1985).

Krugman, P. R., "Differentiated Products and Multi-lateral Trade," 1980, Mimeo.
_____ , "Intra-industry Specialization and the Gains from Trade," *Journal of Political Economy* 89 (1981): 959–73.

Lancaster, K., "Intra-industry Trade Under Perfect Monopolistic Competition," *Journal of International Economics* 10 (1980): 151–75.

Linnemann, H., *An Econometric Study of International Trade Flows* (Amsterdam: North Holland, 1966).

Loertscher, R., and F. Wolter, "Determinants of Intra-industry Trade: Among Countries and Across Industries," *Weltwirtschafliches Archiv* 8 (1980): 280–93.

CHAPTER 8

The Impact of Domestic Environmental Regulatory Policies on U.S. International Competitiveness

Joseph P. Kalt

M icroeconomic regulatory policy making and debate in the United States tend to be conducted in a shifting language that reflects the broader economywide concerns that occupy the public's attention at the moment. In the early 1970s, with the environment at the forefront of political consciousness, practically every regulatory proposal—from certificating a new airline to deregulating stockbrokers—had to be accompanied by a statement of environmental impact. Similarly, the rapid inflation of recent memory put policy makers on an inflation standard of value—with regulation-induced changes in relative prices occasionally ascribed remarkable macroeconomic power. Stagflation and recessions in turn created a jobs standard by which to measure the desirability of regulatory changes.

The new emphasis on international competitiveness in public discussion is placing a trade-balance burden of proof on proponents and opponents of regulatory change. A rise (or fall) in net exports is treated as a significant advantage (disadvantage) of any regulatory policy. Moreover, domestic regulation is often blamed for the secular decline in U.S. trade performance. Folk wisdom holds that U.S. microeconomic regulation is inordinately stultifying to entrepreneurship and management; that regulation has made the United States a

This chapter was initially prepared for the International Competition Conference, Ft. Lauderdale, Florida, March 7-9, 1985. The research assistance of Jay Hamilton, Eric Press, Pamela Rodman, Christopher Murdoch, and David Butler is greatly appreciated.

far more litigious society than its foreign competitors; and that foreign competitors are implicitly subsidized by less stringent regulation of the environment, health, safety, and quality.

The claim that domestic regulation has hampered U.S. trade performance may seem plausible. Much regulation does indeed raise domestic firms' costs. Quality, safety, and environmental regulation, for example, typically requires specific capital investments and/or changes in production techniques. Even traditional price and entry regulation, with no direct control over production methods, can involve administrative, legal, and managerial costs, as well as downstream factor input distortions. At least in the long run, such regulatory effects result in inward shifts in the supply schedules with which affected firms enter international marketplaces. While such shifts may be warranted on grounds of economywide optimality, they will tend to hurt the trade performance of affected firms.

How much domestic regulatory policies affect the international competitiveness of U.S. industries is an empirical issue. The focus of much recent research, however, implies a view that regulation is unlikely to explain trends in either interindustry or aggregate U.S. trade performance. Indeed, other than case studies of individual industries (e.g., U.S. Department of Commerce, 1983; Goedde, 1982), no systematic investigation of the regulation-trade link is available. Most recent attention has focused on the trade-determining role of such obviously significant factors as comparative advantage and relative factor endowments (Bowen, 1983; Bowen and Peltzman, 1984; Stern and Maskus, 1981), macroeconomic developments (Hall, 1983), exchange rate fluctuations (Richardson, 1983), and trade barriers (Deardorff and Stern, 1981). Research on the determinants of factor productivity finds that the "regulatory, legal and human environment" seems to account for 2–4 percent of the general decline in total U.S. factor productivity that has been observed since (roughly) the 1960s (Eads and Fix, 1984; Kendrick, 1981). This finding, however, has not been linked explicitly to international trade performance.

This chapter attempts to assess the power of domestic regulatory costs in explaining both interindustry and aggregate trade performance. The bulk of the quantifiable, disaggregable regulatory costs borne by domestic firms are typically those associated with environmental controls. Consequently, my quantitative analysis focuses on this form of regulation. Using a Heckscher-Ohlin (cum Leamer) framework, I found that the major increase in environmental regulation since the early 1970s has apparently altered U.S. trade patterns significantly—contrary to my (weakly held) prior assumptions. The imposition of environmental controls seems to have left the United States relatively poorly endowed—from the perspective of private actors—with clean air and water, and has put the nation at a comparative disadvantage in the implicit trade that takes place in (embodied) air and water resources. When available information on nonenvironmental regulatory costs is coupled with the more detailed and reliable data on environmental regulatory costs, it appears that the overall impact of domestic regulatory policy on trade performance has been negative, particularly in the manufacturing sector.

In the next section I review evidence on regulatory costs and describe workably narrow definitions of *regulation* and *regulatory costs*. Then I analyze the trade effects that direct environmental regulation costs have had at the two-digit SIC input-output (I-O) industry level. This section also examines the separate trade effects of the total (direct and indirect) costs of both environmental regulation and nonenvironmental, price, and entry regulation. I then investigate a Heckscher–Ohlin framework for assessing changes in relative factor abundance and the direct and indirect impacts of regulatory costs, and conclude with a summary and interpretation.

THE NATURE OF REGULATORY COSTS

Defining Regulation and Its Costs

Regulation might be defined quite broadly to include all microeconomic governmental intervention, from pollution control policy to tariffs on manufactured imports. This definition, however, would not capture the essence of the claims and counterclaims regarding the impact of regulation on trade performance. Here I mean to include in regulation those microeconomic interventions that are directed at domestic policy or economic problems and that are not explicitly trade policies. To be sure, regulatory policies that are ostensibly purely domestic can carry international trade consequences unrecognized by interested parties and policy makers. But the international trade consequences of water pollution policy, the deregulation of trucking, or occupational health legislation have generally been secondary or Machiavellian concerns of the policy sector. Such policies are treated as *regulation* here, as distinct from explicit trade policies of tariffs, quotas, export promotion, and so forth.

Ideally, regulation would be imposed to correct real-world markets' failures to allocate resources efficiently. Such regulation might alter firms' costs and/or behavior so as to remove marketplace deadweight losses. For example, it might represent an improvement in the allocation of national resources to raise the costs of domestic polluting industries, worsen their trade performance, and let other countries consume their own environmental resources in producing (and exporting to the United States) commodities that are pollution intensive. The social cost-benefit assessment of regulation in internationally traded goods, however, is not the focus of this inquiry. I will confine myself to the narrower issue of trade performance.

The costs of regulation—or, more properly, the costs of carrying out a given regulatory policy—are real economic costs. At their normative best, these costs are akin to market transaction costs. They are the resource expenditures incurred to achieve a resource reallocation through nonmarket means. At their worst, they represent welfare-worsening reallocations and/or nonproductive rent seeking. In either case, they represent social expenditures to be minimized.

The various forms of regulation are commonly categorized into two general types. One is traditional economic regulation of price and entry in nonmonopoly and natural monopoly markets. The other is the so-called new social regulation of health, safety, quality, and the environment. The costs associated with these two types of regulation are likely to differ in character.

Most of the costs of price and entry regulation are likely to occur downstream, since directly regulated firms are relatively free in their choices of production techniques and factor inputs, but their (typically) higher prices may distort downstream users' production decisions.[1] As Carlton (1978) has demonstrated, these downstream distortions, appearing as increases in users' costs, map directly into the deadweight allocative (i.e., "triangle") efficiency losses commonly measured in the regulated industry. Compared with these downstream regulatory costs, the administrative and compliance costs of the industry actually subject to price and entry regulation appear to be small.[2] Consequently, a relatively large part of the trade effects of price and entry regulation is likely to appear downstream from the point of regulation. This conclusion is reinforced by the observation that traditional price and entry regulation has been directed most heavily at the (nontraded) service sector and the transportation sector.[3] Thus the trade effects of a regulation-created cartel in domestic trucking would be expected to show up in reduced international competitiveness of U.S. firms that directly or indirectly employ regulated trucking services.

In contrast to price and entry regulation, environmental, health and safety, and quality regulation is likely to impose substantial direct costs on the regulated firms themselves. This form of regulation has almost invariably preferred direct control over firms' operations to price-like regulatory techniques. The resulting increases in costs can hurt the trade of the regulated firms themselves. These costs might also alter the performance of the direct and indirect downstream users of their output.

In the case of environmental regulation, costs incurred in one firm may *reduce* the shadow price of environmental inputs to some other firm or firms. A firm requiring clean air inputs, for example, may incur precleaning costs when pollution by its neighbors goes unabated; environmental regulation would permit it to avoid such costs and improve its trade performance.[4] Unfortunately, available data do not permit us to investigate this effect. It seems plausible, however, that the benefits of any cleaner air and water that has resulted from U.S. regulation have come primarily in the health and aesthetics arena, rather than as reduced costs to internationally traded producing sectors of the economy.[5]

Evidence on the Costs of Regulation

Perhaps the most natural test of the hypothesis that regulation hurts trade performance would be to incorporate some measure of regulatory costs into a cross-industry model of export and import determination. This approach presupposes the existence of sufficiently detailed and comprehensive data on regulation-related costs. Fortunately, certain data are available at the two-digit SIC industry level. These data permit an examination of the direct effects of regulatory costs on trade. Within an input-output-based model, they permit a look at the direct and indirect trade effects of regulation.

The most comprehensive attempt to measure the costs of regulation has been performed by Arthur Andersen and Co. (1979), for the Business Roundtable. The results of this study are summarized in Table 8–1A. Forty-eight firms in twenty two-digit SIC industries

Table 8-1. Cost of Regulation (billion 1977 dollars).

A. Firms' Expenditures on Regulatory Compliance: Six Agencies.

Agency	Total Expenditure	Cost Distribution (percent)				Agency Share of Total
		Capital	Administration	Product	R&D	
Environmental Protection Agency	$2.018	38%	31%	27%	4%	77%
Equal Employment Opportunity	.217	4	96	0	0	8
Occupational Safety and Health Administration	.184	37	56	1	6	7
Department of Energy	.116	24	60	9	7	5
Employee Retirement Income Security Act	.061	0	100	0	0	2
Federal Trade Commission	.026	4	88	0	8	1
Total	$2.622					

Note: Based on a survey of forty-eight firms in twenty two-digit SIC industries.
Source: Arthur Andersen and Company, Cost of Regulation, Study for the Business Roundtable (New York: Arthur Andersen, March 1979).

B. Summary of Regulatory Cost Estimates.

Type of Regulation	Total Cost	Percentage of 1977 GNP
Environmental	$13.4 – 37.9	.7 – 2.0%
Health and safety	7.4 – 17.1	.4 – .9
Economic	13.9 – 35.6	.7 – 1.9
Total	$34.7 – 90.6	1.8 – 4.8%

Source: Robert E. Litan and William D. Nordhaus, Reforming Federal Regulation (New Haven: Yale University Press, 1983).

were surveyed to learn the annualized incremental costs of regulation for the six reportedly most costly federal regulatory agencies or laws. Costs were divided into four categories: (1) capital equipment expenditures, (2) administrative-legal-managerial costs of record keeping and compliance, (3) increases in operating costs (essentially, variable costs) associated with mandated alterations of product design or production system design, and (4) regulation-induced research and development expenditures. The study measured only direct additions to cost that would not have occurred in the absence of regulation. So-called secondary costs associated with changes in productivity, delays and foregone opportunities, and deadweight social losses (or gains) were not counted.

The forty-eight companies in the Arthur Andersen study reported annual regulatory costs of slightly more than $2.6 billion (1977 $s) in 1977. These companies accounted for approximately 8 percent of sales in the manufacturing, mining, trade, service, and communication sectors of the U.S. economy. If the sampled firms' regulatory costs/sales ratio is applied to the rest of the economy, the Arthur Andersen estimates imply economywide regulation costs in the range of 3 percent of gross national product.[6] This figure is comparable to that of Litan and Nordhaus (1983), who summarized all published attempts to measure the costs of regulation (as of 1977). (See Table 8-1B.)

Litan and Nordhaus draw on studies that include virtually all regulatory agencies; they attribute a much smaller proportion of regulatory costs to environmental regulation than does the Arthur Andersen study—although both sources show environmental costs as quite substantial. The discrepancy arises because Litan and Nordhaus's economic regulation category primarily reports academic estimates of the deadweight allocative (triangle) efficiency losses, which do not appear in the individual accounting records of the firms surveyed by Arthur Andersen. In fact, most of the costs of economic regulation reported by Litan and Nordhaus occur in the rail, truck, and airline sectors, reflecting the price-raising effects of price and entry regulation.[7] As noted, regulatory price increases can distort factor proportions and raise the costs of downstream industries, thereby inhibiting their trade performance.

Because the associated costs are so high, it is worth examining the trade effects of environmental regulation separately from regulation

Table 8-2. Direct and Indirect Regulatory Costs and Trade Performance, 1977.

I-O Industry	Direct Environmental Costs[a]	Direct and Indirect Environmental Costs[b]	Direct and Indirect Costs, All Regulation[c]	Net Exports[d]	Export Performance 1967-77[e]
1. Livestock and products	$0.09	$0.72	$ 2.50	-0.31	0.45
2. Other agricultural products	0.00	0.62	1.48	17.64	25.73
3. Forest, fish products	0.00	0.34	0.94	-24.34	-18.63
4. Agriculture service	0.00	0.61	1.71	0.27	2.57
5. Iron, ferroalloy mining	0.95	2.03	14.16	-41.14	-11.35
6. Nonferrous mining	1.06	1.92	13.03	-15.92	-1.92
7. Coal mining	0.19	0.61	13.22	12.07	44.68
8. Crude, petroleum, natural gas	0.39	0.66	1.06	-71.02	-215.64
9. Stone and clay mining	0.00	0.67	1.79	-2.20	-2.39
10. Chemical and fertilizer mining	0.00	1.24	2.68	-0.14	-10.19
11. New construction	0.00	0.59	1.84	.00	0.23
12. Maintenance construction	0.00	0.52	1.50	0.04	0.20
13. Ordnance and accessories	0.20	0.67	1.52	16.12	11.39
14. Food, kindred products	0.19	0.82	2.18	-0.55	0.64
15. Tobacco manufactures	0.09	0.44	1.09	10.83	5.34
16. Fabric, yarn, and thread	0.15	1.18	2.36	0.25	4.36
17. Miscellaneous textiles	0.21	1.34	2.66	-0.68	23.16
18. Apparel	0.03	0.66	1.48	-12.39	-35.81
19. Miscellaneous fabric	0.00	0.77	1.74	0.95	-2.38
20. Lumber and wood products	0.18	0.69	1.69	-4.18	-10.60

21. Wood containers	0.18	0.73	1.86	-5.99	-8.01
22. Household furniture	0.17	0.79	1.90	-2.64	-7.72
23. Other furniture	0.09	0.81	2.10	-2.78	-6.90
24. Paper and allied products	1.33	2.40	3.96	-4.10	-2.70
25. Paperboard container	0.14	1.46	3.03	1.25	3.20
26. Printing and publishing	0.06	0.82	1.88	0.68	-0.35
27. Chemicals	1.73	2.89	5.04	3.31	0.42
28. Plastics and synthetics	0.78	2.36	4.14	6.22	5.09
29. Drugs, cleaning products	0.25	1.04	3.95	1.27	-1.98
30. Paints, allied products	0.23	1.52	3.26	2.46	6.84
31. Petroleum refining	0.96	1.78	4.43	-8.77	-66.94
32. Rubber, miscellaneous products	0.19	1.21	2.54	-2.53	-7.99
33. Leather tan, finish	0.73	1.55	2.80	-0.58	9.05
34. Footwear, leather products	0.07	0.79	1.73	-38.49	-72.40
35. Glass and glass products	0.32	1.13	2.44	0.41	-1.40
36. Stone and clay products	0.73	1.56	3.66	-2.52	-7.19
37. Primary iron, steel	1.28	2.38	5.36	-8.70	-18.44
38. Primary nonferrous	0.72	2.05	4.56	-7.82	-8.65
39. Metal containers	0.23	1.49	3.38	0.27	0.27
40. Fabricated structures	0.10	1.08	2.60	3.25	5.67
41. Metal stamping	0.14	1.14	2.80	2.21	2.05
42. Other fabricated metal	0.22	1.17	2.53	-1.11	-5.54
43. Engines and turbines	0.20	0.98	2.27	14.74	39.79
44. Farm machinery	0.13	0.85	2.10	1.58	-2.87
45. Construction and mining equipment	0.11	0.88	2.15	20.35	33.47

(Table 8–2. continued overleaf)

Table 8-2. continued

I-O Industry	Direct Environmental Costs[a]	Direct and Indirect Environmental Costs[b]	Direct and Indirect Costs, All Regulation[c]	Net Exports[d]	Export Performance 1967-77[e]
46. Material handling equipment	0.06	0.76	1.89	4.70	1.68
47. Metal working machinery	0.06	0.66	1.60	1.02	-2.98
48. Special industry machinery	0.13	0.78	1.80	12.69	4.14
49. General industry machinery	0.10	0.81	1.92	7.53	7.35
50. Machine shop products	0.10	0.65	1.67	0.77	-1.14
51. Office, computer products	0.08	0.60	1.48	12.20	19.61
52. Service industry machinery	0.17	0.93	2.17	8.55	13.62
53. Electric distribution equipment	0.16	0.82	1.90	3.29	-0.27
54. Household appliances	0.17	0.96	2.20	-2.65	-16.05
55. Electric light, wiring	0.19	0.92	2.10	2.65	0.76
56. Radio, tv, communication equipment	0.09	0.58	1.37	-11.14	-21.87
57. Electric components	0.19	0.82	1.82	1.65	-0.77
58. Miscellaneous electric machinery	0.17	0.93	2.25	1.08	-1.07
59. Motor vehicles and equipment	0.14	0.99	6.75	-6.19	-40.54
60. Aircraft and parts	0.10	0.60	1.55	24.26	20.88
61. Other transportation equipment	0.15	0.85	2.09	-1.43	-7.17
62. Professional, scientific equipment	0.09	0.66	1.57	4.37	-3.79
63. Optical, photo equipment	0.28	0.93	1.87	-1.72	-9.44
64. Miscellaneous manufacturing	0.10	0.79	1.97	-12.85	-27.30
65. Transportation, warehousing	0.00	0.95	14.72	7.47	11.80

	a	b	c	d	e
66. Communications	0.00	0.15	0.46	1.86	3.30
67. Radio, TV broadcasting	0.00	0.27	36.47	0.00	0.03
68. Electric, gas, water, sewage	2.34	5.19	10.37	-1.82	-5.69
69. Wholesale, retail	0.00	0.31	1.01	1.83	1.17
70. Finance, insurance	0.00	0.24	1.32	0.08	0.26
71. Real estate, rental	0.00	0.29	0.54	1.34	1.79
72. Hotels, personnel, representatives	0.00	0.42	1.08	0.06	0.11
73. Business services	0.00	0.27	2.67	2.51	4.97
74. Auto repair and service	0.00	0.56	1.99	-0.02	-0.06
75. Amusements	0.00	0.54	1.19	1.66	-0.72
76. Medical, educational	0.02	0.39	1.10	0.05	0.13
77. Federal government	2.58	2.79	4.03	0.98	7.45
78. State, local government	19.81	20.81	22.32	.00	0.01

a. Cents per dollar of industry output.
b. Cents per dollar of final demand.
c. Cents per dollar of final demand.
d. Net exports as percentage of value of shipments.
e. Change in contribution to value added, 1967-77.

Source: Environmental Protection Agency, *The Cost of Clean Air and Water: Report to Congress, 1984* (Washington, DC: EPA, 1984); U.S. Department of Commerce, *Current Industrial Reports* (Washington, DC: U.S. Department of Commerce, various years).

in general. As Table 8–1A indicates, over three-fourths of the reported costs of regulation in the Arthur Andersen sample occurred under
the regulatory authority of the Environmental Protection Agency
(EPA). Roughly half the costs of regulation are attributable to environmental policy in Litan and Nordhaus's data. Fortunately, detailed
industry-level data on the costs of environmental regulation are reported annually by the U.S. Department of Commerce (in its *Current
Industrial Reports*) and the Environmental Protection Agency (1984).
The first two columns of Table 8–2 show these data by industry.

The Commerce and EPA data on pollution abatement expenditures are reported on an SIC basis and have been matched to the
seventy-nine two-digit industries in the 1977 U.S. input-output table.
The first column of Table 8–2 shows the annualized capital, operating, and administrative cost of pollution abatement per dollar of
industry output (shipments) in 1977, representing the direct impact
of environmental regulation. These costs fall most heavily on such
industries as nonferrous metal mining, paper products, nonagricultural chemicals, iron and steel, electric power generation, and the
government sector. The particularly high costs at the state and local
government level reflect the operation of water treatment facilities,
which to some extent are explicitly in the business of pollution
abatement.

The direct incidence of pollution abatement expenditures suggests
which sectors are most intensively affected by regulation, but may
not accurately reflect the impact of such expenditures on the international competitiveness of U.S. industries. To the extent that pollution control costs are not entirely absorbed by the directly spending
industry, they become embodied in the output of industries that purchase the output of the directly spending industries. Short of a full
general-equilibrium model of the incidence of upstream cost changes,
running to seventy-nine equations, the input-output approach provides a viable method of investigating the net impact of regulatory
costs, particularly if we wish to explore the impact of the national
endowment of environmental resources on the pattern of U.S. trade.
Accordingly, column 2 of Table 8–2 reports the total (direct and
indirect) distribution of pollution abatement expenditures at the
two-digit I-O level, determined by multiplying column 1 and the
1977 total requirements I-O table.[8] The incidence of environmental ·
regulation (in cents per dollar of delivery to final demand) now falls
most heavily on industries such as ferrous and nonferrous metal min-

ing, nonagricultural chemicals, paper, plastics, iron and nonferrous metal fabrication, electric power generation, and the government sector.

In political debates, it is often asserted that domestic regulatory policy is particularly detrimental to trade performance because U.S. regulations—particularly environmental regulations—are more stringent than those of other major countries. It might be argued that the pollution control policies of other nations should be taken as given. On the other hand, their willingness to impose a given level of regulatory control may depend on the level of control adopted in the United States. Moreover, even if the United States is becoming absolutely less well endowed (from the perspective of private firms) in environmental resources, it might realize a relative improvement if other countries are simultaneously decreasing the (private) endowment of environmental resources by putting a cost on them.

Table 8–3 suggests that the United States indeed has been more stringent in its environmental policies than have its major trading partners; in 1979 the fraction of its resources devoted to abatement was at the upper end of the distribution (Table 8–3B). The United States was relatively late in instituting pollution control measures, however, particularly in the case of water resources (Table 8–4). In the case of air pollution, enforceable and biting regulation did not begin until passage of the Clean Air Act of 1970.

Thus the environmental policies of the 1970s may have moved the United States from a position of relative factor abundance in air and water resources to a position of relative factor scarcity. If so, the nation would be at a comparative disadvantage in the implicit international trade in embodied pollution. The effect of environmental regulation on industries' costs might also be expected to show up in cross-industry differences in trade performance. These possibilities are investigated explicitly in following sections.

Like pollution control expenditures, Litan and Nordhaus's compilation of nonenvironmental regulatory costs can be allocated across I-O sectors. Great caution in interpretation is needed, however, since these costs are gleaned from numerous, possibly noncomparable sources (i.e., academic deadweight loss analyses), rather than from a systematic collection of plant-level data, as in the case of the pollution control cost data. Bearing in mind the limitations likely in the data, the third column of Table 8–2 shows the calculated direct and indirect incidence of regulation when the "Economic Regulation"

Table 8–3. National Environmental Policies, 1975.

A. National Air Quality Objectives.

Country	SO_2 (ppm)	Particulates (mg/m_3)	NO_2 (ppm)
Japan	0.04	0.10	0.02
Canada	0.06	0.12	0.10
Germany	0.06	na	0.15
Finland	0.10	0.15	0.10
United States	0.14	0.26	0.13
Italy	0.15	0.30	na
Sweden	0.25	na	na
France	0.38	0.35	na

Source: Organization for Economic Cooperation and Development, *Environmental Policies in Japan* (Paris: OECD, 1977).

B. Private Sector Investment in Pollution Control.

Country	Percentage of GDP	Percentage of Total Private Investment
Japan	1.00%	4.6%
United States	0.44	3.4
Netherlands	0.34	1.9
Germany	0.32	1.9
United Kingdom	0.29	1.7
France	0.28	1.4
Finland	0.22	0.9
Norway	0.22	0.7
Sweden	0.19	1.1
Denmark	0.17	0.9

Source: Organization for Economic Cooperation and Development, *The State of the Environment in OECD Member Countries* (Paris: OECD, 1979).

Table 8-4. Enactment Dates of Major Environmental Laws.

Country	Water Pollution	Air Pollution
Belgium	1971	1964
Canada	1970	—
France	1964	1974
Germany	1957	1974
	1976	—
Greece	1978	—
Ireland	1977	1977
Italy	1976	1966
Japan	1958	1962
	1970	1968
Netherlands	1970	1972
	1975	—
New Zealand	1967	1972
	1974	1977
Norway	1970	—
Spain	—	1972
Sweden	1969	1969
Switzerland	1971	—
Turkey	1971	—
United Kingdom	1961	1956
	1974	—
United States	1972	1963
	1977	1970
	—	1977

Source: Organization for Economic Cooperation and Development, *The State of the Environment in OECD Member Countries* (Paris: OECD, 1979).

and "Health and Safety Regulation" costs of Litan and Nordhaus are added to the detailed federal data on pollution control costs.[9] As noted earlier, looking at direct costs alone is likely to miss the nature of economic regulation. The total (direct and indirect) factor allocation shown in Table 8-2 indicates that regulatory costs are most heavily embedded in the output of the mining sector, motor vehicles, transportation, broadcasting, electricity generation, and state and local government.

To provide a first look at possible links between regulation and international competitiveness, the last two columns of Table 8-2 show measures of trade performance. Column 4 shows the net exports of each I-O industry as a percentage of total industry shipments. The correlations between this measure and the costs of regulation shown in columns 1, 2, and 3 are consistently negative, but small: -0.02, -0.01, and -0.07, respectively. The last column of Table 8-2 shows a measure of trade performance suggested by Lawrence (1983): the percentage change in value added attributable to foreign trade over the period 1967-77. It is based on the identity $VA_i = D_i + X_i - M_i$ and is calculated as

$$\Delta VA_i^{XM} = \frac{[(X_{it} - M_{it}) - (X_{it'} - M_{it'})]}{VA_{it'}}, \tag{1}$$

where   subscript i indicates the industry,
         subscripts t' and t indicate the sample years, 1967 and
            1977, respectively,
VA = value added,
X = exports,
M = imports, and
D = domestic use of commodity produced.

This measure of performance is correlated with the three measures of regulatory costs at the levels of 0.002, 0.01 and 0.07, respectively.

The weakness (and inconsistency) of the simple correlations between regulatory costs and trade performance might suggest that regulation is not a determinant of international competitiveness or—more reasonably—that such competitiveness is determined by a multivariate process. In fact, significant regulatory costs are found in a number of industries that, at least by reputation, are poor trade performers *and* have old and/or inefficient capital, low levels of re-

search and development, or poorly skilled labor. Thus direct inference from Table 8-2 is tenuous, at best. I now turn to a more systematic look at the link between trade and regulatory costs.

TRADE PERFORMANCE AND
REGULATORY COSTS

The imposition of stringent environmental regulations in the United
States can usefully be viewed as a decline in the relative abundance
of environmental resources. From the perspective of the producing
sector of the economy, the rise of environmental regulation signaled
the drying up of the "common pool." Federal intervention reduced
the effective endowment of environmental inputs available to producers by imposing a new regime of property rights. Holding other
countries' effective endowments of air and water inputs constant, a
Heckscher-Ohlin view of intercountry trade would indicate an expected decline in U.S. net exports of air and water (i.e., the air
and water used up through pollution and hence embodied in total
output).

The Hecksher-Ohlin theory of international trade has most commonly been tested indirectly through cross-industry analyses of the
link between factor intensity at the industry level and the level of an
industry's net exports of its commodities (e.g., Branson and Monoyios, 1977; Stern and Maskus, 1981). Leamer and Bowen (1981)
have shown, however, that coefficients yielded from a regression of
commodity trade on industry-level factor inputs need not indicate
national-level resource abundance or scarcity. At the industry level,
competitiveness is determined by the relative cost of combining inputs into a composite called output; for any particular industry, the
impact of changes in factor intensities on this relative cost may or
may not be in the same direction as might be inferred from national
factor endowments.

In short, a regression of net trade on industry-level factor inputs
does not provide a definitive test of the Hecksher-Ohlin theory that
an increase/decrease in the national endowment of a factor will cause
the total (embodied) net exports of that factor to increase/decrease.
Such a test (fortunately) is inapposite to the issue of concern here,
namely the impact of a change in the effective endowment of environmental inputs on the net exports of commodities. It is this impact that is measured by the coefficients from a regression of com-

modity net exports on factor inputs—thus providing us with a research design.

The Direct Effects of Regulation on Trade Performance

I begin by examining the effect of direct factor input levels on net exports of industries' outputs. I employ the general framework of Branson and Monoyios (1977) and Stern and Maskus (1981), in which net exports of the ith industry are a function of that industry's use of the national endowment of factors of production. Specifically, net exports are taken to be:

$$NET_i = f(K_i, R\&D_i, HK_i, UNSKILL_i, ABATE_i), \qquad (2)$$

where:

K_i = each industry's use of capital services,

$R\&D_i$ = flow of research and development inputs to each industry,

HK_i = flow of human capital services to each industry,

$UNSKILL_i$ = each industry's claim to the flow of low-skilled labor services, and

$ABATE_i$ = expenditures on pollution abatement services by each industry.

Of course, if environmental policy prices environmental resources at their social cost, $ABATE_i$ measures the input value of air and water resources to each industry. For the moment, indirect inputs and, correspondingly, price and entry types of regulation are ignored.

As suggested in the preceding discussion of the Heckscher-Ohlin theory, the signs of the variables in equation 2 cannot be determined a priori.[10] Bowen (1983), however, provides some guidance as to what might be expected. Looking at trade behavior at several points between 1963 and 1975, Bowen divided industries into top net exporters ($NE_i = NET_i > 0$) and top net importers ($NM_i = NET_i < 0$). For both types of industries, the effect of capital inputs on NET_i was positive by the mid-1970s. The effect of HK_i was positive for the NE_i industries, but negative for the NM_i industries. This pattern was exactly reversed for low-skill labor. Bowen provided no evidence on $R\&D_i$ or, of course, $ABATE_i$.

Data for equation 2 are applied in 1977 for all of the I-O industries listed in Table 8-2. Following previous studies, K_i is measured by the total payments to property-type factors, as reported in the 1977 input-output table. Research and development inputs $(R\&D_i)$ are based on the SIC data reported by the National Science Foundation (1982), reallocated to the I-O industries. The measurement of human capital services (HK_i) is related to the measure introduced by Branson and Monoyios (1977), who measured the human capital stock of each industry by the difference between the industry's average wage and the national average wage, multiplied by the total employment in the industry and divided by a discount rate (10 percent). Here I measure the flow of human capital services as the difference between an industry's average wage and the average wage in the lowest-paying of the two-digit I-O sectors (Other Agricultural Products), multiplied by the industry's full-time equivalent employment. This measure presumes that unskilled labor is best reflected in the wage paid in the lowest-paying sector; and $UNSKILL_i$ is measured by the average wage in this sector, multiplied by total full-time equivalent employment in industry i. Abatement costs $(ABATE_i)$ are total annualized expenditures provided, as in Table 8-2, by the *Current Industrial Reports* of the Department of Commerce and the Environmental Protection Agency (1984).

As discussed by Stern and Maskus (1981) and Branson and Monoyios (1977), we might expect heteroskedasticity in a model based on equation 2. Specifically, Stern and Maskus investigate the possibility that the disturbance term implicit in the linear version of (2) varies systematically with the size, S, of the industry. They find that scaling each variable by $S^{-.5}$ provides a good correction for heteroskedasticity. Some moderate evidence (Glejser, 1969) of heteroskedasticity is found here, with $S^{-.25}$ providing the best fit. I report generalized least squares (GLS) results with this scaling, where S measures total industry shipments. Net exports, NET_i in (2), are as reported by the 1977 input-output table. All variables are in millions of dollars.

Table 8-5 shows results from estimation of equation 2. The model does not perform well when applied to the entire sample of two-digit industries in the seventy-nine-industry input-output table. But when applied to the manufacturing sector (industries 13-64, from Ordnance and Accessories through Miscellaneous Manufacturing), the model has significant explanatory power. The residuals from (2), when applied to manufacturing, consistently show the chemical in-

Table 8-5. Factor Inputs and Net Export Performance, 1977 (*t-statistics in parentheses*).

	Without Heteroskedasticity Correction			With Heteroskedasticity Correction		
	All I-O Industries	Manufacturing I-O Industries	Manufacturing Excluding Chemicals[a]	All I-O Industries	Manufacturing I-O Industries	Manufacturing Excluding Chemicals[a]
Pollution abatement (ABATE)	0.217 (0.00+)	-3.009 (-2.13)	-5.499 (-3.62)	-0.284 (-0.41)	-3.213 (-1.93)	-5.580 (-2.94)
Capital (K)	(0.006) (0.00+)	0.197 (1.20)	0.556 (0.35)	-0.122 (-2.02)	0.230 (1.23)	0.113 (0.61)
R&D	0.211 (0.00+)	1.028 (3.45)	0.773 (2.71)	0.582 (1.25)	1.033 (3.62)	0.858 (3.03)
Human capital (HK)	(0.037) (0.00+)	-0.609 (-3.89)	-0.503 (-3.42)	0.047 (0.35)	-0.433 (-2.59)	-0.343 (-2.09)
Unskilled labor (UNSKILL)	-0.114 (-0.00+)	2.364 (2.04)	2.480 (2.33)	0.134 (0.21)	1.162 (1.02)	1.189 (1.09)
Constant term	-786.608 (-1.03)	341.783 (0.81)	336.497 (0.87)	-167.301 (-0.64)	273.841 (0.87)	286.335 (0.94)
R^2	0.069	0.445	0.536	0.082	0.353	0.413
F-statistic	1.074	7.367	10.406	1.283	5.021	6.340

a. The chemical industry was found to be an outlier; see text.

dustry as an outlier, for reasons that are not entirely clear. Special targeting by the Occupational Safety and Health Administration (whose costs are not captured here) or the receipt of substantial special energy subsidies throughout the 1970s may be at work. Table 8–5 reports results both including and excluding the chemical industry.

Of most central interest, Table 8–5 indicates that pollution abatement regulations have a negative and fairly significant effect on trade performance. The negative sign on *ABATE* is quite stable under alternative specifications, as is the sign pattern across all the variables. As Bowen (1983) found, capital inputs to an industry are positively related to its trade performance, although after accounting for abatement expenditures, it is hard to assign much significance to capital. R&D expenditures are a clearly positive influence on net exports, providing support to Lawrence's (1983) finding that recent U.S. trade performance has been particularly strong in high-tech industries. The positive relationship between R&D and trade performance is also consistent with Stern and Maskus's (1981) results. As a group, the I–O manufacturing industries are net importers (i.e., $\Sigma NET_i <$ 0). In agreement with Bowen's (1983) finding for net importers, *HK* and *UNSKILL* have negative and positive effects, respectively, on trade performance.

Table 8–6 shows results for a restated version of equation 2; here the dependent variable is the change in net exports over the period 1967–77. (This variation was suggested by Lawrence's (1983) performance measure noted in Table 8–2—the change over time in the contribution of trade to value added.) Each of the independent variables is now measured as the change in the variable between 1967 and 1977. The 1967 data are converted to 1977 dollars and are taken from the 1967 input-output table, as well as the sources corresponding to those from which the 1977 data are acquired. Mandated pollution abatement expenditures were negligible in 1967, and data on abatement were not collected until the early 1970s.

The results in Table 8–6 mirror those in Table 8–5. Specifically, with fairly high confidence, it can be concluded that *environmental regulation played a negative role in the evolution of trade performance over the decade.* This result is consistent with the earlier observations that U.S. environmental policy has tended to be more stringent and, by inference, more costly than the policies of its major trading partners. Of the other variables employed to explain the

Table 8-6. Factor Inputs and Changes in the Contribution of Trade to Value Added, 1967–1977 (t-statistics in parentheses).

	Without Heteroskedasticity Correction			With Heteroskedasticity Correction		
	All I-O Industries	Manufacturing I-O Industries	Manufacturing Excluding Chemicals[a]	All I-O Industries	Manufacturing I-O Industries	Manufacturing Excluding Chemicals[a]
Pollution abatement (ABATE)	-0.464 (-0.57)	-2.016 (-1.90)	-2.091 (-2.02)	-0.747 (-1.15)	-2.859 (-2.34)	-2.967 (-2.59)
Capital (K)	-0.106 (-1.44)	0.446 (2.11)	0.428 (2.08)	-0.541 (-4.26)	0.285 (1.05)	0.246 (0.97)
R&D	-0.701 (-0.65)	-0.026 (-0.05)	0.065 (0.13)	-0.392 (-0.53)	-0.128 (-0.31)	-0.019 (-0.05)
Human capital (HK)	-0.012 (-0.12)	-0.744 (-4.09)	-0.783 (-4.38)	0.208 (1.40)	-0.282 (-1.55)	-0.345 (-2.01)
Unskilled labor (UNSKILL)	-0.551 (-1.91)	-0.146 (-0.49)	-0.206 (-0.71)	0.216 (0.51)	0.288 (0.96)	.122 (0.42)
Constant term	-951.049 (-1.67)	562.477 (1.78)	652.013 (2.09)	-29.470 (-0.11)	260.421 (1.50)	306.503 (1.87)
R^2	0.174	0.486	0.514	0.204	0.290	0.335
F-statistic	3.032	8.688	9.535	3.696	3.760	4.527

a. The chemical industry was found to be an outlier; see text.

change in trade performance over the period 1967–77, changes in the level of human capital inputs and perhaps in the flow of capital services have significant explanatory power. The negative impact of human capital is consistent with Bowen's (1983) finding that the U.S. growth rate of skilled labor as a percentage of total labor was one of the lowest in the world over the period 1963–75, as the United States was becoming relatively less abundant in human capital.

So far we have seen a consistently negative relationship between direct environmental regulatory expenditures and interindustry trade performance. Only the direct incidence of mandated pollution abatement costs has been considered. In the following section, the analysis turns to the direct and indirect incidence of regulatory costs, now extended to include the costs of nonenvironmental regulation.

The Direct and Indirect Effects of Regulation on Trade Performance

The preceding analysis of direct cost effects is useful for investigating what would happen to a certain industry's trade performance if the federal government increased the stringency of environmental regulations on that industry. An analysis of both direct and indirect cost effects, however, more readily suggests what would happen to the industry's trade performance if environmental regulation of all industries was made more stringent or if the environmental regulation applied to one of the industry's major upstream suppliers was increased.

The parent specification of equation 2 is again employed, as are the basic data on net exports and factor inputs. Now, however, the factor inputs are passed through the total requirements 1977 input-output matrix, yielding direct and indirect factor inputs for each I-O commodity. Using the Litan and Nordhaus (1983) data on the costs of economic regulation, it is possible to examine the direct and indirect effects of environmental and economic regulatory costs separately.

Table 8–7 reports the results for the application of direct and indirect inputs to equation 2. As before, results are shown with and without correction for heteroskedasticity and with and without the chemical industry (which continues to be an outlier). There was moderate evidence of heteroskedasticity in the GLS results, with $S^{-.25}$ providing the best explanation.

244 / INTERNATIONAL COMPETITIVENESS

Table 8-7. Total Factor Inputs and Net Export Performance, 1977 (t-statistics in parentheses).

	Without Heteroskedasticity Correction			With Heteroskedasticity Correction		
	All I-O Industries	Manufacturing I-O Industries	Manufacturing Excluding Chemicals[a]	All I-O Industries	Manufacturing I-O Industries	Manufacturing Excluding Chemicals[a]
Pollution abatement (ABATE)	-2.818 (-1.32)	-15.766 (-1.64)	-23.389 (-2.36)	-1.910 (-0.83)	-17.742 (-1.87)	-23.063 (-2.34)
Economic Regulation	1.101 (1.30)	0.266 (0.27)	0.709 (0.72)	0.857 (0.83)	0.138 (0.13)	0.442 (0.41)
Capital (K)	0.038 (0.92)	0.180 (0.65)	0.384 (1.35)	0.030 (0.49)	0.292 (1.09)	0.420 (1.53)
R&D	-0.264 (-0.030)	1.284 (3.07)	1.307 (3.25)	0.628 (0.77)	1.280 (3.16)	1.279 (3.22)
Human capital (HK)	-0.197 (-1.22)	-0.355 (-2.18)	-0.302 (-1.90)	-0.251 (-1.25)	-0.235 (-1.33)	-0.203 (-1.17)
Unskilled labor (UNSKILL)	0.943 (1.36)	1.853 (1.67)	1.306 (1.19)	1.136 (1.29)	0.871 (0.75)	0.608 (0.53)
Constant term	-267.812 (-0.41)	322.936 (0.96)	360.074 (1.07)	-151.310 (-0.34)	340.156 (1.28)	352.321 (1.35)
R^2	0.068	0.528	0.564	0.036	0.408	0.437
F-statistic	0.856	8.384	9.488	0.443	5.175	5.690

a. The chemical industry was found to be an outlier; see text.

Under each estimation, mandated pollution abatement expenditures have a negative impact on trade performance. At least in the case of manufacturing, this finding carries moderate but not overwhelming confidence, and its consistency with the pattern of previous findings in this study is noteworthy. Changes in regulatory costs associated with economic regulation cannot be shown to have any significant impact on trade performance at the industry level. The reasons for this result are speculative. The uncertain quality of the data on economic regulatory costs may be a major factor. Litan and Nordhaus (1983) relied on disparate studies employing disparate methods to estimate the allocative efficiency effects of complicated regulatory policies. Many of these studies employ narrow partial-equilibrium analyses. Environmental regulation raised the relative price of environmental resources for all industries, and the effect could reasonably be expected to involve a shift in the economy's mix of outputs away from environment-intensive production. By comparison, the general-equilibrium effects of, say, price and entry regulation in the airline industry seem less predictable and might well not be captured by an analysis based on a given input-output structure.

Total capital inputs have a consistently positive sign in Table 8–7, again in keeping with Bowen's (1983) finding that capital is a positive determinant of trade performance. Very little confidence, however, can be placed in capital's estimated impact on trade performance. Bowen also found that human capital and unskilled labor were negative and positive determinants, respectively, of trade performance in at least those (net import) sectors where the United States revealed a comparative disadvantage. This finding is reflected in Table 8–7 (the manufacturing sector was a net importer in 1977), with the most confidence adhering to the impact of human capital. As in the preceding analysis of direct factor inputs, R&D appears to be a significantly positive determinant of U.S. trade performance.

Conclusion

The analysis of this section has added regulatory costs to a commonly used model of net export performance. The addition of these costs has not upset the general findings of other analysts regarding the role of capital, human capital, unskilled labor, and R&D as determinants of trade performance. This congruence increases confidence in the results regarding regulatory costs, for these costs have made a net contribution to the explanation of trade performance. In particular, the important conclusion of this analysis is that environmental regulation has been a negative determinant of trade performance in the U.S. economy. No evidence has been uncovered to indicate that the same conclusion applies to nonenvironmental, economic regulation.

FACTOR ABUNDANCE, COMPARATIVE ADVANTAGE, AND THE TOTAL IMPACT OF REGULATORY COSTS

It is not particularly startling to find that an increase in the stringency and cost of environmental regulations has a negative effect on trade performance. The direction, if not the size, of the effect is as would be predicted by a comparative static analysis that asks what happens to U.S. firms' competitiveness when their costs are raised while their competitors' costs are held constant. Even in a general-equilibrium setting, the direction of the likely effect of this change seems straightforward: a rise in environmental regulation shifts the United States' output mix toward production of clean air and water (which are not sold directly on national or international markets) and away from those goods (i.e., manufactured goods) that it can buy on the world market. The nation's measured trade balance in goods other than clean air and water thus worsens.

Whatever the trade effect of a unilateral change in regulatory policy, the terms of current policy debate suggest that policy makers and involved parties are at least as interested in knowing whether the U.S. economy is more or less intensively regulated than its international competitors'. For example, we seem to be more willing to regulate the environment, regardless of optimality concerns, if we believe domestic firms are playing on a "level field"—that is, with foreign competitors who have to bear comparable environmental protection costs.

Leamer's (1980) clarification of the Heckscher-Ohlin view of international trade provides a surprisingly direct method for assessing the scarcity of environmental resources (represented by the abundance of regulation, from the perspective of the producing sector) in the United States relative to other factors of production and relative to other countries. In this section, I apply this framework to both environmental regulation and nonenvironmental economic regulation.

The Relative Abundance of Regulation in the United States

Leamer's analysis of the Heckscher-Ohlin theory of trade begins with the observation that, under the assumption of (1) factor price equalization, (2) competitive markets, (3) internationally identical and constant-returns-to-scale production functions, and (4) consumers with identical homothetic preferences worldwide, there exists a set of scalars ω_i for the $i = 1 \ldots I$ countries of the world and a $J \times N$ input-output matrix, A, of total (direct and indirect) J factor requirements for the production of N goods such that the vector of net exports of the ith country, XM_i, is related to the vector of i's endowment of factors, Z_i, by:

$$A \times XM_i = Z_i - \omega_i Z_w \qquad i = 1 \ldots I , \tag{3}$$

where Z_w is the world's factor endowment. Each country's factor endowments go into producing its output Q_i, so that $AQ_i = Z_i$. The fourth assumption means that each country's $N \times 1$ consumption vector, C_i, is proportional to world output such that $C_i = \omega_i Q_w$ (where Q_w is world output). Thus, ω_i is the ith country's claimed share, as a consumer, of the world's output.

Within this framework, one can describe trade in (embodied) factors, as opposed to trade in commodities. Specifically, because $XM_i = Q_i - C_i$, $A \times (Q_i - C_i) = Z_i - \omega_i Z_w$, and for each individual factor z^j ($j = 1 \ldots J$) there is an equation from (3) for each factor:

$$z^j_{xm} = z^j_i - \omega_i z^j_w , \tag{4}$$

where

z^j_{xm} = country i's implicit trade in factor j,

z^j_i = country i's endowment of the factor, and

z^j_w = the world's endowment of the factor.

From this, it follows that a country is a net exporter of z^j if its production makes a larger claim (z^j_i) on the world's endowment of z^j than the claim made by its consumption ($\omega_i z^j_w$). Conversely, the country is a net importer of factor z^j if its consumption employs the factor more intensely than does its production. With each country making a claim on the world factor endowments in proportion to its economic size (from assumptions 3 and 4), this means that country i is well or poorly endowed with factor z^j relative to the rest of the world (as opposed to relative to other factors) when z^j_{xm} is greater or less than zero, respectively.

In the case at hand, equation 4 provides a means of directly measuring whether the United States is implicitly more or less intensely regulated than its international competitors, given its size. If we can interpret the aggregate cost imposed on an industry by environmental regulation as the value of the nation's endowment of pollutable air and water resources claimed by that industry, equation 4 says that a positive value of z^j_{xm} means the nation is implicitly exporting pollutable resources. Actually, if we directly measure only the input-output matrix A for the United States and cannot directly verify assumption 3, a positive value of equation 4 indicates that the domestic production required to replace imported goods would embody less air and water than the goods that the nation exports. Conversely, a negative value would indicate that the nation is a net importer of pollutable air and water.[11]

In pushing this interpretation of environmental regulation, we again encounter the distinction between the *effective* endowment of environmental resources perceived by the producing sector and the true social-costed endowment. Pending a full cost-benefit analysis of U.S. environmental policy, the most that can be said is that the cost of environmental regulation represents the price that the political system has put on the nation's endowment of pollutable resources. Equation 4 then provides only a nonnormative, behavioral statement about the impact of environmental regulation. It is a measure of trade-revealed effective factor abundance.

Interpreting equation 4 as a measure of relative factor abundance may seem more reasonable for environmental regulation than in the case of nonenvironmental, economic regulation. While economic regulatory costs are embodied in U.S. exports and the domestic goods that would have to be produced to replace imports, there is no clear natural referent called "government regulation" that we can readily envision as a factor endowment implicitly embodied in trade, as we can in the case of "the environment." Nevertheless, equation 4 can be used to measure the relation between the costs of economic regulation that are embodied in exports and import-replacing domestic production. In this sense of trade-revealed abundance, (4) can suggest whether the United States is subject to more or less costly economic regulation than are other nations.

In Tables 8–8 through 8–11, the top panels report the values of the Heckscher–Ohlin–Leamer measure in equation 4 of trade-revealed factor abundance. Tables 8–8 and 8–9 apply to the entire seventy-nine-sector I–O economy for 1977 and 1967, respectively. Tables 8–10 and 8–11 report calculations for the manufacturing sector in the same years. To arrive at these tables, the direct costs of environmental regulation from Table 8–2 and Litan and Nordhaus's (1983) sector-by-sector compilation of economic regulatory costs were passed through the total (direct and indirect) requirements input-output table. This yields the factor embodiments shown in the third column of Table 8–2. Multiplication by the vectors of exports and imports yields the results in Tables 8–8 through 8–11.

Tables 8–8 and 8–10 indicate that the United States implicitly imported more pollutable air and water—more environmental costs—than it exported in 1977. This finding holds for both the total economy and the manufacturing sector. From equation 4, this indicates that, given the size of the nation's economy as reflected in ω_i, the nation's producers' endowment of environmental resources was small relative to the rest of the world's. In other words, trading patterns reveal the United States to have relatively more costly environmental policies than its international competitors—as is consistent with Table 8–3B and the relative stringency of U.S. environmental standards.

The plausibility of this result is reinforced by Tables 8–9 and 8–11, which apply to 1967, when no major federal environmental costs had yet been imposed. Although the environment was implicitly being zero-priced in 1967, it is informative to identify the implicit export and import of environmental resources before the rise of regulation. Tables 8–9 and 8–11 analyze this question by assuming that the shadow-valued input of environmental resources that was required directly and indirectly per unit of output in 1967 was the same as the more explicitly costed environmental input requirements in 1977. Based on this assumption, Tables 8–9 and 8–11 indicate that in 1967 the nation implicitly exported more pollutable resources than it imported (or more than would have been embodied in import-replacing domestic production).[12] Thus, it would appear that environmental regulation was a source of shifting comparative advantage over the period 1967–77.

Table 8-8. Heckscher-Ohlin-Leamer Tests of Trade-revealed Factor Abundance, All Industries, 1977 (*million dollars*).

	Total	Factor Dollars per Dollar of Exports/Imports
Pollution abatement costs		
Exported	$ 1,318.5	$0.0094
Imported	-1,800.5	0.0113
Capital costs		
Exported	51,112.4	0.3641
Imported	68,999.9	0.4342
R&D costs		
Exported	5,839.4	0.0416
Imported	4,150.0	0.0261
Human capital costs		
Exported	65,678.1	0.4679
Imported	65,812.3	0.4141
Unskilled labor costs		
Exported	11,572.9	0.0824
Imported	10,770.9	0.0678
Economic regulation costs		
Exported	3,750.2	0.0267
Imported	3,073.4	0.0193

	Factor Intensities in Production Relative to Consumption (ratio of factor i (column) intensity to factor j (row) intensity)					
	Pollution Abatement	Capital	R&D	Human Capital	Unskilled Labor	Economic Regulation
Pollution abatement	1					
Capital	0.9920	1				
R&D	0.9104	0.9177	1			
Human capital	0.9652	0.9730	1.0602	1		
Unskilled labor	0.9601	0.9678	1.0546	0.9947	1	
Economic regulation	0.9434	0.9510	1.0363	0.9774	0.9826	1

Table 8-9. Heckscher-Ohlin-Leamer Tests of Trade-revealed Factor Abundance, All Industries, 1967 (*million dollars*).

	Total	Factor Dollars per Dollar of Exports/Imports
Pollution abatement costs		
Exported	$ 370.0	$0.0102
Imported	-315.4	0.0134
Capital costs		
Exported	12,382.4	0.3424
Imported	8,326.8	0.3530
R&D costs		
Exported	1,393.1	0.0385
Imported	582.5	0.0247
Human capital costs		
Exported	12,610.8	0.3487
Imported	8,087.8	0.3429
Unskilled labor costs		
Exported	6,926.2	0.1915
Imported	4,346.3	0.1843

Factor Intensities in Production Relative to Consumption
(ratio of factor i (column) intensity to factor j (row) intensity)

	Pollution Abatement	Capital	R&D	Human Capital	Unskilled Labor
Pollution abatement	1				
Capital	0.9937	1			
R&D	0.9579	0.9640	1		
Human capital	0.9901	0.9964	1.0336	1	
Unskilled labor	0.9924	0.9987	1.0360	1.0023	1

Table 8-10. Heckscher-Ohlin-Leamer Tests of Trade-revealed Factor Abundance, Manufacturing Industries Only, 1977 (*million dollars*).

	Total	Factor Dollars per Dollar of Exports/Imports
Pollution abatement costs		
Exported	$ 1,032.4	$0.0074
Imported	1,375.6	0.0087
Capital costs		
Exported	30,204.1	0.2152
Imported	38,104.1	0.2398
R&D costs		
Exported	5,604.1	0.0399
Imported	3,968.5	0.0250
Human capital costs		
Exported	47,822.8	0.3407
Imported	54,665.0	0.3440
Unskilled labor costs		
Exported	7,265.2	0.0518
Imported	8,398.3	0.0528
Economic regulation costs		
Exported	1,750.4	0.0125
Imported	2,540.2	0.0160

Factor Intensities in Production Relative to Consumption (ratio of factor i (column) intensity to factor j (row) intensity)

	Pollution Abatement	Capital	R&D	Human Capital	Unskilled Labor	Economic Regulation
Pollution abatement	1					
Capital	0.9869	1				
R&D	0.9214	0.9336	1			
Human capital	0.9832	0.9963	1.0671	1		
Unskilled labor	0.9819	0.9950	1.0657	0.9988	1	
Economic regulation	1.0004	1.0137	1.0858	1.0175	1.0175	1

Table 8-11. Heckscher-Ohlin-Leamer Tests of Trade-revealed Factor Abundance, Manufacturing Industries Only, 1967 (*million dollars*).

	Total	Factor Dollars per Dollar of Exports/Imports
Pollution abatement costs		
Exported	$ 284.6	$0.0079
Imported	−243.9	0.0103
Capital costs		
Exported	7,448.5	0.2060
Imported	−5,861.8	0.2485
R&D costs		
Exported	1,317.0	0.0364
Imported	−540.2	0.0229
Human capital costs		
Exported	9,180.9	0.2539
Imported	6,186.6	0.2623
Unskilled labor costs		
Exported	4,566.2	0.1263
Imported	3,293.1	0.1396

	Factor Intensities in Production Relative to Consumption (ratio of factor i (column) intensity to factor j (row) intensity)				
	Pollution Abatement	*Capital*	*R&D*	*Human Capital*	*Unskilled Labor*
Pollution abatement	1				
Capital	1.0010	1			
R&D	0.9577	0.9567	1		
Human capital	0.9943	0.9933	1.0382	1	
Unskilled labor	0.9988	0.9977	1.0429	1.0045	1

With regard to other sources of shifting comparative advantage, Tables 8–8 through 8–11 indicate that from 1967 to 1977 the United States went from being a net exporter of capital to being a net importer of capital. This finding is consistent with a number of recent studies regarding the changing pattern of U.S. trade (e.g., Lawrence, 1983, and Bowen, 1983). In both 1967 and 1977, the United States was an exporter of R&D—again consistent with an observed comparative advantage in high-tech production (Lawrence, 1983). In 1977, the aggregate U.S. economy had a human capital trade balance of approximately zero. The manufacturing sector, however, showed substantial net imports. These figures represented shifts relative to 1967, when the country implicitly exported considerably more human capital than it imported. This finding does not appear to be consistent with Lawrence's (1983) conclusion that the United States is specializing more in skilled labor-intensive production—although, as noted, product-by-product comparisons of trade and factor intensity of the type Lawrence makes do not provide clear tests of a Heckscher-Ohlin theory of trade. The results of Tables 8–8 through 8–11, coupled with Lawrence's findings regarding human capital, may indicate a sort of Leontief paradox of the type that prompted Leamer's (1980) analysis of factor abundance-trade links in the n-good world. In 1977, the United States manufacturing sector was a net importer of unskilled labor, but the aggregate economy was a net exporter. This aggregate statistic reflects the Other Agricultural Products category, which embodies large amounts of the least skilled labor in the economy. Both the aggregate economy and the manufacturing sector were net exporters of unskilled labor in 1967.

Data on the costs of nonenvironmental, economic regulation are not available for 1967. In 1977, however, the aggregate U.S. economy was a net exporter of economic regulation. That is, the nation's exports embodied more direct and indirect economic regulatory costs than the import-replacing goods it could have produced. In the manufacturing sector, this conclusion is reversed. It is tempting to interpret this result to mean that the U.S. manufacturing sector, at least, is more heavily regulated than the corresponding sectors of its international competitors. But the strongest justifiable conclusion is that the U.S. manufacturing sector is subject to more costly *U.S.-style* economic regulation than its international counterparts; or, even more mildly, that U.S. production for export embodies fewer regulatory costs than import-replacing production. Since the mid-1970s, of course, there have been major acts of deregulation in such previously price-and-entry-regulated sectors as finance, energy, and transportation. Thus even these conclusions may well be inapplicable to the current state of international trade.

Relative Factor Intensities and Revealed Factor Abundance

Within a Heckscher-Ohlin context, the pattern of international trade reflects the abundance of factors relative to one another. To examine factor-by-factor relative abundance in the N-good, I-country world, Leamer (1980) shows that factor z^j is revealed by trade to be abundant relative to factor z^k if and only if:

$$z^j / (z^j - z^j_{xmi}) > z^k / (z^k - z^k_{xmi}) . \tag{5}$$

In our case, these ratios are positive, and equation 5 can be expressed as:

$$\frac{z^j / (z^j - z^j_{xmi})}{z^k / (z^k - z^k_{xmi})} > 1 . \tag{6}$$

The denominator on each side of (5) is simply the factor embodiment in consumption; and (6) says that a country is well-endowed with z^j relative to z^k if there is relatively more z^j embodied in the country's production per unit of z^j embodied in consumption than is the case for z^k.

If my conclusions regarding intercountry factor abundance are valid, they should be confirmed by examination of equation 6. If, for example, the nation is a net importer of pollutable resources because environmental regulation makes at-home pollution so expensive, then (b) should show the nation's environmental endowment per unit of consumption to be lower than the equivalent measure of abundance for other factors. The bottom panels of Tables 8-8 and 8-10 show the evaluation of (6) for each factor in both the aggregate economy and the manufacturing sectors in 1977. The numerator of (6) is the factor noted at the head of each column, with the corresponding row giving the factor represented in the denominator.

The bottom panel of Table 8–8 reveals environmental resources (i.e., pollution abatement expenditures) to be a scarce factor in the United States relative to all other factors in the aggregate economy in 1977 (i.e., the value of (6) is less than unity). This presumably reflects the impact of environmental regulation, for in 1967 the producing sector arguably treated the environment as a substantially free common-pool resource. The bottom panels of both Tables 8–9 and 8–11 calculate (6) for 1967, shadow-valuing environmental resources in that year at their same relative value as in 1977 and assuming that the imposition of environmental regulation left the total requirements input-output matrix unaltered.[13] These calculations suggest that environmental resources would have been scarce relative to all other factors used by the aggregate economy in 1967, and would have been scarce relative to all factors except capital in the manufacturing sector. By implication, the trade pattern for 1967 that is indicated in the top panels of Tables 8–9 and 8–11—net exports of pollutable resources—might have been reversed if the stringent environmental regulation of the 1970s had been imposed earlier.

Table 8–10 indicates that the only "factor" abundant relative to environmental regulation in 1977 was economic regulation (and that only in the manufacturing sector). Moreover, economic regulation was abundant relative to all other factors of manufacturing production in 1977 (i.e., the bottom row in the bottom panel of Table 8–10 is greater than unity in each case). The "abundance" of economic regulation costs in manufacturing is consistent with the implicit trade in such regulation—that is, with the finding in the top panel of Table 8–10 that the United States was an aggregate net importer of goods subject to economic regulation. For the aggregate economy, economic regulation was abundant relative to R&D, but scarce relative to environmental resources, capital, human capital, and unskilled labor (Table 8–8). In short, at least in the manufacturing sector, economic regulation has historically been a source of comparative disadvantage.

At least within the manufacturing sector, economic regulation appears to be even more costly than environmental regulation, and the United States implicitly has difficulty exporting embodied economic regulatory costs (Table 8–9). Yet the costs of economic regulation are the least defensible (on market failure grounds) of the nation's regulatory costs—recall that the economic regulatory costs employed here are based on Litan and Nordhaus's (1983) compilations of the *deadweight costs* of economic regulation. In terms of relative factor abundance, that is, the least desirable of regulatory costs are more burdensome than those of environmental regulation, which may conceivably improve welfare. Many of the reforms of economic regulation since the mid-1970s have been motivated by a view that such regulation had become particularly wasteful and distortive. The results produced here are not inconsistent with this view.

SUMMARY AND CONCLUSIONS

In struggling to explain particular industries' changing net export performance, the political sector has perhaps paid too much attention to the trade effects of domestic regulatory policies—particularly in the making of regulatory policy, as opposed to the making of trade policy. I suspect this is because regulation is viewed (properly) as a choice variable with understandable consequences for firms' costs and hence their potential trade performance. Analyses of inexorable forces of comparative advantage, esoteric discussions of exchange rate fluctuations, and translog descriptions of total factor productivity probably mean little to many interested participants in the regulatory process. In addition, as a choice variable, regulation seems to be viewed as one of the dimensions on which other countries might acquire an "unfair" competitive advantages for their industries. Interested parties have repeatedly sounded this theme in political debate.

There is little systematic evidence on the trade effects of domestic regulation above the level of the case study. In this chapter I have tried to produce some evidence on these effects at a relatively aggregate level. The usefulness of the reported results to the policy process, however, is uncertain. The trade effects of regulation are probably addressed most often on a case-by-case basis, corresponding to the usual case-by-case administration of regulation that follows initial periods of legislation and implementation. Nevertheless, the results of this study suggest certain generalizations.

Domestic environmental regulation appears to have a negative effect on industries' trade performance. Industries with higher direct or indirect costs of pollution control do less well in net export performance. I have found no corresponding evidence that nonenvironmental, price and entry regulation causes poor trade performance.

To the extent that policy makers use trade performance as a criterion for assessing regulatory proposals, the results reported here should make them less interested in stringent environmental control.

It is important to point out however, that environmental policy making should be governed by economic criteria that flow from the definition of allocative market failure and the desirability of optimally internalizing environmental externalities. Trade effects make little sense as an adjunct criterion. Indeed, the lesson may be that the national economic pie, defined as including nonmarket traded environmental resources, is larger if the United States specializes in "clean" goods and allows other countries to pollute themselves while manufacturing our imports.[14]

The imposition of environmental regulation in the early 1970s has been viewed here as a change in the endowment of pollutable environmental resources that the nation makes available to the producing sector of the economy. A Heckscher-Ohlin-Leamer look at this change in factor endowments indicates that, following the imposition of environmental regulation, the United States moved from being a net exporter of polluted, "used-up" environmental resources (as embodied in traded commodities) to being a net importer. That is, environmental regulation has been a source of comparative disadvantage to the United States. Nonenvironmental, economic regulation does not appear to have been a source of comparative disadvantage to the United States in the aggregate, although it may have been so for the manufacturing sector as of 1977. Given recent reforms, nonenvironmental, economic regulatory policy is probably not a continuing source of comparative disadvantage in the manufacturing sector.[15]

NOTES

1. The most obvious likely exception would be the naturally monopolistic industries subject to, for example, effective rate-of-return regulation. For such cases, the reasoning of this discussion would be reversed.
2. For a case study, see Kalt (1981).
3. The obvious exception would be agricultural price supports—if they are considered a form of price and entry regulation. This study does not examine the trade effects of agricultural price supports.
4. Such benefits are a component of the allocative (triangle) efficiency gain that could be measured at the point of regulation in the case of a welfare-improving environmental policy.
5. This judgment probably applies more readily to air pollution than to water pollution.

6. The most widely quoted alternative study of the costs of regulation, by DeFina and Weidenbaum (1978), put regulatory costs at approximately 6 percent of GNP. For a review, see Eads and Fix (1984).

7. See note 1.

8. This use of the input-output approach assumes that the multiple downstream buyers of an industry's output all have the same price elasticities of demand for the factor in question.

9. The midpoints of the Litan and Nordhaus ranges are used here. The sectors for which costs are reported are mining, transportation, broadcasting, financial markets, milk marketing, oil and gas, pharmaceuticals, automobiles, nuclear power, and labor. All but the last are allocated to the corresponding I-O industry. Labor costs (due to OSHA, Davis-Bacon, and the Equal Employment Opportunity Act) are not allocated to Table 8–2 because data on industry-level incidence are not available. Thus labor regulation and agricultural price support programs are the major omissions from Table 8–2.

10. See Leamer and Bowen (1981) for an extended discussion.

11. Note that equation 4 does not provide a direct test of the Heckscher-Ohlin theory, which focuses on the impact of factor endowments relative to one another as determinants of trade. Equation 4 provides a direct test of the classic two-good version of Heckscher-Ohlin only if we think of exports and imports as the only two (composite) commodities being produced. I examine the abundance of factors relative to one another below.

12. As in Bowen's (1983) cross-year comparisons, the 1967-77 comparisons here capture the Rybczynski effect of changing factor endowments on the pattern of goods trade, given input requirements, by using the 1977 input-output table. For a discussion of the effect of changing factor endowments on input requirements, given the pattern of trade, see Bowen (1983).

13. See note 12.

14, The internationalist will be interested in seeing that all countries optimally internalize environmental externalities. Since a clean environment is a demonstrably normal good, however, the implication is still that a wealthy nation should tilt its output mix toward preservation of clean environmental resources and away from embodied pollution. In any case, the economic criteria for environmental regulation should begin with a focus on the externality problem, rather than trade performance.

15. Roughly three-quarters of Litan and Nordhaus's (1983) estimated deadweight losses from economic regulation in 1977 occurred in oil, gas, broadcasting, banking, and transportation; all sectors that have been substantially deregulated in recent years.

REFERENCES

Arthur Andersen and Company, *Cost of Regulation, Study for the Business Roundtable* (New York: Arthur Andersen and Company, March 1979).

Bowen, Harry P., "Changes in the International Distribution of Resources and Their Impact on U.S. Comparative Advantage," *Review of Economics and Statistics* 65 (August 1983): 402–14.

Bowen, Harry P., and Joseph Pelzman, "U.S. Export Competitiveness: 1962–77," *Applied Economics* 16 (June 1984): 461–73.

Branson, William H., and Nikolaos Monoyios, "Factor Inputs in U.S. Trade," *Journal of International Economics* 7 (1977): 111–31.

Carlton, Dennis W., "Valuing Market Benefits and Costs in Related Output and Input Markets," unpublished, Chicago, 1978.

Deardorff, Alan V., and Robert M. Stern, "A Disaggregated Model of World Production and Trade: An Estimate of the Impact of the Tokyo Round," *Journal of Policy Modeling* 3 (1981): 127–52.

DeFina, Robert, and Murray Weidenbaum, *The Cost of Federal Regulation of Economic Activity* (Washington, DC: American Enterprise Institute, May 1978), Reprint No. 88.

Eads, George C., and Michael Fix, *Relief or Reform? Reagan's Regulatory Dilemma* (Washington, DC: Urban Institute Press,1984).

Environmental Protection Agency, *The Cost of Clean Air and Water: Report to Contress, 1984* (Washington, DC: EPA, 1984).

Glejser, H., "A New Test for Heteroscedasticity," *Journal of American Statistics Association* 64 (1969): 316–23.

Goedde, Alan G., "International Diversification and U.S. Regulatory Controls in the Pharmaceutical Industry," *Quarterly Review of Economics and Business* 22 (Spring 1982): 101–10.

Hall, Robert E., "Macroeconomic Policy Under Structural Change," in *Industrial Change and Public Policy* (Kansas City: Federal Reserve Bank of Kansas City, 1983).

Kalt, Joseph P., *The Economics and Politics of Oil Price Regulation: Federal Policy in the Post-Embargo Era* (Cambridge: M.I.T. Press, 1981).

Kendrick, John W., "International Comparisons of Recent Productivity Trends," in *Essays in Contemporary Economic Problems: Demand, Productivity, and Population*, ed. William Fellner (Washington, DC: American Enterprise Institute, 1981).

Lawrence, Robert Z., "Changes in U.S. Industrial Structure: The Role of Global Forces, Secular Trends and Transitory Cycles," in *Industrial Change and Public Policy* (Kansas City: Federal Reserve Bank of Kansas City, 1983).

_____, "Is Trade Deindustrializing America? A Medium-Term Perspective," *Brookings Papers on Economic Activity* 1 (1983): 129–71.

Leamer, Edward E., "The Leontief Paradox, Reconsidered," *Journal of Political Economy* 88 (June 1980): 495–503.

Leamer, Edward E., and Harry P. Bowen, "Cross-Section Tests of the Heckscher-Ohlin Theorem: A Methodological Comment," *American Economic Review* 71 (December 1981): 1040–43.

Litan, Robert E., and William D. Nordhaus, *Reforming Federal Regulation* (New Haven: Yale University Press, 1983).

Maskus, Keith E., "Evidence of Shifts in the Determinants of the Structure of U.S. Manufacturing Foreign Trade, 1958–76," *Review of Economics and Statistics* 65 (August 1983): 415–22.

Organization for Economic Cooperation and Development, *Environmental Policies in Japan* (Paris: OECD, 1977).

_____, *The State of the Environment in OECD Member Countries* (Paris: OECD, 1979).

Richardson, J. David, "International Trade Policies in a World of Industrial Change," in *Industrial Change and Public Policy* (Kansas City: Federal Reserve Bank of Kansas City, 1983).

Stern, Robert M., and Keith E. Kaskus, "Determinants of the Structure of U.S. Foreign Trade, 1958–76," *Journal of International Economics* 11 (1981): 207–24.

U.S. Department of Commerce, Bureau of Industrial Economics, *An Assessment of the Relative Effect of Certain Federal Regulations on the International Competitiveness of the U.S. Petrochemical Industry* (Washington, DC: Department of Commerce, 1983).

DATA SOURCES

Environmental Protection Agency, *The Cost of Clean Air and Water: Report to Congress, 1984* (Washington, DC: EPA, 1984).

National Science Foundation, *National Patterns of Science and Technology Resources, 1982* (Washington, DC: National Science Foundation, 1982).

Ritz, Philip M., "The Input-Output Structure of the U.S. Economy, 1972," *Survey of Current Business* 59 (February 1979): 34–72.

U.S. Department of Commerce, Bureau of the Census, "Pollution Abatement Costs and Expenditures," *Current Industrial Reports MA-200* (Washington, DC: U.S. Department of Commerce, various years).

U.S. Department of Commerce, Bureau of the Census, Foreign Trade Division, "Y.S. Exports by SIC-Based 2-Digit, 3-Digit, and 4-Digit Product Code," unpublished data, 1970–1983.

_____, "U.S. Imports for Consumption and General Imports, SIC Division by SIC-Based 2-Digit, 3-Digit, and 4-Digit Product Code," unpublished data, 1970–1983.

U.S. Department of Commerce, Interindustry Economics Division, "The Input-Output Structure of the U.S. Economy, 1967," *Survey of Current Business* 54 (February 1974): 24-56.

_____ , "The Input-Output Structure of the U.S. Economy, 1977," *Survey of Current Business* 64 (May 1984): 42-84.

U.S. Department of Labor, Bureau of Labor Statistics, *Supplement to Employment and Earnings* (Washington, DC: Department of Labor, various years).

CHAPTER 9

Capital and Ownership Structure: A Comparison of U.S. and Japanese Manufacturing Corporations

W. Carl Kester

Observers of global industrial competition have long noted an apparent decline in the competitiveness of many U.S. corporations vis-à-vis their Japanese counterparts. Of the many reasons offered to explain this trend, a commonly suggested financial one has been the greater use of bank debt by Japanese companies to fund their asset expansion. It is argued that the aggressive use of such a relatively low-cost source of capital creates a potent competitive weapon, enabling Japanese companies to charge lower prices and/or bear higher costs elsewhere in their cost structure than their rivals can.[1] Presumably, such an advantage will result in faster growth, higher market share, and ultimately greater long-term profitability for the Japanese manufacturers.

Using a large sample of manufacturing corporations, this study analyzes Japanese corporate capital and ownership structures and compares them to those of U.S. corporations. Specifically, it tests the hypothesis that Japanese manufacturing is more highly leveraged than U.S. manufacturing and attempts to explain the observed results.

The results of this study indicate that when leverage is measured on a market value basis and adjusted for liquid assets, there are no

This chapter is based on article by the same name that appeared in the Spring 1986 issue of *Financial Management*, pp. 5–16.

significant country differences in leverage between the United States and Japan beyond that which can be explained by variance in such factors as growth, profitability, risk, size, and industry classification. When leverage is measured on a book value basis, significantly higher leverage is found in Japan even after controlling for such factors.[2] However, this result is concentrated in mature heavy industries and does not appear to characterize the rest of Japanese manufacturing.

These results are notable in view of Japanese corporate ownership structures and financial institutional arrangements that tend to facilitate a greater use of debt than might normally be acceptable in the United States. Two hypotheses are advanced as explanations. First, unique Japanese bank-industry relationships thought to support heavy debt financing are more likely to characterize the mature, capital-intensive industries than the more rapidly growing high-technology and other light industries. Second, slower growth since the oil shock of the mid-1970s has resulted in increased internal funding by Japanese corporations and thus a loosening of ties with the major banks. The greater scope for managerial discretion that results may also lead Japanese managers to eschew otherwise attractive debt financing.

The first section of this chapter discusses why, in principle, one would expect Japanese manufacturers to make greater use of debt than U.S. manufacturers. It is followed by a description of the sample and the analysis used in this study. I conclude with a discussion of the empirical results within the context of the financial practices and institutional arrangements of the two countries.

COUNTRY DIFFERENCES IN INCENTIVES FOR USING DEBT FINANCING

An important incentive for using debt financing is the value arising from the tax deductibility of interest expense. However, there is little to suggest that substantial differences in leverage between the United States and Japan would arise from tax motives. Although the tax codes of the two countries differ on many fine points, they are not dramatically different at the corporate level as far as the statutory rates and the deductibility of interest expenses are concerned.[3] The maximum statutory tax rates in Japan, including inhabitants taxes and enterprises taxes, are 44.4 percent on declared dividends and 56.4 percent on all other income. These rates can be compared with a typical statutory rate of 50.3 percent for U.S. corporations, assuming average state and local taxes, which are deductible for federal tax purposes, of 8 percent.

Personal taxes do not seem any less effective an offset to the corporate tax advantage of debt in Japan than in the United States. Interest from corporate debt is taxable as ordinary income in Japan at marginal rates extending up to 75 percent for the national tax (80 percent if prefecture and municipal taxes are also included). Individuals in Japan can save up to ¥14 million in tax-free investments, but only ¥3 million (approximately $12,000) of this total can be invested in corporate fixed-income securities. The balance must be placed in postal accounts, government bonds, and employee benefit trusts to receive a tax exemption. Cash dividends are also taxed as ordinary income in Japan, while capital gains are essentially tax free.

Although it is difficult to establish a compelling tax rationale for higher Japanese leverage, other determinants of capital structure (such as costs of financial distress, agency costs, and asymmetric information) suggest that Japanese companies are capable in principle of suporting more debt than their U.S. counterparts. At the core of this conclusion is the ownership structure of Japanese corporations and the unique relationship that many of them have with commercial banks and other nonfinancial corporations. Specifically, Japanese banks are allowed to own as much as 5 percent of the equity of manufacturing corporations, and manufacturing corporations themselves are characterized by extensive interlocking equity ownership positions.

Table 9–1 presents data pertinent to the ownership structure of the Japanese companies used in this study's sample (described below in more detail). Of particular significance is the high concentration of ownership as reflected in the mean percentage held by the ten largest owners and the high mean fraction of shares held by financial institutions and other corporations.

Comparable ownership structure data for the U.S. sample were not available. However, Vishny and Shleifer (1984) report that their sample of 456 of the Fortune 500 firms had a mean percentage ownership of 14.3 percent for the largest shareholder. The mean for the five largest shareholders was 28.8 percent. At least one shareholder owned 5 percent or more of the firm for 354 companies in their sample. The largest shareholder owned less than 3 percent in only fifteen instances.

Table 9-1. The Ownership of Japanese Manufacturing Corporations.

	Share of Common Equity[a]
Financial institutions	34.48%
Investment trusts	0.88
Securities companies	2.33
Domestic corporations	25.73
Government	0.01
Individuals	29.53
Foreigners	7.04
Total	100.00%
Ten Largest Holders	44.44%

a. Mean percentage for the Japanese sample of 344 manufacturing corporations.
Source: Calculated from data reported in Daiwa Securities Research Institute, *Analyst's Guide: 1983* (Tokyo, 1983).

Although the comparison is not direct, it would appear that the concentration of corporate ownership is not very different between the United States and Japan. The *composition*, however, is quite different: Japanese companies are more heavily owned by banks and other corporations.

The concentration of equity ownership in the hands of one or several large parent companies and a number of major banks (twelve large "city banks" plus the Bank of Tokyo account for approximately 60 percent of the intermediated credit to large corporations in Japan) results in an extended "family" of closely related companies. In essence, such large industrial groups, called *keiretsu*, are modern versions of the prewar *zaibatsu*, which were organized around powerful holding companies. The *keiretsu*, however, are more loosely organized and depend more heavily on bank leadership than was generally true of the *zaibatsu*.

The Japanese corporate ownership structure and banking relationships tend to reduce the costs of financial distress. Such costs should be construed broadly to include the paralysis of corporate strategy and potential loss of competitive position that usually accompanies financial embarrassment even before actual bankruptcy occurs. Temporary financial adversity is often met in Japan by considerable aid from other companies within the industrial group, in the form of stretched receivables, prompt cash payment of payables, favorable discriminatory pricing, or even direct managerial assistance.

More serious financial embarrassment will involve the company's lenders. Usually a troubled company's main bank will coordinate rescue efforts, which can extend from the arrangement of loans from other banks to the arrangement of a merger with another company within the industrial group. If bankruptcy and reorganization become necessary, the main bank will effectively adopt a subordinated position by absorbing all losses itself, thus eliminating the need for protracted negotiations among other claimants. As a typical example of this practice, Suzuki and Wright (1984) note the voluntary repayment of all Kojin Corporation's debt by Dai-Ichi Kangyo Bank, the main lender, when Kojin went bankrupt.

Agency costs associated with debt should also be reduced by Japanese corporate ownership structure and lending practices. As discussed by Jensen and Meckling (1976) and Myers (1977), debt may create adverse investment incentives if opportunities exist to transfer value from creditors to equity owners, or if valuable investment opportunities mature before the outstanding debt.

If lenders are rational, such creditor-owner conflicts will result in residual losses borne by the equity owners, in the form of higher yields on the debt or even in credit rationing. The conflict can be relieved, however, to the extent that ownership and credit extension are embodied within the same entity. As suggested by the data in Table 9–1, such a dual role is a salient characteristic of Japanese lenders. It is not nearly so common in the United States, where banks are prohibited from owning equity and few if any coordinated efforts are made to combine debt and equity ownership beyond the issuance of equity-linked debt securities.

The typical terms and covenants of Japanese debt also seem likely to reduce agency costs more effectively than is the case in the United States. Most of the debt of Japanese companies is short term, and most of that is supplied by banks in the form of promissory notes with 90 to 120 days maturity. These notes are generally rolled over continually for a period of years. Since 1975, interest on the notes has been negotiated independently by each bank with its clients. However, other terms are uniform across banks and borrowers, since virtually all notes conform to the basic model form drafted by the Federation of Bankers' Associations of Japan.[4]

In contrast to the United States, where the most commonly used forms of corporate debt are unsecured, Japanese bank loans and bonds generally require collateral. Real property, securities, obligation rights (i.e., notes and accounts receivable) and inventory are the most common forms, because of their liquidity or explicit title. Long-term bonds that are not explicitly secured generally have indentures containing a standard negative pledge that prohibits the securing of other new or existing obligations ahead of the bonds and/or a financial restriction clause limiting the amount of additional long-term debt that can be obtained. However, they appear to lack most of the other restrictions common among U.S. bond indentures, such as investment and dividend restrictions.[5]

The short-term, secured characteristics of Japanese corporate debt should lower the agency costs normally associated with the use of debt, thus permitting higher leverage than might be observed in the United States. The continual rolling over of short-term debt, for example, is mentioned by Myers (1977) as one means of alleviating the potential underinvestment problem associated with debt. The widespread use of secured debt should also lower agency costs by limiting monitoring costs and reducing the scope for asset substitution. Stulz and Johnson (1983) point out that the funding of new projects with secured debt can also help relieve the underinvestment problem by enabling shareholders to capture a larger fraction of the project's value than might be possible with unsecured financing.

Information effects on capital structure should also favor relatively higher leverage in Japan. Myers and Majluf (1984) show that if company insiders have information about the firm's prospects that is superior to that of rational capital market investors, a new issue of risky securities such as equity will be underpriced from the perspective of insiders as public investors hedge against the possibility that insiders possess unfavorable information. This will cause companies with favorable prospects to rely as much as possible on internal financing and the issuance of safe securities, to avoid the underpricing or the forgoing of an otherwise valuable project. Thus, where capital needs exceed internal cash flow, where low-risk debt can be issued, and where information is held asymmetrically, one would expect to find highly leveraged capital structures.

All these conditions appear more characteristic of Japanese manufacturing than of U.S. manufacturing. Nominal growth has been more rapid in Japan than in the United States, and short-term secured debt, which would certainly be high in the pecking order of financing alternatives, is also used much more heavily in Japan. Information asymmetries between company insiders and public securities markets also appear more pronounced in Japan than in the United States, although the evidence for this conclusion is largely indirect and circumstantial. Japanese corporations face less stringent disclosure requirements than do U.S. companies and are well known for their secrecy. The Tokyo Stock Exchange seems to exhibit characteristics symptomatic of information asymmetries that might further discourage companies from raising equity capital publicly.[6] Bronte (1982, p. 169) makes the following observation:

> ... the lack of public disclosure, the laissez faire attitude taken by government officials on enforcing regulations, the frequent manipulation of stock prices, and the restrictions on free competition can make the [Tokyo Stock Exchange] a hazardous place for the uninformed investor. Many market practices in Tokyo are clearly illegal in other capital markets. . . . These factors often combine to produce highly volatile share price movements.

It should be noted that such information asymmetries are unlikely to be as severe between manufacturing companies and their lenders, particularly the major city banks. These banks maintain very close contact with borrowers, often have board representation, and are frequently involved in major decisions or substantial changes in company policy. In the event of financial distress, banks have virtually unlimited access to corporate records and may place officers directly in top management positions. As far as an information effect on capital structure is concerned, such close relationships between lenders and borrowers in Japan should reinforce a preference for bank debt.

Finally, as often noted, the Japanese financial system is permeated by implicit government guarantees on the liabilities of various financial and nonfinancial corporations. It is claimed that such guarantees exist for companies in certain industries targeted by the government for development and rapid growth, such as steel, electric power, and shipbuilding in the immediate postwar years, or semiconductors, computers, and industrial robots in more recent years.[7] Implicit guarantees also appear to exist for the major banks for which the Bank of Japan has made clear in word and deed that financial failure will be precluded.[8]

In both instances, holders of bank liabilities and securities of companies in targeted industries effectively possess a put option that can be exercised against the government. By reducing or even eliminating default risk, such puts ought to result directly in lower-cost debt and greater debt capacity from the point of view of the issuing corporations than would be the case in the absence of implicit guarantees. To the extent that the resulting lower cost of bank capital is passed on to borrowers through competitive activity, as Wellons (1985) argues, the debt capacity of all manufacturing corporations will be increased, as well as that of targeted industries.

DATA AND METHODOLOGY

In general, Japanese patterns of corporate finance and ownership structure appear conducive to the use of more substantial debt financing than is the common practice in the United States. To determine if this is in fact the case, the empirical part of this study is designed to test the null hypothesis that there are no differences in debt-equity ratios between U.S. and Japanese corporations after controlling for several likely determinants of capital structure: growth, profitability, risk, size, and industry classification. These have been employed in other empirical tests of capital structure differences among countries, with mixed results.[9] A linear model is specified, and coefficients are estimated using ordinary least squares (OLS).

The regression analysis employs April 1, 1982, through March 31, 1983, cross-sectional data for 344 Japanese companies and 452 U.S. companies in twenty-seven industries. The data are drawn from two primary sources. Japanese data are obtained from the *Analyst's Guide 1983* issued by Daiwa Securities Co. Ltd. (1983). All companies contained therein are listed on the first section of the Tokyo Stock Exchange. In addition, Japanese companies are screened so that the final sample includes only manufacturing concerns in industry classifications that contain at least five companies.

The U.S. data are drawn from the *Compustat Annual Industrial File.* Any stock price data missing from the *Compustat* file are taken from the daily CRSP tapes. Only manufacturing concerns with equity publicly traded on the New York and American Stock Exchanges are included.

The industries represented in the sample are listed in Table 9–2. The definition of each conforms to that used by Daiwa Securities in the *Analyst's Guide.* U.S. companies are classified into these industries on the basis of their Standard and Poor's (S&P) industry codes, which are derived from SIC classifications. Generally, there is a close match between the two systems of industry classifications. Occasionally, however, it is necessary to combine two or more S&P codes to match the Daiwa and S&P industry definition properly. Industries for which there are particularly poor matches, because of either definition or dramatic imbalance in the numbers of Japanese and U.S. firms, are excluded.

Composite balance sheets for the sample are shown in Table 9–3. It appears that the sample used in this study conforms to certain stylized images of Japanese and U.S. corporations. That is, Japanese companies appear to be more highly leveraged than U.S. companies on a mean book value basis and make considerably greater use of short-term debt. They are, however, more liquid than U.S. firms insofar as they have higher balances of cash, securities, and receivables, but less inventory, as a percentage of total assets.

Debt Ratios

A number of different debt-equity ratios are specified for use as the dependent variable in regression analysis (see Table 9–4). A set of ratios using book values is employed both to afford comparison with other studies using book ratios and to reflect the difficulty of borrowing against growth options in contrast to real assets in place (see Myers, 1977). In the first of the book value ratios, debt for both countries is defined to include all notes payable, short-term debt, bonds, other types of long-term debt including convertible debt, if any, and capitalized leases. Book equity includes all preferred stock, common stock, and retained earnings.

For Japanese companies, book equity also includes legal reserves, special reserves, and long-term liability reserves. Briefly, the legal reserve is simply a set-aside of retained earnings made at the rate of 10 percent of cash dividends paid until the reserve equals 25 percent of stated capital. Cash dividends cannot be paid out of the legal reserve.

Most of the special reserves and the long-term liability reserve also represent charges against retained earnings, although their use is motivated by the fact that they are tax-deductible provisions. The special reserves are generally tax-deductible provisions designated annually by the government and applicable only to specific industries (e.g., reserves for computer repurchase losses, dry weather, and

Table 9-2. Industry Classification.

	Standard & Poor's Industry Codes Included	Net Debt		Number of Companies in the Sample		
		Book Value Equity	Market Value Equity	Japan	U.S.	Total
Nonferrous metals	3330,3341,3350	3.791	1.106	11	13	24
General chemicals	2800	2.945	1.256	21	16	37
Steel	3310	1.973	1.665	35	35	70
Paper	2600	1.732	1.364	16	25	41
Paint	2850	1.548	0.614	7	5	12
Petroleum refining	2911	1.548	1.117	6	33	39
Audio equipment	3651	1.539	0.631	7	10	17
Textiles	2200	1.405	1.296	29	23	52
Cement	3241	1.298	1.366	6	10	16
Glass	3210,3221	1.213	1.087	5	8	13
Soaps and detergents	2841	1.143	0.683	6	8	14
Apparel	2300	1.021	0.951	14	41	55
Tire and rubber	3000	1.021	0.835	8	14	22
Motor vehicles	3711	0.922	0.594	9	6	15
Plastics	2820,3079	0.843	0.792	18	25	43

Agricultural machinery	3520	0.836	1.082	5	5	10
Electrical machinery	3600,3620	0.813	0.376	14	12	26
Construction machinery	3530,3531	0.688	0.810	6	12	18
Electronic parts	3670,3674,3679	0.614	0.358	19	34	53
Motor vehicle parts	3714	0.488	0.500	20	16	36
Machine tools	3540	0.472	0.425	10	15	25
Photo equipment	3861	0.468	0.222	7	7	14
Alcoholic beverages	2082,2085	0.427	0.284	8	10	18
Communication equipment	3661	0.356	0.186	15	24	39
Confectionery	2065	0.326	0.286	6	5	11
Pharmaceuticals	2380	0.194	0.079	25	23	48
Household appliances	3630	0.102	0.244	13	13	26

Source: Calculated from data reported in Daiwa Securities Research Institute, *Analyst's Guide: 1983* (Tokyo, 1983).

Table 9–3. Common Size Balance Sheet, 1983 (*sample mean percentage of total assets*).

	Japan[a]	United States[b]
Assets		
Cash and securities	18.7%	8.6%
Accounts receivable	14.9	21.4
Notes receivable	10.8	—
Inventory	16.4	25.0
Other current assets	2.5	2.2
Total current assets	63.3	57.2
Net property, plant, and equipment	23.9	35.7
Investments and advances	12.5	5.5
Intangibles	0.2	1.6
Other assets	0.1	—
Total assets	100.0%	100.0%
Liabilities		
Accounts payable	7.5%	8.8%
Short-term debt	15.9	6.4
Notes payable	16.4	—
Taxes payable	—	1.4
Other current liabilities	7.0	8.8
Short-term liability reserves	3.7	—
Total current liabilities	50.5	25.4
Long-term debt	13.5	19.0
Deferred taxes	—	3.3
Other long-term liabilities	0.6	1.9
Long-term liability reserves	4.4	—
Special reserves	0.1	—
Equity		
Preferred stock	30.9%	1.0%
Common shareholders' equity	—	49.4
Total liabilities and equity	100.0%	100.0%

a. 344 companies in sample.
b. 302 companies in sample.
Source: Calculated from data reported in Daiwa Securities Research Institute, *Analyst's Guide: 1983* (Tokyo, 1983).

Table 9-4. Summary Statistics of Debt Ratios, April 1, 1982–March 31, 1983.

Debt/Equity Ratios Using:	Entire Sample (796)			Japan (344)			United States (452)		
	Mean	Median	Standard Deviation	Mean	Median	Standard Deviation	Mean	Median	Standard Deviation
Book value equity									
Gross debt	1.592	0.621	2.872	2.703	1.605	3.822	0.745	0.456	1.332
Net debt	1.153	0.473	2.357	1.910	1.000	3.098	0.577	0.340	1.382
Fully adjusted debt	0.975	0.391	2.168	1.494	0.636	2.860	N.R.	N.R.	N.R.
Market value equity									
Gross debt	1.113	0.639	1.329	1.416	0.949	1.444	0.882	0.490	1.184
Net debt	0.812	0.424	1.164	0.976	0.590	1.174	0.687	0.342	1.142
Fully adjusted debt	0.713	0.356	1.129	0.729	0.371	1.077	N.R.	N.R.	N.R.

N.R. = not relevant.
Source: Calculated from data reported in Daiwa Securities Research Institute, *Analyst's Guide: 1983* (Tokyo, 1983).

special repairs on large ships or blast furnaces). The long-term liability reserve is related to a company's severance indemnity plan and approximates 40 percent of the liability that would be incurred should all employees voluntarily separate at the same time.[10]

Other debt-equity ratios are specified by adjusting debt in several ways. A "net" debt-equity ratio is calculated for both U.S. and Japanese companies by subtracting cash and marketable securities from total debt as previously defined. A "fully adjusted" debt ratio is also calculated for Japanese companies by subtracting notes receivable from net debt (for U.S. companies, which do not report material amounts of notes receivable, "net" debt and "fully adjusted" debt are identical). Notes receivable in Japan are commercial instruments used in intercorporate transactions in lieu of cash settlements. Manufacturers typically discount such notes at banks or occasionally at other companies to meet working capital needs. Since uniform ninety-day notes have been in effect since 1975, these negotiable instruments have become a kind of "semi-currency" among commercial enterprises.[11] As such, a strong case can be made for treating them like cash when measuring financial leverage.

A set of debt-to-value ratios is also calculated for each of the preceding definitions of debt by using the market value of equity rather than the book value. Market values are determined using closing market prices on the last trading day of each company's fiscal year.

Debt-to-value ratios are a better representation of leverage to the extent that substantial differences exist between the market value and book value of real assets in place. This is likely to be true for Japanese companies, which typically carry assets such as land and investments in affiliates at historical cost rather than at current market value. Since the Japanese industrial land price index increased from 100 to 3,288 between 1955 and 1981 (see Elston, 1981), and the Tokyo Stock Exchange index increased sevenfold between 1968 and 1983, this gap in value can be large.

Explanatory Variables

Expected profitability is included as an explanatory variable in the reported regressions since debt policy may be influenced by a company's ability to service debt and fund projects internally with anticipated cash flow. Profitability, therefore, is defined as earnings before interest, taxes, noncash expenses, discontinued operations, and extraordinary items. This sum is scaled by dividing by average gross total assets to yield a return-on-assets ratio.[12] To obtain an estimate of expected profitability for regression purposes, a simple OLS prediction of return on assets is calculated for each company using observations for the five preceding years. The sum of squared residuals from each of these regressions is used in the final regression as a proxy for the volatility or risk, of return on assets.

The growth variable is defined as the compound average annual rate of growth in revenues between 1978 and 1982. Revenues rather than assets are chosen as a basis for measuring growth in order to eliminate variance that might arise exclusively from differences in the historical cost basis used to value most assets carried on the balance sheet. While potential differences in revenue recognition between countries and among individual companies may also introduce biases in the measurement of growth, revenues have the overriding virtue of being measured on a current dollar/yen basis.

The volume of sales, measured in millions of dollars, is included in the regression to test for a possible relation between size and leverage. Yen are converted to dollars using the average spot exchange rate for the twelve months of a given company's fiscal year. While there is no theoretical foundation for a size effect on leverage, size may proxy for other relevant variables in such a way that a positive relation to leverage might be observed. For instance, size may proxy for information asymmetries between inside and outside investors, which are likely to be less severe for large, complex companies. Hence, the incentives to preserve financial slack, as described by Myers and Majluf (1984), may not be as great for large firms.

Dummy variables for twenty-six of the twenty-seven industries are included in the regression to test for industry effects in the determination of capital structure. These might plausibly arise from industry-specific institutional arrangements, tax allowances, or other financial advantages due to government policies. The omitted industry dummy is that for photographic equipment.

Finally, a country dummy is included to test for a significant country effect in the determination of debt-equity ratios. The country dummy takes the value of one for U.S. companies and zero for Japanese companies.

RESULTS

The regression results for each leverage specification are presented in Table 9-5. The country dummy variable has a negative and signifi-

Table 9-5. Summary of Regression Results (t-statistics in parentheses).

Debt/Ratio Specification	Constant	Country[a]	Profit-ability	Risk	Growth	Size	R-Squared	F-Statistics	Degrees of Freedom
Gross debt/book value equity	2.288 (3.32)	-1.844 (-9.65)	-6.551 (-4.49)	-3.475 (-0.35)	1.662 (1.52)	-0.255 E-04 (-1.51)	0.262	8.781	764
Gross debt/market value equity	1.134 (3.72)	-0.418 (-4.94)	-5.920 (-9.18)	-4.392 (-0.99)	1.833 (3.78)	-0.108 E-04 (-1.45)	0.325	11.888	764
Net debt/book value equity[b]	1.615 (2.80)	-1.225 (-7.66)	-6.115 (-5.01)	-5.375 (-0.64)	1.717 (1.87)	-0.222 E-04 (-1.57)	0.233	7.474	764
Net debt/market value equity[b]	0.712 (2.56)	-0.190 (-2.46)	-5.25 (-8.92)	-3.012 (-0.75)	1.990 (4.50)	-0.848 E-05 (-1.25)	0.269	9.056	764
Fully adjusted debt/book value equity[c]	1.291 (2.39)	-0.809 (-5.40)	-5.758 (-5.06)	-5.627 (-0.72)	1.576 (1.84)	-0.213 E-04 (-1.61)	0.202	6.266	764
Fully adjusted debt/market value equity[c]	0.554 (2.02)	0.068 (0.90)	-5.202 (-9.02)	-3.737 (-0.94)	1.786 (4.11)	-0.849 E-05 (-1.27)	0.246	8.076	764

a. The country dummy variable takes the value of 0 for Japanese companies and 1 for U.S. companies.
b. Net debt equals gross debt less cash and securities.
c. Fully adjusted debt equals gross debt less cash, securities, and notes receivable.

cant coefficient when the debt ratio is specified on a book value basis, indicating significantly higher leverage for Japanese companies regardless of how debt is defined and after controlling for other factors. The extent of the difference diminishes, however, when cash and notes receivable are deducted from gross debt.

A negative and significant coefficient for the country dummy variable is also obtained when a market value debt ratio is specified and debt is defined on either a gross or a net basis. However, the estimated coefficient becomes *positive* and *insignificant* for the fully adjusted market value debt ratio. The inference is that there is no significant difference in leverage among U.S. and Japanese corporations beyond that explained by the other factors included in this specification.

Although omitted from Table 9–5, four or five of the estimated coefficients for the industry dummy variables are positive and significant at a 5 percent level of error, the number depending on which specification of the book value debt ratio is used. Roughly twice as many industry dummy coefficients are positive and significant when market value debt ratios are used. Nearly all significant industry dummy coefficients represent industries with average debt-equity ratios above the median for the entire sample. In fact, for the book value specifications, the significant industry dummies are all for industries with average debt-equity ratios in the upper quartile of the sample. Most of these are mature heavy industries, including steel, general chemicals, nonferrous metals, paper, and petroleum refining.

Separate regressions were estimated for the U.S. and Japanese subsamples, and a test of their homogeneity was conducted. The F-ratios were significant for all specifications of leverage at a 1 percent level of error or better.

Finally, to determine if the country effect is concentrated in a few industries or is simply the result of different industrial compositions in the two countries, separate regressions were run for each of the twenty-seven industries. The results generally confirm that only some of the industries, not the broad sample, are characterized by significantly higher leverage for Japanese corporations.[13] Nine of the twenty-seven estimated coefficients for the country dummy variable are negative and significantly different from zero when book value debt ratios are specified. The nine industries are steel, nonferrous metals, general chemicals, paper, petroleum refining, motor vehicles, textiles, glass, and plastics. In contrast to these mature and predominantly heavy industries, the high-technology industries and the various types of machinery industries do not exhibit significant differences in leverage between countries. When market value debt ratios are used, only two estimated coefficients for the country dummy variable are negative and significant (petroleum refining and motor vehicles), while three are actually *positive* and significant (electrical machinery, pharmaceuticals, and household appliances).

DISCUSSION

With the exception of taxes, most of the major financial institutional arrangements in Japan favor greater debt financing than is common in the United States. But the empirical evidence presented here is at variance with this prediction. Significantly higher Japanese leverage does appear to characterize some industries when debt ratios are calculated with book equity. But this is not true for most industries or companies in the sample after correcting for country differences in accounting methods and working capital management, and after controlling for several likely determinants of leverage. When debt ratios are calculated with market valued equity, the evidence of higher Japanese leverage is even less compelling.

Two observations may help explain these results. First, Japanese manufacturing in general, and light industry in particular, appears to be reducing bank borrowing with a concomitant loosening of bank control and an increase in the scope of managerial discretion. Second, those institutional arrangements that contribute to lower costs of financial distress, lower agency costs associated with debt, and fewer informational asymmetries between manufacturers and banks do not necessarily characterize all Japanese industries uniformly. Specifically, large Japanese companies in mature heavy industries may be able to exploit such arrangements more fully than smaller companies in newer light industries.

Diverse Bank-Industry Relationships

Major Japanese banks are themselves a fairly heterogeneous group. At a broad level, they may be classified into three basic types: large "city" banks, trust banks, and long-term credit banks. Regulation and tradition have confined their respective activities to certain types of loans within certain industries and geographic areas. The overall result has been to benefit heavy industries disproportionately.

The three long-term credit banks, for example, are former government financial institutions that maintain very close ties with the government through their high-volume purchases of government bonds, their hiring of retiring senior ministry officials, and their "loans" of staff members to assist in the preparation of government policies. Because of these government ties, their five- to seven-year loans or their participation in a project financing, however small, is often interpreted as evidence of government favor and the existence of a de facto guarantee. Historically, their lending base has been dominated by heavy industries such as electric power, steel, chemicals, oil refining, automobiles, and shipbuilding.[14]

The twelve major city banks and the Bank of Tokyo can be further divided into subsets with different lending bases. Only four of these banks—the Sumitomo, Mitsui, Mitsubishi, and Fuji banks—are directly descendant from the powerful prewar *zaibatsu* banks. These banks continue to extend between 20 percent and 30 percent of their loans to their traditional industrial groups, which are essentially the same set of heavy industries that form the primary lending base of the long-term credit banks. The coordination among banks and clients generally thought to characterize all Japanese manufacturing seems far more prevalent among these former *zaibatsu* banks than the others. The presidents of their industrial groups' core companies, for instance, meet monthly and are formally recognized as policy-coordinating bodies for their groups.

The seven Japanese trust banks were also required to focus their lending activity in heavy industries until 1971. Changes in banking laws during that year permitted them to expand lending in other areas. However, most of this expansion has taken place in the personal housing and consumer finance markets rather than in corporate lending.

Among the remaining major Japanese banks are six "new" city banks formed by mergers during the 1930s and 1940s, two former government banks that became privately owned during the U.S. occupation, and the Bank of Tokyo, which focuses on international finance under a unique charter that, for a time, gave it an exclusive right to engage in foreign exchange transactions. These banks either have not been affiliated with distinct industry groups, as in the case of the Bank of Tokyo and the Hokkaido Takushoku Bank (a former government bank), or have had much looser ties. The new city banks in particular have usually lent to newer and more rapidly growing industries, with less than 10 percent of their loan portfolio being concentrated in their industry froups.

In view of these activities and arrangements of the various bank groups, the uniquely higher leverage of heavy industry in Japan is more easily understood. For the most part, heavy, mature industries appear to have experienced the greatest degree of coordinated activity among *keiretsu* members, the closest contact with main lenders, and the greatest benefit from implicit guarantees within the Japanese financial system. In principle, this should contribute to their willingness and ability to support more debt than their U.S. counterparts or the rest of Japanese manufacturing. To the extent that these heavy industries are also populated by large corporations with significant bilateral bargaining power vis-à-vis the major banks, any benefits derived from implicit government guarantees on bank liabilities are more likely to be appropriated by these large corporations in the form of bigger and/or lower-cost loans.[15] This should contribute further to their relatively high degree of leverage.

Managerial Discretion

A second factor that could contribute to the observed results is that professional Japanese management may be increasingly functioning to maximize its own utility rather than to increase shareholder value. That is, despite the clear value-creating incentives to use debt in Japan, managers may eschew debt financing in order to increase their scope of managerial discretion whenever possible.[16]

Clearly, a drawback of the Japanese financial system from the professional manager's point of view is that bank ownership of equity, the constant close scrutiny of lenders, direct lender involvement in some major decisions, and the occasional insertions of bank officers into management all limit management's independence. Moreover, the shareholder benefits that might accrue from such arrangements are not likely to reward Japanese managers heavily. While some top managers may own equity in their employers, officers are prohibited from owning stock options and explicit profit-sharing contracts are considered socially unacceptable. Executive compensation generally takes the form of a fixed salary plus a bonus paid after the annual meeting. The bonus, however, is only nominally related to performance. Bonuses are fixed within industry norms and are withheld only if the company omits its cash dividend (but are not raised if the dividend is increased). For all practical purposes, bonuses are considered part of regular compensation.

Whether an intended result or a mere by-product of changing capital needs, many Japanese manufacturing companies appear to be escaping the control and discipline imposed by the institutional arrangements accompanying heavy bank borrowing. Indirect evidence of this is provided by the trend toward greater reliance on internal financing and more direct external financing rather than bank loans. Bronte (1982) reports that internal sources provided 34.5 percent of long-term funds raised by Japanese corporations in 1970, but 50.7 percent in 1979. After netting out debt refinancing, internal sources accounted for 50.5 percent of net new capital invested in 1970 and 102.4 percent in 1979, indicating that internally generated cash is being used to retire debt.[17] The trend appears most pronounced in such high-technology industries as electronics, pharmaceuticals, and communications equipment as well as other light industries such as cosmetics and photo equipment. Recently, some companies in these sectors of manufacturing have flatly refused bank nominees for their board of directors.

CONCLUSION

After adjusting for accounting reserves and liquid assets, Japanese manufacturing is not as highly leveraged as it might first appear. Indeed, on a market value basis there is no significant country difference in leverage between U.S. and Japanese manufacturing after controlling for characteristics such as growth, profitability, risk, size, and industry classification.

While a significant country difference exists when leverage is measured on a book value basis, this result is concentrated among the mature capital-intensive industries. It does not appear to be a general characteristic common to all Japanese manufacturing.

It must still be recognized that the *composition* of Japanese capital and ownership structure is quite different from that commonly observed in the United States. Moreover, it is different in ways that could result in a competitive advantage for Japanese corporations even if the overall degree of leverage is not significantly different. By blunting incentives to engage in asset substitution or to underinvest, the rolling over of short-term bank loans and the substantial ownership of equity by major lenders are effective means of promoting optimal investment while funding heavily with debt.

Japanese managers and industrial policy makers should be aware of such beneficial arrangements as corporations loosen their bank relationships and redirect their sources of capital. Despite the potential benefits of such trends, one cost is likely to be the emergence of agent-principal conflicts that have not been of major concern in the past. Depending on how and to what extent they are resolved, the future investment policies of Japanese corporations could be distorted and their competitiveness impaired.

For U.S. managers and policy makers, it should be apparent that the competitive implications of the Japanese financial system and corporate capital structure are by no means straightforward. A comparatively high level of short-term debt carried on the liability side of a Japanese company's balance sheet certainly need not imply financial weakness. But neither can it be interpeted as prima facie evidence that the company enjoys a competitive advantage founded on a low-cost source of capital. In light of the complexities of the Japanese financial system, such a conclusion might safely follow only after the firm's capital structure is analyzed in connection with its asset base, ownership structure, industry group relations, and lending group composition.

NOTES

1. See, for example, Chase Financial Policy (1980), Hatsopolous (1983), and U.S. Department of Commerce (1983).
2. Michel and Shaked (1985) obtain a similar result using nonparametric tests of differences in the distributions of capitalization ratios for U.S. and Japanese manufacturers. This study differs from theirs in its use of a larger sample and several different measures of leverage that adjust for cash and near-cash. It also attempts to isolate a pure country effect by controlling for firm-specific characteristics likely to explain some of the variance in leverage within the sample.
3. The availability of nondebt corporate tax shields also appears comparable between countries. While Japan has only a 7 percent investment tax credit available on energy-saving equipment, less rapid depreciation schedules,

and longer depreciable asset lives than are generally used in the United States. Japanese companies enjoy a host of tax deductions generated through the creation of reserves that are not available in the United States. Net operating losses can be carried back one year and forward five years in Japan, and back three and forward fifteen years (for taxable years ending after December 31, 1975) in the United States. Thus, on balance, interest tax shields do not appear any more or less likely to displace nondebt tax shields in Japan than in the United States.

4. See Kitagawa (1984), vol. 3, II, 4–33.

5. See Kitagawa (1984), vol. 3, VIII, 4.39–4.46, for a model Japanese bond registration statement.

6. An additional factor that may make a public equity issue unattractive is the common practice, enforced by underwriters, of requiring issuing companies to "return" to shareholders the difference between the offering price of new equity and par value in the form of stock distributions over a five-year period. Given the strong tendency of most Japanese companies to maintain fixed dividends per share, such promised stock distributions are tantamount to making cash dividend increases a necessary condition for offering new equity at prices greater than par value. This requirement appears to be descendant from the former practice of raising all new equity through pre-emptive rights issues with par subscription prices. Equity was not raised through a public offering at market prices until a musical instrument manufacturer, Nihob Gakki, did so in January 1969. Although still common, the practice of returning the issue premium appears to be weakening.

7. Elston (1981), p. 513.

8. Suzuki and Wright (1984), p. 5.

9. See Stonehill and Stitzel (1969), Remmers et al. (1974), Toy et al. (1974), and Collins and Sekely (1983). Generally, growth and profitability have been found to be significant determinants of capital structure, but the significance of the other variables has been inconsistent among the several studies.

10. Typically, Japanese companies provide retirement benefits for employees through lump sum settlements at the time of separation rather than through pension plans such as those used in the United States. Unfunded pension liabilities for U.S. companies have not been included in the debt ratios. Clearly, the treatment of such unfunded liabilities as a type of debt would raise U.S. leverage ratios.

11. See Kitagawa (1984), vol. 5, III, 3-2.

12. The adding back of depreciation expense to the numerator and accumulated depreciation to the denominator of this ratio is designed to circumvent differences in depreciation accounting methods among companies,

especially those that might exist between Japanese and U.S. firms. However, the typically higher reporting basis of U.S. corporate assets compared with Japanese probably still imparts a general downward bias to U.S. profitability figures.

13. There is also some evidence that a country difference in industrial composition contributes to the apparent country effect on leverage. The five most highly leveraged industries on a net debt-book value equity basis account for 26 percent of the Japanese sample and 2 percent of the U.S. sample. Thus, the Japanese manufacturing sector appears to be more heavily populated by companies in highly leveraged industries, some of which are still more highly leveraged than their U.S. counterparts.

14. Among the long-term credit banks, the Industrial Bank of Japan plays a particularly prominent and dominant role. Bronte (1982) reports that it lends only to the highest-rated industrial borrowers and cements its relationships through a network of 160 staff members on various boards of directors. Its loans are considered a virtual "corporate life insurance policy" because of the implicit guarantees they carry.

15. Caves and Uekusa (1976) find that debt capital for large Japanese firms costs a third less than for medium-sized and small firms.

16. See Mullins (1984) for a discussion of managerial discretion and its implications for corporate finance in the United States.

17. A preference for this use of excess cash is undoubtedly encouraged by a prohibition of share repurchases in Japan's Commercial Code and the double taxation of dividend incomes.

REFERENCES

Bronte, S., *Japanese Finance: Markets and Institutions* (London: Euromoney Publications Limited, 1982).

Caves, R., and M. Uekusa, *Industrial Organization in Japan* (Washington, DC: Brookings Institution, 1976).

Chase Financial Policy, a Division of the Chase Manhattan Bank, N.A., *U.S. and Japanese Semiconductor Industries: A Financial Comparison* (June 9, 1980).

Collins, J.M., and W.S. Sekely, "The Relationship of Headquarters Country and Industry Classification to Financial Structure," *Financial Management* (Autumn 1983), pp. 45–51.

Daiwa Securities Research Institute, *Analyst's Guide: 1983* (Tokyo, 1983).

Elston, C.D., "The Financing of Japanese Industry," *Bank of England Quarterly Bulletin* (December 1981), pp. 510–18.

Hatsopolous, G.N., *High Cost of Capital: Handicap of American Industry* (Waltham, MA: Thermo Electron Corporation, 1983).

Jensen, M.C., and W.H. Meckling, "Theory of the Firm: Managerial Behavior, Agency Costs and Ownership Structure," *Journal of Financial Economics* 2 (1976): 305-60.

Kitagawa, Z., ed., *Doing Business in Japan* (New York: Matthew Bender, 1984).

Michel, A., and I. Shaked, "Japanese Leverage: Myth or Reality?" *Financial Analysts Journal* (July/August 1985), pp. 61-67.

Mullins, D.W., Jr., "Managerial Discretion, Shareholder Control and Corporate Financial Management," Harvard Business School, 1984.

Myers, S.C., "Determinants of Corporate Borrowing," *Journal of Financial Economics* 5 (1977): 147-75. Myers, S.C., and N.S. Majluf, "Stock Issues and Investment Policy When Firms Have Information that Investors Do Not Have," *Journal of Financial Economics* 2 (1984): 187-221.

Remmers, L., A. Stonehill, R. Wright, and Theo Beekhuisen, "Industry and Size as Debt Ratio Determinants in Manufacturing Internationally," *Financial Management* (Summer 1974), pp. 24-32.

Stonehill, A., and T. Stitzel, "Financial Structure and Multinational Corporations," *California Management Review* 12 (Fall 1969): 91-96.

Stulz, R.M., and H. Johnson, "An Analysis of Secured Debt," University of Rochester, NY, and Louisiana University, LA, February 1983.

Suzuki, S., and R.W. Wright, "Financial Structure and Bankruptcy Risk in Japanese Companies," Keio University, Tokyo, and McGill University, Montreal, 1984.

Toy, N., A. Stonehill, L. Remmers, R. Wright, and T. Beekhuisen, "A Comparative International Study of Growth, Profitability, and Risk as Determinants of Corporate Debt Ratios in the Manufacturing Sector," *Journal of Financial and Quantitative Analysis*, 1974 Proceedings (November 1974), pp. 875-86.

U.S. Department of Commerce, International Trade Administration, *A Historical Comparison of the Cost of Financial Capital in France, the Federal Republic of Germany, Japan, and the United States*, 1983.

Vishny, R.W., and A. Shleifer, "Large Shareholders and Corporate Control," second draft, Massachusetts Institute of Technology, July 1984.

Wellons, P.A., "Competitiveness in the World Economy: The Role of the U.S. Financial System," in *U.S. Competitiveness in the World Economy*, ed. B.R. Scott and G.C. Lodge (Boston: Harvard Business School Press, 1985), pp. 357-94.

CHAPTER 10

Multistage International Competition

Paul R. Krugman

Technologists and business historians assert that industries have a natural life cycle, with several distinct stages. At first there are many small, innovative firms, all of them losing money. As the technology becomes commercial, there is a period during which the leaders earn easy profits. Finally, when the technology becomes well established, ordinary economies of firm scale become dominant and the field narrows to a small-group oligopoly.

This commonplace observation takes on a new, and some would say ominous, meaning when applied to current international competition. In the first half of the 1980s the United States has done badly in virtually all mature sectors subject to international competition. The popular conception is that its remaining strength lies in its ability to innovate. Yet today's new industries are tomorrow's mature ones. Unless the United States can convert initial leadership into a permanent market position, it will reap little benefit from its inventiveness. Many observers see the history of semiconductor memories, where a U.S.-invented technology has become a Japanese-dominated market, as an omen of the future of U.S. industry.

While alarmist views of the U.S. competitive position are easily faulted, it is nonetheless important that economists look closely at the dynamics of multistage international competition. If nothing else, we need to know how to interpret the evidence. If U.S. firms lead an industry in its early stages, but then allow foreign firms to displace them, what does that mean? If foreign firms seem to follow different strategies from those of their American rivals, is this evidence of better management, a superior industrial structure, or simply appropriate responses to differing conditions? Is there a case for government intervention to preserve innovative firms under economic pressure from such sources as a strong dollar?

This chapter attempts to provide a framework for thinking about some of the issues raised by multistage competition for trade policy. The discussion is inspired by issues I encountered while studying the semiconductor industry. I was particularly influenced by the strong argument of Ferguson (1986) that the contrast between the "fragmented" U.S. semiconductor industry and the "coordinated" Japanese one is crucial in explaining U.S. failure. Ferguson's premise is questionable, but the issues he raises deserve attention. This chapter may also be viewed as an effort to go beyond the strategy adopted in Baldwin and Krugman (1986) of viewing each generation of semiconductors as a stand-alone competition. Here we develop a theory of intergenerational spill-over reflecting the role of one round of competition in setting the stage for the next.

I begin with a simple, highly stylized model of international competition in an industry where competition involves two successive "rounds." Firms cannot participate in the second round unless they were players in the first round. This model then serves as a jumping-off point for discussing a variety of cases of multistage international competition and their interpretation. Finally, I turn to the policy question of whether multistage competition offers an argument for government intervention.

THE MODEL

Consider an industry where two countries compete in selling goods to a third market. Following Brander and Spencer (1985), I assume away any domestic demand for the industry's products in either country. This is not a harmless assumption, because it emphasizes the competitive aspect of trade and de-emphasizes the consumer effects that are crucial in assessing real trade policy. As a simplifying strategy, however, it is useful, and as we will see, it is by no means enough to guarantee interventionist conclusions.

Firms from the two countries compete in two periods: an "innovative" period and a "mature" period. In each period they face interdependent demand curves, which for simplicity I assume to be linear. All firms from each country produce identical products, but the products of the two countries are differentiated. This assumption allows us to have a free-entry equilibrium in which firms from both countries are present. Thus we have the following demand system:

$$p_1 = A_1 - B_1 z_1 - C_1 z_1^* \tag{1}$$

$$p_1^* = A_1^* - B_1^* z_1 - C_1^* z_1^* \tag{2}$$

$$p_2 = A_2 - B_2 z_2 - C_2 z_2^* \tag{3}$$

$$p_2^* = A_2^* - B_2^* z_2 - C_2^* z_2^* \tag{4}$$

where p_i, z_i are price and total industry sales in period i and asterisks indicate foreign variables. Values for period 2 are expressed in terms of their present value in period 1. Since a period represents an unspecified stretch of time, and an industry's maturity may last longer than its youth, this discounting by no means implies that the demand in period 2 is smaller than that in period 1.

There is assumed to be free entry by firms, but in making their entry decisions firms are assumed to foresee correctly the profits they will earn after entry. The costs of a representative firm from each country may be divided into first- and second-period costs, both expressed in period 1 present values. For each firm there is a fixed cost of entry, then constant marginal costs are incurred over the individual firm's production, x, thereafter. Thus each firm faces total costs:

$$C_1 = F_1 + C_1 x_1 \quad \text{if } x_1 > 0 \tag{5}$$

$$= 0 \text{ otherwise}$$

$$C_1^* = F_1^* + C_1^* x_1^* \quad \text{if } x_1^* > 0 \tag{6}$$

$$= 0 \text{ otherwise}$$

$$C_2 = F_2 + C_2 x_2 \quad \text{if } x_2 > 0 \tag{7}$$

$$= 0 \text{ otherwise}$$

$$C_2^* = F_2^* + C_2^* x_2^* \quad \text{if } x_2^* > 0 \tag{8}$$

$$= 0 \text{ otherwise.}$$

Total industry sales, z_i, are the sum of individual firm sales, x_i. Since the firms within each country are symmetric, we can simply write

$$z_1 = n_1 x_1 \tag{9}$$

$$z_1^* = n_1^* x_1^* \tag{10}$$

$$z_2 = n_2 x_2 \tag{11}$$

$$z_2^* = n_2^* x_2^* . \tag{12}$$

where n_i is the number of firms producing in period i and asterisks continue to indicate a foreign variable.

We now introduce a linkage between the two periods by the simple assumption that *a firm cannot participate in the second period unless it entered in the first period.* Firms may rationally choose to enter a market early, even though they expect to make a loss, in order to have the option of participating in a potentially lucrative market later. In addition to imposing a constraint on each firm, this condition also imposes a constraint on the aggregate outcome, namely that

$$n_2 \leq n_1 \tag{13}$$

$$n_2^* \leq n_1^* . \tag{14}$$

To focus on the implications of this assumption, other issues of competition will be handled as simply as possible. Within each period, firms will be assumed to engage in Cournot-Nash competition. Integer constraints will be ignored, so that entry will proceed until profits are zero (except in some of the special cases discussed later).

SOLUTION OF THE MODEL

The model will be solved backward in the standard way. For given n_1, n_1^* we solve for the second-period equilibrium. If the constraints (13) and (14) are binding, this equilibrium will involve positive profits. We then solve for the free-entry equilibrium in period 1, where firms take into account the possibility of earning profits in period 2.

For expositional purposes, however, it is useful to begin by considering a particular kind of equilibrium as a reference case, then asking under what circumstances this case fails to obtain.

Consider, then, the possibility of an unconstrained equilibrium—that is, an equilibrium where the constraints (13) and (14) do not bind. Free entry will ensure that no profits are earned by firms in the second period. Therefore a desire to keep open the option of entry in the second period will not be an additional motive for entry in the first period. Thus in the case of an unconstrained equilibrium we can treat each period as a simple stand-alone free-entry Cournot game, a subject that has already been examined by Horstmann and Markusen (1986).

It is sufficient to consider the equilibrium of domestic firms in the first period. Setting marginal revenue equal to marginal cost, their first-order condition is:

$$p_1 + x_1 (dp_1 / dx_1) = c_1 \qquad (15)$$

or

$$p_1 - c_1 = B_1 x_1 . \qquad (15')$$

Their zero-profit condition is

$$p_1 x_1 - c_1 x_1 - F_1 = 0 ,$$

or, by rearranging,

$$(p_1 - c_1)x_1 = F_1 . \qquad (16)$$

Thus we have the equation

$$(p_1 - c_1)^2 = F_1 B_1 , \qquad (17)$$

which implicitly defines a unique price for domestic output. We can similarly find the price of foreign output. The first-order condition (15) gives us the output of a representative firm, which together with the demand conditions gives us the numbers of firms n_1 and n_1^*. A similar calculation will give us the numbers of firms in the second period, n_2 and n_2^*.

We now ask under what conditions this unconstrained equilibrium will obtain. The answer is immediately apparent: if we calculate the unconstrained equilibrium and discover that in fact the inequalities (13) and (14) are satisfied, then this is the correct equilibrium. That is, if enough firms find it profitable to enter the first round of competition even without the lure of an entry ticket to the second round, entry tickets will have no value.

Suppose, however, that in one or both countries the number of firms that could profitably enter the second round is larger than the number that could profitably enter the first. Then the equilibrium is more complex to calculate, but its basic characteristic is clear. Firms will enter in the first period in sufficient numbers that they make losses, in order to be able to participate in the second period and make profits. As long as firms are unconstrained in their ability to borrow, free entry will ensure that the present value of profits is zero.

This clearly leaves us with three generic cases of multistage competition: (1) The entry constraint is binding on neither country, so that the unconstrained equilibrium is in fact the outcome. (2) The entry constraint binds on both countries, so that in both countries firms must accept losses now in order to get profits later. (3) The entry constraint is binding in one country but not in the other.

We now turn to a discussion of the conditions under which each of these cases will occur, and the implications of each.

COMPETITIVE CASES

Entry Constraints Not Binding

In the simplest case of multistage international competition, fewer firms want to enter the second round than have been first-round players. The intertemporal game then breaks into two distinct one-shot games, and our usual static analysis becomes valid.

This case would occur, for example, when scale economies are larger relative to the market in the second round than in the first. If the theorists of industry life cycles are correct, this is a normal case, in which economies of scale eventually lead a highly fragmented industry to become an oligopoly with four or five members. This "shakeout" case may well be viewed as the typical situation for a maturing industry.

Even though the set of eventual oligopolists is a subset of the original set of players, it does not pay for firms to enter just to have the chance to become oligopolists. Enough players are left at the end of the first period to compete away any ex ante profits in the second.

This result is somewhat surprising. It implies that in the normal case, in which an industry comes to have fewer firms as it matures, it does not make sense for firms to adopt too long-sighted a view. It is true that a firm must stay the course to end up a survivor; but the cost of surviving is equal to its benefits.

Entry Constraints Binding in Both Countries

Now consider the opposite case, where in both countries it would be profitable for more firms to enter the second round than can be profitable in the first round. As long as firms are able to borrow freely, extra firms will enter in the first stage. All firms lose money in the first round; however, the entry constraint binds in the second round and thus profits are earned. If the players have perfect foresight, they will earn zero profits in terms of present value.

This scenario would be most likely to arise in a growth industry, where either exogenous shifts in demand or rapidly advancing technology create the expectation of a rapidly expanding market. An example might be biotechnology, where nobody makes money now but the future is believed to hold vast profits for firms that get a head start.

In this case a zero-profit free-entry equilibrium depends on the ability of firms to borrow. If access to the capital market is constrained, some profits may eventually be earned. Differing opinions about the functioning of capital markets are, I would argue, central to differences of opinion about the reasons for Japanese success in semiconductors. I return to this point below.

In competitions that extend beyond two rounds, both case 1 and case 2 may obtain at different times. For example, suppose that an industry begins with an immature technology and a small market; firms that get in on the ground floor are then able to cash in later when the market grows large; but eventually the technology becomes cut-and-dried and the field narrows to only a few firms. During the initial round of competition, firms will accept losses in order to establish a foothold in the industry, but later they will expect to earn compensating profits. One semiconductor expert reported in conversation that "the industry used to focus on market share, but now they're after profitability"; presumably he was talking about just such a transition.

Entry Constraints in Only One Country

Finally, we turn to the case of asymmetry between the countries. Suppose one country's firms expect second-period entry to be constrained by the number of first-period firms, while the other's do not. Then there will be a difference in behavior between the two industries. In one country firms will appear strongly future oriented, accepting current losses in order to stay in the game. In the other, they will appear to follow a strategy of taking the money and running.

In such a situation it would be natural to condemn the management of the unconstrained industry as short-sighted and unstrategic. Yet it is quite easy to imagine circumstances in which one industry truly faces entry constraints while the other does not. For example, suppose that for reasons exogenous to strategic decisions, costs are expected to fall more rapidly in one country's industry than the other's. Then the industry with growing comparative advantage, if unconstrained, might offer room for growing numbers of firms, whereas the other country's industry would not. It would then make sense for firms in one country to enter in the first period despite losses even when it would not make sense for their foreign competitors.

Consider the competition between the United States and Japan in semiconductors. Japanese firms seem to have been willing to lose money in order to establish market position, while U.S. firms have not. Similarly, the two countries' firms respond differently to economic events; when there is a recession or an adverse currency fluctuation, U.S. firms cut back on capital spending while Japanese firms do not. The model makes it clear that such a difference in behavior might be perfectly rational on both sides.

There is also the issue of dumping. Under U.S. law, firms that sell below cost can be ruled to be dumping, even if they charge the same price in export markets as they do domestically. Clearly if Japanese firms view access to later rounds of competition as valuable, while U.S. firms do not, the result will be dumping under U.S. law.

The point is that the differences in behavior that have excited so much attention and served as the ostensible justification for the recent semiconductor pact *could* represent rational behavior in the face of differing circumstances. Such an interpretation of events would be fiercely disputed by many analysts of the semiconductor industry, however. While careful modeling is rare in this field, these researchers have at least implicitly a very different mode of what is happening. Can we offer an alternative interpretation that makes sense? I would argue that the heart of the issue rests on one's view of the functioning of the capital market.

AN ALTERNATIVE VIEW

As we have seen, asymmetry in U.S. and Japanese behavior could be explained by asymmetry in circumstances. Ferguson (1986) and others argue (to oversimplify) that there is no asymmetry in circumstances; firms in both countries should be willing to accept losses to establish market position. The difference in behavior results instead from a difference in industrial structure. Because U.S. firms are independent and concerned about their stock prices, they cannot take the long view; Japanese firms, as part of large vertically and horizontally integrated enterprises with access to long-term bank lending, can afford to take losses for a long period.

In a situation where current losses are required to establish market position, an inability of one country's firms to accept losses in the first round of competition will indeed put them at a disadvantage. A sort of multiplier process will be at work. For any given number of foreign entrants, an inability to ride out losses would discourage entry by domestic firms; this would, however, raise foreign profits, leading to more entrants, which would in turn lead to still fewer domestic entrants, and so on. If foreign and domestic products are sufficiently close substitutes, an inability of domestic firms to ride out the first-period loss would lead to a complete absence of domestic entrants.

In multistage competition, facts have to be interpreted with great care, however. We observe that U.S. firms cede the field to Japanese firms, which appear to be willing to win the market by losing money. This pattern of events may show that something is wrong with U.S. industrial structure and/or capital markets, or it may represent efficient behavior by both sides. (Or it may represent a misjudgment on the part of the Japanese. This remains a real possibility—the profits have not started rolling in yet and may never do so.) We cannot decide which is the true situation without either making independent estimates of future profitability or carefully assessing the functioning of capital markets.

Are U.S. capital markets efficient enough to ensure that inability to ride out losses is not a major problem? Many analysts would point to the sophistication of our markets, as well as the ability to finance start-up industries like biotechnology, as evidence that capital market failure cannot be a source of competitive problems. On the other hand, there is evidence that firms in general place a lower shadow price on investment funds from retained earnings than they do on external funds. This suggests that capital market access may be crucial after all. All we can do here is emphasize that this is the key issue.

GOVERNMENT POLICY

Can a case be made for government promotion of industries subject to multistage competition, especially those in which firms must initially incur losses?

If no capital market failure is present, there is no case for government support. Although price is above marginal cost, any effort at a strategic export subsidy will simply be absorbed by additional entry, in the manner described by Horstmann and Markusen (1985). Thus no rents will be gained, and the entire government subsidy will simply be passed on in lower prices in the export market. Essentially, as long as there is no capital market failure, multistage international competition is no different from single-stage competon. And we know that strategic trade policies do not work when there is free entry.

It would be very easy for policies of government promotion to *appear* successful, however. Suppose that in the absence of a government subsidy firms would enter and lose money in the first round, then make profits as a viable industry in the second round. The outcome will be similar if a subsidy is offered (unless it is so large as to induce enough entry to eliminate second-round profits). After the fact, who will be able to argue that the subsidy was not a successful policy instrument?

On the other hand, if capital markets do not work properly, government promotion might be desirable. Subsidy—or better still lending—could enable firms to reach the green pastures on the other side of the cash flow hill. As usual, however, one needs to ask why, if the government can perceive the benefits of tiding firms over until they can earn profits, private markets cannot do so as well. There may be good reasons, but they need to be spelled out.

Should the government try to make the industrial structure more conducive to long-term action? It is certainly true that a large, integrated firm may be able to provide an internal capital market for its divisions. But is deliberate encouragement of the formation of large firms the right way to make up for an unsatisfactory capital market? Again one must ask why, if integration is such an advantage, it does not happen without government encouragement.

CONCLUSIONS

This chapter has suggested a simple framework for thinking about the process of international competition in industries where competition passes through a series of natural stages. The key assumption is that firms cannot skip stages; they must be present in earlier stages if they want to participate in later stages. Under some, but not all, circumstances this constraint will lead firms to accept losses now in order to have a chance at profits later.

Even a simple model of the dynamics of multistage competition suggests how difficult it can be to interpret evidence. If foreign firms are willing to accept losses but home firms are not, this *could* represent a failure of domestic firms to act in their long-term interests, or unfair foreign competition; but it could equally well represent rational strategies on both sides in the face of shifting comparative advantage.

Among those who discuss the unsatisfactory performance of U.S. industry in international competition, we may define two broad schools: those who attribute these industrial problems to micro-level issues of worker relations, middle management, and so on, and those who emphasize strategic failings, such as an excessive short-term emphasis. This chapter illustrates a point that is common to this whole debate: strategic failure, if it exists, must be tied to some failure of our capital market.

REFERENCES

Baldwin, R., and P. R. Krugman, "Market Access and International Competition: A Simulation Study of 16K Random Access Memories," in *Empirical*

Research in International Trade, ed. R. Feenstra (Cambridge: M.I.T. Press, forthcoming).

Brander, J. A., and B. J. Spencer, "Export Subsidies and International Market Share Rivalry," *Journal of International Economics* 18 (1985): 83–100.

Ferguson, C., "The U.S. Semiconductor Industry in Decline," M.I.T. Department of Political Science, 1986, Mimeo.

Horstmann, I., and J. R. Markusen, "Up Your Average Cost Curve: Inefficient Entry and the New Protectionism," *Journal of International Economics* 20 (May 1986): 225–47.

CHAPTER 11

Bailout: A Comparative Study in Law and Industrial Structure

Robert B. Reich

E conomies are like bicycles: the faster they move, the better they maintain their balance. Changes in consumer preferences, technologies, international competition, and the availability of natural resources all require economies to reallocate capital and labor to newer and more profitable uses. Societies that redeploy their capital and labor more quickly and efficiently than others are apt to experience faster growth and greater improvements in productivity.

Redeployment is particularly difficult in regions that are dependent on a few large manufacturing firms. In such regions, a substantial portion of the plant, equipment, and labor force has been dedicated to making certain products. When markets for these products change radically, capital and labor are not always able to keep up. The investment required to redeploy these resources may involve too many workers and too much plant and equipment, entail too serious risks, and affect too large a portion of the regional economy to be undertaken without substantial sacrifice and dislocation. Failure to adapt, however, raises the specter of sudden liquidation, massive loss of jobs, erosion of the local tax base, and areawide economic decline.

This chapter is adapted from an article by the same name that appeared in the *Yale Journal on Regulation* 2 (1985): 163–224. Copyright © 1985 by the *Yale Journal on Regulation*, Box 401A Yale Station, New Haven, CT 06520. Reprinted from Volume 2:2 by permission. I am indebted to many friends and colleagues for their helpful insights: in particular, Mark Moore, William Hogan, Raymond Vernon, Steven Kelman, Ezra Vogel, George Lodge, Richard Nelson, Owen Fiss, and the members of the Legal Theory Workshop at Yale Law School.

In some instances, the process that might normally be applied to effect the necessary redeployment—a bankruptcy under the protection of a court receiver or even an informal workout among creditors—is perceived to be inadequate. Although such a proceeding might entail concessions from employees, suppliers, and others with a direct stake in the company, it does not involve the participation of other constituents—manufacturers in the area, service businesses, communities dependent on a healthy tax base—who have an indirect stake in a major firm's continued operations. Inevitably, politics has interceded. Governments have been called on to save jobs by "bailing out" the companies.

In recent years the U.S. government has responded with increasing frequency to calls for aid to certain large, distressed businesses. Conrail, Lockheed, Chrysler, and Continental-Illinois Bank are only the most visible bailouts.[1] Tariffs, quotas, and tax and regulatory relief are examples of additional efforts also directed at failing enterprises. These responses have released a storm of criticism and debate. Some people, recoiling from the ad hoc nature of these government actions, have called for a new government institution to aid troubled industries and companies.[2] They typically point to Japan's Ministry of International Trade and Industry (MITI) as a model.[3] Opponents of this approach typically point to the failures of Britain's National Enterprise Board or similar institutions.[4]

The debate to date has had a strange, disembodied quality, as if its participants were arguing over the best way to start up an old machine. There has been too little discussion of the social context in which economic change occurs—the vast network of rules, informal codes, shared understandings, and values that help determine how economies adapt. Broad policies cannot be borrowed wholesale from Japan or anywhere else. But smaller-scale rules and social understandings *can* be altered, if only incrementally. By understanding the detailed context of economic change, we can perhaps begin to face these more subtle possibilities.

The underlying question, then, is not that which many economists and policy analysts want to ask: "Are bailouts *good?*" It is a fact of social and political life that governments inevitably will respond to such calls for help. This essay, therefore, is less a search for normative judgments than a quest for explanations and hypotheses. What accounts for the differences in how societies have responded to roughly similar problems? What are the underlying social realities? Perhaps most importantly, what can we learn through these comparisons about our own system of economic adaptation, and about its limitations and possibilities? This chapter is organized into three parts. The first examines in detail four large manufacturing companies—AEG-Telefunken, A.G., in West Germany; British Leyland in Great Britain; Toyo Kogyo in Japan; and Chrysler in the United States—and the "rescues" that were arranged to bail them out. Each of these major regional employers began to experience substantial losses at some time during the last decade, but for one reason or another did not make the investments required to shift its resources to potentially more profitable uses. Then I analyze the responses to these four crises and identify various underlying patterns in their politics, economics, and administration. In each case, the company dismissed employees, reduced capacity, and shifted some employees and assets to new, more productive uses after the bailout was initiated. However, the extent and pace of such shrinkage and shifting varied. The concluding section discusses possible explanations for these differences.

CASES

The four cases described in this section are not intended to be representations of how these political-economic systems typically redeploy people and capital within normal business reorganizations. To the contrary, the four cases are atypical; they depict systems under stress. These major business failures threatened, or were perceived to threaten, entire regions of the country and, to some extent, the entire national economy. Each case occurred during a particularly turbulent economic period. Each was perceived as exceptional and generated controversy, debate, complex negotiations, and a search for new solutions. Each case tested the system of normal political and economic arrangements among finance, labor, management, and government, and thereby illuminated the detailed rules and understandings that normally shape relationships among these groups.

Typically, we see only the gross movements—the large deals, lawsuits, statutes, and economic aggregates—and mistake them for the social organization lying beneath them. It is only when the system is under stress, when the normal institutional relationships are stretched and tested, that we can see the underlying patterns more clearly, and understand what is unique about them and why their uniqueness matters.

The comparisons drawn in the following pages are not intended as a controlled experiment, in the sense that differences in how each of these large-firm crises was handled clearly indicate systemic differences among these four political-economic systems and their capacities to adapt to economic change. No such experiment is possible, because an almost infinite number of variables might have affected public and private approaches to these four cases and their eventual outcomes. Instead, the comparisons are intended merely to suggest systemic differences in the approaches and outcomes, and in social organization.

AEG-Telefunken, A.G.

AEG-Telefunken, A.G., was founded in Berlin in 1883.[5] After World War II, the company was dismembered because 90 percent of its production facilities were in East Germany. But the company capitalized on the consumer boom of the 1950s and 1960s, becoming a giant conglomerate. It bought up small companies that made washing machines, ranges, and household appliances. By 1970, it was the second-largest electronics manufacturing company in West Germany, after Siemens, and the fifth-largest in Western Europe. It also was responsible for approximately 1 percent of the nation's GNP.

In the mid-1970s, AEG's successes began to wane. Japanese manufacturers of consumer products started to invade the West German market, cutting into AEG's sales. The deutschemark rose relative to foreign currencies, making imports even more attractive and AEG's exports even less so. Moreover, having never fully digested its various acquisitions or imposed any coherent management structure on them, the firm seemed incapable of cutting costs. The many acquisitions also had left the company deeply in debt. As costs rose, the company dipped into pension reserves, creating a large deficit in the pension fund.

The crisis came in 1979. Losses for that year mushroomed to $580 million. In October, management presented to the company supervisory board a plan to reduce costs. The plan included elimination of 20,000 jobs, 13,000 to occur in 1980 alone. Labor representatives on the board strongly opposed the plan.

AEG's labor leaders met in Bonn with Count Lambsdorff, minister of economics in Helmut Schmidt's coalition government, and Hans Matthöfer, minister of finance. They argued that the government should invest in the firm, possibly taking over the company, and thereby saving jobs. Matthöfer, a union member and also a leading member of the Social Democratic party, was sympathetic, but concerned about the government's mounting deficits. Lambsdorff, a Free Democrat and economic conservative, opposed the plan. There was no agreement on a remedy for AEG's problems.

The Dresdner Bank, AEG's lead bank and the second-largest bank in West Germany, then took the initiative. In December, Dr. Hans Friderichs, chief executive of Dresdner and a director of AEG's supervisory board, hosted a meeting of sixty-six of West Germany's most powerful business and financial leaders at the bank's headquarters in Frankfurt. Friderichs's message was clear: AEG needed financial help. If the help did not come from the banks, insurance companies, and other industrial giants assembled there, it would have to come from the government. If help came from the government, it would come with strings, and the strings would be tied to organized labor, giving it more power within management. One managing director of the Dresdner Bank put the matter bluntly: "Let's face it, either we are going to provide the subsidy or the State will, and if the State does then the State will want control . . . and there are certain voices in our political system that will be happy to ease the way."[6]

The assembled financiers and industrialists also were aware of mounting public concern about the powerful role banks played in the West German economy.[7] The government was then considering legislation to limit the amount of equity any bank could hold in a given company. The bankers feared that an admission that they could not handle the crisis without state intervention would raise serious questions about why they should enjoy such sweeping power in corporate boardrooms.[8]

The meeting produced a plan to aid AEG. Under the plan, a consortium of twenty-four banks would provide the company with the equivalent of $376.2 million in new equity, bringing the banks' combined holdings to around 65 percent of the firm's outstanding shares. The banks also would reschedule about $1.16 billion of the company's long-term debt and some $700 million in short and medium-term debt. Insurance companies would subscribe to $90 million in unsecured bonds at a rate 1 percent below that on long-term government bonds; other large industrial firms would subscribe to about $125 million in similar bonds. In addition, shareholders would be asked to approve a two-thirds reduction in the nominal value of the company's stock. The company, in turn, would reduce its West German work force by 10 percent in 1980 and would replace its chief executive with Heinz Dürr.

The plan proved to be inadequate, and losses continued to mount. In 1981, the firm lost $260 million on sales of $6.2 billion. Nearly the same results befell the firm in 1982. Accumulated debt rose to $3.2 billion. Equity shrank to 10 percent of indebtedness. The 1981 recession, coupled with high interest rates, was partly to blame; the firm was still struggling to repay loans for its 1960s expansion.

Once again, the Dresdner Bank took the initiative. It sought to get the group of lenders to reschedule the existing debt and provide new loans. This time, however, the government's help would be needed. The company's debt was now too large, and its future too precarious, to rely any longer on a private-sector solution.

In the spring of 1982, Hans Friderichs and Heinz Dürr met with Count Lambsdorff and the new finance minister, Manfred Lahnstein. The recession had pushed unemployment up to more than 7 percent from an average rate of 3.5 percent between 1977 and 1980. Prospective job losses were on everyone's mind. Friderichs and Dürr proposed that the government become involved in the company's plight. The banks would write off the firm's 1982 debt repayments of $105 million and would provide new loans up to $800 million. But the government would have to guarantee to repay the loans if the firm went into bankruptcy. Labor leaders met separately with the government officials to ask for government assistance, but argued, as they had three years before, that in return the government should obtain an ownership interest in the company.

A few months later the government announced its decision. It would immediately provide AEG with loan guarantees equivalent to $239 million for the purpose of financing export sales, on condition that the banks provide $100 million in new loans. Additional loan guarantees would be made available to the company on the condition that an independent audit showed that the firm was still viable and could survive without aid in two or three years' time. Lambsdorff made it clear, however, that any solution to the company's problems was primarily the responsibility of the company and of West German industry, not of the state.[9]

AEG then dropped the other shoe. On August 9, 1982, after an emergency meeting of its supervisory board, the firm announced that it had run out of cash, that its losses for the year could be as much as $200 million, and that it would therefore seek reorganization under a court proceeding known as *Vergleich*, a type of partial bankruptcy under which 60 to 65 percent of a company's debt can be written off so long as the company's reorganization plan is approved by a majority of creditors holding among them at least 75 percent of the debt.[10] If successful, the reorganization would wipe the company's slate clean of more than $2 billion of debt. Reorganization would have the added advantage of eliminating $520 million of unfunded pension liabilities, which would be taken over by the Pension Security Association, a semipublic corporation established in the early 1970s to insure the pensions of employees of insolvent companies. In addition to seeking reorganization, the company announced that 20,000 employees would be laid off.

The announcements shocked the West German financial community and labor unions. Labor leaders again called on the government to buy the company in order to stop job losses. The government held firm, although Chancellor Helmut Schmidt's Social Democrats were about to face an important contest with the Christian Democrats in the State of Hesse, in which labor support was crucial. The conservative Free Democrats, on whom Schmidt depended to maintain his increasingly fragile coalition government, opposed state intervention. The unions were philosophical. "The times have changed," stated Eugen Loderer, a chief of the labor union, IG Metall. "A cave-in has occurred that cannot be handled in the usual bombastic way. Union policy must accept the realities."[11]

Several weeks later the government formally agreed to guarantee up to $440 million of new loans to the firm. The independent audit commissioned by the government had concluded that the firm had a good chance of survival so long as the court-supervised settlement of AEG's current debts was approved, the new loans were provided, and the company continued to slim down. Half of the loan guarantees would come from individual state governments, in proportion to their share of AEG's work force. In addition, certain states agreed to provide low-interest loans. For example, the State of Hesse would grant loans of up to $400,000 at subsidized rates to any AEG supplier headquartered within the state.

AEG's creditors approved the reorganization plan. The banks then came up with more than $800 million of new loans, half of which were guaranteed by the government. The crisis seemed to be over. Indeed, in 1983, AEG appeared to be back on a relatively even keel. Its stock price had rebounded to around $47 a share, up from a low of around $12 in 1979. Its worldwide payroll was down to 76,500 people—60,000 of them in West Germany. Although the company celebrated its hundredth birthday with losses of just under $333 million for 1982, it cut its losses to less than $13 million in 1983, and approached the breakeven point in 1984.[12]

British Leyland

British Leyland (BL) was created in 1968 when Harold Wilson's Labour government decided that the only way to preserve a strong British automobile industry that could compete worldwide was to merge the two remaining British-owned automobile companies, British Motor Company and Leyland Motor Company, into a larger-scale enterprise.[13] The government, therefore, offered funds to induce the change.

The merger occurred on paper only. The two companies, which themselves resulted from more than thirty mergers over the years, remained fragmented. There were more than seventy plants scattered around England, many too small to achieve economies of scale. More than 200,000 employees were divided among eight divisions, seventeen different unions, and 246 bargaining units. In 1970, five million work-hours were lost to strikes and work stoppages; by 1972, the loss had reached ten million work-hours. Fierce interunion rivalries also existed because many of the companies that were merged into BL had been rivals for decades. According to one industry executive, "the people at Longbridge [where Austins were made] wouldn't talk to the people at Cowley [the Morris plant], and the snobs at Jaguar wouldn't speak to any of them."[14]

Despite these problems, BL managed during the early 1970s to coast along on rising automobile sales generated largely by the government's decision to lift restrictive credit and tax measures. BL sold all the cars and commercial vehicles it could produce, though profit margins were extraordinarily low: in 1973, it sold 1.2 million cars, but earned the equivalent of $66 million on $3.8 billion of sales (a paltry 1.7 percent).

Then came the oil crisis and soaring inflation of the mid-1970s. BL's costs were so high relative to other auto companies, and its quality so poor, that it could not compete. It began to lose money. The Austin 1300 sedan became one of the few cars ever to be awarded a "silver lemon" by the West German Automobile Club, a dubious honor bestowed for "horrible" mechanical faults. BL's share of the British market tumbled from 45 percent, just before the 1968 merger, to 33 percent in 1974; its share of the continental European market declined from 10 to 7 percent.

In July 1974, BL executives met with the firm's principal bankers—Barclays, Lloyds, Midland, and National Westminster—to ask them to lend the company the equivalent of $1.2 billion for new investment over the next six years. The company already had borrowed $315 million. The banks, however, were unwilling to extend any more loans. By September BL's cash position was deteriorating quickly. Losses for the fiscal year amounted to $46.2 million. With its share capital valued at only $360 million, the company had a worrisome debt-to-equity ratio of approximately one to one.

The crisis was deepening. In a few months, BL would not be able to pay its bills. BL executives and their bankers met in late November with Tony Benn, secretary of state for industry in the Wilson government. On December 6, 1974, Benn announced that the government would seek Parliament's approval for public aid to the company, perhaps including some degree of public ownership. He immediately appointed a team of business and labor leaders, under the direction of Sir Don Ryder, a noted industrialist, to assess both BL's present situation and its future prospects, and report back to Parliament.

The Ryder Report, issued on March 26, 1975, blamed BL's troubles on inadequate capital investment, poor labor-management relations, and inefficiently organized production.[15] According to the report, however, the situation was not hopeless: the company could become profitable again with an infusion over the next seven years of the equivalent of $6.2 billion for new investment. Half of this money would come from the government; the other half would be generated internally. Through its purchase of old and new shares, the government would own a majority of the company. In addition, the report proposed the establishment of a new structure of "industrial democracy" within the company, in order to take advantage of the ideas and enthusiasm of the work force and overcome hostilities. It also suggested reorganizing the company into four separate profit centers with responsibility, respectively, for cars, trucks and buses, international sales, and other special products.

On April 24, 1975, Prime Minister Harold Wilson, the leader of the Labour Party, described the government's plan to rescue BL to a packed and somber House of Commons. Wilson explained that the company's importance to the national economy necessitated such a vast investment.[16] After a bitter and acrimonious debate, Parliament agreed.[17] BL announced in a letter to its shareholders that it had accepted the plan. The company's managing director resigned and was replaced with a new chief executive. BL's aged chairman, Lord Stokes, was given the figurehead position of president, and a new chairman was installed.

The government immediately provided BL with the equivalent of $426 million of new equity capital; the rest would come in stages, as BL met certain performance benchmarks. The National Enterprise Board (NEB), a semi-independent government agency, then headed by Sir Don Ryder, would provide these funds. The board soon began working with BL's new management, restructuring the company along the lines that had been suggested in the Ryder Report.

Labor disputes increased as a result of these efforts. Ryder's plan for industrial democracy involved a complex hierarchy of plant committees, divisional committees, and senior councils. Shop stewards, who had the greatest power under the old arrangement, feared that the new system would create a rival channel of communication. A compromise was reached that gave the shop stewards responsibility for putting forth a slate of worker delegates to the committees and councils.

There were other problems. Middle managers felt excluded from the process, while senior managers had all they could do to attend the 760 weekly meetings of the various groups. Confidential company information leaked out to the press. Rank-and-file workers continued to engage in wildcat strikes. There were stoppages at the Triumph works over track speed, at Bathgate over pay, at Coventry's Jaguar plant over a management decision to install a new paint shop at Castle Bromwich—which the workers feared would jeopardize the independence of Jaguar. Moreover, workers continued to complain about salaries and responsibilities, as well as about other company policies.

Productivity in 1977 was lower than in the crisis year of 1974. The company estimated that strikes and work stoppages reduced production by 225,000 vehicles. Losses amounted to the equivalent of $110.5 million. The company sold 785,000 vehicles (down from 1.2 million in 1973), and BL's share of the British automobile market slipped to 23 percent (from 33 percent at the time of the Ryder Report). The National Enterprise Board continued to hand out money, but the government threatened to review and revise the entire Ryder plan.

A turning point of sorts came in the fall of 1977, when Leslie Murphy took over from Don Ryder at the NEB. Among Murphy's first acts was to dismiss BL's chief executive and its chairman. The NEB appointed Michael Edwardes to both positions. As chief executive of Chloride Group, Britain's largest battery maker, Edwardes had earned something of a "whiz kid" reputation; he had also been one of the first members of the NEB.

Edwardes immediately set out to reduce BL to profitable size. He revised the firm's production targets downward to 800,000 vehicles and 25 percent of the British market, and announced the need for a corresponding cut in employment. He offered workers bonuses of up to $3,000 if they would leave the company voluntarily. Simultaneously, Edwardes took a tough line with the unions. He closed the Speke plant in Liverpool, which had been plagued by work stoppages and poor workmanship, thereby laying off 3,000 workers. When the machinists at Scotland's Bathgate truck and tractor factory went out on strike, Edwardes announced a $70 million cut in planned investment at the plant.

By late 1979, as Margaret Thatcher moved into Downing Street and the Conservatives took over the reigns of government, BL's share of the British auto market had fallen for the first time to under 20 percent. Only 625,000 vehicles were manufactured, down from 785,000 in 1977, and 1.2 million in 1973. The company had slimmed: it now employed 165,000 people (down from 211,000 in 1975). With under 2 percent of the world's automobile market, BL was the smallest full-range automobile manufacturer on the globe. Losses for the fiscal year ending in September were the equivalent of $242 million, double the losses for 1977 and almost four times the losses for the crisis year of 1974. All told, the Labour government had invested more than $1 billion and lent the company more than $500 million.[18]

It was now the Tories' turn to deal with BL's problems. Union leaders met with Keith Joseph, the new secretary of state for industry, and argued for more government assistance. Joseph opposed generous concessions to BL. Edwardes announced that substantial new public investment was needed both to launch new models and to encourage voluntary layoffs. He warned that, without the funds, BL would be forced into bankruptcy and he would resign. He also unveiled a plan to scale back BL still further by closing thirteen more plants and cutting an additional 25,000 workers from the payroll. Joseph relented. The Conservatives agreed to provide the equivalent of an additional $660 million in cash.

However, this new infusion of capital did not help. Although 1979 had been a bad year for BL, 1980 was even worse. Losses were $1.2 billion on sales of $6.5 billion. The world auto industry was generally in a slump. BL had invested a substantial portion of the government's money in developing new models, but they were still months away from appearing in showrooms. In the meantime, new cash was needed desperately. After a stormy meeting of the Cabinet in February 1981, Joseph announced that the government would provide BL with another cash infusion—this one the equivalent of $1.2 billion. One ministerial colleague commented dryly, "There's a job waiting for Sir Keith Joseph in Oxford Street. He's been practicing the role of Father Christmas."[19]

The rest of the story is more upbeat. Losses for 1981 were slightly less than the year before. By 1982, losses had been reduced to $275 million, and in 1983 the company nearly broke even. Certain divisions, like Land Rover and Jaguar, actually turned a profit. The new models were enormously successful. The Metro became Britain's most popular compact. The Maestro, a five-door hatchback, was introduced to much acclaim in early 1983. News reports featured Mrs. Thatcher at the wheel, proudly motoring up and down Downing Street for the cameras. BL's share of the British market bounced back almost to 20 percent. Productivity was up, and the company was now considerably leaner. Capacity had been reduced to roughly a half-million vehicles; employment was down to 100,000. Industry observers predicted a rosy future, and indeed by 1985 the company was safely back in the black.

Toyo Kogyo

Toyo Kogyo, founded in 1920 in Hiroshima, began as a manufacturer of cork products.[20] The company's first automobile, introduced in 1931, was little more than a wagon attached to a motorcycle. During World War II the company produced rifles, rock drills, and gauges to measure the accuracy of precision-engineering instruments. When the United States dropped the atomic bomb on Hiroshima on August 6, 1945, Toyo Kogyo's factory and its 10,000 workers were shielded by a small hill separating them from the rest of the city.

Tsunjei Matsuda, son of the company's founder, took over as president in 1951. The company became one of Japan's leading truck makers under the brand name Mazda, a contraction of Matsuda. Matsuda was intent on using Toyo Kogyo's expertise in engineering to compete with the much-larger Toyota and Nissan automobile companies. In 1960, the firm produced its first "real" car, a tiny sixteen-horsepower two-seater.

Soon thereafter Toyo Kogyo turned for help to the Sumitomo Bank, one of Japan's largest banks. Until that time Toyo Kogyo's lead bank had been the Hiroshima Bank, but the firm was now sufficiently large that it needed the backing of a larger financial institution. The new relationship proved auspicious. Shozo Hotta, the chairman of Sumitomo Bank, introduced Matsuda to West Germany's Konrad Adenauer, and Adenauer in turn arranged for Toyo Kogyo to obtain from Audi-Wankel a license to produce a rotary engine that Audi engineers had just designed.

By 1967, Toyo Kogyo was the world's only commercial manufacturer of cars equipped with rotary engines. The cars were wildly successful: rotary engines produced relatively little pollution (an important advantage, as the Japanese government progressively tightened pollution-control standards in the 1970s), were snappy and responsive, and were novel.

Before introducing rotary engine models, Toyo Kogyo produced about 150,000 cars and trucks a year; after it began to concentrate on rotary engines, production increased dramatically. By 1973, Toyo Kogyo was building 740,000 vehicles annually and had become Japan's third-largest automaker. Its export sales, mostly to the United States, were booming. It was expanding its facilities to accommodate annual production of one million vehicles. Its work force also expanded rapidly, reaching 37,000 by 1973—4.5 percent of the working population of Hiroshima prefecture. If component suppliers are included in the calculation, 7.4 percent of total jobs in the prefecture derived from Toyo Kogyo, one-quarter of the total manufacturing employment. Hiroshima's other major industry, shipbuilding, was in steep decline, so that the regional economy was growing even more dependent on Toyo Kogyo.

Toyo Kogyo's success was abruptly shattered by the oil crisis of the mid-1970s. With all their advantages, rotary engines had one telling disadvantage: they were inefficient. According to a 1974 report of the U.S. Environmental Protection Agency, Mazdas with rotary engines got only ten miles per gallon in city driving.[21] Rapidly rising oil prices therefore meant rapidly falling sales. In 1974, U.S. sales of Mazdas declined by more than 43,000 cars, and Japanese sales also plummeted. Inventories bulged.

Nevertheless, throughout 1974 Kohei Matsuda, the president of the firm and grandson of the founder, continued to make rosy projections. Late in the year he called a press conference to announce that a new rotary engine with 40 percent better fuel efficiency would be in production before the end of 1975. (In fact, it took Toyo Kogyo engineers six more years to achieve this feat.) Despite declining sales, Matsuda refused to cut production, with the result that by the end of 1974 the company was left with 126,000 unsold cars. Not surprisingly, the company's performance in 1974 was a disaster; it lost the equivalent of more than $75 million on $2 billion of sales. The firm had sunk even more deeply into debt than normal for debt-laden Japanese firms. By the end of 1974, the firm's bank indebtedness had grown to $1.5 billion, and its debt-equity ratio had mushroomed to four to one.

Sumitomo Bank officials were not standing idly by. They suggested to Kohei Matsuda that the firm cut production and stop its expansion program, but Matsuda would not listen. Meanwhile, Toyo Kogyo dealers from around Japan expressed their concerns about the company to bank officials. The dealers' lack of confidence, coupled with Matsuda's intransigence and the rapidly deteriorating position of the firm, forced the bank's hand.

In October 1974, the bank sent two of its senior officers to Toyo Kogyo to join the firm's management temporarily. This action was intended to "strengthen the company's financing operations [and] prepare for a possible deterioration in the company's business."[22] The Sumitomo officers took charge of the biggest trouble spots: financing the ballooning inventories of unsold Mazdas in the United States and projecting the firm's performance over the next year or two. These emissaries were followed by others. In all, over the next two years, Sumitomo Bank and Sumitomo Trust Company placed eleven of their top-level executives in key positions within Toyo Kogyo. These included Tsutomu Murai, managing director of the bank, who took over as executive vice president of the automaker. Murai described the changeover bluntly: "For now, we're an army of occupation. Active intervention is unavoidable."[23]

The Sumitomo rescue team acted quickly. Kohei Matsuda, Toyo Kogyo's president, was made chairman of the company without any operating duties. Two-thirds of the company's section chiefs were shifted to new positions. Costs were slashed in all areas. Production was cut back, expansion plans were dropped, $54 million in stock and real estate was sold off, dividends were reduced by 20 percent for three years, hiring of new assembly workers was halted for four years, pay levels were frozen for all managers at the rank of section chief or above (about 4 percent of the total payroll), directors' salaries were cut and bonuses ended for three years, and the union accepted pay raises lower than those received by auto workers at other automobile companies.

One major cost remained. With production cut, the company no longer needed one-quarter of its workforce. Ten thousand employees were now redundant. Rather than lay off the workers, the new Toyo Kogyo managers devised a scheme for training them as auto salesmen and sending them to Mazda dealers around Japan to sell the excess cars door-to-door. About 5,000 employees, mostly from the shop floor, took part in the plan between 1975 and 1980. (The other 5,000 employees gradually retired from the firm over the five years.) Each participating employee spent two years in sales work before returning to his factory job. Most were assigned to Tokyo and Osaka, hundreds of miles north of Hiroshima. The company paid each participant his incidental expenses, provided a supplemental wage in order to match his factory salary, and housed him in company-owned dormitories.

Mazda dealers were delighted to have the extra help. It is common in Japan to sell automobiles door-to-door, and a larger sales force means more sales. The displaced workers, however, were less enthusiastic. The two-year shift often meant absence from family and friends. Many found the transition from production to sales to be difficult. Hayato Ichihara, who later became president of the company's union, explained why workers went along: "We feared that if we didn't accept the proposal the company would demand we accept dismissals of workers in exchange for wage increases. And union members did understand that there were too many workers for the work that existed."[24]

Simultaneously with their cost-cutting efforts, Toyo Kogyo's new managers shifted the firm's competitive strategy. Rather than compete solely on the basis of engineering, the company henceforth would compete on the strength of its sales organization and its low costs. But the new managers also knew that Toyo Kogyo's future would depend on new models. The company continued to hire engineers and pour money into developing cars both with conventional piston engines and with rotaries. Between 1977 and 1980 Toyo Kogyo introduced five new models, including a fuel-efficient rotary.

Sumitomo Bank financed much of this transition and arranged financing for the rest. By 1976, when Toyo Kogyo's accumulated debt reached the equivalent of $1.6 billion, the bank's share reached $256 million, 16 percent of the total. The following year it boosted its lending by $70.9 million, to a peak of $327 million. When the other sixty banks and insurance companies that had lent money to Toyo Kogyo threatened to cut off future credit, Ichiro Isoda (later president of Sumitomo Bank and then an executive in charge of the Toyo Kogyo account) called the other lenders to a meeting at Sumitomo's headquarters in Osaka and assured them that regardless of what happened to Toyo Kogyo in the future, the Sumitomo Bank would "stand by the company to the end" and would be making additional loans in the near future.[25] Isoda then asked the other lenders not to desert Toyo Kogyo either, and promised them that all creditors would share equally in repayment of any new loans. In the end, only a few of the lenders came forth with additional loans, but none called in the loans then outstanding.

Sumitomo Bank also twisted arms. Members of the Sumitomo *keiretsu* provided additional loans.[26] They bought most of the $54 million in stocks and real estate that Toyo Kogyo was forced to sell. They also purchased large numbers of Mazdas from Toyo Kogyo's bloated inventories. Sumitomo Bank branch offices around Japan steered bank customers to Mazda dealers. The bank also provided a large loan to C. Itoh, a major trading company that was not a member of the *keiretsu*, on condition that Itoh take over Toyo Kogyo's sales organization in the eastern United States and purchase its inventory of 10,000 unsold cars. Finally, in 1979 the bank arranged for Ford Motor Company to purchase 25 percent of the outstanding shares of Toyo Kogyo, a move that dramatically improved Toyo Kogyo's cash position.

Additional help came from the city of Hiroshima. Business leaders formed an association called a *Kyoshinkai* (Home Heart Group) to promote Toyo Kogyo sales in the region. The prefectural government cooperated by enacting a new and far stricter pollution-control law. Because rotary engines produced less pollution than conventional engines, this change had the effect of reducing the pollution tax on rotary-engine vehicles relative to the tax on conventional engine models. These efforts served to raise Toyo Kogyo's share of the regional market from 20 to 35 percent, and further reduced inventories.

The national government did not intervene directly, but its presence was felt. From the beginning Sumitomo Bank officials understood that the Ministry of Finance was vitally concerned about the future of the company and that the central bank would make every effort to cooperate. The Ministry of International Trade and Industry (MITI) at first considered merging Toyo Kogyo with Mitsubishi or Honda. However, in a widely circulated speech Tomatsu Yoguro, vice minister of MITI, announced that MITI would not look favorably on a merger. MITI also encouraged Toyo Kogyo's large suppliers, such as Mitsubishi Steel, to continue their dealings on normal terms. The Ministry of Finance encouraged major banking institutions like the Industrial Bank of Japan and the Long-Term Credit Bank, to provide Toyo Kogyo with additional credit. In 1979, MITI obligingly cleared away legal hurdles for Ford's purchase of one-quarter of Toyo Kogyo.

Toyo Kogyo's new models were successful and, because they could all be produced on the same production line at the same time, the company had the flexibility to vary its output while fully utilizing its plant and equipment. This new organization of production fueled productivity improvements, from nineteen cars a year per worker in 1973 to forty-three cars in 1980.

By 1980 the company was profitable once again. Its debt had been reduced to the equivalent of $943.5 million, and the infusion of new equity from Ford had reduced its debt-to-equity ratio to under two to one. It sold more than one million vehicles, slipping past Chrysler to become the world's ninth-largest auto maker.

Successes continued. Export sales ballooned. Ford began to rely on Toyo Kogyo's supply of subcompacts and components. In 1983, its most popular export model, the Mazda 626, was named U.S. "Import Car of the Year" by *Motor Trend* magazine.[27] That year the company sold 1.2 million vehicles, earning the equivalent of $91.4 million on $4.3 billion of sales. In the fall of 1983, looking back on nine years of rebuilding the company, Satoshi Yamada, general manager of Sumitomo Bank's credit department and one of the bank executives who had spent time at Toyo Kogyo, said: "It was a difficult period. Many people sacrificed. We didn't know how it would come out in the end. We are very pleased."[28]

Chrysler

The Chrysler story began in 1922 when several bankers, worried about their outstanding loans to the faltering Maxwell Motor Company, persuaded Walter P. Chrysler to take over management of the auto company.[29] The company had expanded too rapidly and haphazardly during World War I and the short boom following it. It had been unprepared for intense competition from other upstart automakers and a decline in demand when the market returned to normal. Chrysler persuaded the bankers to extend new loans to Maxwell and forgive much of the old debt in exchange for stock and stock options. He also raised more funds by hurriedly redesigning Maxwell's old line of cars and slashing the price. In 1924, he unveiled a new car with a high-compression engine capable of extraordinarily quick starts. More than 32,000 Chryslers were sold that year at a profit of over $4 million, and the name of the company was changed to the Chrysler Corporation. The company continued to flourish, purchasing Dodge in 1928. It weathered the Depression better than most businesses.

Chrysler's performance after World War II was less impressive. Walter Chrysler was gone. The company was slow to ready new models to meet the postwar boom; its historical strength lay in engineering rather than in marketing and styling, which were now the keys to capturing Americans' growing demand for autos. It gained 22 percent of the U.S. automobile market in 1951, but then entered a long downward trend that would take its share below 10 percent in 1962. It bounced back a bit in the mid-1960s under the direction of Lynn Townsend, who emphasized design and sales. Townsend also launched Chrysler on an ambitious expansion program, which drained the firm of cash and made it vulnerable to sudden changes in demand.

Chrysler's first brush with bankruptcy came in 1970, when it lost $27 million in the first quarter and plunged deeply into debt. The Penn Central bankruptcy that year made investors wary of any company with heavy debt and current losses. A rescue mission was mounted by John McGillicuddy, then a vice chairman of Manufacturers Hanover Trust Co., Chrysler's lead bank. He organized a syndicate of banks to pump $180 million into Chrysler's critical financial subsidiary, which in turn continued to provide loans to car buyers. The firm got a second wind.

However, the oil shock and the 1974 recession caused auto sales to plummet. Chrysler went into a tailspin. Lynn Townsend was replaced by John Riccardo, whose strategy was basically to keep the company solvent by selling off the foreign subsidiaries that Townsend had created and closing marginal factories around the United States. Eventually, even these cuts proved to be insufficient. In 1978, the firm lost $204.6 million on under $13 billion in sales.

By the summer of 1979, Chrysler's lenders had become extremely worried. The firm by now owed more than $1 billion to almost 400 separate financial institutions spread around the globe. Chrysler needed more loans, but its creditors were in no mood to accommodate. McGillicuddy, now chairman of Manufacturers Hanover, persuaded Chrysler to host a meeting of its major creditors to allay their fears. The meeting was held at Chrysler's headquarters; one participant described it as little more than a pep rally, in which no new information was forthcoming but Chrysler executives expressed determination and confidence.[30] The bankers agreed to keep available to Chrysler $750 million in short-term credit, but warned that they could not arrange additional funding. Their fears and warnings mounted in July after Riccardo announced Chrysler's performance for the second quarter: the company had suffered a loss of $207 million on sales of $3 billion. This loss was worse than the total losses for 1978.

Politicians also were becoming worried. Chrysler had closed a number of plants in 1978, and more closings seemed imminent. The firm directly employed 140,000 people, and hundreds of thousands more worked for suppliers. Most of the workers were concentrated around the Great Lakes. Riccardo hoped that the new Democratic administration would be sympathetic to Chrysler's problems and the hardships that would result from massive layoffs. Since President Carter's election, Riccardo had made repeated trips to Washington, seeking financial assistance to modernize certain plants and relief from fuel efficiency and environmental regulations. At first, his requests fell on deaf ears. As the company's position deteriorated, however, senators and representatives from affected states became increasingly active. In June 1979, Riccardo met with administration officials to seek legislation that would permit the company to convert its mounting tax losses into a $1 billion cash advance, but the Carter administration still was not receptive. The Treasury Department feared that any such plan would pervert the tax code and open the floodgates to other companies in dire straits. Nevertheless, Treasury officials organized a task force to gather information on Chrysler and devise alternatives.

By August, the Carter administration had decided to help Chrysler. It was likely that Congress would act even if the administration did not. In addition, Douglas Fraser, president of the United Auto Workers Union, and Coleman Young, mayor of Detroit, had impressed on the president and his immediate staff the importance of maintaining Chrysler jobs. With an election little more than one year away, their advice struck a responsive chord. On August 9, 1979, G. William Miller, the newly appointed secretary of the treasury, met with Chrysler's board of directors. He told them that the administration would support neither the tax plan nor regulatory relief, but might be persuaded to introduce legislation guaranteeing up to $750 million in new loans if the company came up with an acceptable restructuring plan, including financial concessions from lenders, employees, dealers, and state governments. Another requirement—well understood, although unstated—was that John Riccardo would step down as chairman of the company.[31]

Riccardo resigned, and Lee Iacocca, who had come to Chrysler from Ford in 1978, took over. The firm hired an investment banking firm and a management consultant to help devise its restructuring plan. It also shifted its public-relations strategy: the firm no longer argued that relief was warranted by the burdens of the government's tax and regulatory policies; instead, it blamed itself for past failures, but warned that a bankruptcy would force 600,000 people out of work. It also shifted its lobbying efforts from Congress's tax committees to the banking committees.

Chrysler and the Treasury negotiated throughout October 1979. Secretary Miller continued to demand that the plan include larger financial concessions from the banks and employees, and that the earnings projections on which the plan was based be better substantiated. The Treasury commissioned several independent studies of Chrysler, the automobile industry, and the possible effects of a Chrysler bankruptcy. Meanwhile, Chrysler's cash situation continued to deteriorate. Its losses for the third quarter exceeded $450 million. No company in history had lost so much money in so short a time. Chrysler was approaching default on its loans. Its share of the U.S. automobile market was now down to less than 9 percent.

Chrysler's congressional allies were growing impatient. Senator Don Riegle and Representative James Blanchard, both from Michigan and both members of their respective chambers' banking committees, introduced loan guarantee legislation. Both committees held hearings at which Lee Iacocca, Douglas Fraser, and Coleman Young argued for loan guarantees. John McGillicuddy of Manufacturers Hanover explained that Chrysler executives have "substantially exhausted their remedies in the private sector, from a lending point of view, and are now in a position where they need Federal assistance if they are to implement their plan and bring their organization back on its feet."[32]

On November 1, 1979, Secretary Miller announced the administration's support for a $1.5 billion loan guarantee. He explained that the administration's original estimate of $750 million was far short of what was needed to put Chrysler back on a sound footing.[33] Immediately, Chrysler swung into action, seeking congressional relief before the end of the year. Chrysler dealers, members of the United Auto Workers (UAW), and key suppliers all visited congressional offices, armed with print-outs showing Chrysler and Chrysler-related jobs in each district. There was no organized opposition, save for relatively weak lobbying by the National Association of Manufacturers, the National Taxpayers Union, and Ralph Nader's Congress Watch.

Nevertheless, certain members of Congress did press for specific provisions in the loan guarantee legislation. At the behest of Senator Russell Long, the proposal was amended to include an employee stock ownership plan.[34] Senators Richard Lugar and Paul Tsongas held out for greater concessions from the employees.[35] Other members simply opposed the whole idea on the basis that the "free market" should be allowed to work its will.[36]

The final bill was enacted on December 20 in the House and on the following day in the Senate.[37] A few weeks later, in a subdued

White House ceremony, President Carter signed the Chrysler Loan Guarantee Act while Douglas Fraser and Lee Iacocca watched. The law provided guidelines for approximately $2 billion of financial concessions required of the banks, employees, dealers, suppliers, and states, to be matched by $1.5 billion of federal loan guarantees.[38] It also established a loan guarantee board composed of the secretary of the treasury, the chairman of the Federal Reserve Board, and the comptroller general to monitor the company's compliance with the legislation and to authorize issuance of guarantees on finding that the company continued to be "viable."[39]

Chrysler's losses for the year totaled $1.1 billion. Iacocca said, "The hard part starts now—getting the various groups to agree to come up with $2 billion worth of concessions.[40] Chrysler's workers were the first to cooperate. Annual pay increases specified in the industrywide "pattern" contract (which Chrysler workers already had agreed to delay in their October contract talks) would be postponed further, putting Chrysler workers six months behind Ford and General Motors employees that year and another five-and-one-half months behind the next year. The 250-member Chrysler Council approved the new contract on January 9, 1980; three weeks later it was approved by more than 75 percent of the workers voting in seventy-five Chrysler locals. One UAW official explained the large margin of victory: "The debate in Congress over federal aid and all the publicity convinced them. They voted to save their jobs."[41] In addition, the UAW leaders agreed to allow Chrysler to postpone its periodic payment to the union pension fund. Chrysler viewed this as a "contribution" worth $413 million, even though the government, as insurer of pensions through the Pension Benefit Guarantee Corporation, ultimately would pick up the tab should Chrysler fall into bankruptcy.[42]

Creditors were more recalcitrant. The act required that creditors contribute $650 million in loan concessions.[43] But by January Chrysler had stopped paying both principal and interest on its outstanding debt. It was now technically in default, and some lenders argued that their forebearance from seeking bankruptcy was a form of contribution. Many of the 400 lenders were convinced that Chrysler eventually was going to fail. They feared that the government loan guarantee, which had priority over their claims, would only drain away assets that might otherwise go to the banks at liquidation. The banks also fought among themselves: European banks, and some small U.S. banks, demanded payment in full from the larger U.S. lenders. Some banks seized funds Chrysler had deposited with them and applied the funds against Chrysler's debts. The larger U.S. lenders insisted that every lender must sacrifice directly in proportion to its outstanding loans. Negotiations dragged on through March and April, with Chrysler and Manufacturers Hanover executives trying to strike a deal with the others. Eventually the lenders agreed to defer certain debt payments until after 1983, in exchange for $200 million in Chrysler preferred stock.

The new plan that Chrysler submitted to the Loan Board at the end of April did not meet the legal requirements set out in the Loan Guarantee Act. State and local governments had not yet committed funds; suppliers and dealers had agreed only to "softer" terms on purchases; the lenders' agreement to defer payments did not represent "new" money for Chrysler. Nevertheless, the Loan Board conditionally approved the plan.[44] Chrysler would receive $500 million in loan guarantees so long as the various parties actually came up with the sacrifices to which they had agreed.

Despite the Loan Board's leniency, the deal almost fell through. A few small banks and several foreign banks still held out. By June, Chrysler was without cash. It stopped paying its suppliers. Had they then stopped supplying Chrysler, the company would have shut down. Secretary Miller and his staff, now firmly committed to Chrysler's plan, applied pressure. They met with the bank officials, explained that with anything less than 100 percent participation the entire deal would unravel, and subtly threatened retaliation.[45]

Final agreement was reached on June 24. Chrysler received its $500 million loan guarantee. The Loan Board approved a second draw-down of up to $300 million on July 15, 1980.[46] The transaction, said Lee Iacocca, represented "the most complex financial restructuring program in history . . . for one purpose—to protect the jobs of 600,000 American workers who build American cars for American buyers."[47]

Throughout this period, Iacocca and other Chrysler executives reported monthly to Secretary Miller, and daily to the Loan Board staff. "We were like a board of directors," Miller said. "I tried to convince them that they could no longer be a big car company, offering a full range of models. They had to downsize the firm. They resisted the notion at first."[48] This resistance, however, soon disappeared. Chrysler abandoned the full-size car business, cut its production, and concentrated on compacts and subcompacts, including the much-vaunted K-car. Plants were closed, with corresponding cuts in employment. When a UAW official charged in October 1980 that the Loan Board was putting "undue pressure on Chrysler Corporation to strip down its operations," Secretary Miller insisted that the board's "sole objective" was to put Chrysler back on a "sound financial and operative plan."[49]

Despite the new money, Chrysler's plight did not improve. The K-car did not sell, in part because the Federal Reserve Board was drastically restricting the money supply, forcing interest rates to more than 20 percent and thereby discouraging automobile sales. By the end of 1980, Chrysler was back to the Loan Board for a third installment. This time Secretary Miller and the board demanded even greater sacrifices from the constituent groups. The board held all the cards: if it did not approve additional loan guarantees soon, responsibility for resolving the situation would shift to the Reagan administration, which was not likely to be sympathetic.

Miller summoned Chrysler executives, bankers, and union officials to an eleventh-hour meeting at the Treasury Department in early January 1981. There he met separately with representatives of each group, squeezing them for more concessions. In the end, the union agreed to cut wages by $1.15 an hour and freeze them at that level until September 1982; the banks agreed to convert $1 billion of Chrysler's $2 billion debt into preferred stock, and accept repayment on the other half at a rate of thirty cents on the dollar. No one was happy with the deal. William Langley, an executive from Manufacturers Hanover, claimed that the banks had been forced to the wall and had borne the brunt of the sacrifice.[50] Douglas Fraser called it "the worst economic settlement we ever made. The only thing worse is the alternative—which is no jobs."[51] The board approved a final installment of $400 million in loan guarantees.

Chrysler came back from the dead, earning a small profit in 1982. Helped by the strong upturn in the U.S. car market in 1983, the company earned over $700 million, a swing of more than $1 billion from the same period two years before. Chrysler had cut its long-term debt from $2.15 billion in 1983 to $1.07 billion, paid $116.9 million in back dividends on preferred stock, strengthened its capital structure by exchanging $1.1 billion in preferred stock and warrants for common shares, and retired 14.4 million warrants held by the

Treasury for $311 million. Its share price rose to $35 during the summer of 1983—more than seven times higher than its low in 1982.

The company was now "lean and mean," in the words of Lee Iacocca.[52] Its production capacity had been slashed to approximately 750,000 cars, down from a peak of almost 1.6 million in 1968. Its total employment was down to approximately 70,000, from 160,000 just five years before (U.S. employment shrank from 110,000 to 60,000). It produced far fewer models, had no foreign subsidiaries (except for a plant in Mexico), had a far smaller budget for developing new models and technological innovations (though it was now producing several new models, including a highly successful mini-van), and was relying heavily on Japanese producers to fill out its product line and supply it with technology. Nevertheless, the company had survived and had, according to Iacocca, "won its long battle for independence."[53]

PATTERNS

These four cases appear to have a great deal in common. Each manufacturing company had been highly successful in the past. Each expanded rapidly during the boom years of the 1960s, becoming extremely large by the start of the 1970s. Each had difficulty consolidating and digesting its expansion. Each became deeply in debt. In each case, the combination of past successes and a rapid build-up made the company unable or unwilling to change direction, even in light of signs that the market for its products was leveling off or declining. Each company therefore was highly vulnerable to the oil shocks, deep recessions, and sharp changes in international competition that characterized the middle and late 1970s.

In addition, each of these companies was a major regional employer. By the early 1970s, each accounted for 5 to 10 percent of the manufacturing jobs in areas like the State of Niedersachsen in West Germany, the British Midlands around Coventry and Liverpool, the Hiroshima Prefecture in Japan, and the Great Lakes region around Detroit and northern Ohio. Each also purchased a significant percentage of materials and components produced within the region or in regions nearby. Although estimates of indirect employment vary, each of these companies clearly had a pivotal position within at least one regional economy, producing the largest item of trade between the region and the national and world economies, and thereby supporting countless smaller businesses producing both goods and services.[54]

In each instance, the first clear sign of crisis was a shortage of cash that compelled company executives to seek additional short-term credit from the company's lead bank. Within months, the shortage of operating capital grew significantly. Losses ballooned. Company executives denied the extent of the crisis. They continued to view it as a temporary cash-flow problem that would sort itself out as soon as the economy improved, when the company developed a technical fix for its declining competitiveness, or when its new product line was unveiled. In each case the lead bank forced the company's hand by refusing to make additional loans.

As the crises deepened, control of each company shifted out of the hands of the incumbent executives to a third party that oversaw the transition to a new management team. This third party also negotiated with the various interests who had a continuing stake in the company, seeking financial sacrifices from them in order to keep the company going. In return, the third party agreed to bear a considerable share of the cost itself, including the investment of new money. Although government was involved in every case, the third party was the lead bank for AEG-Telefunken and Toyo Kogyo; for British Leyland and Chrysler the third party was a government agency.

A deeper set of comparisons may also be drawn. In none of these four cases was the company formally liquidated. Although AEG-Telefunken resorted to a limited type of formal reorganization under court protection, in no case did a receiver or trustee oversee a full, formal reorganization under the bankruptcy laws. Nevertheless, a reorganization of sorts did take place. The companies were refinanced and reorganized, assets were redeployed, new products were developed, and various parties had to sacrifice in the short term for the sake of longer-term rewards. Parts of the companies were liquidated in the sense that certain assets were sold off and employees let go. In each case the bailout was effected by a mix of shrinking the company and shifting some workers and assets. Each ultimately succeeded in restoring the company to solvency.

Shrinking the Company

Given the size and importance of these companies, the groups requesting government aid argued that the free market and the profit motive on which market transactions are based could not be relied on to ensure the well-being of citizens dependent on the enterprise. And yet, paradoxically, each of the companies ended up substantially smaller than it was originally.[55] This paradox appeared repeatedly in public discussions and debates over what to do about these companies: the company had to be saved because so many people were dependent on it, but the only way to save it was to reduce its size drastically and thereby harm the very people who depended on it. Market processes, including bankruptcy, would result in a significant portion of the company being sold off or liquidated for scrap, so it was necessary to subsidize the company while it sold off or liquidated a significant portion of itself.

The bailout of AEG-Telefunken is a case in point. Count Lambsdorff justified the West German government's decision to provide AEG-Telefunken with loan guarantees by emphasizing the firm's importance to the West German economy.[56] His secretary, Otto Schlecht, pointed to the hundreds of thousands of workers who depended on the company and the 30,000 separate companies that provided it with materials and supplies, and noted that a "[bailout] in this instance is less costly for Germany than bankruptcy."[57] But Lambsdorff ultimately approved the loan guarantees only after an independent audit concluded that the company could survive as long as it continued to cut its size and payroll drastically.

We see a similar apparent inconsistency in the case of Toyo Kogyo. Tsutomi Murai, managing director of the Sumitomo Bank, who took over as vice president of Toyo Kogyo, made the rounds of business leaders in Hiroshima to assure them that the bank's intention in taking over the troubled company was to save jobs. The bank also requested assistance from the prefecture on the same grounds. The new Toyo Kogyo managers then proceeded to cut employment. "Obviously, we had to reduce costs," one bank official later explained, "and labor costs are among the most important to reduce."[58]

The same tension was present in the British Leyland case. The initial debate in Parliament clearly pitted Conservative against Labour, free-market ideology against the socialization of costs.[59] The conservatives argued that the free market should be allowed to function, that letting BL go bankrupt would facilitate the redeployment of labor and capital to more efficient uses. Labour countered by focusing on the hardships such a bankruptcy would impose on the many people dependent on the automaker.[60] Not surprisingly, the initial Labour plan for British Leyland relied on a combination of new investment and more participation by the workers in company management to restore the company to profitability.[61] There was no mention of reducing the size of the company and cutting its work force. Indeed, Lord Stokes, British Leyland's chairman, publicly criticized this lack as the "worst aspect" of the plan."[62] Just two years and more than $500 million later, the Labour government's National Enterprise Board hired a new chief executive for the company who, with the full approval of the government, set about slashing its work force.[63] By then it was clear that such cuts were the only way to save the company.

When the Conservatives regained power in 1979, the reduction in employment at BL was well under way. Job cuts accelerated over the next two years. At the start of 1981, however, Margaret Thatcher's government decided to give British Leyland more than $2.4 billion, a far larger infusion of new equity than had ever been contemplated by the Labour Party, because Sir Geoffrey Howe, the chancellor of the exchequer, had determined that liquidation of the firm would increase unemployment in Britain by 150,000 people (including the employees of suppliers), and thereby boost public welfare spending by approximately $7 billion a year.[64] Keith Joseph, the industrial secretary who approved the payment, told the press: "We tried to find a middle way but there was no middle way. Whether we accepted or rejected [British Leyland's request for more aid] the taxpayers would have been clobbered."[65]

The debate in the United States over Chrysler followed a similar path. In the congressional hearings on the loan guarantee, Detroit's Mayor Coleman Young cited estimates that a Chrysler bankruptcy would double the number of unemployed in Detroit to about 20 percent of the city's population.[66] Other cities would be hit hard as well: the Wilmington, Delaware–Newark, New Jersey area would lose 14,000 jobs; St. Louis would lose more than 25,000; Syracuse, New York, and Huntsville, Alabama, would have their unemployment rates doubled; Newcastle, Indiana, would lose one-third of its jobs;

Kokomo, Indiana, faced a 40 percent cut in its jobs.[66] The individual suffering caused by such losses would be considerable:

> Although economic theoreticians may be comforted by the fact that over the long term our economy would adjust, this is no comfort to those in so many of our cities who face the loss of a job. Because of age, some of those, as a matter of reality, will never be able to find a job again, or at least will never be able to find a job at anything close to comparable wage rates or in the places where they now live.[67]

Congressman Jim Wright, the House majority leader, urged his colleagues to support the aid bill, arguing that a Chrysler bankruptcy would cost the federal government $14 billion to $15 billion and plunge the nation into a full-scale recession. The $15 billion figure included $11 billion in lower taxes and higher welfare and unemployment payments, a $1.1 billion drain on the Pension Benefit Guarantee Corporation, and a $3 billion rise in the trade deficit as foreign cars picked up much of Chrysler's market share. Wright warned that the failure of Chrysler would trigger an economic calamity. A loan guarantee would be in keeping with the tradition that says if "your neighbor's barn caught fire and burned down, then all of the rest of those who lived in the community would provide a little bit of their substance to help and that that was part and parcel of the American spirit."[68]

These sentiments were opposed by those who urged that the market be allowed to work its will. Walter Wriston, the chairman of Citicorp, testified against the loan guarantees:

> There is no avoiding the fact that it is an attempt by the Government to move economic resources to places where they would not otherwise go. Such distortions inevitably lead to less, not more, productivity—and therefore to fewer jobs, less return on investment, and fewer bona fide lending opportunities for banks and everyone else.[69]

Peter G. Peterson, chairman of the investment banking firm of Lehman Brothers Kuhn Loeb, Inc., and a former secretary of commerce under the Nixon administration, warned that a loan guarantee would make Chrysler a permanent ward of the state: "There is clearly a grave danger here that the ultimate costs of government assistance may escalate far beyond the initial projections and that even then, the problem will not have been resolved." Peterson implied that he would let Chrysler fail rather than set a precedent for other federal bailouts.[70] His sentiments were echoed by the Business Roundtable, a group of chief executives of very large companies, which issued a statement opposing the loan guarantees: "Whatever the hardships of failure may be for the particular companies and individuals, the broad social and economic interest of the nation are best served by allowing this system to operate as freely and as fully as possible."[71]

The proponents of the loan guarantee, many hoping to save jobs, won the legislative battle. Once administration of the loan guarantee program was firmly in place within the Treasury Department, however, a different viewpoint seemed to predominate. Treasury officials were bent on restoring Chrysler to competitive health as soon as possible, thereby protecting the government's investment. "My job was to make sure that the government was protected," said Brian Freeman, who served as executive director of the Loan Guarantee Board. "That meant making sure that Chrysler was viable."[72] The objective of restoring Chrysler to quick health required that the firm cut costs and lay off workers. Treasury officials pushed Chrysler to reduce its size drastically. G. William Miller, who was secretary of the treasury at the time, talked about the difficulties involved:

> The truth is Lee [Iacocca] didn't want a downsized company when we started this; we had to fight for it. We weren't on the same wavelength. The first proposal he gave me I just slid . . . back across the table and said, "you haven't thrown any ballast off yet. When the ship starts to sink, the first thing you do is get rid of ballast.[73]

In the end, the Treasury view prevailed, and Chrysler shrank to almost half its size.

One way to explain the apparent shift in objective, from saving jobs at the expense of efficiency to saving the company at the expense of jobs, is to view the reorganization process as moving from a political to an administrative frame of reference. At the political stage, the company's plight is described as a public problem requiring a public response. Bankruptcy would result in huge social costs, falling disproportionately on certain groups of people. Such a result would be unfair, and in any event would require vast public assistance. Therefore, it is far more equitable, and less costly to the public, for the company to be given special aid.

With the political battle won, the problem then becomes one of administering aid to the troubled company. Financial specialists now take charge. Their professional training is in helping companies to improve their cash flow and balance sheets, not in keeping people employed. They are judged by how quickly they restore companies to financial health, not by how well they maintain the income streams of employees and subcontractors. They work within ministries of finance, treasury departments, and commercial loan departments of large banks—institutions whose traditional roles involve ensuring fiscal responsibility and prudence, rather than promoting social welfare or distributional justice. These administrators naturally come to see their task as making a financial "deal" similar to other deals with which they have been associated. Former Secretary of Treasury G. William Miller described the Chrysler loan guarantee from the vantage point of the Treasury Department:

> It was just a professional reorganization outside of bankruptcy. One of the problems of doing it as public policy is that you can't count on every administration to have people in place who can do that sort of thing. We happened to have a set of industrialists and lawyers who were not strangers to deals like this.[74]

Because the political mandate to save jobs inevitably is short-lived, and because political agendas are crowded and public attention can be focused on such a problem for only a short time before other issues predominate, administrators have considerable leeway in shifting to the objective of saving the company and minimizing the financial exposure of their own institution, even at the expense of jobs. Moreover, a goal like "saving jobs" is difficult to define and measure with certainty; by the time the crisis is apparent, many jobs already will have been lost, and additional job losses are to be expected.

This shift from a political to an administrative frame of reference, however, cannot explain the administrators' apparent willingness to pour additional funds into the company and their corresponding reluctance to allow the company to fall into bankruptcy, even when it showed no signs of revival. This tenacity is particularly interesting in the two cases in which governments ostensibly committed to the free market significantly increased public assistance to companies that seemed destined for eventual bankruptcy: AEG-Telefunken under a fragile coalition between the Social Democrats and the conservative Free Democrats, and British Leyland under the Conservatives. When asked to explain their sharp departures from party ideology and rhetoric, both West Germany's Count Lambsdorff and Britain's

Keith Joseph pointed out that providing government assistance to the company was far cheaper than providing it to all the people who would be unemployed in the event of a bankruptcy.[75] Each government had every incentive to do its calculation carefully, taking full account of any segments of the company that probably would find another use in short order. Nevertheless, each determined that company assistance would be cheaper than social assistance.

This conclusion may seem curious, coming as it does from conservative leaders who were not particularly dependent on labor support. To be sure, the rather generous programs of assistance for unemployed workers in these countries are themselves the results of earlier political compromises. But even with these social programs firmly in place, it seems strange that these governments would have preferred subsidies for the ailing companies. Though costly, unemployment insurance at least would permit workers to find alternative employment eventually. Bankruptcy at least would allow assets of the ailing company to be released into the economy, eventually to be put to better use. The bailout alternative might be a permanent drain on public resources, and a permanent misallocation of resources in the economy. One would expect free marketeers to argue that though in the short term it may be more expensive to allow the company to go under, in the long term this route is far cheaper than any other.

The surest explanation of free market advocates' support for corporate bailouts is that company assistance was not seen as a permanent subsidy. It was, rather, a means of *slowing down* the inevitable shrinkage of the enterprise. If administrators move too quickly to restore the company through cuts in employment, the issue may move back into the political realm. We see elements of this constraint in all four cases. In the AEG-Telefunken rescue, Dresdner Bank officials justified an industry-led bailout to other banks and insurance companies on the ground that continued rapid job losses otherwise would force a political solution. When this "private" bailout itself began to result in rapid job losses, labor leaders pushed for nationalization of the company.[76] In the British Leyland case, after the National Enterprise Board finally acceded to substantial job cuts, the Labour Party grew deeply divided over the proper course of the rescue, with back-benchers calling for a change in management.[77] As Sumitomo Bank executives began to shrink Toyo Kogyo, leaders of Hiroshima expressed growing concern, with the implicit threat of political recourse if the situation grew markedly worse.[78] When the Loan Guarantee Board began to press Chrysler to reduce its size, labor leaders pressed Congress and the Carter administration to intercede.[79] Under this view, the threat of political intervention caused these administrators to temper their enthusiasm and slow down their efforts to save the company by cutting labor costs.

There was also an economic justification for slowing down the shrinkage. If the company suddenly dissolved its least competitive parts, large numbers of workers in particular regions of the country would simultaneously lose their jobs. This sudden burst of unemployment would have devastating effects on the economy, with multiplier effects as suppliers and services lost customers and could not collect on accounts. By extending the decline over a longer period of time, however, policy makers could ease the adjustment. Fewer people would be out of work at any given time, and growing businesses might be able to absorb many of them. Suppliers might lose the failing company as a customer, but would have time to develop alternative customers. Fewer workers and small businesses would face a credit crunch, and this would reduce the pressure on other small businesses, services, and lending institutions. Seeing the coming decline, creditors and shareholders also could make gradual adjustments, writing down their loans and altering their portfolios with minimal disruption. In short, given the size and importance of these companies to their economies, bankruptcy would release vast resources far more quickly than the market could absorb them. What was needed, therefore, was *slow* bankruptcy.

In sum, both political and economic exigencies dictated that these companies' demises be slowed. If the shrinkage were too rapid and the resulting unemployment too great within a particular time period, there would be political demands to preserve the status quo. These demands in turn would make it difficult, if not impossible, to reduce the firm down to a viable size. The administrators' goal, therefore, was to shrink the company as fast as politics would permit in order to regain solvency and protect their institutional investment. But the administrators might equally have been responding to the economy's limited ability to adjust to extremely rapid change. Operating under this limitation, the administrators tried to shrink the company only as fast as the economy would permit, in order to ease the process of economywide adjustment.

The British Leyland bailout seems to have moved from concern with politics to concern with economics over its seven-year course. Between 1975 and 1977, when the issue of saving British Leyland jobs was highly politicized, there were almost no layoffs. Between 1977 and 1979, still under the Labour government, the National Enterprise Board and BL's new executives cut employment by about 30,000, a pace that was as fast as these administrators could manage without politicizing the issue once again. Between 1979 and 1981 the Conservatives, unconcerned about union support, cut employment by almost 50,000. However, in 1981, faced with the possibility of an even more rapid dissolution, the Tories held back. The social costs of unemployment were rising, not just for former BL employees and subcontractors, but for the nation as a whole, and it seemed that a quicker decline would imperil the entire economy. The Thatcher government decided to give BL a major infusion of new capital. Job cuts thereafter slowed to the earlier pace of around 15,000 per year.

The Chrysler pattern is slightly different. In this case, the greatest number of layoffs—30,000 of them—came in 1979, the very year that Chrysler was ostensibly seeking government assistance to save jobs. The magnitude of the layoffs put Chrysler on the political agenda. In 1980 and 1981, after the issue had moved from Congress to the Treasury Department, the pace of layoffs slowed. About 17,000 workers were laid off during those two years. As we have seen, once the loan guarantee legislation was passed, the treasury secretary and the staff of the Loan Board urged Chrysler to slim down. By then, however, Chrysler had already done most of its slimming. Had Chrysler maintained the same pace of layoffs in 1980 and 1981 that it had in 1979, the company would have ended 1981 with a mere 10,000 employees—fewer than were expected to be employed after a formal bankruptcy. Presumably the company would have cut back its suppliers to a similar degree. However, given the problem of high and rising unemployment, particularly in the Midwest and the industrial belt of the Northeast, the social costs of such a sudden demise would have been prohibitive.

Shifting Workers and Assets

So far we have assumed that the only reason for subsidizing these companies was, paradoxically, to shrink them, but to do so more slowly than would have been possible had they been left to the market and bankruptcy. The evidence suggests this pattern, although it is unclear whether it was attributable to financial administrators who were engaged in a kind of tug-of-war with politicians, or to economic ministers who were keeping a watchful eye on how quickly the economy could adjust to the company's gradual demise, or to some combination of both. To round out our discussion, however, we need to recognize another pattern in these cases. It concerns the shift that occurred within each company toward more competitive products and processes, and better use of employees.

If the market for the company's products had irrevocably declined, or if the company had simply grown too large and ungainly to serve its market profitably, then we could understand the crisis simply as a failure of the company to shrink in a timely manner. In this scenario, resources would have been kept too long, as if the company had erected a dam to block their natural outward flow toward more profitable uses. By the time the crisis appeared, the company was huge, and the dam extraordinarily high. If the dam broke, the pent-up resources would have inundated the economy, or else politics would have interceded to shore up the dam at all costs. The challenge was to reduce the reservoir of misallocated resources gradually, so that they could be absorbed elsewhere without igniting more political demands.

But this metaphor is too tidy. Markets change; new markets develop. Each company might have shifted its research, plant, equipment, cash, and employee resources in the direction in which the markets seemed to be moving or in the direction of new emerging markets. In other words, the company whose old market was declining need not have watched passively as its productive resources flowed out to more profitable uses. It could have put its resources to better uses internally by shifting them to new products and more efficient processes. Even after the crisis occurred, the company still had the option of shifting instead of shrinking. The reservoir of misallocated resources lying behind the dam could have been rechanneled in other directions rather than simply allowed to flow out.

In each of our cases, some such shift occurred after the crisis broke. AEG-Telefunken invested anew in telecommunications and defense-related technologies. British Leyland developed new automobile models and improved the quality of its Land Rover and

Jaguar. Toyo Kogyo invested in new models and the development of a fuel-efficient rotary engine. Chrysler developed several new compacts and a new mini-van. All these shifts appear to have been successful. All adapted to new markets. All entailed a redeployment within the company of certain resources, including people, that otherwise might have flowed out. All the shifts were encouraged by the financial administrators who presided over the reorganization.

Shifting resources, however, requires money. New products must be designed and tested, plant and equipment converted, employees retrained, the production system reorganized, dealers prepared, and consumers reoriented. The well-managed company, highly sensitive to potential changes and new opportunities in the market, is constantly investing in such shifts. On the other hand, the company that has disregarded such changes and new opportunities, or is caught unaware by a sudden shock to the market (such as that brought about by the introduction of a path-breaking technology or a substantial increase in the price of a raw material), may need to make a dramatic shift all at once, but lack the large sums necessary to do so. This was the problem faced by all four of our companies. Once the crisis became apparent each of them shifted, but the shifts were only partial. The companies could not redeploy all of their resources internally because they did not have enough money to make a complete transition. In addition, because their market shares were declining and almost all their divisions were losing money, there was no likelihood of finding another company to purchase all or a substantial part of the ailing company.[80]

To some extent, shrinking and shifting are complementary strategies for companies in distress. Liquidating the most costly and least profitable operations, enhances cash flow. The new cash can then be invested in shifting the remaining resources to more profitable uses. This shrink-and-shift strategy was used by all four companies to some degree. All cut their payrolls and, as we have seen, some of the revenues resulting from these changes were invested in new products and improved manufacturing processes.

The irony, of course, is that shrinking and shifting ultimately are inconsistent. Human and capital assets that flow out of the company no longer are available to be shifted. Even if the shrink-and-shift strategy is enormously successful—so much so that the shrunken company finds itself growing rapidly once again—the company may have difficulty summoning back old suppliers, employees, dealers, customers, and certain specialized assets. Time has elapsed. The discarded employees and suppliers are likely to have linked up with other companies in the interim. Having once been jettisoned by the old company, they may be unwilling to resume what seems to be a precarious relationship. Under these circumstances it may be more costly for the company to bid them back and shift them to new uses than simply to find new suppliers, employees, dealers, customers, and specialized assets.

If markets adjusted to such changes with ease, and transactions such as these were relatively costless, then it would not matter what combination of shrinking and shifting was chosen. The company could be as profitable after a great deal of shrinking and a small bit of shifting as the other way around. The economy as a whole could adapt as easily to a dramatic shrinkage in one of its largest companies as to a major shift.

The selection of a balance between shifting and shrinking does matter, however. Markets do not always adjust with ease. Market transactions are costly because parties often have difficulty getting adequate information. Individual suppliers, employees, and other participants may find it difficult to attempt a shift for themselves— locating new uses for their services, determining precisely what retraining they need, and ferreting out reliable buyers and sellers. On the other hand, networks of suppliers, managers, employees, dealers, and customers who have dealt with one another over a long period of time may have a sufficiently subtle understanding of one another's needs and performance that transactions among them are highly efficient. Under these circumstances, it is likely to be less costly for the company to shift them as a group than for individual actors to engage in a large number of "retail" transactions among strangers.

Besides potential efficiency advantages of internal redeployment, there may be social advantages as well. Companies like these exist at the center of intricate social networks. They anchor communities and define relationships and obligations over time. They shape community values as they order social life. Their sudden demise may rend the community irreparably.

This is not to suggest that shifting is always preferable to shrinking, either for the company or for society as a whole. Even if workers, financial intermediaries, and other constituents are perfectly willing to invest in a wholesale shift, there simply may be no profitable alternative for the specialized networks of people that would justify the investment. The point is that shifting is *sometimes* preferable.

Such shifts nevertheless are unlikely to take place if the company's constituencies are unwilling to sacrifice, each waiting for other constituents to make the first move or appropriating assistance for its own outside uses. Under this logic, the outside assistance provided in the cases described above should have been used for shifting. Merely compensating employees, suppliers, creditors, or other parties for sacrifices they were making in light of the company's current cash crisis would simply transfer wealth from one group (taxpayers or shareholders of the lead bank) to those being compensated. No real shift would occur.

The tension between wealth transfer and investment exists to a degree in all of our cases. For example, Alfred Kahn, then chairman of the Council on Wage and Price Stability, caused a stir when he pointed out that the initial deal struck between the United Auto Workers and Chrysler, while saving the firm between $203 million and $206 million in wages and benefits relative to the old contract, nevertheless would cost the company $1.3 billion over current wages during the three years of the contract.[81] This amount was just shy of the $1.5 billion loan guarantee that the company was seeking. Without more sacrifice from the union, therefore, it appeared that the government assistance would merely go into the pockets of Chrysler workers, leaving the company unchanged. As we might expect, more sacrifices were demanded as a condition of the loan guarantee. British Leyland, by contrast, did not have to cope with an Alfred Kahn. The bulk of government assistance to the troubled company in that case went to the workers for salary increases and severance payments, rather than toward new products and processes.

To the extent that the tacit goal of the assistance was simply to slow the pace of shrinkage, it did not matter that funds were diverted from investment into such payoffs. After all, the payoffs accomplished approximately the same underlying objective—they helped ease the pain of adjusting to a much smaller company by compensating those who otherwise would be hurt. But to the extent that new investment and internal redeployment was considered socially preferable to an "orderly" shrinkage and external redeployment, then the diversion was perverse. It prevented internal shifts.

Of all our cases, Toyo Kogyo shifted the most and shrank the least. Its employment declined by only 27 percent during the crisis. At the same time it completely transformed its manufacturing process and produced a wide array of new models. Most of the assistance provided to the company by the Sumitomo Group, and indirectly by the regional and national governments, was invested in the shift. There were no payoffs to constituents, aside from continued interest payments to the banks on the company's accumulated debt. Suppliers and dealers continued to absorb losses; managers and employees took major cuts in wages and benefits; 5,000 production employees were temporarily transferred to dealers. Even when Toyo Kogyo sold its stock and real estate holdings to raise additional cash, it maintained the ability to summon these resources back to the fold, the purchasers being other members of the Sumitomo Group, which in effect merely held these assets until Toyo Kogyo was able to reclaim them.[82] Thus, Toyo Kogyo managed better than the other companies in our sample to preserve its network of people and assets during the crisis, and simultaneously to shift them to new production.

At the other end of the spectrum lies British Leyland, which shrank more than it shifted. It cut the size of its workforce by more than half during its crisis, but did not fundamentally alter its products, manufacturing processes, or organization. As we have seen, most of the assistance was diverted into payoffs. Neither the employees, suppliers, dealers, nor banks bore any special sacrifice. Most of the bailout amounted to a simple transfer by which British taxpayers compensated those who otherwise might have been burdened by the company's contraction.

EXPLANATIONS

We have identified two related phenomena in the four crisis-ridden companies—shrinking and shifting. Once the company received extraordinary assistance, the pace of its shrinkage was linked both to the likelihood of continued political interference in financial administrators' efforts to return the company to solvency, and to the economy's overall ability to absorb idled resources. The extent to which the company shifted its resources to more profitable pursuits rather than simply let them flow out, seems to have been related to how tightly the extraordinary assistance was tied to company investments instead of payoffs to its constituents.

Interestingly, the two relationships appear to have moved in the opposite direction: the slower the pace of shrinkage, the smaller the proportion of resources ultimately shifted. British Leyland's overall pace of shrinkage while it received assistance was the slowest of our four examples, and it also shifted the least. Toyo Kogyo's pace of shrinkage during its crisis was faster than that of British Leyland, and it shifted the most. AEG-Telefunken and Chrysler were in the middle on both scales.

Explanations are not difficult to find. The Japanese economy was performing relatively well during this period. Its unemployment averaged under 2.5 percent of the labor force, and overall productivity was improving 3.8 percent a year.[83] So we might expect that such adjustments—substantial internal shifts of resources coupled with the rapid release of whatever marginal resources could not be used even if the shift were highly successful—would characterize many large companies. On the other hand, during British Leyland's crisis, the British economy was performing poorly, with unemployment averaging 6 percent of the labor force and creeping upward. Yearly productivity improvements averaged only about 0.1 percent.[84] Under these circumstances rapid shrinkage was politically problematic, and shifts were far more difficult to negotiate because every major transaction was a zero-sum game.

It seems equally plausible, however, that cause and effect ran in the opposite direction. Perhaps one explanation for Japan's relatively low unemployment and high rates of productivity improvement during these tumultuous years of oil shocks, world recessions, and rapid technological changes was the capacity of its large manufacturing enterprises to respond very rapidly—in our parlance, to shrink quickly and shift substantially. And perhaps one explanation for Britain's relatively poor performance lay in the comparative inability of its large manufacturers to do the same. The United States and West Germany, whose economic performance during these years fell between the two poles, also occupied intermediate points in the relative responsiveness of their larger manufacturers to rapid economic change.

Viewed in this light, the important distinction among our examples is not in the intensity of political demands to save jobs—the pressures were intense and the governments highly responsive in all four cases. Rather, the important distinction is how the companies, and the set of institutions of which they were a part, responded to these demands. Toyo Kogyo's response was to jettison quickly a relatively small number of jobs and to shift the rest. British Leyland's response was to jettison slowly many of its jobs and to shift few of the remaining ones. AEG and Chrysler each attempted some of both.

How can we account for these differences in the patterns of response? A rescue was organized in all four cases, but the rescues were substantially different. Key institutions—labor, finance, and government—assumed different sets of responsibilities and undertook them in different ways. These variations resulted from the formal laws and informal understandings that governed the relationships among key institutions. The following sections explore some of these differences and their effects on the nature of the bailout in each instance.

Information and Control

One important difference is found in the timeliness and accuracy of information received about the company's difficulties by those with sufficient resources or influence to effect a rescue. Presumably, the earlier, more reliable, and more detailed that information, the easier it was to set a new course by shifting resources. If information came much later, or was of poorer quality, the rescuers were less able to do more than preside over a gradual shrinkage.

In the Toyo Kogyo case, the Sumitomo Bank knew of the firm's problems almost at once. Toyo Kogyo had done well in 1973, but the rapid rise in oil prices during the year made 1974 a disaster, causing the company to post a loss of $75 million. By October 1974, the bank had sent two of its senior officials over to Toyo Kogyo to take on financial management of the firm temporarily. These officials thereafter supplied the bank with highly detailed information about all aspects of the firm's problems and paved the way for a larger rescue team that took over day-to-day management entirely.[85]

It was somewhat more difficult for the Dresdner Bank to get timely and accurate information about AEG's problems. Although the bank's chief executive also served as director of AEG's supervisory board, the board was slow to obtain detailed information, large-

ly because of the tensions between labor and management representatives on the board.[86] Losses mounted steadily for six years before
they reached the crisis level of $580 million in 1979, finally forcing
Dresdner Bank's hand.

Chrysler's problems were even better hidden. Manufacturers Hanover Trust Co. received the same quarterly reports that investment
analysts and shareholders received, but these merely summarized
Chrysler's gradually worsening position, without explanation. Sometimes the figures masked reality. In 1978, for example, when slump-
ing car sales began to push the company into the red and forced it to
halt production at many plants and slash dividends by 60 percent,
the company still managed to project a fourth-quarter profit. Thanks
to a little-noticed actuarial adjustment, Chrysler merely changed the
assumed rate of return on its employee pension portfolio to 7 percent from 6 percent, reducing pension costs and adding about $50
million to its profits.[87] Manufacturers Hanover did not receive even
moderately accurate projections of the firm's earnings or explanations of its problems until the Treasury Department's audits and
research began to obtain better information as a condition for the
loan guarantee.[88] By then, the crisis was well under way.

British Leyland is the extreme case. Although news that the firm
had problems came relatively early, there was very little information
about the problems themselves or the prospects for solving them.
When the firm went to the government at the end of 1974, its losses
for the year were only $46 million—small by comparison with those
of AEG-Telefunken or Chrysler. BL's banks, which had just refused
to provide the company with any more loans, knew only that the
firm's cash position was deteriorating rapidly. The government there-
upon appointed a special commission to investigate, but the resulting
Ryder Report contained no detailed assessments or projections. Its
authors had done little more than ask BL management what new
strategies the firm would pursue if money were no object, and report
the results back to the House of Commons.[89] Nor was the National
Enterprise Board equipped to diagnose BL's disease and prescribe a
remedy, since it dealt with BL's managers at arm's length. Moreover,
although BL officials filed reports with the NEB, the NEB—in sharp
contrast to Sumitomo Bank—had no staff with particular expertise
in the automobile industry.

The four sets of rescuers also differed considerably in their ability
to effect a change in management or impose a new direction on the

firm. Both the Sumitomo Bank and Dresdner Bank took the initiative in removing top managers who had presided over the firms' deepening problems and found new managers to replace them. The Sumitomo Bank continued to maintain tight control over Toyo Kogyo's rescue; the Dresdner Bank had a less direct role. At British Leyland, the National Enterprise Board selected the company's chief executives, but had no direct role in managing the company; the banks played no part. In the Chrysler case, the government also initiated the change by making it clear to Chrysler's board of directors that a management change was a precondition for a loan guarantee. The government, however, had no direct role in selecting a successor or in managing the company. As with BL, the banks to which Chrysler was indebted played no part.

These differences are attributable largely to differences in the relationships between banks, companies, and governments in the four nations, a subject to which we now turn.

Financial Linkages: Japan. In Japan, the lead bank for a company plays a key role in its long-term development, as well as that of other companies in the same industrial group. Banks are permitted to lend substantial portions of their capital to individual companies and may also hold up to 5 percent of the outstanding shares of any company. Other companies within the industrial group also hold shares in the bank and in one another.[90] In 1975, at the start of Toyo Kogyo's crisis, the Sumitomo Bank was responsible for more than 16 percent of Toyo Kogyo's accumulated debt, and it held 5 percent of Toyo Kogyo's shares. Toyo Kogyo held 3 percent of the shares of the bank. Given these relationships, it is not surprising that Toyo Kogyo routinely shared confidential information with the bank, and that when the crisis occurred Kohei Matsuda, the company's president, put up only minor resistance to the bank's rapid takeover.

In addition to close relations to companies, Japanese banks are linked tightly to government agencies—the Ministry of Finance, the Ministry of International Trade and Industry, and the central bank. Banks are the primary intermediaries between savers and borrowers, but the banks must rely on the central bank for some of their capital. Because government officials set interest rates at the central bank lower than the demand for funds otherwise would dictate, the banks must depend on the discretion of the central bankers and government authorities for the amount of funds they receive. This "window guidance" makes bank officials particularly sensitive to the inclinations of policy makers and politicians.[91] In the Toyo Kogyo case it was clear that government officials were concerned about the firm's future and wanted to restore its competitiveness, but they also wanted to preserve jobs.

These two binding relationships—between the lead bank and its client companies on the one hand, and the lead bank and the government on the other—make the lead bank one of the major channels between government and individual companies in Japan. Rescues of companies in distress are timely and effective largely because of this deeply entrenched public role of the lead bank. Commenting on the Sumitomo Bank's rescue of Toyo Kogyo, one of the bank executives who had temporarily managed the troubled firm explained:

> In Japan, banks are private profit-making operations. But at the same time, banks have a social obligation to make sure that their clients are healthy. Had Sumitomo Bank merely tried to get its loan to Toyo Kogyo repaid, it might have succeeded by forcing the company into bankruptcy. But the bank would have been criticized by society. It would have gotten a reputation for being unreliable. One of the bank's goals is to avoid that kind of criticism.[92]

Financial Linkages: West Germany. The relationship between banks and companies in West Germany is similar to that in Japan. West German banks exercise extraordinary control over company access to capital; there are few other institutions that channel savings to borrowers.[93] By law, the banks can represent shareholders who deposit their shares with the banks.[94] Because only the banks are allowed to trade on the floor of the West German stock exchanges, and therefore have the best knowledge of stock performance, most shareholders take advantage of this service. In 1974, the latest date for which such data are available, West German banks held proxies for 63 percent of the shares of the nation's seventy-four largest publicly held companies.[95] Banks are also permitted to purchase directly up to 100 percent of the shares of a company, although it is considered imprudent for them to invest substantial portions of their capital in any single company.[96]

As a result of these linkages, the banks in West Germany control a majority of the shares of companies to which they lend money. In 1974, for example, banks were represented on practically all of the supervisory boards of the seventy-four largest companies in the nation, and bank representatives chaired half of them.[97] Control is further centralized in West Germany's three largest banks—the Deutsche, Commerz, and Dresdner—which in 1974 supplied two-thirds of the bankers chairing such supervisory boards and voted 35 percent of the outstanding shares of the largest companies.[97]

The banks' control of AEG-Telefunken fits this pattern. At the height of the firm's crisis, the Dresdner Bank was its chief creditor; the bank also directly held more than 18 percent of the company's outstanding shares. With the proxies of AEG shares deposited with the bank or lent to it by other banks, the Dresdner Bank effectively controlled a majority of the company's shares. This explains why Hans Friderichs, the bank's chief executive, also came to be the chairman of AEG's supervisory board. It also helps explain why the bank assumed responsibility for arranging first the "private" bailout of the firm, and then the public one: the bank simply had too much at stake in AEG to let the firm go under all at once.

In these respects, the relationship between the Dresdner Bank and AEG paralleled that between the Sumitomo Bank and Toyo Kogyo. There were important differences, however. The Dresdner Bank did not have access to information about AEG of the same quality that Sumitomo had about Toyo Kogyo, or at quite such an early stage of the crisis. The Dresdner Bank could neither place bank officers in key positions within AEG, as Sumitomo had done with Toyo Kogyo, nor accomplish the dramatic changes that the Sumitomo Bank managed at Toyo Kogyo in a relatively short time.

The ability of Dresdner Bank to control outcomes at AEG was also compromised by divisions on AEG's supervisory board. As AEG's financial position deteriorated in the middle and late 1970s, its board was unable to agree on a diagnosis or a plan of action. Not trusting the bank representatives to act in the best interest of labor, the representatives of labor on the board withheld certain information in their possession. Not trusting labor to maintain confidentiality, management and the bank representatives also withheld information.[98] As the crisis deepened in 1979, the board was deadlocked. The Dresdner Bank refused to seek assistance from the government because it feared that such a move would give labor a greater voice in the management of the company and ultimately in the management of the economy. It therefore turned for help to other banks, industrial companies, and insurance companies, while labor simultaneously sought help from the government. Even by 1982, when the bank was forced to go to the government, it negotiated separately from labor.

In short, the ongoing power struggle in which the Dresdner Bank found itself impaired its ability to manage AEG's rescue.

West German banks are not politically accountable for their major decisions, despite all their power over the economy.[99] The Dresdner Bank thus never assumed the same public responsibilities for West German economic development that the Sumitomo Bank assumed for Japanese development. Unlike the Sumitomo Bank, the Dresdner Bank was not an agent of government policy.

Financial Fragmentation: United States.   Banks in the United States maintain arm's-length relationships both with companies and with the government. This helps to explain why Chrysler's lead bank, Manufacturers Hanover, had neither early warning of Chrysler's problems nor the ability to solve the problems even if it had received warning. The arm's-length relationship between banks and companies is required by law. In general, financial institutions in the United States may not hold shares in separate business enterprises.[100] National banks, bank holding companies, and insurance companies are typically permitted to engage (either directly or through a subsidiary) only in businesses bearing a close relationship to traditional banking or insurance functions.[101] In addition, the Glass-Steagall Act limits the role of commercial banks in underwriting and purchasing securities and specifically prohibits them from making investments in corporate securities for their own account.[102] Further restrictions on bank investments were embodied in the Bank Holding Company Act, which was designed to extend the principle of separation of banking from commerce to entities that own or control banks.[103] Similar restrictions on investments by state-chartered banks exist under various state laws.[104] Although insurance companies are generally permitted to make equity investments under state laws, such laws frequently require the investments to be made in corporations with a specified level of financial performance and strength.[105]

In addition to these limitations on equity ownership, banks in the United States may not extend loans that exceed 10 percent of the bank's capital to an individual company.[106] Moreover, banks generally may not do business in more than one state.[107] On the other hand, specialized investment banks are permitted to hold shares, but, because they are not allowed to accept deposits, they have comparatively few resources to invest.[108] Such banks function primarily to maintain secondary markets for commercial paper and corporate bonds.

Most of these restrictions originated in the 1930s to help ensure bank solvency and credibility, and some are gradually succumbing to the forces of deregulation and competition.[109] These restrictions have fragmented and decentralized financial intermediaries in the United States, so that no large company is particularly dependent on any single financial institution, or vice versa. Chrysler was indebted to more than 400 separate banks; it also had substantial amounts of commercial paper and corporate bonds outstanding. By the same token, even Manufacturers Hanover, Chrysler's chief lender, regarded Chrysler as but one of a large number of clients about whom the bank knew relatively little. The loan officer in charge of the Chrysler account had no particular knowledge about Chrysler or the automobile industry; indeed, his portfolio of accounts was organized geographically, rather than by industrial sector.[110] He periodically reviewed Chrysler's balance sheets and income statements to assure that they technically conformed to bank credit requirements. He was not trained to analyze financial projections or strategic plans, even had Chrysler been willing to give them to him.[110]

Even if bank managers possessed the skills, knowledge, and authority needed to deal with problems such as those experienced by Chrysler, it was not clear that they would have wanted to become deeply involved in developing a solution. U.S. financial institutions that wish to participate in the debtor's management risk creating a relationship that will cause them to be deemed "in control" of the debtor. This may subject them to substantial liability under U.S. bankruptcy, securities, and tax laws.[111] Even if a lender is not actually in control of a debtor, allegations that such control exists can result in expensive litigation.

In addition, corporate laws of various states draw a relatively sharp distinction between the fiduciary duties owed creditors and those owed shareholders.[112] Chrysler managers had a legal responsibility to act in the best interest of Chrysler shareholders, not in the best interest of the bank's shareholders.[113] Had the bank required as a condition of a loan that Chrysler change its management or take some other action that might harm Chrysler shareholders—for example, selling off a valuable property to pay off corporate debts—Chrysler's shareholders could have a right of action against the bank.[114]

These fiduciary obligations obviously constrain the banks from asserting control over distressed companies. During the years immediately preceding Chrysler's crisis, the chairman of the board of Manufacturers Hanover, Gabriel Hauge, also was a member of Chrysler's board of directors—an interlocking relationship of the sort that flourished between Sumitomo Bank and Toyo Kogyo, and Dresdner Bank and AEG-Telefunken. Unlike the situations in Japan and West Germany, however, this relationship was purely cosmetic. It may have impressed a few shareholders or smaller creditors, but as a practical matter Hauge had to be careful not to pass information he learned at the Chrysler board meetings to the commercial loan department of the bank, lest he place himself in a conflict of interest and thereby invite a suit by Chrysler shareholders.[115]

The U.S. government, like the West German government, has no particular substantive authority over the banks, although it closely regulates them to ensure solvency and prudence. The government collects a large amount of information about individual companies in tax filings, securities filings, reviews of regulatory compliance, and reviews of proposed mergers and acquisitions. Most of these data, however, are in the wrong form to provide adequate warning that a major company is in trouble, or are dispersed among so many agencies that they often cannot be reconstructed without contravening laws that protect confidentiality.[116] This inadequacy explains why, when Chrysler came to the White House seeking help, the Carter administration had to commission a variety of studies by private accountants, investment bankers, and management consultants in order to elicit useful information about the company's plight and future prospects, rather than rely on data already in the government's possession.

Financial Fragmentation: Great Britain. If anything, British banks are even further removed from the companies to which they lend money than are U.S. banks. The City of London, Britain's Wall Street, is oriented to an international financial market in which capital is highly mobile. As a result, financial relationships are fragmented. Loans tend to be short term (more than 80 percent are due to be paid within a year),[117] and British companies typically finance their expansion through retained earnings and new issues of stock.[118] In addition, the fiduciary obligations governing banks and company managers are at least as strict as those in the United

States.[119] For these reasons, the banks play no significant role in monitoring or rescuing large firms in distress. British Leyland's major creditors had no inside information about the company's mounting problems and no particular capacity to do anything about them.[120]

Sacrifice

Even if a rescuer has early and reliable information about a company's growing problems and asserts managerial control over the company, the rescue still is more likely to be an orderly shrink than a substantial shift, unless the other participants cooperate. In particular, workers must be willing to accept lower pay, at least for a time, and to shift to new jobs within the company. Lenders must maintain their outstanding loans even in the face of higher risks and perhaps advance additional credit. Without these sacrifices, new funds from the rescuer merely preserve the status quo for a time—maintaining existing wages and commercial credit while the company gradually shrinks.

The four cases represent a spectrum of sacrifice, with Toyo Kogyo and British Leyland once again occupying the extreme positions. Toyo Kogyo workers accepted major pay cuts, and many of them agreed to transfer temporarily to automobile dealers hundreds of miles away from Hiroshima. Similarly, Toyo Kogyo's banks, insurance companies, and suppliers agreed to maintain loans or advance credit. On the other hand, British Leyland workers resisted pay cuts and changes in work rules and job classifications, while private lenders called in their loans and refused to make new ones. AEG and Chrysler lie in between: AEG's lenders sacrificed, but its workers balked at major reductions in wages and benefits; Chrysler's lenders and workers both sacrificed, but only to a limited extent. This section attempts to account for these differences in the degree of sacrifice parties were willing to undertake.

Financial Interdependency. One explanation is found in the structures of national financial markets. For the same reasons that lead banks in Japan and West Germany receive more timely and detailed information about their clients than do arm's-length banks in the United States and Britain, they also are more committed to maintaining their clients. In these countries, even a gradual liquidation would be likely to impair the value of the bank's equity and jeopardize its major loans, both with the distressed company and also with a larger network of suppliers and industrial purchasers that depend on the company. These lead banks therefore are more likely to finance resource shifts than are banks in the United States or Great Britain.

In addition, these lead banks are linked financially and strategically to other banks, insurance companies, and trade creditors. The lead banks, therefore, can facilitate the agreement of these other lenders to maintain their own outstanding loans to the troubled company and even on occasion to provide new financing. These interdependent networks function as systems of mutual aid. Lenders, in effect, insure one another against relatively sudden market changes that might threaten their survival.

In 1975, at the start of Toyo Kogyo's crisis, the Sumitomo *keiretsu* as a whole held almost 11 percent of Toyo Kogyo's shares, and Toyo Kogyo had considerable holdings in other group members. The Sumitomo Bank also held 9 percent of the shares of C. Itoh, the trading company outside the group on which the bank later called to help Toyo Kogyo. In addition to this financial tie, several members of the Sumitomo *keiretsu* supplied parts to Toyo Kogyo, or had common technological needs and therefore were engaged in joint ventures or joint purchasing arrangements. These financial and strategic ties enabled the bank to spread the cost and risk of the Toyo Kogyo rescue among many cooperating institutions. They also enabled the bank to make credible guarantees about the company's survival and thereby reduce the perceived riskiness on new loans. Given all these interdependencies, the Sumitomo Bank's announcement that it would stand by Toyo Kogyo made other lenders more willing to maintain their outstanding loans and commercial credits with the company.[121]

Like Sumitomo in the Toyo Kogyo case, the Dresdner Bank was able to call on other banks and insurance companies to help AEG. For some of these participants the stake was more direct: twenty-four of these banks held almost 50 percent of the AEG's outstanding shares; the Deutsche Bank alone held 9 percent. The Dresdner Bank could also count on the support of a small group of industrial companies. Although this group was not as formally organized and integrated as the Sumitomo Group, its ties were similarly strategic and financial. Through its close relationship with AEG, the Dresdner Bank gradually had developed expertise in the electronics and capital goods industries in which AEG competed; the bank therefore organized its industrial loan department along these sectors.[122] In this way, over time, many AEG suppliers and industrial purchasers became clients of the bank. These interdependencies were reinforced as the bank took equity positions in these companies.

There was no similar, mutually dependent network on which Chrysler or British Leyland could rely. As we have seen, British Leyland's banks backed out early in the crisis. Chrysler's banks agreed to extend the maturity of some notes in 1980, and in 1981 they agreed to convert approximately one-third of the company's outstanding debt to equity and to write down another one-third. The banks, however, demanded full payment on the final one-third, and throughout the crisis they adamantly refused to extend new loans to the company. The few concessions they did make came largely as a result of pressure from the Treasury Department and the Federal Reserve Board.

To some extent, the comparative reticence of U.S. and British banks can be explained by differing auditing practices and financial regulations. Auditors and bank examiners in Japan and West Germany take a far more lenient view of nonperforming loans than do their colleagues in the United States and Britain. In Japan and West Germany, debtors may violate loan covenants or miss interest payments without necesarily forcing the bank to write down the asset on its books. Because the debtor may well shift into a more profitable line of business, the loan is not necessarily considered to be riskier, or of lesser value, than it was before.[123] For the same reason, the bank also may advance new loans to such a company and carry the new loan as an asset.

In the United States and Britain, on the other hand, bank auditors and regulators are more concerned about the risk of inadequate capitalization. A bank typically is required to write down its nonperforming loans; it also may have to expand its loan-loss reserves in coming years.[124] These items are charged off against earnings. If the distressed company subsequently repays the loan and any lost interest, these payments can be applied against whatever provisions have been made for the losses.[125] In the interim, however, the damage has already been done to the bank's reported profits, thereby impairing its ability to raise more capital. By the same token, new loans to a distressed company are scrutinized carefully; the bank probably would not be able to carry them as assets.

This cautious approach obviously makes banks more reluctant to accept temporary sacrifices. A Manufacturers Hanover vice president in charge of problem loans explained that the bank would never extend a new loan to a distressed company except as part of a plan to reduce the bank's overall embedded debt. Indeed, the bank followed this rule with respect to Chrysler, and other banks took the same position.[126] Such a rule ultimately favors shrinkage over shifts.

Financial structures are only part of the story, of course. To understand why sacrifices were more widespread in Toyo Kogyo than in British Leyland—with AEG and Chrysler in between—we also need to examine the organization of labor.

Labor Interdependency. By a variety of formal and informal rules, Japanese workers are tightly linked to their companies. The links are somewhat more attenuated in large West German companies. In the United States and Great Britain, such links are almost nonexistent. These patterns are evident in the ways unions are organized, in the relations between unionized workers and managers, and in ways of providing job security and regulating wage differentials among workers.

In each of the four countries, workers are organized at several levels. At the bottom are local shop-floor organizations, which are aggregated into company unions or affiliates, then into industry unions, and finally into multi-industry labor federations. The locus of control differs in each country, however. In Japan, company unions predominate; most of the important decisions about wages and working conditions are made at this level.[127] Company unions also are important in West Germany. Unlike their Japanese counterparts, West German workers also participate through their unions in national negotiations over wages and macroeconomic policies.[128] Company unions are less important in the United States and Great Britain. In the United States, most bargaining occurs at the level of the industry union.[129] In Britain, bargaining occurs both at the shop floor and at the industry level.[130]

Formal relations between managers and unionized workers within the company are structured quite differently in the four countries. In most large Japanese companies there is no sharp distinction between supervisors and blue-collar workers. Japanese companies typically employ elaborate systems of joint consultation through which confidential management information is shared with lower-level employees. Japanese company unions include many white-collar supervisors, and the links between management and labor are reinforced by the fact that many company directors were once union leaders.[131] In West Germany, distinctions between production workers and supervisors are more clearly drawn, yet there exist a variety of consultative mechanisms. By law, union representatives occupy one-third to one-half of the seats on company supervisory boards, which have responsibility for major decisions affecting the company.[132] In the United States and Great Britain, on the other hand, managers and workers are sharply separated.

The National Labor Relations Act (NLRA), for example, presumes a fundamental conflict between managers and employees. Section 8(a)(2) makes it an unfair labor practice for employers to "dominate or interfere with the formation or administration of any labor organization or contribute financial or other support to it."[133] This provision has been construed broadly to bar management from supporting certain formal mechanisms of worker participation.[134] By the same token, supervisory employees are excluded from the provisions of the NLRA on the theory that the supervisor-employee relationship is necessarily adversarial and supervisors represent management; union membership, it is assumed, would involve them in a conflict of interest.[135] An American employer is under no obligation to open its financial records to its unions unless the company specifically pleads an inability to pay during collective bargaining.[136] Nor do employers have a duty to bargain about management decisions to close part of an operation.[137] The cumulative effect of these rules is to maintain an arm's-length, adversarial relationship between management and employees.

Like American labor law, British labor law seems to presume a fundamental tension and separation between management and labor. For example, although British employers are obligated to disclose to the trade unions information without which the union representatives' collective bargaining efforts would be severely hampered, this obligation is subject to numerous qualifications and exceptions.[138] The ability of workers to obtain data from management is further compromised—and thus the separation between workers and management is preserved—by the uncertainty of the procedures for enforcing whatever obligations do exist.[139] British employers are required to give trade unions advance notice of and the reasons for plant closings; however, like their American counterparts, they are under no affirmative duty to bargain over such managerial decisions.[140]

Finally, important differences also exist among these four countries in ways of providing job security and regulating wage differentials among workers. In Japan, employees of most large companies are hired directly from high school and expect to remain with the company until retirement; their wages and benefits depend largely on their age.[141] In West Germany job security is built into most labor contracts within large firms, as are generous severance payments in the event of necessary layoffs. Wage and benefit levels rise with the number of years the employee has served. In both West Germany and Japan, employers are required to provide employees with at least one month's advance notice of a plant shutdown. In addition, employees have substantial rights in the event of an employer's insolvency: In West Germany, employees have a priority in bankruptcy, entitling them to 68 percent of their average pay for one year; in Japan, they receive full wages for two years and 80 percent of the first three months' salary is provided by the state.[142]

In the United States and Great Britain, job security and relative wages have been more closely linked to job classifications, work rules, and seniority; rights and benefits vary with the category in which a worker is classified. Particularly in the United States, income-security provisions have substituted for job security. The government administers unemployment insurance, which pays approximately 60 percent of previous wages.[143] In many industries these benefits have been supplemented by unemployment benefits built into wage contracts.[144] If the company cannot then offer "suitable employment," workers who are at least forty-five years old can collect regular pensions, plus $400 monthly supplements until they become eligible for Social Security.

These different patterns of organization presumably influence workers' willingness to sacrifice in order to help a distressed company shift. Such shifts require flexibility in wages, benefits, and work responsibilities as alternatives to layoffs. Shifts also require external *inflexibility*—meaning that employees tend not to move between firms, but to remain with the same firm during the course of their career. This combination results in a great deal of mutual dependence between the company and the employee; both sides can draw on a reservoir of trust and simultaneously rely on the discipline of future dealings. In consequence, unionized workers will be more willing to reduce wages and shift jobs during bad times than they would be otherwise.[145]

Japan's system of company negotiations, combined with lifetime job security (in the largest firms) and age-based wages, is the most internally flexible of the four. When a Japanese company suddenly begins to lose money, it can quickly reduce its workers' wages and benefits, and shift job responsibilities. The Japanese system is also externally rigid: with lifetime employment as the norm, it is difficult for a worker to leave one large company and find employment with another. Like those of the lead banks, workers' fates are linked to that of the company. Toyo Kogyo's company union accepted pay raises lower than those received by workers at other automobile companies and agreed to the transfer of 5,000 workers to Toyo Kogyo dealers.

AEG's workers were less inclined to accept wage and benefit reductions. In West Germany, national labor negotiations may have reduced the flexibility of the company union. Officials at IG Metall, the national union that represented many of AEG's workers, were concerned that any concession at the company level might strengthen the hand of management nationally, not only with regard to wages and benefits of workers in other companies but also with regard to larger questions about the role of financial institutions in shaping economic development. AEG's workers had not participated in planning either the initial private rescue or the subsequent federal loan guarantee; the unions viewed both actions as disturbing precedents.

Chrysler's workers resisted wage cuts even more adamantly. The United Auto Workers did not want to depart from "pattern bargaining" in which wages and benefits are established for the entire industry. Nor was the union willing to give up work rules and job classifications, a move that would have permitted Chrysler management to shift workers to other responsibilities. Under the pressure of the Loan Guarantee Board, the union ultimately acceded to wage cuts in 1981, but only after tens of thousands of Chrysler workers already had been laid off.

Indeed, at no point in Chrysler's crisis did the union express a willingness to exchange wage concessions for job guarantees. The union seniority system may have been partly to blame for this, since the axe would fall on younger workers with less influence in the union. The majority of union members who voted on wage concessions knew that they were less likely to be laid off. This dynamic was most apparent in the fall of 1982, when Chrysler's workers were offered a no-raise, no-layoff contract. Fifty thousand Chrysler workers, including 45,000 still on the job and 5,000 most recently laid off, were entitled to vote; a majority of them wanted pay raises. But

42,000 Chrysler workers were not allowed to make this choice between pay raises and job security. This group had been laid off for so long that they had lost their union voting rights. Had they voted, the results might have gone the other way, and many of these laid-off workers might have gotten their jobs back.

Workers at British Leyland were the least cooperative of all. Many of their disputes were not with BL management, but with other workers. With seventeen unions arranged into 246 bargaining units, and an elaborate system of work rules and job classifications, every negotiation over wages and benefits for one group potentially altered the relative positions of every other group. The firm was wracked by disputes over union jurisdictions and pay differentials. Shop stewards vied for control. With so many groups and individuals competing for leadership and influence, none could risk appearing to concede too much. In the end, most of the rescue money went to maintaining wages and providing lump-sum severance payments. Shrinking was far easier to accomplish than shifting.

CONCLUSION

The broader lessons that emerge from this study must be stated tentatively. We have, after all, investigated only four cases and explored only some of the plausible explanations for their patterns and outcomes. Nevertheless certain conclusions seem warranted.

First, the cases suggest that these sorts of large manufacturing enterprises are more than mere productive enterprises. They are also the centers of vast social and economic networks of suppliers, dealers, financial institutions, employees, and service industries. They anchor communities, define relationships, and structure social obligations. How these companies respond to crisis is therefore intimately conditioned by, and profoundly affects, the way these social systems respond. When large companies that employ substantial portions of a region's work force begin to falter, political pressures invariably mount to "save jobs." Even if politics did not intercede initially, rapid dissolution of such companies might so disrupt social and economic life that governments and other institutions would be compelled to respond. The fact that they did respond in the four cases thus is less interesting than the differences in how they responded.

Second, the responses can be arranged along a continuum. Some responses merely slow down the company's inevitable shrinkage. Other responses help the company to shift its resources internally to more profitable pursuits. At the extremes, Toyo Kogyo quickly jettisoned a relatively small number of its jobs and shifted the rest; British Leyland slowly jettisoned most of its jobs and shifted comparatively few. Yet the British government intervened far more directly to save British Leyland jobs—effectively nationalizing the company— than did the Japanese government to save Toyo Kogyo jobs. Chrysler and AEG both lie midway on this continuum; both companies shrank considerably after they were rescued, although the Chrysler and the AEG loan guarantees also were premised on saving jobs.

Third, the pattern of response seems related to the laws and detailed understandings that shape relationships between management, finance, and labor. There are other possible explanations, of course. Some have to do with the overall pace of economic activity surrounding these companies. Presumably shifts are easier to negotiate when the economy is expanding and all participants can anticipate a larger income in the future. Culture also obviously plays a part; shifts are probably easier to arrange if people think of themselves more as group members—as in Japan—than as isolated individuals—as in the United States.

Between economics and culture, however, lies a detailed set of laws, regulations, and social norms that frame institutional relationships. These formal and informal rules both establish and represent responsibilities. They define institutional loyalties and shape patterns of negotiation among different groups of people. They thereby give rise to different types of transactions—some between parties that perceive their dealings to be only temporary and convenient, others between parties whose ties to one another arise from perceived mutual dependencies stretching over long periods of time.

At one extreme we find companies that are tied to lead banks, and through the lead banks to other financial and industrial units, and regional and national governments. This network functions as a system of early warning and mutual aid. It insures against unexpected changes in the market, helping companies restructure themselves by shifting their resources internally at the first sign of trouble. The corresponding organization of labor is internally flexible, but externally inflexible. Although wages, benefits, and responsibilities can vary significantly within the company from one period to the next, employees find it relatively difficult to leave one company and obtain a new job at another. Employees' fates are as inextricably linked to the fate of the company as is the fate of the lead bank. This overall organization of finance and labor, typified by the case of Toyo Kogyo, strongly favors shifts over shrinkage, internal over external redeployment.

At the other extreme, we find companies that have no special ties to any particular financial institution, and financial institutions that are similarly fragmented and distanced from one another, from other companies, and from governments. Most of the financial transactions in this system are at arm's length; parties deal with one another on the basis of information available to them at the time and do not necessarily assume repeated dealings in the future. Each separate company or institution takes responsibility only for its own profitability. The corresponding organization of labor is internally inflexible, but externally flexible. Wages, benefits, and responsibilities do not vary significantly within the company from one period to the next, but employees find it relatively easy to leave the company. Management and labor deal at arm's length, because they are presumed to have conflicting agendas. As a result, neither employees nor financial institutions are especially dependent on the fate of a particular firm. Furthermore, neither can draw on a reservoir of trust or rely on the discipline of future dealings. This overall organization of finance and labor, typified by the case of British Leyland, favors shrinkage over shifts, external over internal redeployment.

Fourth, the government's role in rescuing large failing companies is likely to be far more visible and targeted when management, finance, and labor deal with each other at arm's length than when these groups are more tightly linked. When tightly linked to the firm, both financial and labor organizations are likely to be actively involved in responding to the crisis. Government therefore can do its work indirectly through these mediating groups. It can act on behalf of affected communities merely by supporting the financial institutions or the labor organizations that already have a stake. In contrast, when they are at arm's length from the firm, neither financial nor labor organizations are necessarily involved in the crisis. Much of the real burden of redeployment therefore falls on individuals, some of whom have no direct contractual relationship with the firm, and on local governments and relief organizations. These individuals and institutions in turn make political demands for national government intervention to save jobs and communities. The irony, as the BL case reveals, is that government can do little more than slow the pace of shrinkage without the active cooperation of finance and labor.

Finally, the analysis suggests that the practical question in these circumstances is not whether the government should intervene to save jobs, but how it might intervene to preserve social networks. The answer to that question has a great deal to do with how finance and labor are organized. There are some reasons why internal redeployment might be preferable to external for very large companies whose activities and employment are concentrated in certain regions. If internal redeployment is preferred, then centralized planning boards or national development banks, as have been suggested by some proponents of "industrial policy,"[146] may be less useful than changes in the detailed rules and understandings by which financial institutions and labor organizations undertake their day-to-day responsibilities—changes that strengthen the bonds between the company's workers, managers, and financial institutions.

NOTES

1. The U.S. government's response to the problems of several failing northeastern and midwestern railroads is embodied in the Regional Rail Reorganization Act, 45 U.S.C. secs. 701–97 (1982). For a discussion of Conrail's return to profitability, see "Making More Hauling Less," *Fortune* August 23, 1982, p. 7. The bailout of Lockheed Aircraft Corp. was effectuated through the Emergency Loan Guarantee Act, 15 U.S.C. secs. 1841–52 (1982). The bailout of the Chrysler Corp. is discussed later in this chapter. For a discussion of the problems at the Continental Illinois Bank, see, for example, *Wall Street Journal*, July 19, 1984, p. 1.

2. See Eizenstat, "Reindustrialization Through Coordination or Chaos?" *Yale Journal on Regulation* 2 (1984): 39, 49; Weil, "U.S. Industrial Policy: A Process in Need of a Federal Industrial Coordination Board," *Law and Policy in International Business* 14 (1983): 981.

3. See C. Johnson, *MITI and the Japanese Miracle: The Growth of Industrial Policy, 1925–1975* (Stanford, CA: Stanford University Press, 1982), pp. 30–32, 305–24; Weil, op. cit., pp. 994–97.

4. Many commentators have warned against the United States following the lead of Great Britain or other Western European countries in the industrial policy area. See, for example, Krauss, "Europeanizing the U.S. Economy: The Enduring Appeal of the Corporatist State," in *The Industrial Policy*

Debate, ed. C. Johnson (San Francisco: ICS Press, 1984), pp. 71–90 ("European experience shows that the real myth is the notion of an efficient industrial policy in the first place."); Miller, Walton, Kovacic and Rabkin, "Industrial Policy: Reindustrialization Through Competition or Coordinated Action?" *Yale Journal on Regulation* 2 (1984): 1, 23–27.

5. This case study is based on data obtained from a wide variety of sources, including company reports of AEG-Telefunken, interviews, news accounts, and other materials. For the reader interested in learning more about this case one very useful source is D. Anderson, "AEG-Telefunken, A.G.," Harvard Business School Case No. 1-381-187, July 1981. For the purposes of this case and the cases that follow (see notes 13, 20, and 29), all foreign currencies have been converted into equivalent dollar values at the exchange rate applicable when the transaction discussed occurred.

6. D. Anderson, op. cit., p. 15.

7. Ibid., pp. 12–15. The role German banks traditionally play in the economy is discussed later in this chapter.

8. *Wall Street Journal*, November 26, 1979, p. 16.

9. *Wall Street Journal*, July 15, 1982, p. 34.

10. Vergleichsordnung secs. 7, 20, 73, 74, 1935 Reichsgesetzblatt (RGB1) I 321 (West Germany).

11. "Labor Is Bracing for AEG's Collapse," *Business Week*, September 6, 1982, pp. 42–43.

12. *German Tribune*, January 8, 1984, p. 7; company reports, 1984, 1985.

13. The sources for this case study, as for the study of AEG, are too numerous to list comprehensively. See generally G. Lodge, "British Leyland: The Ryder Report," Harvard Business School Case No. 9-376-052, February 1982; D. Ryder, R. Clark, S. Gillen, F. McWhirter, and C. Urwin, *British Leyland: The Next Decade* (1975), an abridged version of a report presented to the secretary of state for industry by a team of inquiry led by Sir Don Ryder, hereafter cited as Ryder Report; British Leyland, *1974 Report and Accounts* (1975).

14. *Wall Street Journal*, April 11, 1975, p. 1.

15. See note 13.

16. *New York Times*, April 25, 1975, p. 45. See also Ryder Report, p. 3: "Vehicle production is the kind of industry which ought to remain an essential part of the UK's economic base. We believe, therefore, that BL should remain a major vehicle producer, although this means that urgent action must be taken to remedy the weaknesses which at present prevent it from competing effectively in world markets."

17. 892 Parliamentary Debate, House of Commons (5th ser.) 1542 (1975). See also note 60.

18. The poor performance could no longer be blamed entirely on the company. Sales of North Sea oil had strengthened the pound, thereby making

all British exports less attractive. At the same time, higher oil prices dampened demand for larger cars, on which BL made its highest profits.

19. "BL: It's the Thought that Counts," *Economist*, January 31, 1981, p. 48.

20. This case study is based on data obtained from a wide variety of sources including company reports of Toyo Kogyo, interviews, news, accounts, and other materials. See, for example, "The Turnaround at Mazda—Is There a Lesson for Chrysler?" *Los Angeles Times*, October 25, 1981, sec. 5, p. 1; Toyo Kogyo, *Summary of Toyo Kogyo*, company report, 1983.

21. U.S. Environmental Protection Agency, *1974 Gas Mileage Guide for Car Buyers: Fuel Economy Test Results for Automobiles and Light-Duty Trucks* (1974), pp. 4-5.

22. *Wall Street Journal*, October 3, 1974, p. 11.

23. "Where Is Toyo Kogyo Going?", *Toyo Kezai the Oriental Economist*, February 14, 1976.

24. "Hard Times Make Tenjin a Top Auto Salesman," *Los Angeles Times*, October 25, 1981, sec. 5, p. 1.

25. Interview with Satoshi Yamada, general manager of Sumitomo Bank, in Japan, September 16, 1983, hereafter cited as Yamada interview.

26. *Keiretsu*, groups of companies united by stock ownership and financial support, are the postwar descendants of the great *zaibatsu*, whose hand in the Japanese war effort led to their dissolution during the American occupation after World War II. The four most famous prewar *zaibatsu*—Mitsubishi, Mitsui, Sumitomo, and Yasuda—included firms in every sector of the economy from heavy industry to banks, each bearing the *zaibatsu's* name and all centered on a single holding company exercising strict control. Unlike the *zaibatsu*, the *keiretsu* is centered on a large bank, which exercises considerable influence over the *keiretsu's* members. The power of this lead bank is assured not only by its debt and equity arrangements with the firms in the *keiretsu*, but also by the interlocking financial and operating linkages among the firms and by the efforts of the group's trading company. See R. Caves and M. Uekusa, *Industrial Organization in Japan* (Washington, DC: Brookings Institution, 1976), pp. 62-68; K. Haitan; *The Japanese Economic System: An Institutional Overview* (Lexington, MA: Lexington Books, 1976), pp. 120-25. The main role of the lead bank within a *keiretsu* is to guarantee a member's debt and thereby permit heavy leveraging of investment. See Johnson, op. cit. (note 3), p. 206.

27. *Motor Trend*, April 1983, p. 9.

28. Yamada interview.

29. The data on which this case is based were obtained from company reports, interviews, and news accounts. A much more detailed version of this study appears in R. Reich and J. Donahue, *New Deals: The Chrysler Revival and the American System* (New York: Times Books, 1985).

30. Interview with officials of Manufacturers Hanover Trust Co. (names withheld by request), in New York City, January 10, 1984, hereafter cited as Manufacturers Hanover interview.

31. Interview with G. William Miller, former secretary of the treasury, in Washington, DC, January 17, 1984, hereafter cited as Miller interview.

32. *Chrysler Corp. Loan Guarantee Act of 1979: Hearings on H.R. 5805 Before the Subcommittee on Economic Stabilization of the House Committee on Banking, Finance and Urban Affairs*, 96th Cong., 1st sess. (1979), hereafter cited as House hearings, p. 824 (statement of John McGillicuddy, chairman, Manufacturers Hanover Trust Co.).

33. *New York Times*, November 2, 1979, p. 1.

34. *Congressional Record* 125 (1979): 27, 180–81.

35. *Congressional Record* 125 (1979): 36, 638–44.

36. See, for example, *Congressional Record* 125 (1979): 37, 059 (statement of Senator Goldwater, "I think this [bailout of Chrysler] is probably the biggest mistake that Congress has ever made in its history"); *Congressional Record* 125 (1979): 36, 220–22 (extension of remarks of Representative D. Crane, "Clearly, such largesse [to the Chrysler Corp.] would be the end of the free enterprise system").

37. Chrysler Corporation Loan Guarantee Act of 1979, Pub. L. No. 96–185, 93 Stat. 1324 (1979) (codified at 15 U.S.C. secs. 1861–75). The authority of the Loan Guarantee Board to issue new guarantees for loans to Chrysler expired on December 31, 1983. 15 U.S.C. sec. 1875 (1982).

38. 15 U.S.C. sec. 1863(c) (1982) (requiring $1.43 billion in concessions from creditors); sec. 1865(a)(1) (requiring $462.5 million in concessions from Chrysler employees); sec. 1867 (limiting Board authority to extend loan guarantees to $1.5 billion).

39. 15 U.S.C. sec. 1862 (1982).

40. *New York Times*, January 8, 1980, p. D1.

41. *Detroit Free Press*, February 2, 1980.

42. 29 U.S.C. secs. 1301–9 (1982).

43. 15 U.S.C. sec. 1863(c)(1) (1982) (requiring at least $500 million from U.S. banks, financial institutions, and other creditors in the form of new loans or credits); sec. 1863(c)(2) (requiring at least $150 million from foreign banks, and other creditors).

44. The conditions are set forth in Staff of Subcommittee on Economic Stabilization of the House Committee on Banking, Finance and Urban Affairs, 96th Congress, 2nd sess., *Findings of the Chrysler Corporation Loan Guarantee Board* (Comm. Print, 1980), pp. 39–45.

45. Interview with Wendell Larsen, former Chrysler vice president for public affairs, in Chicago, February 14, 1984. Legislation affecting bank regulation was pending in Congress; in addition, one member of the Loan Board

was Chairman Paul Volcker of the Federal Reserve Board, the government agency that directly regulated many of the banks.

46. Staff of Subcommittee on Economic Stabilization of the House Committee on Banking, Finance and Urban Affairs, 96th Congress, 2nd sess., *Report of the Chrysler Corporation Loan Guarantee Board* (Comm. Print, 1980), pp. 10–14.

47. L. Iacocca, statement at press ceremony, June 25, 1980.

48. Miller interview.

49. *New York Times*, October 21, 1980, p. D5.

50. Interview with William Langley, executive vice president of Manufacturers Hanover Trust Co., in New York City, January 10, 1984.

51. *New York Times*, January 25, 1981, sec. 3, p. 15.

52. Interview with Lee Iacocca, president of Chrysler Corp., in New York City, November 9, 1983.

53. *New York Times*, February 24, 1984, p. 3.

54. "AEG: Weltfirma am Abgrund," *Der Spiegel*, November 19, 1979, p. 75 (discussing the role of AEG in the West German economy); Ryder Report, app. B, p. 74 (discussing regional employment by BL); interview with Ichiro Maeda, assistant general manager of Toyo Kogyo for corporate planning, in Hiroshima, Japan, September 16, 1983, hereafter cited as Maeda interview (discussing effects on Japan); *The Chrysler Corp. Financial Situation: Hearings before the House Subcommittee on Economic Stabilization of the House Committee on Banking, Finance and Urban Affairs*, 96th Cong., 1st sess. (1979) (report on the employment and economic effects of a shutdown or major reduction of business by Chrysler), pp. 187–227.

55. AEG-Telefunken shrank from 105,000 West German employees at the start of the crisis to 60,000 by the time it was over (a 43 percent drop in employment); British Leyland, from 211,000 to slightly more than 100,000 (52 percent); Toyo Kogyo, from 37,000 to 27,000 (27 percent); and Chrysler, from 110,000 U.S. employees to around 60,000 (45 percent).

56. *Financial Times*, July 15, 1982, p. 1.

57. Schlecht, "Darf der Staat sanierungsreifen Unternehmen helfen? (Should the Federal Government Support Enterprises That Have Economic Problems?)," *Wirtschaftsdienst*, September 1982, pp. 423, 425.

58. Yamada interview.

59. 892 *Parl. Deb.*, H.C. (5th ser.) cols. 1419-1538 (May 1975).

60. Enoch Powell summed up the Conservative view (Ibid., pp. 1481–84):

    [W]hat bankruptcy brings about, and it does so harshly, is to make it possible for the resources which have been devoted to making a loss to be reapplied in ways which are more likely to make a profit.

We use the terms "loss" and "profit," but they disguise a much cruder reality—and that cruder reality is destruction and creation. When men are employed in an undertaking which, year after year, is making a loss, those men—who are the last people to blame—are actually destroying that which their fellow workers are creating. Less is going out than comes in; they are involuntary parasites upon the economy. The benefit which bankruptcy confers, the benefit which makes it indispensable, is that it enables resources which would otherwise be locked in the work of destruction to be released for different applications, different combinations, different circumstances, in which they can again be creative.

Immediately, however, public money comes upon the scene, immediately public money is to be injected into an undertaking, all the criteria which would otherwise be brought to bear fly out of the window and are replaced by a very different outlook. The private, cautious, calculated, experienced, almost cynical estimation of the likely prospects for the future is replaced by the public commitments, by the political pressures and by the freedom from responsibility which comes out of spending public money, money which is there to hand. . . .

[B]ankruptcy is indispensable and . . . there is no substitute for the judgment of bankruptcy and for the liberating power of bankruptcy.

Tony Benn, secretary of state of industry in the Labour government, responded to Powell and several other Tories (Ibid., p. 1493):

I am listening intently to the hon. Gentleman, who speaks with great clarity and seriousness on these matters, but the more I listen to him the more I am utterly convinced that his argument leaves out of account that there is not only the balance sheets but the ballot box. He speaks of people as if they can be moved at the behest of the owners of industry without regard to the political and social factors which are the basis of our standing in the House . . . [T]he people represented through the ballot box intend to exercise, and do exercise, a countervailing power to the use he would wish to make of them as pawns in a financial game.

Soon after the Parliamentary debate, Keith Joseph, a member of the Conservative shadow cabinet who was to be secretary of state for industry in the Thatcher government, condemned Benn's position: "In order to preserve jobs in over-manned, inefficient British Leyland, Mr. Benn will take astronomic money from the rest of the country and thus cause many other firms to fail. . . . Mr. Benn is the real manufacturer of poverty" (*Financial Times*, May 3, 1975, p. 1).

61. "Our Very Own British Leyland," *Economist*, April 26, 1975, p. 88.
62. *Financial Times*, May 8, 1975, p. 1.
63. Ball, "Saving Leyland is a Job for Hercules," *Fortune*, July 3, 1978, pp. 58, 61.
64. "BL: It's the Thought That Counts" (see note 19), p. 48; "Brighter Future for British Cars?" *Newsweek*, February 9, 1981, p. 77.
65. *Brighter Future for British Cars?*, p. 77.
66. *Chrysler Corporation Loan Guarantee Act of 1979: Hearings on S. 1965 and S. 1937 Before the Senate Comm. on Banking, Housing and Urban Affairs*, 96th Cong., 1st Sess. (1979), pp. 1032–33, hereafter cited as Senate hearings.
67. House hearings, p. 343 (statement of Coleman Young, mayor of Detroit).

68. Ibid., p. 684 (statement of Rep. Wright).
69. Senate hearings, p. 1286 (statement of Walter Wriston, chairman, Citicorp).
70. Ibid., pp. 777–78 (statement of Peter G. Peterson, chairman, Lehman Brothers Kuhn Loeb, Inc.).
71. *Congressional Quarterly* 37 (December 1, 1979): 2752.
72. Interview with Brian Freeman, former executive director of the Chrysler Loan Guarantee Board, in Cambridge, Massachusetts, February 2, 1984.
73. Miller interview.
74. Ibid.
75. See "Shrinking the Company," above.
76. See, for example, "Labor Is Bracing for AEG's Collapse," *Business Week*, September 6, 1982, pp. 42–43; *Financial Times*, August 12, 1982, p. 16.
77. "Can British Leyland Survive?" *New Statesman*, January 27, 1978, pp. 108–9.
78. Yamada interview.
79. Interview with Douglas Fraser, former president of the United Auto Workers, in Washington, DC, October 19, 1983.
80. Occasionally, parts of large failing firms may be sold off to other companies or groups of investors, who expect that—because of their superior managerial acumen or "synergistic" aspects of their other businesses—the newly spun-off divisions will offer a better return to them than they did as part of the failing firm. This occurred to a limited extent in Chrysler, which sold off its tank division; it occurred to a substantial extent in AEG-Telefunken, which sold off its consumer-products divisions. In these transactions, titles to plant, equipment, and employees are transferred to the new owners. From a social standpoint, there has been no change, particularly no net loss of jobs. Wholesale transfers like these, therefore, may represent a socially preferable alternative to shrinkage.
81. Senate hearings, p. 701 (statement of Alfred Kahn, chairman, Council on Wage and Price Stability).
82. Yamada interview.
83. For an analysis of all four countries' economic performances over the past five years, see U.S. Department of Commerce, Bureau of the Census, *International Economic Indicators* 10 (1984).
84. Ibid.
85. Yamada interview.
86. See "Financial Linkages: West Germany," below.
87. *Wall Street Journal*, June 20, 1980, p. 1.
88. Manufacturers Hanover interview.
89. See generally Ryder Report.
90. See Anti-monopoly and Fair Trade Maintenance Act, art. 11 (Japan), reproduced in Z. Kitagawa, *Doing Business in Japan*, 1984, app. 7a-16.

91. See J. Zysman, *Governments, Markets, and Growth: Financial Systems and the Politics of Industrial Change* (Ithaca, NY: Cornell University Press, 1983), pp. 248–50.

92. Yamada interview.

93. See J. Carrington and G. Edwards, *Financing Industrial Investment* (New York: MacMillan, 1979), pp. 117, 120.

94. Aktiengesetz sec. 135, 1965 Bundesgesetzblat [BGB1) I 1089 West Germany.

95. *Schriftenreiche des Bundesministeriums der Finanzen, Bericht der Studienkommission, Grundsatzfragen der Kredidwirtschaft*, heft 28 (1979).

96. Aktiengesetz in der Fassung, sec. 135, 1965 BGB1 I 1089 West Germany.

97. *Schriftenreiche des Bundesministeriums der Finanzen*, heft 28.

98. Interview with an official of the Dresdner Bank (name withheld by request), in Cambridge, Massachusetts, January 12, 1984, hereafter cited as Dresdner interview.

99. See, for example, J. Zysman, p. 260 (note 91).

100. The Bank Holding Company Act, 12 U.S.C. sec. 1843 (1982), generally prohibits bank holding companies from engaging in nonbank activities.

101. See, for example, Bank Holding Company Act, 12 U.S.C. sec. 1843(c)(8) (1982) (a bank holding company may invest in a company that the Board of Governors of the Federal Reserve determines "to be so closely related to banking or managing or controlling banks as to be a proper incident thereto"); N.Y. Banking Law sec. 96.1 (McKinney 1971 and Supp. 1984) (banks may "exercise all such incidental powers as shall be necessary to carry on the business of banking"); N.Y. Insurance Law sec. 46-a1(a) (McKinney 1971 and Supp. 1984) (insurance companies may invest in subsidiaries engaged in insurance or investment related business); Connecticut General Statutes sec. 38–146a (1983) (Connecticut mutual life insurance companies can invest in subsidiaries engaged in insurance or investment-related business).

102. 12 U.S.C. sec. 24 (1982). Under 12 U.S.C. sec. 335, the provisions of 12 U.S.C. sec. 24 also apply to restrict the investment of state member banks of the Federal Reserve System.

103. Section 4(c)(5) of the Bank Holding Company Act (BHCA), 12 U.S.C. sec. 1843(c)(5) (1982), permits a bank holding company to invest in "shares which are of the kinds and amounts eligible for investment" by a national bank under 12 U.S.C. sec. 24 (thus embodying the limited exceptions to the Glass-Steagall Act). Section 4(c)(6) of the BHCA, 12 U.S.C. sec. 1843(c)(6) (1982), permits a holding company to own no more than 5 percent of the outstanding voting shares of any company. Although an equity investment of up to 5 percent might be insignificant, investments of 5 percent each by a number of bank holding companies could be substantial in the aggregate. However, there is a substantial risk that such joint

investments of less than 5 percent each could be unprotected by sec. 4(c) (6). See 12 C.F.R. 225.137 (1984) ("the exemption was not intended to allow a group of holding companies, through concerted action, to engage in an activity as entrepreneurs"). Section 4(c)(2) of the BHCA provides an exemption to bank holding companies or any of their subsidiaries for shares acquired in satisfaction of "a debt previously contracted." 12 U.S.C. sec. 1843(c)(2) (1982). Unless such shares represent less than 5 percent of the total outstanding shares, they may only be held for a period of two years (which may be extended at the discretion of the Federal Reserve Board).

104. For example, New York banks generally may not purchase the stock of other corporations. Although Section 97.5 of the New York Banking Law provides that a New York bank may acquire "so much of the capital stock of any other corporation as may be specifically authorized by the laws of this state or by resolution of the banking board upon a three-fifths vote of all its members," the investments that are "specifically authorized" are not numerous. A provision similar to the exemption in 12 U.S.C. sec. 1843(c)(2) is also present in the New York statute, New York Banking Law sec. 97.5 (McKinney 1971 and Supp. 1984).

105. McCarran-Ferguson Act, 15 U.S.C. sec. 1011 (1982) (states given authority to regulate the business of insurance). Under New York law, an insurance company may not invest in common stock unless the issuing institution earned enough in the aggregate to pay a dividend of 4 percent on all stocks and shares outstanding for each of the seven years preceding the acquisition by an insurer. N.Y. Insurance Law sec. 81(13)(a) (McKinney Supp. 1984): Various limitations are also placed on such equity investments in terms of a percentage of the insurer's total assets. See N.Y. Insurance Law sec. 81(13)(b) (McKinney Supp. 1984).

106. This restriction applies only to national banks. See 12 U.S.C. sec. 84(a)(2) (1982).

107. 12 U.S.C. sec. 36(c) (1982).

108. Banking Act of 1933, secs. 20–21, 12 U.S.C. secs. 78, 377, 378 (1982): see also F. Solomon, W. Schlighting, T. Rice and J. Cooper, *Banking Law* sec. 80.22(3) (1984); Clark and Summers, "Judicial Interpretation of Glass Steagall: The Need for Legislative Action," *Banking Law Journal* 97 (1980): 721.

109. See, for example, "Nationwide Banking: Barriers Fall," *New York Times*, June 4, 1983, p. 29; "America's Debut in Offshore Banking," *New York Times*, November 22, 1981, p. F1.

110. Interview with Manufacturers Hanover Trust Co. loan officer (name withheld by request), in New York City, January 10, 1984.

111. Under the Bankruptcy Code, "insiders" are subject to possible recovery preferences during the one-year period preceding the commencement of a

bankruptcy case, while other persons are subject to such recoveries only during the ninety-day period preceding the commencement of a case. 11 U.S.C. sec. 547(b)(4) (1982). An "insider" is defined to include a director, officer, or person in control of the debtor. 11 U.S.C. sec. 101(25) (1982). Moreover, the bankruptcy court has the power to subordinate one claim to another on considerations of equity and fairness. 11 U.S.C. sec. 510(c) (1982). A creditor in control of a debtor can expect that it will be met with allegations that its claim should be equitably subordinated if not disallowed.

Although there is no specific statutory definition of "control" in either the Securities Act of 1933, 15 U.S.C. sec. 77b (1982), or the Securities Exchange Act of 1934, 15 U.S.C. sec. 78c (1982), the Securities and Exchange Commission broadly defines control as 'the possession, direct or indirect, of the power to direct or cause the direction of the management and policies of a person, whether through the ownership of voting securities, by contract, or otherwise." 17 C.F.R. 230.405 (1984). Therefore, a creditor that directly participates in or selects management runs the risk of being considered to be in control of the debtor. See, for example, *In re Falstaff Brewing Corp. Antitrust Litig.*, 441 F. Supp. 62 (E.D. Mo. 1977) (lender that controls the daily affairs of borrower corporation can be held liable for corporation's Securities Exchange Act of 1934 violations).

112. The fiduciary duty of corporate directors and officers to stockholders includes a duty to act loyally, in good faith, and without assuming any position in conflict with the interest of the corporation. 19 C.J.S. *Corporations* sec. 761 (1940). No such fiduciary duty automatically exists with respect to creditors; directors and officers are merely agents of the corporation. 19 C.J.S. *Corporations* sec. 837 (1940).

113. See, for example, Newman v. Forward Lands, Inc. 418 F. Supp. 135, 136 (E.D. Pa. 1976) (the directors "had a duty to exercise in managing [the company's] affairs, but the duty was owed only to the corporation itself and not to" those outside the corporation); Rosebud Corp. v. Boggio, 39 Colo. App. 95, 561 P.2d 367 (1977) (managers of solvent corporation are primarily responsible to the corporation, through managers of insolvent corporation may be trustees for the entity and for its creditors).

114. See, for example, State National Bank of El Paso v. Farah Mfg. Co., Inc., 678 S.W.2d 661 (Tex. App. 1984) (creditor held liable to debtor for damages resulting from creditor's efforts to prevent one individual from becoming chief executive officer and to retain in his place management more sympathetic to the creditor's concerns); Connor v. Great Western Savings and Loan Association; 68 Cal.2d 850, 864–66, 447 P.2d 609, 616–17, 73 Cal. Rptr. 369, 376–77 (1968) (lender became participant in home construction enterprise by entering business relationships with the devel-

oper as well as lending capital, and thus was liable to the home buyers for structural defects).

115. Interview with Paul Hunn, vice president, Manufacturers Hanover Trust Co., in Cambridge, Massachusetts, March 7, 1984, hereafter cited as Hunn interview.

116. Most agencies forbid interagency and intergovernmental flow of information. For example, in the Tax Reform Act of 1976, Congress provided that all tax returns and information were confidential and thus not routinely subject to disclosure to federal or state agencies. 26 U.S.C. sec. 6103 (1982). Similarly, information gathered by the Federal Trade Commission is confidential and may be shared with other federal agencies only in disaggregated form, with limitations on the use of such data. 15 U.S.C. sec. 57b–2 (1982). The Bureau of the Census may not disseminate census data in any form whereby an individual establishment might be identified, or use the data for other than statistical purposes. 13 U.S.C. sec. 9(a) (1982).

117. Carrington and Edwards, p. 129 (see note 93).

118. J. Zysman, p. 193 (see note 91).

119. For a comprehensive analysis of fiduciary duties in England, see H. Sheldon and P. Fidler, *Sheldon and Fidler's Practice and Law of Banking*, 11th ed. (London: Basil Blackwell, 1982), p. 1.

120. Although the relationships between a troubled company and its bank, and the bank and the government, are more attenuated in Great Britain than in our other examples, the relationship between distressed companies and the government is closer. Britain is the only nation of the four to have embraced public ownership as a general solution to the problem of large companies in distress, or to have permanently created a special institution of government to oversee such rescues. Perhaps the two phenomena are related: with the banks unwilling to back up such companies or help oversee their revival, the burden has fallen entirely on government to meet resulting political demands for special assistance.

    The National Enterprise Board, which oversaw most of the rescue of British Leyland, was conceived as a kind of state "holding company" whose purpose, according to its guidelines, was to "combine the advantages of public sector financial resources and the private sector's entrepreneurial approach to decisionmaking" (National Enterprise Board, *Annual Report and Accounts 1977*), pp. 56–59. Board members were appointed by the secretary of state for industry; the director and deputy of the board during this period were drawn from industry, and four of the nine part-time members were trade unionists. The board was authorized to make loans to troubled companies only at "commercial" rates of interest, and only to companies that eventually could become viable on their own. Lord Don Ryder, its first director, who presided over the initial stages of the

British Leyland rescue, stated that "it is not part of NEB's policy to prop up non-viable companies simply to maintain jobs." National Enterprise Board, *Annual Report* 3 (1976), cited in W. Grant, *The Political Economy of Industrial Policy* (1982), p. 106, n. 13.

In addition, the NEB was not equipped to anticipate problem companies or to monitor and supervise the restructuring of the sort that a large company such as BL required. The board had no particular knowledge of individual companies or industries; its relationship with BL, for example, was entirely by way of the chief executives whom the board selected. The government could only approve or disapprove company decisions on the basis of limited financial data. Every request for funds or for additional funds, therefore, became a choice between acceding to the company or allowing it to fail. See W. Grant, pp. 104–10.

121. Yamada interview; Maeda interview.

122. Dresdner interview.

123. Yamada interview; Hunn interview; see also Commercial Code, art. 281 (Japan), reproduced in Z. Kitagawa, app. 5a–104 (see note 90).

124. See Solomon et al., sec. 44.08(2) (see note 108).

125. Hunn interview.

126. Ibid.

127. See, for example, W. Gould, *Japan's Reshaping of American Labor Law* (1984), p. 2; R. Clark, *The Japanese Company* (1979), pp. 50-55, 98-139.

128. E. Cullingford, *Trade Unions in West Germany* (Boulder, CO: Westview Press, 1976), pp. 17, 21–22; C. Hanson, S. Jackson, and D. Miller, *The Closed Shop: A Comparative Study in Public Policy and Trade Union Security in Britain, the USA, and West Germany* (New York: St. Martin's Press, 1982), p. 191.

129. See E.O. Smith, *Trade Unions in the Developed Economies* (London: Croom Helm, 1981), pp. 169–70, 172–73.

130. See K. Coates and T. Topham, *Trade Unions in Britain* (Spokesman, 1980), pp. 166–67.

131. Gould, op. cit., p. 4 ("of 313 major Japanese companies . . . 74.1 percent had at least one executive director who once had served as a labor union leader"). See also R. Clark, op. cit., p. 109.

132. Betriebsverfassungsgesetz, 1952 BGB1 I 681 (West Germany); Mitbestimmungsgesetz, 1976 BGB1 I 1153 (West Germany).

133. See 29 U.S.C. sec. 158(a)(2) (1982).

134. See, for example, Homemaker Shops, Inc., 261 N.L.R.B. 441 (1982); Kaiser Foundation Hospitals, Inc., 223 N.L.R.B. 322 (1976); Midwest Piping and Supply Co., 63 N.L.R.B. 1060 (1945). When the United Auto Workers' president, Douglas Fraser, took a place on Chrysler's board of directors as a condition of union cooperation with the troubled company, the general counsel of the National Labor Relations Board declined to

issue a complaint. The general counsel refrained largely because the appointment created no financial ties between the company and the union. See N.L.R.B. Advice Memorandum, Case 7-CB-4815 (October 22, 1980).

135. Justice Douglas's dissenting opinion in Packard Motor Co. v. NLRB, 330 U.S. 485 (1947), appears to have formed the rationale for the exclusion of supervisors under the 1947 Taft-Hartley amendments to the NLRA. In that case, Douglas argued that foremen should not be included as "employees" because a foreman's act—if attributable to management—might be an unfair labor practice, although—if the foreman were characterized as an "employee"—management would not be similarly liable. See id. at 496–497 (Douglas, J., dissenting).

136. NLRB v. Truitt Mfg. Co., 351 U.S. 149 (1956).

137. First Nat'l Maintenance Corp. v. NLRB, 452 U.S. 666 (1981).

138. Employment Protection Act, 1975, ch. 71, secs. 17–21. One of these exceptions excuses the employer from disclosure "where the compilation or assembly [of the requested information] would involve an amount of work or expenditure out of useful proparation to the value of the information in the conduct of collective bargaining." Employment Protection Act, 1975, ch. 71, sec. 18(2)(b).

139. See P. Davies and M. Freedland, *Labour Law: Test and Materials* (1979), p. 154; Civil Service Union v. Central Arbitration Committee, *Industrial Relations Law Report* (1980), p. 274 (giving a broad reading to the exceptions to the disclosure requirement).

140. The elimination of jobs through plant closings in England is governed by the Redundancy Payments Act of 1965, codified in the Employment Protection Consolidation Act, 1978, chap. 44, secs. 81–92. The Redundancy Payments Act was designed to increase managerial freedom in the elimination of jobs, by providing lump sum payments to workers to make the dismissals more palatable (Davies and Freedland, p. 166). Although constraints on managerial discretion were imposed in 1975, see Employment Protection Act, 1975, chap. 71, secs. 99–107, British managers remain free of the duty to bargain over plant closings.

141. Gould, op. cit., pp. 1–11 (see note 127).

142. See generally I. Magaziner and R. Reich, *Minding America's Business* (New York: Harcourt, Brace, Jovanovich, 1983), pp. 143–54.

143. Unemployment insurance is administered jointly by the federal and state governments. Because the states administer the programs—setting eligibility requirements and compensation rates—the benefits paid may vary from state to state. Most states pay unemployment benefits at a rate equal to about 60 percent of a worker's salary before loss of employment, subject to certain limits. See, for example, Connecticut General Statutes, sec. 31–231a (1983); Michigan Comprehensive Laws sec. 421.27(b)(1) (West Supp. 1984). The states collect taxes to pay unemployment benefits; these

taxes are then paid into the federal government's Unemployment Trust Fund, from which the states are reimbursed for their expenditures. 42 U.S.C. sec. 1104 (1982). The federal government also disburses funds to the states to help pay the costs of administering unemployment benefit programs. 42 U.S.C. secs. 501–503 (1982).

144. In steel, aluminum, and can making, for example, workers with twenty years of service are guaranteed supplemental unemployment benefit (SUB) payments for two years, even if the union's own SUB funds are exhausted.

145. A moment's reflection will suggest how this relationship works. Suppose that a firm's managers contend that demand has declined and that workers therefore should reduce their wages. If the workers agree, the firm can have the same work as before but at a lower cost. But why should the workers believe the managers? They might believe them if they had built up a long-term relationship of trust and confidence, and the managers had shared company data with the union. But if the workers did not believe the claim, they could reduce the rewards to misrepresentation by refusing to cut their wages and forcing the firm to reduce its wage bill by cutting employment instead. For a general treatment of this subject, see Goldberg, "Relational Exchange: Economics and Complex Contracts," *American Behavioral Scientist* 23 (1980): 347.

146. See, for example, Eizenstat, op. cit., p. 49; Weil, op. cit., p. 981 (see note 2).

CHAPTER 12

The Technology Game and Dynamic Comparative Advantage: An Application to U.S.-Japan Competition

Ryuzo Sato

C ountries that are leaders in technology, like the United States, Germany, France, and the United Kingdom, have generated scientific breakthroughs and innovations in the past through endogenously determined research and development (R&D) activities. Latecomers like Japan, South Korea, and most of the developing countries, in contrast, have imported technology from the technological leaders. Technological leaders tend to invest a larger share of R&D funds in basic research. The latecomers, on the other hand, invest relatively more in applied research and development. First by imitation, then by improvements on the processes and products imported, the latecomers may gain a competitive edge in export markets as they learn to produce the same (or similar) goods at a lower cost and export them to the world market. This aspect of international competition can best be explained in terms of the dynamic comparative cost analysis of basic and applied innovations in the trading countries.

I will argue that these developments do not reflect malicious behavior on the part of the developing nations, but are the natural result of technological competition. Moreover, as countries like Japan

The author acknowledges, with appreciation, useful comments by A. Michael Spence, Richard Zeckhauser, Avinash Dixit, Gilbert Suzawa, and other participants in the Harvard Conference on International Competition. An earlier version of this chapter is circulated as NBER Working Paper No. 1513, "R&D Activities and the Technology Game," December 1984.

and South Korea achieve greater industrial prominence, we can predict certain systematic changes in the worldwide pattern of R&D expenditures.

International competition often depends on competition to develop technologies specific to the products traded. A question of major current policy interest in many nations is how coordination in R&D policies might promote the economic wealth of nations. I demonstrate that such coordination may prove helpful in two areas: (1) avoiding duplicative applied research and (2) fostering a more appropriate and, in this instance, higher level of basic research. (This analysis assumes the coordination costs of such a strategy are zero.)

A possible counterintuitive consequence of a national coordination strategy—(when viewed in a game theoretic context) is that to the extent basic research is a significant public good, one nation may benefit if another works out a coordinated strategy. The larger is the nation pursuing a coordinated strategy, the more likely is such a result.

I begin by reviewing the post–World War II Japanese R&D activities, emphasizing some unique characteristics. The next section compares R&D expenditures on basic and applied research in the United States and Japan. After schematizing the process of science-related technological innovation as an endogenous process of creating stocks of basic knowledge and applied knowledge (Sato and Suzawa, 1983), I then present a model of a technology (differential) game between two countries. The concluding section provides an intuitive interpretation of our analysis.

The differential game model presented in this chapter has several unique characteristics. The monopolistic firms in the two countries produce similar products and export them to the world market. These firms also engage in R&D activities: the firm in the first country produces both basic and applied technologies or technological innovations, whereas the firm in the second country imports basic technology from the firm in the first country and makes improvements in the form of process innovations. Production and generation of these innovations are basically dynamic, and the firms in the two countries engage in the technology differential game of long-run profit maximization. More specifically I consider the effects of three relevant parameters on the market share outcome between the two nations: (1) the index of diffusion of basic technology; (2) the index of relative efficiency of applied technology; and (3) the index of cost sharing of basic research. The model describes a variety of cases, depending on whether the game is played with a closed or open strategy. In the closed-strategy game, the firm with the advantages in applied research may not necessarily dominate the export market.

EMPIRICAL TRENDS IN JAPANESE R&D ACTIVITIES

Japanese R&D activities since World War II may be divided into three periods: (1) importation of foreign technology; (2) adaptation and improvement of foreign technology; and (3) development of indigenous high technology.

During the 1950s, the import of foreign technology into Japan increased markedly, rising at an average annual rate of more than 30 percent. Expenditures on foreign technologies constituted 45 percent of total R&D expenditures. This proportion declined to 24 percent in the 1960s and to 10 percent in the 1970s, as Japan gradually adopted different R&D strategies (see Table 12–1).

The Japanese government allowed only a small number of large firms to import foreign technology. The government did not permit any firm to monopolize the foreign technology, nor did it allow every firm to obtain or seek foreign technology. Here the govern-

Table 12-1. Trends of Foreign Technology Imports in Japan.

	Annual Percentage Change in Foreign Technology Imports (A)	Total R&D Expenditure Growth Rate (B)	Foreign Technology Imports' Share of Total R&D Investment	Elasticity = A/B
1953–59 (average)	30.8%	25.6%	44.9%	1.61
1960–69	20.7	21.1	24.0	0.97
1970–74	9.8	20.6	16.5	0.53
1975–79	6.0	10.9	12.1	0.73

Source: Statistical Division, Japanese Prime Minister's Office; Bank of Japan statistics. See also R. Wakasugi, "R&D and Economic Policy," presented at the Economic Policy Conference, Tsukuba, Japan, 1983.

ment's aim was to create oligopolistic cooperation and competition. It adhered to this policy until 1968, when it completely lifted restrictions on technology import.

Japanese R&D expenditures grew rapidly, at over 20 percent per year, in the 1960s. The sales of Japanese companies also expanded quickly. Among the industries that enjoyed phenomenal growth were chemicals, textiles, petroleum, machinery, consumer durables, electric, and automobiles. In these industries, R&D expenditures went toward improvements and adaptations of processes rather than basic research.

In the early 1970s, the character of Japanese R&D activities changed dramatically. R&D activities shifted from the chemical, steel, and other heavy industries to the so-called high-technology industries, including computers, semiconductors, and electronics. This is the area of endogenous technical progress in which Japan had a comparative advantage. At the same time, Japan started to export technologies, particularly to other Asian countries. The ratio of technology exports to technology imports exceeded unity in the 1970s, indicating that Japan was rapidly expanding production of its own technologies and innovations, for export, as well as domestic, purposes.

INTERNATIONAL COMPARISONS

Certain difficulties are inherent in any international comparisons of economic statistics. Different countries define the same concept in different ways, or use identical definitions for different concepts. For example, what one country calls *basic research* may be considered *applied research* in another. Nonetheless, a comparison of R&D expenditures in Japan and the United States is at least suggestive of actual differences in the two countries' pattern of spending.

Figure 12–1 compares the trends of various categories of R&D expenditures in the United States and Japan for the period 1973–82. Whereas the United States has spent an almost constant proportion of GNP on basic research, Japan has shifted its research effort to applied research. In the mid-1970s, Japanese R&D expenditures on basic research were almost 30 percent below the level of 1973. Not until 1981 did basic research expenditures regain their 1973 level.

Various statistics suggest that the thrust of science education in Japan is away from the basic toward the applied. Japanese universi-

Figure 12-1. R&D Expenditures, Japan and United States, 1973–1982.

A. Japan

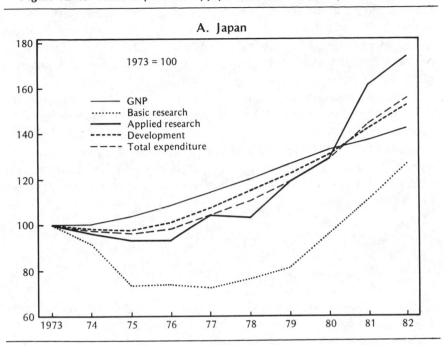

Source: *Science and Technology White Paper*, Government of Japan, 1984.

B. United States

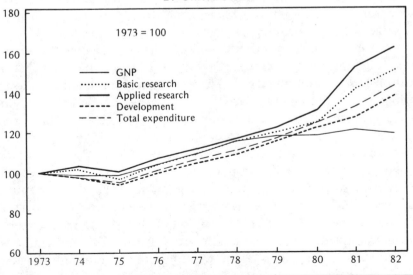

Source: Calculated from National Science Foundation statistics.

ties produce a staggering number of engineers—a total greater than that of the United States, which has five times as many university students. Among graduates, the ratio of engineers to scientists is 6.4 in Japan and 0.8 in the United States. Only 3 percent of Japan's students go on to further university training, whereas the U.S. figure is closer to 18 percent.

We may conclude that Japan has emphasized applied research and development, while the United States has focused more heavily on basic research. In the theoretical part of this chapter, we shall take account of these differences in R&D activities, and try to formulate a dynamic model of technology competition when one country conducts both basic and applied research while the other country conducts only applied research.

A MODEL OF THE TECHNOLOGY GAME

Science-related Innovations

Research and development is today a relatively integrated process. The national R&D effort can be viewed as a science-based technological change enterprise. Each country (or a typical firm in each country) engages in R&D activities to generate technological change in the form of process and/or product innovations. Each country competes in the world market with the best innovations available. The success of international competition hinges crucially on the success of R&D investment in each country.

Although most economists would agree that there is a cause-and-effect relationship between R&D and profit gains, the extent of the relationship remains unclear.[1] There is no temporal stability to the various stages of science-related technological innovations. In some cases, a stream of R&D expenditures leads relatively quickly to improvements in profits and market shares, but not in others. In other words, lags are variable. Moreover, the production of new basic and applied knowledge is a highly uncertain activity. The production relationship between scientific and engineering inputs and the output of new knowledge is not a deterministic one. There is no way to assure that new knowledge will be the outcome. Most R&D endeavors represent an exploration of the unknown. Together, the uncertainty of outcome and the variable lag between inputs and outcomes make it extremely difficult to verify the relationship between R&D and gains in profit and market share.

Technological innovation may be usefully viewed as the outcome of investment. For example, the firm reinvests a fraction of present profit in R&D in order to improve the efficiency of its production technology and reap future cost-saving benefits. As long as R&D investment produces a higher rate of return (adjusting for differences in risk) than other forms of investment, the firm's investment resources will tend to flow into R&D activities. The process of technological innovations should therefore be studied within the context of the efficient allocation of limited resources under institutional, technological, and market constraints. Technological innovations may be regarded as endogenous change generated by the motives of long-run profit maximization and market control.[2]

Innovations and Profit Maximization

The ideas presented in the previous section can be formalized. We assume that certain levels of the same basic and applied knowledge are needed to produce an output regardless of the location of the firms. For instance, to produce automobiles in the United States or in Japan, one needs to know how gasoline engines work (basic knowledge) and how workers and managements need to cooperate to produce automobiles (applied knowledge). The problem to be analyzed here is how companies in the two countries can generate new flows of basic and applied knowledge (technology) so as to enable them to compete in the world automobile market.

The process of accumulating knowledge and developing new technology is endogenous. The firm may alter its stocks of basic knowledge and applied (technical) knowledge by producing flows of the two types of knowledge through basic and applied research. Hence, the firm may alter the levels of basic and applied technologies by optimal allocation of research and development expenditures. Basic knowledge is considered to be an intermediate product in the production of new applied technology.

In the production of a given product, we assume that there are two countries (or two monopolistic firms, one in each country). Country I's firm engages in the full range of research and development, in the sense that it performs both basic and applied research.

Country II's firm concentrates on applied research and imports the basic technology developed in Country I.

Country I's R&D Activities. Let $A^I(t)$ and $B^I(t)$ be respectively the stocks of applied and basic knowledge at time t for the firm in Country I. The production (flow) of basic and applied knowledge is subjected to the following dynamic innovation functions:

$$\dot{B}^I = f(L^I_B, B^I_B) - \mu B^I \tag{1a}$$

$$\dot{A}^I = h(L^I_A, K^I_A, B^I)A^I - \mu A^I , \tag{1b}$$

where $\mu > 0$ is the rate of depreciation in basic knowledge and $v > 0$ is the rate of depreciation in applied knowledge. The depreciation factor takes into account the fact that part of the effort to produce knowledge is aimed at renewing and transferring knowledge. An increase in the stocks of basic and applied knowledge depends on the innovation functions, f and h. Thus the rate of change (flow) of basic knowledge ($\frac{dB^I}{dt} = \dot{B}^I(t)$) is positively related to the specialized research workers, L^I_B, employed to produce basic research, and to the research capital K^I_B, but that rate is negatively related to the depreciation rate μ. In the same way the rate of change (flow) of applied knowledge ($\frac{dA^I}{dt} = \dot{A}^I(t)$) depends on the specialized workers, L^I_A, and research capital K^I_A. It is assumed here that the innovation functions satisfy the concavity and other regularity conditions. We furthermore assume that basic knowledge is an essential input into the production of applied knowledge.[3] More formally, we assume

$$h(L^I_A, K^I_A, 0) = 0 \tag{2a}$$

$$\frac{\partial h}{\partial B}(L^I_A, K^I_A, 0) = +\infty . \tag{2b}$$

As noted earlier, the innovation production functions are usually not deterministic functions. Thus there exists technical uncertainty with respect to outcome. For simplicity, and also for mathematical tractability, we ignore technical uncertainty inherent in the production process of basic and applied knowledge.

In the innovation functions (1a) and (1b), the assimilation of basic knowledge is reflected only by the partial derivatives term $\frac{\partial h}{\partial B}$. This term represents the impact of *current* changes in the stock of basic knowledge on the rate of change of applied knowledge. This depiction of the relationship between basic knowledge and applied knowledge is incomplete. In fact, the generation of new applied knowledge is a function not only of current additions (net investment) of basic knowledge, but also of past additions of basic knowledge.[4]

The cumulative effects of research investment are defined by: flow of new technology at $t = \sum\limits_{\tau=-\infty}^{t}$ past research investment effects at τ. By writing the past research investment effects as the weighted product of the potential technological progress function and the time-delay (weighting) function, and by substituting for the discrete summation Σ, the continuous summation (integration), we formally express the actual flow of both basic and applied knowledge as:

$$\dot{B}^{\mathrm{I}} = \int_{-\infty}^{t} f[L_B^{\mathrm{I}}(\tau), K_B^{\mathrm{I}}(\tau)] W_B^{\mathrm{I}}(t-\tau)d\tau - \mu B^{\mathrm{I}} \tag{3a}$$

$$\dot{A}^{\mathrm{I}} = \int_{-\infty}^{t} b[L_A^{\mathrm{I}}(\tau), K_A^{\mathrm{I}}(\tau), B^{\mathrm{I}}(\tau)] A^{\mathrm{I}}(\tau) W_A^{\mathrm{I}}(t-\tau)d\tau - v A^{\mathrm{I}} . \tag{3b}$$

The weighting functions W_A^{I} and W_B^{I} satisfy the property

$$\int_{-\infty}^{t} W_i^{\mathrm{I}}(t-\tau)d\tau = 1, \quad i = A, B .$$

These equations simply state that it takes time to develop new technology and new innovation.

R&D Activities in Country II. Let $A^{\mathrm{II}}(t)$ and $B^{\mathrm{II}}(t)$ be the stocks of applied and basic knowledge at time t for the firm in Country II. Here we make the crucial assumption that Country II does not engage in basic research, or at least engages in very little basic research. The firm in Country II acquires basic knowledge from the firm in Country I. Assume that the flow of basic knowledge in Country II is proportional to the flow of basic knowledge produced in Country I.

$$\dot{B}^{\mathrm{II}} = \gamma \dot{B}^{\mathrm{I}}, \quad 0 \leqslant \gamma \leqslant 1 , \tag{4}$$

where γ is the proportionality coefficient, which in turn depends on the amount of money paid as royalty and licensing fees, and so on. In general, γ is not constant, but varies depending on the nature of the agreement between the firms in the two countries. The index γ may be looked upon as the index of diffusion of basic knowledge.

When $\gamma = 0$, we have the case of *technology embargo*; when $\gamma = 1$, the case of *perfect dissemination of basic knowledge*. In general, we assume that γ is a function of cost of acquiring $\dot{B}^I$. If the flow of basic knowledge in Country I is of an academic and very fundamental nature, the cost of acquiring it may be minimal. For example, the costs of technical and academic journals may be all that Country II has to pay. Insight into the level of basic knowledge in a foreign country can be obtained by importing goods produced there; an understanding of the general principles of instant photography can be obtained by the purchase of a Polaroid camera. In extreme cases, the flow of basic knowledge in Country I may be obtained through illegal practices such as industrial espionage. The primary source of basic knowledge may be an opportunity for employees and trainees of the Country II (foreign) firm to study abroad.

The flow of applied knowledge in Country II is generated from the same type of *innovation function* as Country I's, because Country II is producing a product identical or almost identical to that of Country I. Hence, we have

$$\dot{A}^{II}(t) = \int_{-\infty}^{t} \delta b \left[L_A^{II}(\tau), K_A^{II}(\tau), B^{II}(\tau) \right] A^{II}(\tau) W_A^{II}(t - \tau) d\tau - \upsilon A^{II}$$

(5a)

where L_A^{II} = specialized workers in Country II in production of applied technology, K_A^{II} = capital used in producing the flow of applied knowledge, and W_A^{II} is the wrighting function representing cumulative delayed or lag effects of R&D investment. The technical progress function in Country II is in general different from that in Country I. To simplify the analysis, we have assumed

$$b^{II} = \delta b^I = \delta b, \quad \delta = \text{constant} > 0 .$$

(5b)

If δ is greater than unity, Country II is more efficient in producing the flow of applied knowledge; if it is less than unity, Country II is less efficient than Country I. We also assume that $W_A^I = W_A^{II}$.

In addition, if the diffusion index of basic technology γ is constant, then $B^{II}(t) = \gamma B^I(t)$, and the production of applied technology may be written as

$$\dot{A}^{II} = \delta \int_{-\infty}^{t} b \left[L_A^{II}(\tau), K_A^{II}(\tau), \gamma B^I(\tau) \right] A^{II}(\tau) W_A^I(t - \tau) d\tau - \upsilon A^{II}$$

(5c)

Technology Game

The firm in each country produces an identical (or slightly differentiated) product $Y^i(t)$ with the aid of factor inputs in each country and sells it in the world market at the price $P(t)$. The world market demand function is given by

$$P[t, Y^*(t)] = P[t, Y^I(t) + Y^{II}(t)] \ , \tag{6}$$

where Y^* = the world production of $Y = Y^I + Y^{II}$, and Y^i, (i = I, II), indicates the quantities of Y produced by Country I and Country II respectively. The independent variable t in P represents the exogenous factors affecting the demand function.

The cost function for each firm is given by

$$C^i = \frac{G[w^i(t), r^i(t)] \, Y^i(t)}{A^i(t)} \ , \quad i = \text{I, II} \ . \tag{7}$$

Here we implicitly assume that the production function of output Y^i is of the constant-returns-to-scale type and that each firm engages in cost-reducing process innovation with the stock of applied knowledge. That is, an increase in A^i will proportionately decrease the cost of producing Y^i. In equation 7 $w^i(t)$ and $r^i(t)$ represent, respectively, the wage rate and the return to capital in each country, i = I, II.

Cournot-Nash Dynamic Game. Each firm's objective is to choose output Y^i and flows of basic and applied knowledge so as to maximize long-run profits. Each firm allocates resources under perfect information (in that it knows the values of all current (state) variables of basic and applied knowledge). The time paths of output and resources are chosen according to either a closed- or open-loop control strategy.[5] We assume that the technology game played by the two firms is a Cournot-Nash differential game.

Closed- and Open-Loop Strategies. The difference between the open- and closed-loop strategies depends on the assumed structure of information available to the firms at every instant of time. The closed-loop strategy takes into account both information on a firm's own actual performance at every point in time, and information on its rival's strategies and the current value of the rival's state variables (i.e., basic and applied knowledge variables). For the open-loop strategies, on the other hand, the firms entirely ignore this information.

The closed-loop strategy is perhaps the more appealing one because it takes account of all available information useful for decision making—the structure of perfect information pattern (Basar and Olsder, 1982). In many cases, however, it may still be appropriate to assume that each firm adopts an open-loop control strategy of imperfect information structure, since the cost of getting more information is nonnegligible. Moreover, even if there is no such direct cost, it may be technically very complicated for the firm to estimate the value of the current state correctly.

Price Expectations. In making decisions about the choice of physical output and research outputs, each firm must know the future course of the price of output Y^i and input prices in each country. Here we assume that the firm's perception of the future course of these prices is based on the rational expectations hypothesis. In particular, we assume that firms in each country use available information in formulating their expectations of the future course of prices. In the absence of uncertainty and significant information costs (which the present analysis abstracts from), firms will formulate accurate price expectations. We assume that the commodity price $P(Y^*)$ is increasing at the same rate, α, as the prices of inputs in the R&D sector in each country, whereas the wage rate and the return to capital both grow at rate β_i.[6] These assumptions will ensure the existence of a long-run Cournot-Nash equilibrium. We also assume that the social discount rate in each country is the same and equal to σ, and that output price is increasing as fast as the input prices of research factors, but does not exceed the social discount rate, whereas the input prices of regular factors increase at least as fast as the output price (because of technical progress); that is,

$$\sigma \geq \beta_i \geq \alpha \geq 0 . \tag{8}$$

Using these assumptions, we now consider the technical progress index in real (net) terms. Let $g(t)$ be defined by

$$g^i(t) = \frac{A^i}{e^{(\beta_i - \alpha)t}} \qquad i = \text{I, II} . \tag{9}$$

The term $g^i(t)$ measures the real effect of technical change in applied technology.

Cost Sharing of Basic Research. Earlier, in discussing the diffusion process of basic knowledge, we assumed that Country II does not engage in basic research but pays royalties and licensing fees to Country I. Let us assume that the two firms have a long-term agreement to share the cost of developing basic technology. Assume that θ percent of the annual cost of developing basic technology is financed by the firm in Country II. Hence, the cost of acquiring $\dot{B}^I$ in the second country is equal to

$$
\begin{array}{cc}
\text{Cost of acquiring } \dot{B}^I & = \quad \theta \times \text{ cost of producing } \dot{B}^I \\
\text{in Country II at } t & \text{in Country I at } t.
\end{array} \tag{10}
$$

Under these assumptions we now present the technology game. To simplify the notation, the subscripts t and τ will be suppressed from the equations. The firm in Country I seeks to

$$
\underset{\substack{L_A^I,\, L_B^I \\ K_A^I,\, K_B^I,\, Y^I}}{\text{Max}} \quad \int_0^\infty e^{-\rho t} \Big[\overline{P}(Y^*) Y^I - \frac{Y^I}{g^I} - (\overline{P}_{L^I} L_A^I + \overline{P}_{K^I} K_A^I)
$$

$$
- (1 - \theta)(\overline{P}_{L^I} L_B^I + \overline{P}_{K^I} K_B^I) \Big] \, dt \tag{11a}
$$

subject to the technological constraints

$$
\dot{g}^I = \eta_I g^I + \int_{-\infty}^t e^{-\epsilon_I(t-\tau)} g^I b(L_A^I, K_A^I, B^I) W_A^I(t-\tau) d\tau, \tag{11b}
$$

and

$$
\dot{B}^I = -\mu B^I + \int_{-\infty}^t f(L_A^I, K_B^I) W_B^I(t-\tau) d\tau \tag{11c}
$$

$$
\eta_I = \beta_I - \alpha + \upsilon, \quad \epsilon_I = \beta_I - \alpha, \quad \rho = \sigma - \alpha,
$$

given the optimal paths of the variables determined by the firm in Country II. Country II's firm seems to

$$
\underset{\substack{L_A^{II},\, L_B^{II} \\ K_A^{II},\, K_B^{II},\, Y^{II}}}{\text{Max}} \quad \int_0^\infty e^{-\rho t} \Big[\overline{P}(Y) Y^{II} - \frac{Y}{g^{II}} - (\overline{P}_{L^{II}} L_A^{II} + \overline{P}_{K^{II}} K_A^{II})
$$

$$
- \theta(\overline{P}_{L^I} L_B^I + \overline{P}_{K^I} K_B^I) \Big] \, dt \tag{12a}
$$

subject to the technological constraints

$$\dot{g}^{II} = -\eta_1 g^{II} + \delta \int_{-\infty}^{t} e^{-\epsilon_2 (t-\tau)} g^{II} h (L_A^{II}, K_A^{II}, B^{II}) W_A^I (t-\tau) d\tau$$

and (12b)

$$\dot{B}^{II} = \gamma [\theta (\overline{P}_{L^I} L_B^I + \overline{P}_{K^I} K_B^I)] \dot{B}^I \tag{12c}$$

$$\eta_{II} = \beta_{II} - \alpha, \quad \epsilon_{II} = \beta_{II} - \alpha, \quad \rho = \sigma - \alpha,$$

given the optimal paths of the variables determined by the firm in Country I.[7]

There are three crucial parameters in this differential game: δ = the relative efficiency parameter for applied technology, γ = the diffusion index of basic technology, and θ = the index of cost sharing of basic research. Their relative magnitudes will determine how the market evolves in the long run.

Technological Competition and Market Shares

A simplified version of the dynamic game described above is solved in the appendix of this chapter. Here I present "local" results, in that the general model is simplified by assuming the linearity of the world demand function and quadratic cost functions. While the conclusions that follow may not be universally true, they provide some useful insights regarding the technology game taking place in the real world. The main result is that market performance depends crucially on the types of strategies the two firms employ. The closed-loop strategy yields the most interesting results. For instance, the firm with relative efficiency in applied technology does not necessarily control the market, even if the cost of sharing expenditures on basic research is very small. This is certainly a paradox. For instance, this implies that even though the Japanese firms have advantages in producing output because of relative efficiency in applied research and/or essentially free inflow of basic technology, they need not necessarily control the world market.

Closed-Loop Strategy. Relative market shares depend on how efficient each country (firm) is in applied technology. Thus, if relative

Figure 12-2. Market Share and Competition.

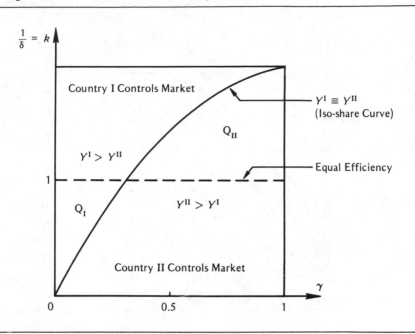

(real) efficiencies are identical ($g^I \equiv g^{II}$), market shares are identical ($Y^I \equiv Y^{II}$). In general, we have

$$Y^I \gtrless Y^{II} \text{ as } g^I \gtrless g^{II} . \tag{13}$$

The relationship between the index of relative efficiency of applied research, δ, and the index of diffusion of basic research, γ, in the steady state is summarized in Figure 12–2. The curve $Y^I \equiv Y^{II}$ is an iso-share curve on which the world market is equally divided by the firms in the two countries. Any point above this line shows that Country I's firm controls the market with $Y^I > Y^{II}$, while any point below that line indicates that Country II's firm controls the market with $Y^{II} > Y^I$. The iso-share curve is a monotonically increasing function of the diffusion index γ. Consider a situation in which only the second country (Japan) employs the closed-loop strategy. Then it is possible that the second country's firm can control the market, even though its firm is relatively inefficient in applied technology compared with the first country's firm. This is illustrated by Q_{II} in

Figure 12-3. Effect of Changes in Cost Sharing of Basic Technology.

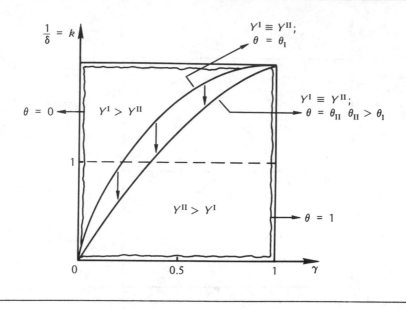

Figure 12-2. On the other hand, if the diffusion index is small, the relatively efficient applied technology in Country II is not enough to overcome the lack of essential basic technology (point Q_I). This is due to the asymmetric closed-loop effect.

What will happen if the index of cost sharing of basic technology changes? Figure 12-3 shows that an increase in the cost sharing of basic technology by Country II will shift the iso-share curve downward. This is reasonable, since by paying more royalties to Country I, Country II loses the competitive edge in production and trade. The extreme case of $\theta = 1$ will result in absolute control by Country I when the iso-share curve coincides with the horizontal axis. The other extreme case, $\theta = 0$, will result in the total loss of the market by Country I, or the absolute monopoly by Country II.

Open-Loop Strategy. When the firms do not completely use all available information, as in the case of open-loop strategies, the results are quite different. As shown in Figure 12-4, the iso-share curve always approaches the equal-efficiency point where $\delta = 1$. Hence the firm inefficient in applied technology cannot possibly control the

Figure 12-4. Open-Loop Strategy and the Share of the Market.

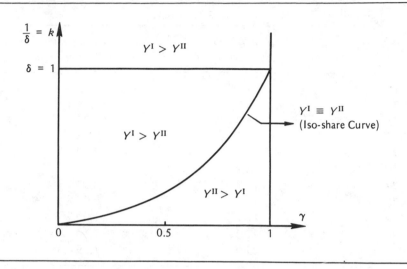

market. It is more likely that Country I's firm will control the market by restricting the diffusion index to a lower value.

The analysis presented here by no means covers all possible outcomes of the technology game in which two countries can engage. However, it does represent some aspects of the real world. The country with relatively efficient applied technology and information structure can overcome diffusion handicaps, while the country with relatively inefficient applied technology can also control the market by restricting the information and/or by forcing the other country to share in the cost of basic technology.

An Application

Few expect that a highly sophisticated and abstract model like the one presented above can be directly subjected to empirical verification. Nevertheless, it is of interest to see how some of the more general conclusions of the model can be tested. It is widely believed that Japan gained competitive advantage in the world automobile market during the 1970s by introducing dynamic process innovation. We illustrate the relevancy of such a model by comparing the trend of Japan's share in the automobile market with the trend of its relative efficiency in applied technology.

Table 12-2. Japanese Share of U.S. Auto Market and Relative Efficiency of Applied Technology.

	Japanese Share of U.S. Auto Market	δ = Relative Efficiency of Applied Technology of Japan
1971	7.1%	0.55
1972	6.8	0.61
1973	5.3	0.72
1974	8.1	0.83
1975	8.6	0.82
1976	8.9	0.86
1977	13.3	0.92
1978	13.2	0.96
1979	17.7	1.00
1980	22.0	1.10
1981	23.0	1.29

Note: The diffusion index, δ, is assumed to be approximately equal to one.

Source: Calculated from productivity data in R. Sato and G. Suzawa, *Research and Productivity, Endogenous Technical Progress* (Boston: Auburn House Publishing Co., 1983) and data supplied by Toyota Corporation.

Even in a mature industry such as automobiles, the diffusion index of basic technology may not be equal to unity. This means that the United States still has an advantage in the basic technology. For instance, Japan is still importing some inventions for the electric circuit of an automobile. We shall, however, assume that the diffusion index is close to unity. Table 12-2 shows the Japanese share of the U.S. auto market and the relative efficiency (or inefficiency) of the applied technology of Japan for the period 1971-81. We see a clear association between the increase of Japan's share and the rise of its relative efficiency for this period. Were it not for import restrictions initiated in 1981, Japan's share would probably have followed this increasing trend up to the present.

SUMMARY AND CONCLUDING REMARKS

We have developed a game-theoretic model of international technology competition. Country I (the United States), a technologically mature country pursuing R&D in both basic and applied technologies, competes in the world market with Country II (Japan), which specializes in research on applied technology. The model assumes that the technologically mature country has a dynamic comparative advantage to the extent that it can control the flow of information or the diffusion index of the basic technology, while the technologically less mature country may have a comparative advantage in applied technology if the flow of information is adequate.

The outcomes of the technology game depend on the strategies the two countries employ—an open-loop strategy or a closed-loop strategy. If they adopt the open-loop strategy in their technology development and if the diffusion index is sufficiently high (close to unity), which means that Japan receives full information on basic research from the United States under some predetermined agreement between the two countries (say $\theta = 0.5$, an equal sharing of the cost of basic research), then control of the world market depends on which country enjoys greater efficiency in the development of applied technology.

A paradox may occur when the closed-loop strategy is adopted. If again the diffusion index = 1 and $\theta = 0.5$, the country with no domestically produced basic research now can win the technology game even if its efficiency in applied technology is lower than that of the country producing basic research. To the technologically mature country it will seem that the other country is participating in unfair competition. But this is a logical conclusion consistent with the type of closed-loop strategy.

An intuitive explanation of such a paradox is not easy, but may be possible if we introduce the concept of informational efficiency. Because it concentrates on applied research, Country II has a smaller amount of information to deal with. (The technically oriented reader can see that there exists an asymmetry of the Hamiltonian functions in the appendix. Basic research B^I appears not only in H^I but also in H^{II}.) Informational efficiency is usually higher, the smaller the number of state variables the player has to deal with, because the cost (implicit) of acquiring information and using it for the next-period strategy increases as the number of state variables increases. By importing the information on basic technology under a predetermined agreement, Country II is informationally more efficient, which may compensate for any inefficiency in applied technology.

This analysis raises two policy issues, one having to do with international cooperation, the other with the development of basic technology in a technologically less mature country. Inasmuch as basic knowledge and basic technology are considered public goods, Country I may find it difficult to control the information on basic technology. International cooperation among countries could both avoid duplicative applied research and foster a more appropriate and, in this instance, higher level of basic research.

The development of basic technology requires a more cooperative arrangement than competition. A technologically less mature country can play an apposite role by sharing in the cost of basic research as much as possible.

MATHEMATICAL APPENDIX

Here I solve the technology game presented in this chapter for a special, but very important case. For simplicity we make four assumptions: (1) One of the factor inputs of specialized and professional categories in the two countries L_j^i, K_j^i (i = I, II, and j = A, B), say K_j^i, is fixed so that in each country the control variables are reduced to L_A^i, K_B^i, and Y^i. (2) Explicit solutions are given in the neighborhood of the steady-state equilibrium. Hence the relevant functions are reduced to either quadratic or linear functions. (3) In view of the Sato-Nôno theorem (see Sato, 1981; Sato and Nôno, 1982), the integro-differential equations for the technical progress functions are reduced to ordinary differential equations with appropriate weights. (4) The model is reduced to a convenient simplified form by introducing the concept of effective marginal costs, $C^i = \dfrac{1}{g^i}$, and by changing the control variables to Y^i and to the true derivatives of the of the marginal costs and of the basic technology (i.e., $\dot{C}^i$ and $\dot{B}^i$). Hence the model that has been explicitly worked out is expressed by the system of the Hamiltonian functions for the two countries:

$$H^I = P(Y^*)Y^I - C^I Y^I - S(C^I, B^I, U^I) - (1 - \theta)T(B^I, V^I)$$
$$+ \lambda_I^I U^I + \lambda_{II}^I U^{II} + \pi^I V^I , \tag{A-1}$$

$$H^{II} = P(Y^*)Y^{II} - C^{II} Y^{II} - \frac{1}{\delta} S(C^{II}, \gamma B^I, U^{II}) - \theta T(B^I, V^I)$$
$$+ \lambda_I^{II} U^I + \lambda_{II}^{II} U^{II} + \pi^{II} V^I \tag{A-2}$$

where $U^I = \dot{C}^I$, $V^I = \dot{B}^I$, and $U^{II} = \dot{C}^{II}$. Also S and T are the cost functions of applied technology and basic technology expressed by the quadratic forms. Finally, λ_j^i and π^i are the respective shadow prices of the control variables. The discussions in the body of the chapter are based on the above model with the three explicit parameters δ, γ, and θ.

By the maximum principle we have:

Country I (for example, the United States)

$$\frac{\partial H^{\mathrm{I}}}{\partial Y^{\mathrm{I}}} = -P_{\mathrm{I}}(Y^*)Y^{\mathrm{I}} + P(Y^*) - C^{\mathrm{I}} = 0, P_{\mathrm{I}}(Y) = \frac{dP}{dY^*} \qquad (\text{A-}3\text{a})$$

$$\frac{\partial H^{\mathrm{I}}}{\partial U^{\mathrm{I}}} = -\dot{S}\,(C^{\mathrm{I}}, B^{\mathrm{I}}, U^{\mathrm{I}}) + \lambda_{\mathrm{I}}^{\mathrm{I}} = 0, \dot{S} = \frac{\partial S}{\partial U^{\mathrm{I}}} \qquad (\text{A-}3\text{b})$$

$$\frac{\partial H^{\mathrm{I}}}{\partial V^{\mathrm{I}}} = -(1-\theta)T_{\mathrm{II}}(B^{\mathrm{I}}, V^{\mathrm{I}}) + \pi^{\mathrm{I}} = 0, T_{\mathrm{II}} = \frac{\partial T}{\partial V^{\mathrm{I}}}. \qquad (\text{A-}3\text{c})$$

Country II (for example, Japan)

$$\frac{\partial H^{\mathrm{II}}}{\partial Y^{\mathrm{II}}} = P_{\mathrm{I}}(Y^*)Y^{\mathrm{II}} + P(Y^*) - C_{\mathrm{II}} = 0 \qquad (\text{A-}4\text{a})$$

$$\frac{\partial H^{\mathrm{II}}}{\partial U^{\mathrm{II}}} = -k\dot{S}\,(C^{\mathrm{II}}, \gamma B^{\mathrm{I}}, U^{\mathrm{II}}) + \lambda_{\mathrm{II}}^{\mathrm{II}} = 0; \quad k = \frac{1}{\delta}. \qquad (\text{A-}4\text{b})$$

Using (A-3a) and (A-4a), we get

$$Y = H(C^{\mathrm{I}}) = H(C^{\mathrm{I}} + C^{\mathrm{II}})$$

or

$$Y^i = G\,[C^i, H(C^i)], \quad i = \mathrm{I, II}. \qquad (\text{A-}5\text{a})$$

Also we obtain:

$$V^{\mathrm{I}} = \phi(B^{\mathrm{I}}, \pi^{\mathrm{I}}; \theta) \qquad (\text{A-}5\text{b})$$

$$U^{\mathrm{I}} = \zeta(C^{\mathrm{I}}, B^{\mathrm{I}}, \lambda_{\mathrm{I}}^{\mathrm{I}}) \qquad (\text{A-}5\text{c})$$

$$U^{\mathrm{II}} = \psi(C^{\mathrm{II}}, \gamma B^{\mathrm{I}}, \lambda_{\mathrm{II}}^{\mathrm{II}}/k). \qquad (\text{A-}5\text{d})$$

Open-Loop Strategy

Country I (United States)

$$\dot{\lambda}_{\mathrm{I}}^{\mathrm{I}} = \rho\lambda_{\mathrm{I}}^{\mathrm{I}} - \frac{\partial H^{\mathrm{I}}}{\partial C^{\mathrm{I}}} = \rho\lambda_{\mathrm{I}}^{\mathrm{I}} + Y^{\mathrm{I}} + S_{\mathrm{I}}(C^{\mathrm{I}}, B^{\mathrm{I}}, U^{\mathrm{I}}), S_{\mathrm{I}} = \frac{\partial S}{\partial C^{\mathrm{I}}} \qquad (\text{A-}6\text{a})$$

$$\dot{\lambda}_{II}^{I} = \rho\lambda_{II}^{I} - \frac{\partial H^{I}}{\partial C^{II}} = \rho\lambda_{II}^{I} \tag{A-6b}$$

$$\dot{\pi}^{I} = \rho\pi^{I} - \frac{\partial H^{I}}{\partial B^{I}} = \rho\pi^{I} + S_{2}(C^{I}, B^{I}, U^{I}) + (1 - \theta)T_{I}(B^{I}, V^{I}),$$

$$\tag{A-6c}$$

$$S_{2} = \frac{\partial S}{\partial B^{I}}, \quad T_{I} = \frac{\partial T}{\partial B^{I}},$$

Country II (Japan)

$$\dot{\lambda}_{I}^{II} = \rho\lambda_{I}^{II} - \frac{\partial H^{II}}{\partial C^{I}} = \rho\lambda_{I}^{II} \tag{A-7a}$$

$$\dot{\lambda}_{II}^{II} = \rho\lambda_{II}^{II} - \frac{\partial H^{II}}{\partial C^{II}} = \rho\lambda_{II}^{II} + Y^{II} + kS_{I}(C^{II}, \gamma B^{I}, U^{II}), S_{I} = \frac{\partial S}{\partial C^{II}},$$

$$\tag{A-7b}$$

$$\dot{\pi}^{II} = \rho\pi^{II} - \frac{\partial H^{II}}{\partial B^{I}} = \rho\pi^{II} + k\gamma S_{II}(C^{II}, \gamma B^{I}, U^{II}) + \theta T_{I}(B^{I}, V^{I}),$$

$$\tag{A-7c}$$

$$S_{II} = \frac{\partial S}{\partial(\gamma B^{I})}, \quad T_{I} = \frac{\partial T}{\partial B^{I}}.$$

Closed-Loop Strategy

Country I (United States)

$$\dot{\lambda}_{I}^{I} = \rho\lambda_{I}^{I} - \frac{\partial H^{I}}{\partial C^{I}} - \frac{\partial H^{I}}{\partial Y^{I}}\frac{\partial Y^{I}}{\partial C^{I}} - \frac{\partial H^{I}}{\partial Y^{II}}\frac{\partial Y^{II}}{\partial C^{I}} - \frac{\partial H^{I}}{\partial U^{I}}\frac{\partial U^{I}}{\partial C^{I}}$$

$$- \frac{\partial H^{I}}{\partial U^{II}}\frac{\partial U^{II}}{\partial C^{I}} - \frac{\partial H^{I}}{\partial V^{I}}\frac{\partial V^{I}}{\partial C^{I}} \tag{A-8a}$$

$$\dot{\lambda}_{II}^{I} = \rho\lambda_{II}^{I} - \frac{\partial H^{I}}{\partial C^{II}} - \frac{\partial H^{I}}{\partial Y^{I}}\frac{\partial Y^{I}}{\partial C^{II}} - \frac{\partial H^{I}}{\partial Y^{II}}\frac{\partial Y^{II}}{\partial C^{II}} - \frac{\partial H^{I}}{\partial U^{I}}\frac{\partial U^{I}}{\partial C^{II}}$$

$$- \frac{\partial H^{I}}{\partial U^{II}}\frac{\partial U^{II}}{\partial C^{II}} - \frac{\partial H^{I}}{\partial V^{I}}\frac{\partial V^{I}}{\partial C^{II}} \tag{A-8b}$$

$$\dot{\pi}^{I} = \rho\pi^{I} - \frac{\partial H^{I}}{\partial B^{I}} - \frac{\partial H^{I}}{\partial Y^{I}}\frac{\partial Y^{I}}{\partial B^{I}} - \frac{\partial H^{I}}{\partial Y^{II}}\frac{\partial Y^{II}}{\partial B^{I}} - \frac{\partial H^{I}}{\partial U^{I}}\frac{\partial U^{I}}{\partial B^{I}}$$

$$- \frac{\partial H^{I}}{\partial U^{I}}\frac{\partial U^{II}}{\partial B^{I}} - \frac{\partial H^{I}}{\partial V^{I}}\frac{\partial V^{I}}{\partial B^{I}} \ . \tag{A-8c}$$

Country II (Japan)

$$\dot{\lambda}_{I}^{II} = \rho\lambda_{I}^{II} - \frac{\partial H^{II}}{\partial C^{I}} - \frac{\partial H^{II}}{\partial Y^{I}}\frac{\partial Y^{I}}{\partial C^{I}} - \frac{\partial H^{II}}{\partial Y^{II}}\frac{\partial Y^{II}}{\partial C^{I}} - \frac{\partial H^{II}}{\partial U^{I}}\frac{\partial U^{I}}{\partial C^{I}}$$

$$- \frac{\partial H^{II}}{\partial U^{II}}\frac{\partial U^{II}}{\partial C^{I}} - \frac{\partial H^{II}}{\partial V^{I}}\frac{\partial V^{I}}{\partial C^{I}} \tag{A-9a}$$

$$\dot{\lambda}_{II}^{II} = \rho\lambda_{II}^{II} - \frac{\partial H^{II}}{\partial C^{II}} - \frac{\partial H^{II}}{\partial Y^{I}}\frac{\partial Y^{I}}{\partial C^{II}} - \frac{\partial H^{II}}{\partial Y^{II}}\frac{\partial Y^{II}}{\partial C^{II}} - \frac{\partial H^{II}}{\partial U^{I}}\frac{\partial U^{I}}{\partial C^{II}}$$

$$- \frac{\partial H^{II}}{\partial U^{II}}\frac{\partial U^{II}}{\partial C^{II}} - \frac{\partial H^{II}}{\partial V^{I}}\frac{\partial V^{I}}{\partial C^{II}} \tag{A-9b}$$

$$\dot{\pi}^{II} = \rho\pi^{II} - \frac{\partial H^{II}}{\partial B^{I}} - \frac{\partial H^{II}}{\partial Y^{I}}\frac{\partial Y^{I}}{\partial B^{I}} - \frac{\partial H^{II}}{\partial Y^{II}}\frac{\partial Y^{II}}{\partial B^{I}} - \frac{\partial H^{II}}{\partial U^{I}}\frac{\partial U^{I}}{\partial B^{I}}$$

$$- \frac{\partial H^{II}}{\partial U^{II}}\frac{\partial U^{II}}{\partial B^{I}} - \frac{\partial H^{II}}{\partial V^{I}}\frac{\partial V^{I}}{\partial B^{I}} \ . \tag{A-9c}$$

From $\dfrac{\partial U^{II}}{\partial C^{I}} = \dfrac{\partial Y^{II}}{\partial B^{I}} = \dfrac{\partial V^{I}}{\partial C^{I}} = \dfrac{\partial V^{I}}{\partial C^{II}} = \dfrac{\partial Y^{I}}{\partial B^{I}} = \dfrac{\partial U^{I}}{\partial C^{II}} = 0$ and

from (A-3) and (A-4), the closed-loop solutions can be reduced to:

Country I (United States)

$$\dot{\lambda}_{I}^{I} = \rho\lambda_{I}^{I} - \frac{\partial H^{I}}{\partial C^{I}} - \frac{\partial H^{I}}{\partial Y^{II}}\frac{\partial Y^{II}}{\partial C^{I}} \tag{A-8a'}$$

$$\dot{\lambda}_{II}^{I} = \rho\lambda_{II}^{I} - \frac{\partial H^{I}}{\partial Y^{II}}\frac{\partial Y^{II}}{\partial C^{II}} - \frac{\partial H^{I}}{\partial U^{II}}\frac{\partial U^{II}}{\partial C^{II}} \tag{A-8b'}$$

$$\dot{\pi}^{I} = \rho\pi^{I} - \frac{\partial H^{I}}{\partial B^{I}} - \frac{\partial H^{I}}{\partial U^{II}}\frac{\partial U^{II}}{\partial B^{I}} \ . \tag{A-8c'}$$

Country II (Japan)

$$\dot{\lambda}_I^{II} = \rho\lambda_I^{II} - \frac{\partial H^{II}}{\partial Y^I}\frac{\partial Y^I}{\partial C^I} - \frac{\partial H^{II}}{\partial U^I}\frac{\partial U^I}{\partial C^I} \tag{A-9a'}$$

$$\dot{\lambda}_{II}^{II} = \rho\lambda_{II}^{II} - \frac{\partial H^{II}}{\partial C^{II}} - \frac{\partial H^{II}}{\partial Y^I}\frac{\partial Y^I}{\partial C^{II}} \tag{A-9b'}$$

$$\dot{\pi}^{II} = \rho\pi^{II} - \frac{\partial H^{II}}{\partial B^I} - \frac{\partial H^{II}}{\partial U^I}\frac{\partial U^I}{\partial B^I} - \frac{\partial H^{II}}{\partial V^I}\frac{\partial V^I}{\partial B^I} \; . \tag{A-9c'}$$

Looking at the open-loop and closed-loop solutions we immediately recognize that $\dot{\pi}^I$ in (A-6c) and $\dot{\pi}^{II}$ in (A-7c) are symmetric, which partly explains why there would be no paradoxical solutions. On the other hand, $\dot{\pi}^I$ in (A-8c') and $\dot{\pi}^{II}$ in (A-9c') are *asymmetric* under the closed-loop strategy: that is, the term $\dfrac{\partial H^{II}}{\partial V^I}\dfrac{\partial V^I}{\partial B^I}$ appears only in equation (A-9c'). Looking at the steady-state solutions under the open-loop strategy, we have

$$\lambda_{II}^I \equiv \lambda_I^{II} \equiv 0 \; , \tag{A-10}$$

while under the closed-loop strategy we have

$$\lambda_{II}^I \neq 0, \; \lambda_I^{II} \neq 0 \tag{A-11a}$$

and

$$\pi^I \neq \pi^{II} \neq 0 \; . \tag{A-11b}$$

The examples in the text are calculated from:

$$P = a - bY \tag{A-12a}$$

$$S = \frac{1}{2}\alpha_{11}(C^i)^2 + \alpha_{12}C^iU^i + \frac{1}{2}\alpha_{22}(U^i)^2 + \frac{1}{2}\alpha_{33}(B^i)^2$$
$$+ \alpha_{13}C^iB^i + \alpha_{23}U^iB^i - \alpha_1 C^i - \alpha_2 U^i - \alpha_3 B^i + \alpha_0 \tag{A-12b}$$
$$i = I, II$$

$$T = \frac{1}{2}\beta_{11}(B^I)^2 + \beta_{12}B^IV^I + \frac{1}{2}\beta_{22}(V^I)^2 + \beta_0 \; . \tag{A-12c}$$

The asymmetric closed-loop effect $\dfrac{\partial H^{II}}{\partial V^{II}} \dfrac{\partial V^{I}}{\partial B^{I}}$ in this special case is derived from:

$$\frac{\partial V^{I}}{\partial B^{I}} = -\frac{\beta_{I\,II}}{\beta_{II\,II}} B^{I} < 0 \ .$$

NOTES

1. For a more extensive discussion of the relationship between scientific knowledge and its practical applications, see Carter and Williams (1957).

2. For a discussion of the relationship between R&D and productivity gains, see Sato and Suzawa (1983).

3. These assumptions are quite realistic. Elementary language and numerical skills, for example, fall in the category of basic knowledge. In this case, equation 2a states that a researcher who has no basic knowledge of a certain computer language could not possibly produce useful programs written in that language. Equation 2b simply states that the marginal productivity of the first unit of basic knowledge in the production of applied knowledge is extremely large.

4. The delayed or lag effect in technological development is known as the dynamic Böhm-Bawerk effect in the recent literature (see Sato and Suzawa, 1983).

5. The mathematical implications of a Cournot-Nash dynamic differential game under different strategies are discussed in detail in Sato and Tsutsui (1984a, 1984b).

6. More formally, we assume:

$$P[t, Y(t)] = e^{\alpha t}\overline{P}\,[Y(t)], \quad Y = Y^{I} + Y^{II} \ ;$$

$$r^{i}(t) = e^{\beta_i t}\overline{r}^{\,i} \ ; \quad w^{i}(t) = e^{\beta_i t}\overline{w}^{\,i} \ ;$$

$$P_{L^i}(t) = e^{t}\overline{P}_{a^i} \ ; \quad P_{K^i}(t) = e^{t}\overline{P}_{K^i} \ ;$$

where $\overline{P}, \overline{r}^{\,i}, \overline{w}^{\,i}, \overline{P}_{L^i}, \overline{P}_{K^i}\ 0, \quad i = I, II$.

7. For simplicity we have normalized the initial values of $\overline{r}^{\,i}$ and $\overline{w}^{\,i}$ to unity, and thus production cost in each country is simply equal to $\dfrac{Y^i}{g^i}$.

REFERENCES

Basar, T., and G. I. Olsder, *Dynamic Noncooperative Game Theory* (London: Academic Press, 1982).

Carter, C. F., and B. R. Williams, *Industry and Technical Progress: Factors Governing the Speed of Application of Science* (London: Oxford University Press, 1957).

Flaherty, M. T., "Industry Structure and Cost-Reducing Investment," *Econometrica* 48 (1980): 1187–1209.

Foly, M. H., and W. E. Schmitendor, "On a Class of Nonzero-Sum Linear-Quadratic Differential Games," *Journal of Optimization Theory and Applications* 7 (1971): 357–77.

Freeman, C., *Economics of Industrial Innovation* (Cambridge: M.I.T. Press, 1982).

Government of Japan, *Science and Technology White Papers* (1982, 1983, 1984).

Krugman, P. R., "Intra-industry Specialization and the Gains from Trade," *Journal of Political Economy* 89 (1981): 959–73.

National Science Foundation, *Research and Development in Industry* (1977).

_____ , *Science Indicators* (1978).

_____ , *National Patterns of Science and Technology* (1981).

Nelson, R., M. Peck, and E. Kalachek, *Technology, Economic Growth and Public Policy* (Washington, DC: Brookings Institution, 1967).

Sato, R., *Theory of Technical Change and Economic Invariance: Application of Lie Groups* (New York: Academic Press, 1981).

Sato, R., and T. Nôno, *Invariance Principles and the Structure of Technology, Lecture Notes in Economics and Mathematical Systems*, vol. 212 (Berlin–Heidelberg–New York–Tokyo: Springer-Verlag, 1982).

Sato, R., and G. Suzawa, *Research and Productivity Endogenous Technical Progress* (Boston: Auburn House Publishing Co., 1983).

Sato, R., and S. Tsutsui, "Technical Progress, the Schumpeterian Hypothesis and Market Structure," *Journal of Economics*, suppl. 4 (1984a).

_____ , "The Evolution of the Market Structure through R&D Competition and Exit," manuscript (1984b).

Spence, M., "Cost Reduction, Competition and Industry Performance," *Econometrica* 52 (January 1984): 101–21.

Spencer, Barbara, and J. Brander, "International R&D Rivalry and Industrial Strategy," *Review of Economic Studies* 50 (October 1983): 707–22.

Wakasugi, R., "R&D and Economic Policy," presented at the Economic Policy Conference, Tsukuba, Japan, 1983.

CHAPTER 13

Tax Policy and International Competitiveness

Lawrence H. Summers

International considerations are coming to play an increasingly important role in U.S. tax policy debates. Policy discussions of tax provisions bearing on foreign investment in the United States and American investment abroad have long focused on the competitiveness question. Recently, reductions in taxes on business investment have been advocated on the grounds that they will increase American competitiveness. Excessive tax burdens are frequently blamed for the poor international performance of some American industries. Indeed the President's Commission on International Competitiveness recently urged business tax relief as a major element in a strategy directed at improving the trade position of the United States. Meanwhile, tax increases to reduce looming budget deficits are often defended on the grounds that they will reduce trade deficits.

While economists have long recognized that increased international competitiveness is not necessarily a good thing, because it is the mirror image of a decline in a nation's terms of trade, it is nonetheless an important policy goal. An analysis of the interrelationships between tax policy and competitiveness therefore seems worthwhile.

I have benefited from useful discussions with Richard Cooper, Rudi Dornbush, and Jeff Sachs. This chapter draws in part on earlier work with John Earle. I am indebted to Fernando Ramos and Mark Sundberg for valuable research assistance. This paper is forthcoming as L. Summers, "Tax Policy and International Competitiveness," in J. Frenkel (ed.), *International Aspects of Fiscal Policies*, © 1988 by The National Bureau of Economic Research. All rights reserved.

This chapter provides such an analysis, stressing the crucial role of capital mobility in determining the impact of tax reforms on an economy's traded goods sector. I begin by examining theoretically the relationship between tax changes and competitiveness under various assumptions about international capital mobility. Finding the conclusions sensitive to those assumptions, I then consider empirically the extent of international capital mobility. Drawing on both the theoretical and empirical analysis, I attempt to assess the likely impact of alternative tax reforms on international competitiveness.

The common assumption of unimpeded international flows of capital leads to striking conclusions regarding the effects of tax policies. Tax measures that stimulate investment but do not affect saving will inevitably lead to declines in international competitiveness as long as capital is freely mobile internationally. The economic mechanism is simple. Measures that promote investment attract funds from abroad, leading to an appreciation in the real exchange rate and a reduction in the competitiveness of domestic industry. By accounting identity, the current account equals the difference between national saving and national investment; therefore increases in investment will be associated with decreases in the trade balance, other things equal. Conversely, tax policies that promote saving but do not have a direct impact on investment will improve trade performance.

These results challenge the commonly expressed view that reductions in tax burdens on business will improve competitiveness by enabling them to undertake more productivity-enhancing investment. They also raise an interesting question in political economy: why do firms in the traded goods sector lobby in favor of investment incentives when their competitiveness will be hurt by the associated capital inflows? Consideration of this question leads naturally to an examination of the premise of free international capital mobility that underlies the arguments in the previous paragraph. If capital is not internationally mobile, stimulus to investment will not lead to capital inflows and therefore will not be associated with trade balance deterioration.

While there certainly is a large pool of internationally mobile capital, Feldstein and Horioka (1980) and Feldstein (1983) have pointed out an important puzzle raised by the hypothesis of perfect international capital mobility. If capital can flow freely, there should be no systematic relationship between domestic saving and investment rates. Yet among the OECD nations there is a very strong positive correlation between saving and investment rates. Over long periods of time, cumulative current account deficits or surpluses are quite small despite large variations in domestic saving rates. On a very consistent basis, high-saving countries are also high-investment countries, while low-saving countries like the United States have relatively low rates of investment.

The strong association between domestic saving and investment rates can be interpreted as suggesting that tax policies that raise saving are likely to increase domestic investment significantly. Similarly, policies directed at investment are unlikely to lead to permanent increases in investment unless domestic saving is increased as well. Alternatively, as many international economists argue, the cross-sectional correlation between national saving and investment rates may be a statistical artifact that does not call into question the international mobility of capital. Resolving the issue requires some interpretation of the close cross-sectional linkages between national saving and investment.

I consider three alternative hypotheses regarding the apparent international *immobility* of capital. The first is the hypothesis advanced by Feldstein and Horioka that institutional and legal restrictions of a variety of types preclude substantial international capital flows. Second is a possibility advanced by Obstfeld (1985) among others that the high correlation between domestic saving and investment rates is an artifact of common factors, such as high population growth, that affect both savings and investment. The third hypothesis is that capital is mobile internationally but that countries systematically use economic policy tools to achieve approximate current account balance, so that large sustained capital flows are not observed. My conclusion is that the third hypothesis provides the most satisfactory available explanation for the observed correlations between domestic savings and investment rates. I suggest several reasons why countries might find it desirable to maintain external balance.

This conclusion raises an important question. Given that policies to limit net capital mobility are frequently pursued, how should the effects of tax policy reforms that affect saving or investment be evaluated? If no other policy measures are undertaken, their effects should be analyzed under the assumption that capital is perfectly mobile. But the historical record suggests that current account imbalances are likely to be offset by other policy actions. Both these issues have obvious relevance to the current situation in the United States, where business tax reductions appear to have stimulated a significant amount of capital formation and drawn capital in from abroad in large quantity, but where the trade deficit is seen as a major problem.

The first section of this chapter examines theoretically the effects of alternative tax policies on competitiveness under different assumptions about international capital mobility. It suggests some possible explanations for the paradox that firms in traded goods industries frequently support tax policies that seem likely to reduce their competitiveness. Then I consider the extent of international capital mobility and document the very high correlation between domestic saving and investment rates across the OECD nations. After exploring alternative hypotheses, I conclude that this phenomenon is most likely the result of national economic policies directed at maintaining external balance. Possible reasons why nations might pursue such policies are considered. The final section considers the implications of the results for tax policy in general and the current American situation in particular.

TAX POLICY IN AN OPEN ECONOMY

This section examines theoretically the effects of various tax policies in an open economy where capital is mobile. It is crucial here to distinguish between taxes on saving and on investment. As I use the terms here, taxes on saving refer to taxes on capital income received by home country residents regardless of where the capital is located. The U.S. interest income tax is an example of such a tax. Conversely, taxes on investment refer to taxes levied on capital within the home country regardless of its ownership. The corporate income tax is an example of an investment tax. In closed economies it is clear that there is no important difference between saving and investment taxes. But in open economies, where capital flows are possible, they will have quite different effects. The model presented below makes it possible to analyze the short- and long-run effects of both pure saving and investment taxes. A variety of complexities are involved in mapping real-world tax structures, with their complex foreign tax credit and deferral provisions, into the pure saving and investment taxes treated here. I bypass these problems.

The main conclusions of the formal analysis presented below may be motivated by considering the national income accounting identity $X - M = S - I$. This identity holds that the trade balance, exports less imports, must equal domestic saving less domestic investment. Equivalently, as the balance of payments must balance, the current account, $(X-M)$, must be just offset by the capital account, $(S-I)$. Therefore policies that increase national investment without increasing national saving must necessarily lead to increases in imports or decreases in exports. In either event, the traded goods sector of the economy will contract. Conversely, policies that increase national saving without affecting national investment will improve the current account and, in a fully employed economy, lead the traded goods sector to expand.

These results apply in the short and intermediate run. Ultimately they will be reversed. Consider again the case where investment is increased with no change in saving. Foreigners who finance the excess of investment over saving will accumulate claims on the domestic economy. Ultimately these claims must be paid back, and this will require that the home country run a trade surplus, exporting more than it imports. Similarly, increases in domestic saving without changes in investment will lead ultimately to trade deficits as domestic residents liquidate their claims on foreign economies.

Modeling the Linkages between Tax Policy and Competitiveness

While a number of studies, notably Feldstein and Hartman (1979) and Hartman (1983) have examined the effects of tax policy on capital intensity, they have assumed that there is only one internationally produced good, thus making it impossible to study issues relating to competitiveness. Goulder, Shoven, and Whalley (1983) examine the implications of international capital mobility within the context of a computable general-equilibrium model and show that international considerations can have important implications for tax policy. Because the model they consider is not grounded in intertemporal optimization, it is not possible to distinguish the short- and long-run effects of tax policies. Lipton and Sachs (1983) examine a two-country growth model with two sectors producing traded and nontraded goods and with investment function-based adjustment costs. Their model is sufficiently complex that it must be solved by numerical simulation.

Here I follow very closely Bruno (1981) and less closely Sachs (1981, 1982) in considering a two-period model in which the first period corresponds to the short run and the second period corresponds to the long run. Consideration of a more realistic infinite-horizon model would be analytically intractable. I treat the case of a small open economy that takes both the price of the traded good and the interest rate as given. The analysis could be modified to treat the case of an economy large enough to affect world markets.

Consider a two-commodity, two-period framework. Tradables Q_f are produced in each period according to the production function $Q_f^t = Q_f(L_f^t, K_f^t)$, which is assumed to have constant returns to scale. The nontradable domestic good Q_d is produced with the constant-returns-to-scale production function $Q_d^t = Q_d(L_d^t, K_d^t)$. The price of tradables is taken as the numeraire, and price of the domestic good is denoted π. Increases in π correspond to real appreciations of the local currency. Production of tradable goods is allocated between consumption C_f, investment I, and net exports X, which may be negative. Production of nontradable goods is divided between private consumption C_d and public consumption G. This is examined further below. The assumed sectoral specialization of investment and government spending simplifies the analysis and does not alter the basic conclusions.

Total labor supply $\overline{L}$, in each period t is fixed at L^{-t}, ($L^{-t} = L_d^t + L_f^t$). Total capital is fixed in the first period and cannot be reallocated between sectors. First-period investment or disinvestment augments the second-period capital stock, ($K_d^2 - \overline{K}_d + K_f^2 - \overline{K}_f = I$). Since for simplicity it is assumed that capital does not depreciate, it is reasonable to allow I to be negative. No new capital goods are produced in the second period since it represents posterity.

Firms maximize the present value of profits after corporate tax:

$$PV = (1 - \tau)[Q_f^1 + \pi^1 Q_d^1 - w^1 L^1 + 1/R (Q_f^2 + \pi^2 Q_d^2 - w^2 L^2)] - I^1$$

where $R = (1 + r)$, r is the interest rate, t is the tax rate, and w is the wage rate. Note that since capital does not depreciate, the firm is allowed no tax depreciation allowances. Maximization subject to the production functions and factor accumulation constraints yields standard first-order conditions:

$$\pi^t \frac{\partial Q_d^t}{\partial L_d^t} = \frac{\partial Q_f^t}{\partial L_f^t} = w^t \qquad t = 1,2 \qquad (1)$$

$$R = (1 - \tau)\pi^2 \partial Q^2 / \partial K_d^2 = (1 - \tau)\partial Q_f^2/dK_f^2 \qquad (2)$$

Figure 13-1. The Long-Run Effects of a Corporate Tax Increase.

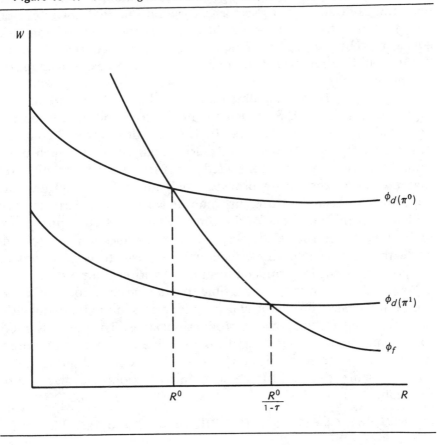

where equality of first-period marginal products at the point K_d, K_f has been assumed.[1]

At this point, we are ready to examine the implications of a corporate tax change for factor and product prices in the long run. Figure 13-1 depicts the factor price frontiers in the two sectors under the assumption that the traded goods sector is more capital intensive. Production occurs at the intersection of the two frontiers. The relative price of the nontraded good, π, shifts until the factor price frontiers intersect at the world interest rate. Now consider a corporate tax increase. The factor price frontier for the tradable good does not shift, but the required pretax return on capital is increased from R^0 to $R^0/1 - \tau$. This necessitates a change in π to shift the domestic goods factor price frontier. It is clear from Figure 13–1 that under our assumption that the traded good sector is more capital intensive than the nontraded goods sector, a corporate tax will lower capital intensity in both sectors and reduce the relative price of domestic goods, thereby causing the traded goods sector to contract. The last result would be reversed if the opposite factor intensity assumption was maintained.

Leamer (1980) presents some rather dated evidence on the relative capital intensities of U.S. traded and nontraded goods in the context of a study of the Leontief paradox. His data, drawn from Leontief's original work, indicate that the traded goods sector is much more capital intensive than the nontraded goods sector. However, he notes that the more recent data provided in Baldwin (1971) suggest the opposite conclusion. At present, I am unaware of more satisfactory evidence on this question for the United States. It seems appropriate to be agnostic on the relative capital intensity question and to conclude that capital intensity effects will not lead to large effects of tax policies on the long-run composition of national output.

As just demonstrated, it is possible to examine the impact of a corporate tax change on factor and product prices in the long run without specifying anything about product demands. To address the sectoral composition of output and employment, and to consider short-run issues, one must specify how demand is determined. For simplicity, I assume that consumers maximize a Cobb-Douglas utility function:

$$U = \alpha 1 n C_f^1 + (1 - \alpha) 1 n C_d^1 + D[\alpha 1 n C_f^2 + (1 - \alpha) 1 n C_d^2] \qquad (3)$$

where D is a discount factor, and α is the share of consumption-expenditure devoted to the foreign good.

Households maximize utility subject to their budget constraint, which holds that:

$$\Omega = C_f^1 + \pi^1 C_d^1 + \frac{1}{(1 - \theta)R} (C_f^2 + \pi^2 C_d^2) \qquad (4)$$

where Ω represents the present value of their endowment in terms of the foreign good, and θ is the tax rate levied on savings. Net household wealth Ω is given by:

$$\Omega = Q_f^1 + \pi^1 Q_d^1 + \frac{1}{(1 - \theta)R} (Q_f^2 + \pi^2 Q_d^2) - T - I \qquad (5)$$

where $T = T^1 + \dfrac{1}{(1-\theta)R} \; T^2 \; = \; \pi^1 G^1 + \dfrac{1}{(1-\theta)R} \; \pi^2 G^2$ is the total cumulative revenue of the government. Since $C_d^t + G^t = Q_d^t$, it follows that:

$$\Omega = Q_f^1 + \pi^1 C_d^1 + \frac{1}{(1-\theta)R} \; (w^2 L^2 + \pi^2 G^2) + \overline{K}_d + \overline{K}_f \qquad (6)$$

where it can be assumed that Q_f is a negative function of π^2.

At this point we are ready to solve the model using the very ingenious graphical technique developed in Bruno (1982). Equation 6 and the assumption of Cobb-Douglas utility imply that:

$$\pi^1 C_d^1 \; = \; b\Omega[\pi^1, R(1-\theta), G^2] \; . \qquad (7)$$

The $b\Omega$ function is negatively related to all three of its arguments. It is plotted as the line marked $b\Omega$ in Figure 13-2. To characterize first-period equilibrium we add a supply function for the total value of C_d:

$$\pi^1 C_d^1 \; = \; \pi^1 Q_d^1 - \pi^1 G^1 \; . \qquad (8)$$

This curve is depicted in quadrant I of Figure 13-2.

Together these two schedules permit us to characterize the determination of first-period equilibrium. Any policy that reduces first-period consumption, such as a reduction in the individual tax rate θ, will lead to a reduction in π^1 and an increase in the size of the tradable goods sector. Likewise a decrease in public consumption will lead to a reduction in π and an increase in competitiveness.

In the following discussion it will be useful to examine the behavior of domestic saving S. Note that $S_1 = Y_f - C_f^1$. Given our assumption of Cobb-Douglas utility, C_f^1 is proportional to $\pi'C_d^1$. Drawing in the schedule βY_f, where $\beta = (1-\alpha)/(\alpha)$, we can see that saving is proportional to the vertical distance between this schedule and the $b\Omega$ schedule. Note that the βY^f schedule is steeper than the $b\Omega$ schedule because $b < \beta$.

We are now ready to consider second-period equilibrium and the determination of investment. The determination of second-period factor and product prices has already been discussed. These serve to determine capital-labor and capital-output ratios uniquely in both sectors. In quadrant 2 of Figure 13-2, the relationship between

Figure 13-2. The Determination of Long-Run Equilibrium.

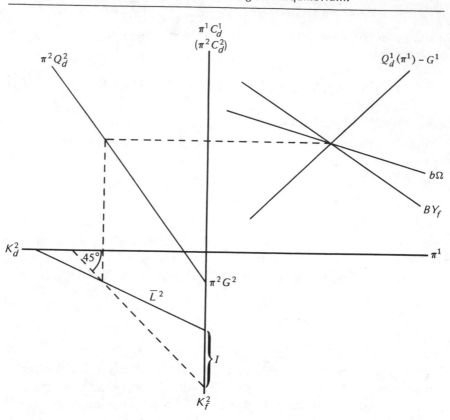

Note: The level of investment is the vertical distance between the $\overline{L}$ schedule's and the $45°$ lines K_f^2 intercept. Saving is proportional to the vertical distance between the BY^f and $b\Omega$ schedules. The current account is $S-I$.

$\pi^2 C_d^2$ and K_d^2 is depicted. The slope of this schedule increases with the period 2 capital-output ratio, and the intercept is $\pi^2 G^2$. It is possible to put $\pi^1 C_d^1$ and $\pi^2 C_d^2$ on the same axis because they are proportional by the Cobb-Douglas assumption.

The requirement of full employment in period 2 is expressed as the L^{-2} schedule in quadrant 3. It will be less (more) steep than the $45°$ line as the nontraded goods sector is more (less) capital intensive than the traded goods sector. The equation of this schedule is $\lambda_d^2 K_d^2 + \lambda_f^2 K_f^2 = L^{-2}$, where λ_i represents the labor-capital ratio in sector i, which is determined by factor prices. The level of investment can be read as the vertical distance between the L^{-2} schedules and the 45° line's K_f^2 intercept.

The schedules in Figure 13–2 along with the factor price frontiers in Figure 13–1 fully characterize equilibrium. Notice finally that the current account, CA, is given by $S-I$, which can be read from Figure 13–2.

Saving Incentives

At this point, we are ready to consider the effects of policy changes. The effect of a decrease in period 1 public consumption is depicted in Figure 13–3. As already noted, the relative price of nontradables, π, declines. Employment in the traded goods sector increases, while decreasing in the nontraded sector. National saving increases. None of the schedules in the other quadrants shifts. It is apparent that in the long run K_d^2 increases and K_f^2 decreases. Since capital-labor ratios are unchanged, it follows that employment in the traded goods sector will decline in the long run after its initial increase. Investment will increase (decrease) as the traded goods sector is less (more) capital intensive than the nontraded goods sector. As long as the nontraded goods sector is not "far" more capital intensive than the traded goods sector, saving will increase more than investment and a current account surplus will result.

The effects of a decrease in θ, which reduces private consumption, parallel those of a reduction in public consumption. They cannot be neatly analyzed diagrammatically because a change in θ breaks the proportionality between $\pi^1 C_d^1$ and $\pi^2 C_d^2$. Note, however, that a saving incentive will raise $\pi^2 C_d^2$ and give rise to second-period effects very similar to those of a change in government spending. The traded goods sector will expand in the short run and contract in the long run. Investment may rise or fall but it is unlikely to change a great deal.

Investment Incentives

The effects of an investment incentive, treated here as a decline in τ, are depicted in Figure 13–4. The solution is most easily achieved by working backward. With capital mobile, the long-run effect of an investment incentive will be to raise capital intensity in both production sectors and to raise real wages. Thus the L^{-2} schedule in the

Figure 13-3. The Effect of a Saving Incentive.

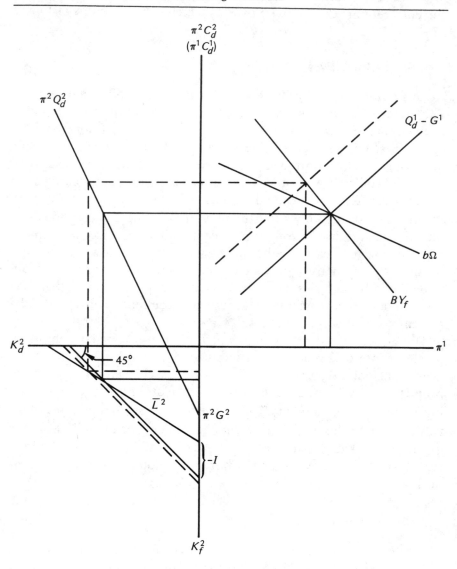

Figure 13–4. The Effect of an Investment Incentive.

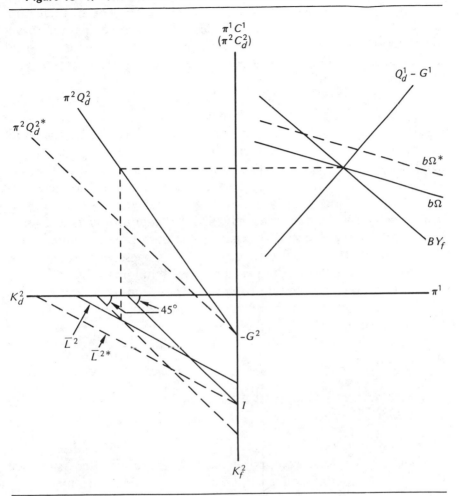

third quadrant shifts downward. The shift will be parallel in the special case depicted here where the elasticities of substitution in the two sectors are equal. The capital-output ratio in the domestic goods sector must increase, shifting the $\pi^2 C_d^2$ schedule down and to the left. Finally, the increase in second-period real wages increases human wealth and shifts the $b\Omega$ schedule in the first quadrant upward.

The effect of an investment incentive is to reduce short-run competitiveness and to reduce domestic savings. Long-run capital intensity is increased, so the current account unambiguously declines. An investment incentive has an ambiguous effect on π^2, the relative price of nontradables, depending on the relative capital intensities of the two sectors. In the special case where the two sectors have equal capital intensity, an investment subsidy will increase long-run employment in the traded goods sector. More generally, however, the result is ambiguous.

In assessing the implications of this theoretical analysis, a crucial question arises. How much real time corresponds to the short and long run in the stylized two-period model considered here? The issue is difficult to judge, but it seems likely that the model's short-run predictions are applicable over fairly long horizons. Policies directed at increasing the domestic capital stock are likely to lead to increased net investment for many years as new capital is accumulated. The available evidence, while weak, suggests that capital adjusts relatively slowly to its desired level. Likewise simulations of the type presented by Summers (1979) and Chamley (1981) suggest that households will take up to a decade to adjust their wealth holding fully following a change in the available rate of return. These considerations suggest that with a horizon of a decade or less it is probably appropriate to use the short-run predictions of the economy for tax reforms. The simulation results of Lipton and Sachs (1983) are consistent with this suggestion.

The Political Economy of International Competitiveness

Why is business tax relief so frequently advocated as a vehicle for increasing international competitiveness? The analysis here suggests that tax reduction measures, which encourage investment, inevitably reduce competitiveness and hurt firms in the traded goods sector as long as capital is mobile internationally. In part, advocacy of tax relief must result from a failure to consider its general-equilibrium ramifications. With fixed real exchange rates, tax relief does help the traded goods sector. Its advocates may fail to take account of the increase in real exchange rates that necessarily accompanies capital inflows. But economists should be reluctant to assume that self-interested parties are advocating positions contrary to their interests. It is therefore worthwhile to consider other reasons why those in the traded goods sector might advocate tax relief.

One possibility is that they are motivated by long-run considerations. Accumulating debt to foreigners will eventually require that we run a trade surplus. But it seems unlikely that such a long-run consideration plays an important role in current policy debates. A second explanation starts with the recognition that the traded goods sector is not monolithic. Tax reforms that benefit firms in some but not all of the traded goods sector may increase their competitiveness even as the total traded goods sector is shrinking. For example, incentives to invest in plant and equipment might benefit American manufacturers at the expense of farmers. The corporate sector is so large a fraction of the traded goods sector that this seems unlikely to be the whole story.

A third explanation is that advocates of investment incentives to increase competitiveness suspect that these incentives will not in fact lead to prolonged capital inflows, either because capital mobility is limited or because governments will not permit large trade deficits to continue for long periods of time. In either case, tax incentives will raise the after-tax profits of firms in the traded goods sector and will not lead to significant declines in competitiveness. I explore the extent of international capital mobility in the remainder of this chapter.

NATIONAL SAVINGS AND
NATIONAL INVESTMENT

As we have seen, the assumption of perfect international capital mobility has important implications for the analysis of competitiveness. It also is important for other fiscal questions. With internationally mobile capital, taxes on investment will all be borne by labor. Government budget deficits will not affect national levels of investment, but will instead reduce investment around the world. More generally, policies that increase national saving will have no effect on national investment.

In provocative recent papers, Feldstein and Horioka (1980) and Feldstein (1983) point out that if national saving does not affect national investment as the capital mobility hypothesis implies, one would not expect to see any strong relationship between national saving and investment rates. Yet, as Table 13-1 demonstrates, there is a very close association between levels of national savings and na-

Table 13-1. Net Saving and Investment, 1960–1983.

Country	Net Savings ÷ GDP	Net Investment ÷ GDP	Investment-Saving ÷ GDP
United States	.065	.066	.001
Iceland	.071	.113	.042
United Kingdom	.074	.070	-.004
Sweden	.008	.102	.013
Ireland	.091	.174	.083
Canada	.098	.110	.012
Denmark	.098	.128	.030
Belgium	.105	.115	.010
Spain	.108	.122	.014
Finland	.110	.124	.014
Italy	.112	.115	.003
France	.112	.121	.009
Turkey	.118	.153	.035
Norway	.126	.144	.018
Germany	.129	.124	-.005
Netherlands	.142	.129	-.013
Austria	.145	.152	.007
Australia	.146	.165	.019
New Zealand	.150	.188	.038
Greece	.155	.179	.024
Switzerland	.182	.159	-.023
Portugal	.191	.265	-.074
Japan	.196	.191	-.003

Source: Organization for Economic Cooperation and Development.

tional investment. While the long-run average net saving rate varied across countries between 6.5 and 19.6 percent of GDP, the largest average current account deficit was 8.3 percent and the largest surplus was only 2.3 percent. The correlation between domestic saving and investment rates was .92.

Table 13-2 presents regressions of the national investment rates on national saving rates for a number of different intervals. Using both net and gross measures, the data suggest a strong relationship between investment and saving.[2] In all cases, the saving variable is highly significant. Although institutional barriers to international capital mobility have been broken down over the past twenty-five

Table 13-2. The Correlation between National Investment and National Saving.

Period	Intercept	S_i	R^2
Net			
1960–64	.015 (.013)	.962 (.095)	.821
1965–69	.043 (.016)	.750 (.106)	.687
1970–74	.042 (.017)	.777 (.099)	.733
1975–79	.025 (.024)	.941 (.185)	.528
1980–83	.024 (.018)	.960 (.164)	.586
Gross			
1960–64	.029 (.017)	.920 (.073)	.879
1965–69	.047 (.023)	.834 (.093)	.783
1970–74	.049 (.026)	.835 (.106)	.755
1975–79	.065 (.042)	.789 (.185)	.439
1980–83	.086 (.032)	.679 (.152)	.464

years, there is no evidence that the impact of national saving on national investment has declined through time. There is some evidence however, that the correlation between savings and investment rates, has apparently declined.

Comparisons of the size of actual capital flows with those that might be expected highlight the apparent lack of capital mobility. Consider a policy that raises the return on domestic investment by 20 percent. This is about the right order of magnitude for the 1981 and 1982 United States tax reforms. Assuming a Cobb-Douglas production function with a capital share of .25, an increase of about 20 percent in the capital stock would be required to equalize the return on domestic and international investment. With a capital-output ratio of 1.5, this would mean a capital inflow of close to 30 percent of GNP. Only one OECD nation, Portugal, experienced a capital inflow of this magnitude over the 1975–81 period. To state the point differently, the observed capital flows do not seem to be large enough to have very large effects on rates of return.

A number of papers including Sachs (1981, 1982), Feldstein (1983), and Caprio and Howard (1984) have examined the relationships between changes in domestic saving and investment rates. While the approaches taken in these papers differ somewhat, several conclusions emerge. There is a positive relationship between changes in domestic saving and changes in domestic investment that is weaker than the relationship between saving and investment levels. Also, it appears that shocks to both domestic saving and domestic investment have significant effects on the current account, although their relative importance is a subject of debate. Finally, there is very weak evidence that the degree of international capital mobility has increased somewhat in recent years. But none of the time series analysis calls into question the proposition that domestic saving and investment rates are closely linked.

Some degree of association between domestic saving and investment rates could be accounted for by the fact that countries are not perfectly "small" on the world capital market. A share of each country's savings would be invested domestically, even if capital was perfectly mobile. It seems unlikely that this observation can account for a large part of the correlation between saving and investment rates, however. Even for the United States, a dollar of saving would be expected to produce only about 25 or 30 cents of domestic investment if capital were really perfectly mobile. Moreover, this point has no force in explaining the cross-sectional association between domestic saving and investment rates.

Another possible source of association between domestic saving and investment is Keynesian effects. Increases in investment that raise domestic income temporarily would be expected to increase domestic saving as well. The fact that saving and investment rates are about equally highly correlated over short and long periods of time suggests that this factor has limited importance.

It is not clear how to interpret the observation that saving and investment rates are highly correlated across countries. The questions of policy interest concern the allocation of the marginal dollar of domestic saving, or the financing of a marginal dollar of domestic investment. It is conceivable that incremental saving is invested in a very different way from the average dollar of saving. This view is suggested by the fact that the linkages between changes in saving and changes in investment are weaker than those between levels. An argument of this kind must explain, however, why ongoing capital flows are not observed between countries with stable high and low saving rates. In the next section we consider alternative explanations for the close association between saving and investment rates across nations. These explanations have differing implications for the hypothesis of marginal capital mobility and for the effects of fiscal policies.

EXPLAINING APPARENT CAPITAL MOBILITY

This section considers three possible explanations for the very high correlation between national saving and investment rates: (1) that capital mobility is greatly limited by institutional factors; (2) that the correlation between national saving and investment rates is a spurious reflection of third factors; and (3) that apparent capital immobility reflects the endogenous adjustment of saving and investment rates. While there is some element of truth in each of these explanations, the third one seems to be the primary reason for the close association of domestic saving and investment rates.

Capital Immobility

A natural hypothesis to explain the observed saving and investment patterns is that most capital is immobile. Perhaps, although some capital can flow freely, restrictions in financial institutions, capital controls, and the perceived risks of foreign investment greatly reduce the flow of capital. As Feldstein and Horioka (1980) suggest,

> official restrictions impede the export of capital. Moreover the fear of future capital export controls by potential host countries . . . deters investors. . . . Important institutional rigidities also tend to keep a large segment of domestic savings at home. The most obvious of these in the United States is the

savings institutions that are required by law to be invested in mortgages on local real estate.

There is, of course, a large pool of very liquid international capital. The argument is that only this money is freely mobile, and other saving is immobile. This raises an immediate problem. If only a particular pool of "hot money" were available to arbitrage large international return differentials, one would expect it all to end up in one place. As long as some mobile funds are located almost everywhere, there is a presumption that rates of return must be equalized.

It is also difficult to accept the related argument of Feldstein and Horioka that returns on short-term financial assets are arbitraged but returns on longer-term investments are not equalized. Arbitrage, like equality, is transitive. As long as there are institutions in each country (e.g., Citibank) that hold different types of domestic assets and also hold some foreign assets, we can be sure that the returns on domestic and foreign assets are arbitraged. Equalization of returns does not require that any agent make long-term investments both at home and abroad. As long as the standard assumption of marginal domestic capital mobility is maintained, the existence of investors at interior solutions holding any domestic and any foreign assets is sufficient to ensure marginal capital mobility on an international basis.[3]

Observed net flows of capital are relatively small but reflect large offsetting gross flows, suggesting the mobility of capital internationally. If capital were immobile, one would expect to see small gross as well as net flows. Unfortunately data on foreign investment by domestic firms and domestic investment by foreign firms are not available on a consistent international basis. Therefore, Table 13–3 presents some information on gross and net flows of investment for the United States. In 1982, both capital inflows and outflows for the United States were more than ten times the net flow of capital. Even these figures underestimate the true flows because they fail to take account of replacement investment by Americans abroad and foreigners here.

Large reciprocal gross investment flows also call into question Feldstein's (1983) argument that subjective uncertainties inhibit capital flows. Feldstein and Horioka (1980) argue that foreign investment is typically directed at exploiting specialized opportunities rather than the general pursuit of higher returns. This claim is difficult to reconcile with the large volume of portfolio investment and

Table 13-3. Net and Gross Flows in the United States (*billion dollars*).

	1981	1982
Current account balance[a]	4.5	-8.1
Net foreign investment	4.1	-4.6
Increase in U.S. assets abroad[b] (capital outflows)	109.3	118.3
Increase in foreign assets in the United States[b] (capital inflows)	77.9	84.5

a. The current account balance and net foreign investment are conceptually the same, differing only by the allocations of Special Drawing Rights ("capital grants" in the National Income Product Accounts) and some small definitional differences.

b. The net increase over the year; that is, conceptually, the difference between the value of assets at the end of the year and the value at the year's beginning.

Note: The difference of the gross flows is not equal to the reported net flows due to sizable statistical discrepancy.

Source: *Survey of Current Business*, March 1983, pp. 13 and 51.

with Hartman's (1983) demonstration that foreign direct investment is very sensitive to tax considerations. Recall that no foreign direct investment is necessary for international arbitrage to equalize returns. Even granting that direct foreign investments represent special situations, it is still reasonable to expect that increased domestic saving that reduces domestic rates of return would lead to more specialized foreign investments.

This discussion suggests that there exist capital flows with the potential to equalize rates of return around the world. A more subtle explanation for capital immobility, which accommodates this observation, might suggest that *total* net capital mobility is limited by fears of expropriation. This is the essential idea lying behind the burgeoning literature on international debt. It was first treated formally by Eaton and Gersovitz (1981). In this view, while capital can be freely moved, investors are aware that if a country has imported too much capital, the gains from expropriating it will exceed the costs that can be imposed. Marginal investors then will not invest abroad even if foreign assets are yielding higher returns. At the margin, capital will be immobile. Changes in domestic saving will affect international capital flows only insofar as they affect countries' debt capacity by affecting the size of the punishment that can be inflicted on them for defaulting.

Arguments of this type seem more applicable to developing countries than to the OECD nations, where expropriations are implausible. One way of testing this explanation for apparent capital immobility is to examine the association between saving and investment across a broad range of countries. If expropriation fears are a major cause of capital immobility, one would expect to see saving and investment rates even more closely associated among developing countries than among the OECD nations. This hypothesis was tested by examining World Bank data on national saving and investment rates for 115 countries.

A regression of investment rates on saving rates using data arranged over the 1973–80 period yields:

$$I/Y = 18 + .311 \, (S/Y) \qquad R^2 = .24$$
$$\quad (1.1) \quad (.051)$$

These results were almost unchanged when the OECD countries were excluded from the sample. As a further check, the equation was re-estimated dropping observations with residuals with absolute value greater than two and three times the standard error of the regression. Results remained much the same. One possible explanation for the low correlation between saving and investment is that aid flows drive a wedge between investment and saving even though capital is immobile. However, subtracting aid flows from investment had little effect on the results. It might be argued that the low correlation between domestic saving and investment is the result of measurement error. This seems unlikely. In most cases, domestic saving is estimated as a residual. When this method is used, measurement error may result in a spurious positive correlation between measured saving and investment.

The results suggest a much greater degree of capital mobility when a large sample of countries is considered. Similar results are reported by Fieleke (1982) and Frankel (1985). This provides evidence against the hypothesis of capital immobility, but runs against the expectation that capital should be most mobile between politically allied developed countries with well-functioning capital markets.

It does not seem reasonable to conclude that the close association between national saving and investment rates is explained by capital immobility. I therefore turn to other possible explanations.

Common Factor Explanations

Is the fallacy of the common cause at work here? Perhaps some third factor determines both saving and investment, leading them to be highly correlated even though exogenous changes in saving would have only very small effects on investment. Two such factors suggest themselves. Countries with high rates of population or productivity growth would be expected to have high investment rates because of the opportunities created by a rapidly growing labor pool. Life cycle saving considerations suggest that such countries should also have high saving rates, as young savers are more numerous and have more lifetime income than older dissavers. Thus growth could be a common factor accounting for associations between saving and investment. Obstfeld (1985) provides a rather elaborate example illustrating this point.

A second factor that could lead to a positive association of saving and investment is initial wealth. A nation ravaged by war, for example, would be expected to have a high investment rate because of the destruction of its capital stock, and a high saving rate because of households' desire to rebuild their wealth holdings. Any source of initial differences in national wealth-income ratios would tend to work the same way.

The growth explanation for the strong association between saving and investment rates is easily tested by adding measures of the rate of growth to a regression of the investment rate on the saving rate. Using the data in Table 13-1, a regression of the net investment rate on the net savings rate and the rates of population growth and productivity growth yields:

$$I/Y = -.015 + 1.02 \, S/Y - .002n + .0026g \qquad R^2 = .703$$
$$(.023) \quad (1.39) \qquad (.01) \qquad (.001)$$

Similar results are obtained by reversing the equation, using gross rather than net concepts, and varying the sample period. Adding growth variables actually increases the coefficient on S/Y. This implies that variations in saving that are uncorrelated with variations in growth actually have more relation to investment than do variations explained by the growth variables. Growth is not the spurious factor accounting for the strong correlations between national saving and investment rates.

No single variable can capture the possible effects of initial conditions on both saving and investment. Therefore it is necessary to take a less direct approach. Estimating the basic investment-saving relationship with instrumental variables, using as instruments any varriable expected to affect saving but not investment, will yield a consistent estimate of the "pure" correlation between saving and investment. Feldstein and Horioka (1980) report a number of estimates of this type using social security variables as instruments, and find little effect on the estimated saving coefficient. Indeed, in several cases it actually increases. Frankel (1985) presents some corroborating evidence.

To examine this issue further, the basic saving-investment relationship was re-estimated using the government budget deficit as an instrument. Because of data limitations, a smaller sample (fourteen countries) and a shorter time period (1973–80) were used in the estimation. For this sample the net result of an OLS regression was:

$$I/Y = .02 + .97 \, (S/Y)$$
$$(.03) \quad (.13)$$

Using the government deficit (as a share of GDP) as an instrument, the result was:

$$I/Y = -.10 + 1.45 \, (S/Y)$$
$$(1.10)$$

This result is surprising. The coefficient on the saving variable rises substantially rather than declining. It attains an implausible value exceeding one. On the "spurious factor" explanation, one would have expected the saving coefficient to decline.

There is no evidence here to support the "spurious factor" explanation for the close association of national saving and investment rates. But the last equation does raise a puzzle. Why should purging the saving and investment variables of the effects of their common causes cause their estimated association to increase? Clearly the answer must have something to do with the properties of the deficit variable. This issue is explored next.

The Maintained External Balance Hypothesis

So far we have assumed that national saving and investment rates are exogenously determined. Feldstein and Horioka (1980) treat differences in national saving rates as a consequence of "basic structural differences among countries." In their formal model (p. 324), the level of public saving is an exogenous variable affecting the national saving rate.

An alternative view is that countries consistently manipulate the levels of economic policy with a view to maintaining external balance. Such an argument has been made by Fieleke (1982) and Tobin (1983) among others. In this case capital appears immobile only because countries pursue policies that bring saving and investment into balance. Possible rationales for this behavior are discussed below.

The endogeneity of budget policy can easily explain the empirical results in the preceding section. Consider the special case where capital is completely mobile on world markets and countries set budget deficits according to:

$$D_i = \alpha(PS_i - I_i) + u_i, \text{ with } 0 \leqslant \alpha \leqslant 1, \tag{9}$$

where D_i is the deficit, PS_i is private saving, and u_i represents the effect of other factors on the deficit of country i. The assumption that deficits are exogenous corresponds to $\alpha = 0$ in this formulation. Standard calculations suggest that the coefficient on saving in our basic equation will equal:

$$\hat{\delta}_{\text{OLS}} = \frac{(1 - \alpha)\sigma_{PS,I} + \alpha\sigma_I^2}{(1 - \alpha)^2 \sigma_{PS}^2 + \alpha^2 \sigma_I^2 + 2\alpha(1 - \alpha)\sigma_{PS,I} + \sigma_u^2} \tag{10}$$

In the special case where $\alpha = 1$ and $\sigma_u^2 = 0$, $\hat{\delta} = 1$, and with Feldstein and Horioka's implicit assumptions that $\alpha = 0$ and $\sigma_{PS,I} = 0$ in a perfect capital market, $\hat{\delta} = 0$. As these polar cases suggest, increases in α and reductions in σ_u^2 will tend to raise the value of $\hat{\delta}$. Direct estimation of (9) yields:

$$D_i = -.01 + .715 (PS_i - I_i) \qquad R^2 = .77 \tag{11}$$
$$(.004) \ (.107) \qquad\qquad\qquad \sigma_u^2 = .00024$$

Using this estimated value of α and the observed sample moments tautologically yields the OLS estimate for δ. If we re-evaluate (10) assuming that $\alpha = 0$ and that $\sigma_u^2 = \sigma_d^2$, the implied value of δ is .597. This confirms that the strength of the Feldstein and Horioka (1980) results arises partly from deficit policy actions directed at maintaining external balance. Feldstein (1983) admits that some positive association between PS_i and I_i is to be expected, arising from factors, such as growth rates, that simultaneously affect both PS_i and I_i. And other policy levers besides deficits may be used to bring saving and investment into balance. Hence the remaining correlation of .6 should not be treated as evidence of the immobility of capital.

The maintained-external-balance hypothesis also explains the paradoxical results obtained when D_i is used as an instrument. In this case, the probability limit of the coefficient of interest is given by:

$$\hat{\delta}_{IV} = \frac{\sigma_{D,I}}{\sigma_{D,S}} = \frac{\alpha\sigma_I^2 - \alpha\sigma_{PS,I}}{\alpha^2 \sigma_I^2 - \alpha(1-\alpha)\sigma_{PS}^2 + \alpha(1-2\alpha)\sigma_{PS,I} + \sigma_u^2},$$

which will be greater than unity as long as:

$$\alpha(1-\alpha)\ \text{var}\ (I - PS) > \sigma_u^2$$

The estimates of δ_{IV} and σ_u^2 reported above imply that this condition is satisfied in practice.

The maintained-external-balance hypothesis explains how the observed high correlation of national saving and investment rates could occur in a world with perfect capital mobility. It also explains an additional finding, the high degree of capital mobility among less developed countries, which seems anomalous if capital is internationally immobile. In these nations the pressure to maintain external balance is much weaker, and so fiscal policy actions are not taken to prevent capital flows. As a consequence, greater current account imbalances and capital mobility are observed.

The evidence considered here suggests that the maintained-external-balance hypothesis is the most plausible explanation for the high cross-sectional correlation between domestic saving and investment rates. It is intrinsically difficult to test, since levels of national saving and investment are affected by a wide variety of policy levers, making it difficult to evaluate any given country's stance of policy toward saving and investment. Below I discuss a number of reasons why nations might seek to maintain external balance. The fact that countries so frequently resort to capital controls that force saving and investment into balance makes it very plausible that they also use other policy levers to achieve the same purpose.

Capital will be effectively immobile internationally if nations act so as to avoid either capital outflows or capital inflows. Either would be sufficient to preclude capital flows. Consider first the incentives nations might have to avoid capital outflows. The fundamental reason would be that the social return to domestic investment exceeds the social return to foreign investment even when their private returns are equated. Most obviously, this will be the case where there are taxes on domestic investment. More subtly and more importantly, there is the risk associated with capital expropriation by government action or by labor.[4] Keynes (1924) puts the argument well:

> Consider two investments, the one at home and the other abroad with equal risks of repudiation or confiscation or legislation restricting profit. It is a matter of indifference to the individual investor which he selects. But the nation as a whole retains in the one case the object of the investment and fruits of it; whilst in the other case both are lost. If a loan to improve South American capital is repudiated we have nothing. If a Poplar housing loan is repudiated, we as a nation still have the houses.

The phrase *legislation restricting profit* covers a host of possibilities far short of outright nationalization. Capital expropriation might also take the form of actions by workers to raise wages and capture the rents that can be earned from irreversible capital investments. Together these possibilities seem likely to be of substantial importance. They provide a motivation for countries that find themselves exporting capital on a substantial scale to pursue measures directed at spurring domestic investment. Insofar as they suggest that the social return to foreign investment may be rather low, they also suggest the possible desirability of reducing saving when it is primarily flowing abroad. Certainly this was Keynes's view regarding the huge British capital outflows in the early part of this century.

Capital-exporting nations tend to be large countries with substantial international power. The British in the Victorian era and the United States after World War II are obvious examples. The current Japanese situation is less clear. Capital outflows made by dominant international powers may confer external benefits that raise their social return by increasing international influence. Large countries may also regard themselves as relatively immune from expropriation risks. The striking feature of Table 13-2 is that almost all of the small countries are capital importers. With large countries unwilling to export capital in large quantities, however, the scope for international capital mobility is relatively limited.

Keynes (1924) went on to provide an additional reason why a nation might want to limit its capital exports.[5] He wrote that

> Foreign investment does not automatically expand our exports by a corresponding amount. It so affects the foreign exchanges that we are compelled to export more in order to maintain our solvency. It may be the case—I fancy that it now is the case—that we can only do this by lowering the price of our products in terms of the products of other nations, that is by allowing the ratio of real interchange to move to our disadvantage.

This consideration, which is important only for countries with some market power, may also help to explain why large capital outflows are so rare. A possible example is provided by the efforts of the United States to limit capital outflows in the early 1960s so as to maintain the value of the dollar. It is not clear whether the motivation for maintaining the value of the dollar was to enjoy favorable terms of trade.

There are also reasons why countries would be reluctant to accept large capital inflows. Where these are associated with large movements in real exchange rates, they are likely to damage an economy's traded goods sector severely. This may generate political pressures to increase domestic saving or to reduce the rate of investment. These pressures are likely to be particularly serious in situations where the real exchange rate changes quickly or where the traded goods sector is not benefiting from the capital inflows. It should not be surprising that capital inflows into Canada to finance development of its natural resources have proved more politically acceptable than recent inflows into the United States to finance budget deficits.

These arguments suggest why we see such a small volume of net international capital mobility. An evaluation of their relative importance is left for future research. In the next section, we tentatively accept their validity and explore their implications for economic policy.

CONCLUSIONS

Our analysis of the experience of the last twenty years suggests that capital was internationally mobile but that governments acted so as to permit only relatively small capital flows. This makes it difficult to analyze the effects of tax policy changes. Such changes, if not accommodated by other policies, would lead to significant capital flows with associated implications for competitiveness. But the historical record suggests that other policy changes would be adopted to maintain external balance. If such changes are always adopted, capital is effectively immobile. National investment cannot be increased without increasing national saving. The effect of any policy depends on the policies it engenders. Consider, for example, an investment tax credit. The resulting capital inflow would lead to a trade deficit. If this created pressures that led to an increase in public saving, the ultimate result would be more domestic investment and only small effects on the traded goods sector. But if other countries responded to their capital outflows by strengthening capital controls, the result would be increased domestic interest rates and only relatively small investment increases. In this case short-run competitiveness might actually be improved by investment tax incentives.

Clearly there are no general principles that can be used to judge the effects of different policies in all situations. Neither the analytic benchmark of perfect capital mobility nor the polar opposite assumption that capital is immobile seems appropriate in assessing the effects of tax reforms.

These points are well illustrated by considering the current American situation. The dollar was extremely strong through 1985, rising by about 60 percent between 1981 and 1985. This led to the large trade and current account deficits that we are still suffering, which many observers regard as a cause for grave concern. Beyond the direct effects on industries producing traded goods, they fear that the United States is becoming a debtor nation and that our national commitment to free trade is weakening. Following the Reagan tax incentives, an increase of close to 25 percent in the capital stock would be necessary to bring the after-tax return to capital back to its former level. Since the United States is not a small country on the world capital market, not all of these funds would come from abroad even if capital were perfectly mobile. But with mobile capital, one would have to predict a cumulative current account deficit in excess of 15 percent of GNP in response to the 1981 tax cuts. This is on top of any current account deficit attributable to federal budget deficits. It seems unlikely that such large sustained capital inflows will be allowed to materialize. Some combination of increased saving through reduced budget deficits and expansionary monetary policy is likely to be used to restore external balance. Thus, the recent U.S. experience is in a sense the exception that proves the validity of the maintained external balance hypothesis.

This hypothesis resolves the riddle of why firms producing traded goods favor investment incentives. If they expect them to be coupled with other policies directed at stabilizing the current account, they are rational in advocating investment incentives. This is true if investment incentives are accommodated by increased public saving, expansionary monetary policies, or even protectionist policies. This point may well be illustrated by the evolution of the U.S. economy over the next few years.

NOTES

1. The formulation here requires that capital invested in either sector earn the world rate of return R in period 2. As Frankel (1986b) has stressed, there is no reason to expect that real interest rates measured relative to a domestic price index that includes both tradable and nontradable goods will be equalized across countries. Indeed as long as purchasing power parity fails as a description of exchange rate behavior, real interest rates cannot be adjusted relative both to price changes in tradable goods and for the domestic consumption basket. In the model considered here, despite capital mobility, real interest rate equalization, measured in the standard way using general domestic price indexes, does not occur.

2. There is no obvious reason for regressing investment on saving rather than running the reverse regression. The interested reader can compute the coefficient that would be obtained from the reverse regression by dividing the reported coefficient into the regression's R^2. The reverse regression coefficients tend to be a little smaller than the reported coefficients.

3. Zeira (1986), in a very perceptive analysis, notes that this conclusion is correct only if assets are perfect substitutes in individual portfolios. The empirical importance of this qualification is open to question, however, given the findings of Frankel (1985) that the standard capital asset pricing model, along with reasonable assumptions regarding risk aversion, implies that assets are in fact very close substitutes.

4. I am indebted to Jeff Sachs for bringing Keynes's discussion of this issue to my attention.

5. This chapter has benefited from discussions with Roger Corden.

REFERENCES

Baldwin, Robert E., "Determinants of the Commodity Structure of U.S. Trade," *A.E.R.* 61 (March 1971): 126-46.

Blanchard, O., and L. Summers, "Perspectives on High World Real Interest Rates," *Brookings Papers on Economic Activity* 2 (1984): 273-324.

Bruno, M., "Adjustment and Structural Change under Supply Shocks," NBER Working Paper 814 (Cambridge, MA: National Bureau of Economic Research, 1981).

Caprio, G., and D. Howard, "Domestic Saving, Current Accounts, and International Capital Mobility," International Finance Discussion Paper 244, Washington, DC, Federal Reserve Bank, 1984.

Chamley, C., "The Welfare Costs of Capital Taxation in a Growing Economy," *Journal of Political Economy* (June 1981): 468-96.

Eaton, J., and M. Gersovitz, "Debt with Potential Repudiation: Theoretical and Empirical Analysis," *Review of Economic Studies* 48 (April 1981): 289-309.

Feldstein, M., "Domestic Savings and International Capital Movements in the Long Run and the Short Run," *European Economic Review* (March 1983): 129-51.

Feldstein, M., and D. Hartman, "The Optimal Taxation of Foreign Source Investment Income," *Quarterly Journal of Economics* 93 (November 1979): 613-29.

Feldstein, M., and C. Horioka, "Domestic Savings and International Capital Flows," *The Economic Journal* 90 (June 1980): 314-29.

Fieleke, N., "National Saving and International Investment," in *Saving and Government Policy*, Conference Series no. 25 (Boston: Federal Reserve Bank, 1982).

Frankel, J., "International Capital Mobility and Crowding Out in the U.S. Economy: Imperfect Integration of Financial Markets or of Goods Markets," in *How Open is the U.S. Economy?* (St. Louis: Federal Reserve Bank, 1986).

_____ , "The Implications of Mean-Variance Optimization for Four Questions in International Macroeconomics," *Journal of International Money and Finance* 5 (Supplement) (March 1986): 553-75.

Goulder, L., J. Shoven, and J. Whalley, "Domestic Tax Policy and the Foreign Sector," in *Behavioral Methods in Tax Simulation Analysis*, ed. M. Feldstein (Chicago: University of Chicago Press, 1983).

Hartman, D., "Domestic Tax Policy and Foreign Investment: Some Evidence, NBER Working Paper 784 (Cambridge, MA: National Bureau of Economic Research, 1983).

Keynes, J. M., "Foreign Investment and National Advantage," *The Nation and Athenaeum* (August 1924).

Leamer, Edward E., "The Leontief Paradox, Reconsidered," *Journal of Political Economy* 88 (June 1980): 495–503.

Lipton, D., and J. Sachs, "Accumulation and Growth in a Two Country Model: A Simulation Approach," *Journal of International Economics* 15 (1983): 135–59.

Obstfeld, M., "Capital Mobility in the World Economy: Theory and Measurement," Carnegie Rochester Public Policy Conference, 1985.

Sachs, J., "The Current Account and Macroeconomic Adjustment in the 1970s," *Brookings Papers on Economic Activity* 1 (1981): 201–82.

_____ , "The Current Account in the Macroeconomic Adjustment Process," *Scandinavian Journal of Economics* 84 (1982): 147–59.

Summers, L., "Tax Policy in a Life Cycle Model," NBER Working Paper 302 (Cambridge, MA: National Bureau of Economic Research, 1979).

Tobin, James, "Comments: 'Domestic Saving and International Capital Movements in the Long Run and the Short Run' by Feldstein" *European Economic Review* 21 (April 1983): 153–56.

Zeira, J., "Risk and the Current Account," Jerusalem, Hebrew University, 1986, Mimeo.

Index

About the Editors

A. Michael Spence, dean of the Faculty of Arts and Sciences at Harvard University, oversees the finances, organization, and educational policies of Harvard and Radcliffe Colleges, the Graduate School of Arts and Sciences, and the Office of Continuing Education. Spence earned his undergraduate degree in philosophy at Princeton, summa cum laude, and was selected for a Rhodes Scholarship. He was awarded a B.A.-M.A. from Oxford and earned his Ph.D. in economics at Harvard. After teaching at Stanford, he returned to Harvard in 1977 as a professor of economics and in 1979 was named a professor of business administration at the Business School. In 1983 he was named chairman of the Economics Department and George Gund Professor of Economics and Business Administration. Spence was awarded the John Kenneth Galbraith Prize for excellence in teaching and the John Bates Clark medal for a significant contribution to economic thought and knowledge.

Heather A. Hazard is a research fellow of the Center for Business and Government at the John F. Kennedy School of Government at Harvard University. Her doctoral work focuses on the productive resolution of conflicts in international trade and industrial organization. Hazard was trained in systems analysis and transport engineering at the Massachusetts Institute of Technology as a General Motors Scholar. As a Canadian open fellow she completed her master's degree in civil engineering at the University of Toronto. She then returned to the United States to work in a private consulting engineering firm. In 1982 she returned to academics to pursue her interest in applied economic analysis, first at the Woodrow Wilson School for Public and International Affairs at Princeton and later at the Kennedy School of Government at Harvard. Between the two she worked for the Economics Department of Unilever PLC in London as a specialist in Industrial Organization.

About the Contributors

Richard E. Caves is a professor of economics and business administration at Harvard University. He chairs the Ph.D. in Business Economics program, which is a joint activity of Harvard's Department of Economics and School of Business Administration. Professor Caves' recent books include *Multinational Enterprise and Economic Analysis* and *Competition in the Open Economy* (co-authored with M. E. Porter and A. M. Spence). His research deals with applied topics in the fields of industrial organization and international trade.

Kim B. Clark is a professor at the Harvard Business School, where he teaches a course in developing and managing technology. He received his B.A., M.A., and Ph.D. degrees in economics from Harvard University. Professor Clark has served on the secretary's staff at the U.S. Department of Labor, on the Committee on the Status of High-Technology Ceramics in Japan of the National Materials Advisory Board, and as a research associate of the National Bureau of Economic Research. His current research focuses on management and productivity at the plant level, and the product/process development cycle. He has written several books, including *The Uneasy Alliance: Managing the Productivity-Technology Dilemma* (edited with Robert Hayes and Christopher Lorenz, 1985) and numerous journal articles, among them "The Interaction of Design Hierarchies and Market Concepts in Technological Evolution" (1985) and "Why Some Factories are More Productive than Others" (1986).

David J. Collis is an assistant professor specializing in business, government, and competition at the Harvard Graduate School of Business Administration. He received an M.A. in economics from Cambridge University, an M.B.A. from Harvard Business School, and a Ph.D. in business economics from Harvard University. He taught at Columbia University before joining the Harvard faculty. Previously, he worked for the Boston Consulting Group in London, specializing in corporate strategy. He has conducted research and written a number of cases on competition in other global industries. Currently his research is on the sources of systemic competitive advantage, and competition in transactions-based businesses.

Richard N. Cooper is the Maurits C. Boas Professor of International Economics at Harvard University. He received an A.B. from Oberlin College, an M.Sc. from the London School of Economics, a Ph.D. from Harvard University, and an honorary LL.D. from Oberlin College. He has served both the academic and government communities, as provost and the Frank Altschul Professor of International Economics at Yale University, and as the undersecretary of state for economic affairs, the deputy assistant secretary of state for international monetary affairs, and senior staff economist on the Council of Economic Advisors. Cooper is a current director of the Center for International Affairs and the Institute for International Economics. He has written numerous books and professional articles, including *Economic Policy in an Interdependent World* (1986) and *The International Monetary System* (1987).

Avinash Dixit is a professor of economics at Princeton University. He received his Ph.D. from the Massachusetts Institute of Technology, and served on the faculties of the University of California at Berkeley, Oxford University, and Warwick University. He was co-editor of the *Bell Journal of Economics* and has been an associate editor for *Econometrica*, the *Journal of Economic Theory*, and the *Review of Economic Studies.* He was elected fellow of the Econometric Society in 1977. He has published *Optimization in Economic Theory* (1976), *The Theory of Equilibrium Growth* (1976), *Theory of International Trade* (1980) (with Victor Norman), and several articles in professional journals. His next book is *Strategic Thinking and Action* (with Barry Nalebuff).

Robert G. Gregory is a professor at the Research School of Social Sciences at the Australian National University. He was educated at the University of Melbourne (B.Comm.) and the University of London (Ph.D.). He has also been the chair of Australian studies at Harvard University and an assistant lecturer at the London School of Economics. His research is primarily in labor economics, structural change, and international trade.

Elhanan Helpman is a professor of economics at Tel Aviv University. He has been associated with the Department of Economics at Tel Aviv University since 1974 and has been a visiting professor at the University of Rochester, Harvard University, and MIT. He holds a B.A. degree and an M.A. degree from Tel Aviv University and a Ph.D. degree from Harvard University. He is a fellow of the Econometric Society, co-editor of the *Journal of International Economics*, and associate editor of a number of other journals. He has written extensively on problems of international trade and international macroeconomics, including two books: *A Theory of International Trade Under Uncertainty* (1978) (with Assaf Razin and *Market Structure and Foreign Trade* (1985) (with Paul Krugman).

Joseph P. Kalt is professor of political economy and assistant director for Natural Resources at the Energy and Environmental Policy Center, Harvard University. He received a B.A. from Stanford University and an M.A. and Ph.D. from the University of California at Los Angeles. His research focuses on exploring the economic implications of government regulation of U.S. markets. Professor Kalt has published widely in the area of natural resources economics and policy. He is the author of *The Economics and Politics of Oil Price Regulation: Federal Policy in the Post-Embargo Era* (1981) and co-editor of *Drawing the Line on Natural Gas Regulation: The Harvard Study on the Future of Natural Gas* (1987).

W. Carl Kester is an associate professor in the Finance Area at the Harvard Business School and teaches in Harvard's M.B.A. program and its Corporate Financial Management Program for executives. He holds degrees in economics from Amherst College (B.A., summa cum laude) and the London School of Economics (M.Sc.), an M.B.A. from Harvard Business School, and a Ph.D. in Business Economics from Harvard University's Graduate School of Arts and Sciences. He has been a consultant and seminar leader for a wide variety of financial and manufacturing corporations in the United States and abroad. The focus of his current research is the theory and practice of international finance, with special emphasis on Japanese corporate finance. He has published a number of papers and cases on corporate finance topics, and is an associate editor of *Financial Management*. Professor Kester was awarded the 1987 O'Melveny and Myers Centennial Grant for research on Japanese merger and acquisition activity.

Paul R. Krugman is a professor of economics at MIT. In 1982 and 1983, on leave from MIT, he served as the chief international economist on the staff of the Council of Economic Advisers. He is a research associate of the National Bureau of Economic Research. Krugman is one of the founders of the "new international economics," which emphasizes economies of scale and strategic behavior by firms and governments as determinants of international trade along with the traditional forces of comparative advantage. He has many important academic contributions in this area, including the edited volume *Strategic Trade Policy and the New International Economics* (1985), and has also written extensively on international monetary and macroeconomic issues.

Robert B. Reich teaches political economy, law, and management at the John F. Kennedy School of Government. He is the author or co-author of numerous books, including, most recently, *Tales of a New America* (1987), and *The Power of Public Ideas* (1987), and articles that have appeared in *Harvard Business Review, Foreign Affairs, The Atlantic, The New Republic, Commentary*, and scholarly journals. Reich served as director of policy planning for the Federal Trade Commission in the Carter administration and as assistant to the U.S. Solicitor General in the Ford administration. He was educated at Dartmouth College, Yale Law School, and Oxford University, where he was a Rhodes Scholar.

Ryuzo Sato is the C.V. Starr Professor of Economics and director of the Center for Japan-U.S. Business and Economic Studies at New York University's Graduate School of Business Administration. He also teaches at Harvard University's John F. Kennedy School of Government as an adjunct professor of public policy and is a research associate at the National Bureau of Economic Research. He was formerly a professor of economics at Brown University and a visiting professor at both Kyoto University and the University of Bonn. Dr. Sato is the author of *Theory of Technical Change and Economic Invariance* (1981), and several books on current issues concerning Japan-U.S. problems, mostly in Japanese. He received his bachelor of economics and doctorate of economics from Hitotsubashi University in Tokyo, and his Ph.D. from John Hopkins University.

Lawrence H. Summers is a professor of economics at Harvard University, where he specializes in macroeconomics and the economics of taxation. Previously he was an assistant and associate professor of economics at M.I.T. and served as a domestic policy economist on the President's Council of Economic Advisers. He has also served as a consultant to the Department of Labor and the Treasury in the United States as well as to the governments of Jamaica, Indonesia, and Mexico, and a number of prominent U.S. corporations. The first social scientist to receive the National Science Foundation's Alan T. Waterman Award, he is a member of the Brookings Panel of Economic Activity, a fellow of the American Academy of Arts and Sciences, and a research associate at the National Bureau of Economic Research. In addition to his academic research, Dr. Summers writes a monthly newspaper column on economic policy.